*Community Relations and
the Administration of Justice*

Administration of Justice Series

INTRODUCTION TO THE ADMINISTRATION OF JUSTICE
Robert Blanchard, Volume Coordinator
Riverside City College and the American Justice Institute

PRINCIPLES AND PROCEDURES OF THE JUSTICE SYSTEM
Harry W. More, Volume Coordinator
San Jose State University, San Jose

LAW AND THE ADMINISTRATION OF JUSTICE
Vernon Rich, Volume Coordinator
Southern Illinois University, Carbondale

EVIDENCE AND PROCEDURE IN THE ADMINISTRATION
OF JUSTICE
Kenneth Katsaris, Volume Coordinator
Tallahassee Community College, Tallahassee

COMMUNITY RELATIONS AND THE ADMINISTRATION
OF JUSTICE
David P. Geary, Volume Coordinator
University of Wisconsin, Milwaukee

Community Relations and the Administration of Justice

DAVID PATRICK GEARY
Volume Coordinator
Associate Professor, Coordinator: Criminal Justice Program
University of Wisconsin, Milwaukee

John Wiley & Sons, Inc.
New York   London   Sydney   Toronto

Credits for Photographs

The South Carolina Department of Corrections,
Columbia, South Carolina, Ken Sturgeon,
Special Projects Officer: Figures 13-1, 13-2,
and 13-3.

The New York City Police Department, Bureau
of Public Information: Figure 3-1. *Spring 3100*:
Figure 2-1a.

The Los Angeles County Sheriff's Department:
Figure 4-1.

The New York City Fire Department, F. W.
Johnstone: Figure 3-2. Charles Gatewood:
Figures 1-1, 3-3, 8-1, and 9-1.

Ken Heyman: Figures 2-1b and 13-1.

Library of Congress Cataloging in Publication Data:
Main entry under title:

Community relations and the administration of justice.

(Administration of justice series)
Includes bibliographies.
1. Public relations—Police. 2. Police—United
States. 3. Criminal justice, Administration of—United
States. I. Geary, David Patrick, 1928-   ed.
II. Series.

HV7936.P8C66   363.2   74-13437
ISBN 0-471-29485-3

Printed in the United States of America

10 9 8 7 6 5 4 3 2 1

This book is dedicated to Mary
and our men, Pat, John, Dan, and Pete

Contributors

David Patrick Geary:
Volume Coordinator

Betty Bosarge:
Rewriter

Professor Egon Bittner
Brandeis University

Major Tyree Broomfield
Dayton, Ohio

Professor Robert M. Brown, Jr.
University of Southern California

Professor Alex J. Cade
Michigan State University

Chief Victor I. Cizanckas
*Menlo Park Police Department,
California*

Dr. George Fox
Riverside, California

Judge Victor Manian
Wauwatosa, Wisconsin

Professor Don Mathews
San Jose State University

Major Norman E. Pomrenke
*Baltimore Police Department,
Maryland*

Susan Schein
*The University of Wisconsin—
Milwaukee*

Professor Stephen A. Schiller
University of Illinois

Professor Jay Sykes
Milwaukee, Wisconsin

Professor Larry L. Tifft
*University of Illinois at
Chicago Circle*

Professor Harold Vetter
Loyola University

Steven M. Ward
University of Southern California

Introduction to the Series

Wiley has undertaken a significantly different approach to the development of five textbooks. The "Administration of Justice" series responds to the belief that teachers should be given an opportunity to state their textbook needs and to define how the organization and contents of a textbook can best serve these needs. Although teachers are generally asked to react to a book after it is published, we sought advice before final decisions were made.

Traditional textbook publishing has assumed that an author is all-knowing about the content of his book and how the content should be organized. The results often have been disappointing for the following reasons.

1. Some books are very long because they attempt to ensure that there will be something for everyone in the text.
2. Some books are written with one type of student or one section of the United States in mind.
3. Other books reflect an author's strengths and weaknesses; they are sound in some areas (where the author is strong) and superficial in other areas.

We began by working with five tentative outlines that were sent to hundreds of educators and professionals within the criminal justice system. Feedback on the outlines—on how they could be strengthened and improved —was excellent and encouraged us to sponsor a series of meetings throughout the United States. Many participants helped us to synthesize the comments received on the outlines, and each participant prepared revised outlines based on the responses evoked by questionnaires. We especially thank the participants. The books could not have been produced without the help and enthusiasm of Bernard Barry, Scott Bennett, Bob Blanchard, John Boyd, Wordie Burrow, Tom Cochee, Bill Cusack, Stan Everett, Matt Fitzgerald, Ed Flint, Jack Foster, George Gaudette, Dave Geary, Henry Guttenplan, Karl Hutchinson, Keith Jackson, Ken Katsaris, Art Kingsbury, Roger Kirvan, Martha Kornstein, Harry More, and Vern Rich.

Several sets of new outlines resulted from the regional meetings, and these outlines were further expanded and refined at a final meeting. Responsibility for the final outlines was placed with the following educators, who managed the process of evolving the outlines into books with great care, professionalism, and perseverance.

Robert E. Blanchard, Riverside City College and the American Justice Institute, *Introduction to the Administration of Justice.*

Harry W. More, San Jose State University, *Principles and Procedures in the Administration of Justice*

Vernon Rich, Southern Illinois University, *Law and the Administration of Justice.*

Kenneth Katsaris, Tallahassee Community College, *Evidence and Procedure in the Administration of Justice.*

David P. Geary, University of Wisconsin, Milwaukee, *Community Relations and the Administration of Justice.*

Volume coordinators identified leading national figures whose area of particular competence is represented by a chapter in each volume. Specialists throughout the United States brought their insight and experience to bear on the writing of individual chapters, which met the goals and requirements of our advisory groups. These chapter authors are listed on page vii. Thus, five highly authoritative, highly current, exceptionally interesting textbooks have resulted.

Individual chapters were examined by the volume coordinator and then were assigned to professional writers. Joseph Schott, Jim George, Charlotte Shelby, Irvin Lee, and Betty Bosarge worked hard and well on homogenizing the volumes. In addition to the responsibility of rewriting two volumes, Charlotte Shelby devoted considerable effort, imagination, and skill to enhancing the clarity and excitement of the other volumes.

Our approach to the development of this series, I believe, has resulted in five important textbooks. It will be for the students and instructors to determine how well we have done. Write to me and tell me how the books might be made even more useful to you.

Alan B. Lesure, Editor
John Wiley & Sons, Inc.

Preface

In considering the contents of this volume the first question to be asked is why have such a book? The answer is that the need for such a systematic and thorough treatment of the topic is great. Our cities are filled with people whose problems become the burden of the police when all else has failed. Rarely are the men and women of the police given adequate training and education to be truly skilled professionals in understanding people in our complex, dynamic society.

This book introduces students to some of the principles of lasting importance in community relations. Rather than concentrating on short-lived public relations fads, we have chosen topics that are basic concepts. Police–community relations is not a study isolated from other subjects; it requires the understanding of many disciplines. We have included material from the fields of history, psychology, communication skills, law, and sociology, and have combined them logically and comprehensively, with major emphasis on the behavioral sciences. Our overall plan has been designed to stress an understanding of human beings and how to operationalize this understanding in a practical way for police and for the citizens they serve and protect.

The student must understand that both the science and practice of understanding police–citizen relationships are relatively new, and that they must continually be analyzed, updated, and reexamined. Unlike the physical sciences, which study matter with constant properties, this book recognizes the importance of meeting the challenge of change that confronts all criminal justice practitioners—police, probation, parole officers, and those in the courts.

It is important to recognize that police–community relations is a title that can mean many different things. To some, it means elaborate public relations activities and community meetings. To others, the topic is synonymous with better recreational programs, especially with youth. Another would insist on a psychological emphasis, as in deciding on nonmilitary-style blue blazer uniforms. Philosophers argue that basic concepts regarding the rule of law and the rights of the citizens are paramount in this subject. In reviewing these definitions of police–community relations, we must conclude that all have merit and constitute a legitimate and necessary part of the whole. This study of police–community relations, therefore, will consider many aspects of the topic.

Chapter 1 explains the police role historically, and why we have police. Chapter 2 shows the development of our country from a rural to an urban society and the effects of these changes on police work. Chapter 3 examines the different role concepts for police in working with citizens. Chapter 4 presents the changes that are taking place in policing and suggests ways to help police cope with change and keep it in perspective. Chapter 5 attempts to focus on how individuals perceive police and the interaction between individuals and groups. Chapter 6 presents the different ways in which people communicate with each other. Chapter 7 identifies some of the factors that interfere with communication, such as bias, prejudice, police military image, and scapegoating. Chapter 8 discusses police relations with the mass media, especially with the press. Chapter 9 shows how an image-building program—public relations—differs from programs in understanding; that is, community relations. Chapter 10 examines some police functions that are counterproductive and destroy public support. Chapter 11 discusses the effects of an officer's discretion on his decision-making. Chapter 12 concerns itself with some of the methods currently being considered or employed in community control of the police. Chapter 13 presents background material useful in dealing with militant organizations and dissident groups. Chapter 14 discusses crisis situations and conflict management. Chapter 15 covers the criminal justice system and some of its dysfunctions and projects into the future status of police, courts, and corrections.

Much more could be said about each of these topics. Many national groups urge police to have a four-year college degree that would include separate courses on the subject matter covered in many of these chapters. Our purpose in putting this book together is to show how they are related. We hope that a larger goal will be served with this volume; that of providing aid to police professionals and, ultimately, more help to the citizenry that officers dedicate their lives to serving.

David Patrick Geary

Contents

Community Relations and
the Administration of Justice

The study of this chapter will enable you to:

1. Describe the foundation of modern law.
2. Show how legal philosophers provide us with a description of a police officer's responsibility.
3. Name at least three of the most enduring codes of conduct.
4. Write a short essay on why we have police.
5. Describe what the U.S. Constitution and the Magna Carta have in common.

1

Historical Perspectives on the Justice System

The modern police officer walks a tightrope between the right of the community to be protected and the right of the individual to be left alone by government. Because this is a nation of laws, not of men, most citizens honestly attempt to obey the law voluntarily. The entire legal justice system is based on the concept that most people voluntarily obey the law and police themselves: If they did not, many more policemen would be necessary to maintain order.

The police officer in today's society is not only expected to apprehend bank robbers and murderers; he is also expected to direct traffic, transport the sick and injured to the hospital, help children cross streets on their way to and from school, man polling places on election day, provide shelter and care for drunks and drug abusers, investigate accidents, settle family disputes, locate missing and runaway children, and a host of other things. He must be all things to all people. He is expected not only to maintain law and order but to dispense justice as well.

When he gathers evidence or apprehends criminals, he must be scrupulously fair. He must never violate an offender's constitutional rights under penalty of having the evidence suppressed in court. He must be professionally detached from the violence and tragedy that he sees on his daily tour of duty. He is expected to be not only honest and fair in fact, but to constantly give the appearance of honesty and fairness. He must have a professional knowledge of the criminal law in order to ensure that he protects the rights of those he apprehends. He must be a professional in every sense of the word—calm, detached, knowledgeable, and dedicated.

The police officer is, for most people, their only contact with the law. What the officer says, thinks, and does reflects on the total community. If the citizen feels that his police are honest and fair, the entire criminal justice system will appear to him to be honest and fair. Whether the officer walks a beat or works under cover, he bears the awesome responsibility of the executive branch of the government. He is not the lowest level of that branch. On the contrary, he is the primary level of the executive function when it comes to the administration of criminal law. Almost every prosecution of a criminal offender begins with an arrest by a police officer. His skill and knowledge will determine, for the most part, the success of the prosecution. As crimes become more complicated and the means of committing them become more sophisticated, the work of the police becomes more challenging. Despite all of the scientific advances and the development of new tools to combat crime, personal contact, forensic skill, and legwork, are still the hallmarks of an effective police department.

A successful police department must have the respect and confidence of the community, which it can earn and maintain by exercising the restraints placed upon it by the Bill of Rights. The concepts expressed in the Declaration of Independence are not ideals—they are a way of life. As crime becomes more complicated and the apprehension of criminals more difficult, the truths expressed by the framers of the Constitution still apply. If we are all to remain free, we must all be concerned with any violation of any person's constitutional rights. The denial of justice to even one person, like ripples on a pond, spreads wider and wider until all are touched.

Every police officer in every community in the United States has an awesome array of might to back his every decision. By means of executive agreements and constitutional authority, each officer represents the full power of the government. An officer attempting to control a situation in a particular case may call upon other members of his department for assistance. If the department's strength is not sufficient, adjacent departments may be called upon for help. If more assistance is needed, the governor of the state may empower the state militia to assist. If the situation is still out of control, the President may authorize the commitment of federal troops to assist. In reality, the entire military—the army, navy, air force, and marines—may, when appropriate, be used to enforce the law. The individual police officer, like the "point-man" on a combat team, leads the forces of the government in maintaining domestic tranquility in the various communities, large and small, throughout the United States.

Great power requires great responsibility. The individual officer has a mandate to use the authority and power granted to him in a reasonable manner. Such responsibility is not merely expected, it is demanded. The use of the executive power means simply that the officer be honest and just. But what is justice? What is truth? These questions are a continuous enigma to mankind.

Over the centuries, man has attempted to regulate himself within the confines of the society in which he lives. Every society, whether it be a primitive tribe or a complex civilization, provides some form of government. In a primitive tribe, the government may simply be a chief whose decisions become the law. In a sophisticated society, the government consists of a legislature, an executive branch, and a judiciary. The form that such government takes may vary from society to society and nation to nation. Some nations have as their leader a monarch; others have a dictator or a troika; still others have a representative leader elected by the population. Some governments have combinations of the various systems.

Figure 1-1. The police officer must be all things to all people. He is expected to dispense justice, as well as to maintain law and order.

Now we shall examine some of the philosophies that have provided the base for our system of government.

The Early Origins

The United States Constitution was drafted in an era when gentlemen were required to be familiar with the sciences, humanities, philosophers, agriculture, and business. The breadth and scope of this great document shows that the authors were well versed in these disciplines and were visionaries as well. Looking toward the future and the great western territories that lay beyond the thirteen colonies, they wrote with firm conviction and were confident in the glorious future of a great nation.

The authors of the Constitution had a great storehouse of material to draw upon, which they used well. They drew their philosophy and guidance from such sources as God and John Locke. It may be helpful to briefly review the philosophical antecedents upon which they relied.

The Bible

And God said, Let us make man in our image, after our likeness: and let them have dominion over the fish of the sea, and over the fowl of the air, and over the cattle, and over all the earth, and over every creeping thing that creepeth upon the earth.

So God created man in his own image, in the image of God created he him; male and female created he them.

And God blessed them and God said unto them, be fruitful, and multiply, and replenish the earth, and subdue it: and have dominion over the fish of the sea, and over the fowl of the air, and over every living thing that moveth upon the earth." (Genesis 1:27-29)

The Philosophers

The ancient Greeks and Romans, whose society rivaled and even (in some respects) surpassed modern government in its regulations and philosophy, contributed heavily to the development of our system of government.

Justinian, the great Roman emperor, developed a complex system of government. The number 12 appeared prominently in his scheme of regulations and is thought to be the basis of our present practice of using 12 jurors in cases tried by a jury. Present law, at least in the Western world, has been greatly influenced by the Justinian model of law.

Demosthenes is credited with saying, "Every law is a discovery, a gift of God—a precept of wise men." Aristotle taught that to make the law supreme is to invest it with God and reason; to make a man supreme as a ruler is to introduce a beast, as desire is something bestial. Even when the best of men are in authority, they are sorely tempted and liable to be corrupted by passion. In contemporary terms: "Power corrupts; absolute power corrupts absolutely." Aristotle believed that with the law as the final authority there is reason without passion, and that the law is therefore preferable to any individual.

Aristotle also taught that "an unjust law is not a law." This thought was echoed recently by civil rights demonstrators and objectors to the Vietnam conflict, who claimed that certain laws were unjust and therefore unenforceable, and need not be obeyed.

Cicero, among the brightest and most eloquent of the philosophers, contended that a true law is synonymous with right reason. A just and fair law must be harmonious with nature; it must reflect eternal truths and be constant; it must be such that those to whom it applies are willing and duty bound to obey it; and it must restrain and not create evil by what it prohibits.

The legislative body, Cicero said, has a sacred duty not to attempt to create the law in contradiction of this principle. There is a law, later referred to as the "higher law" by other philosophers, which is natural to man and which his conscience can accept. No senate, ruler, or even the people can release anyone from this higher law. It is universally applicable and is the same today as it is tomorrow—eternal and unchangeable. It needs no interpreter nor anyone to explain its necessity because it is simple truth. A classic example is the prohibition against murder.

Law is not just a set of rules and regulations to guide the mechanics of society; it is justice for which we are all born—an institution of nature. If law is construed as utility only, it may for the same reason be overturned. Cicero proclaimed a sort of natural law that may be discovered, which is a permanent part of human nature. It is a law that goes beyond and is higher than mere rules and regulations for the sake of expediency. Any law that is to be supported voluntarily by the people must embody this positive law.

The statement attributed to Cicero that is perhaps more remembered than any other is: "The laws are the foundation of liberty which we enjoy; we all are slaves to the law that we may be free." Cicero held that true law is a rule of distinction between right and wrong according to natural experience. If law were merely what kings and rulers said it was, or even what the majority of the people say it is, without regard to what the conscience of man knows is right and wrong, "then all that would be necessary in order to make robbery, adultery, or the falsification of wills right and just would be a vote of the multitude."

Finally, Cicero stated, "Reason is the universal possession of mankind which leads to the doctrine of equality of mankind and this in turn paves the way for the translation of natural law into natural rights."

As time passed, religious convictions and moral principles influenced the drafting of codes of conduct. Religious beliefs heavily influenced government. The explosive defiance of the reformers Luther and Calvin against the authority of the Pope (or any other secular leader) over the spiritual lives and liberty of the masses rekindled the desire for individual freedom of thought. In the early 1500s, Luther attacked the authority of the Pope as a temporal authority. He made the distinction between the civil government, which he taught was a creation of God for secular authority; and the church's authority, which he denied had the authority to make secular laws. Luther claimed that the civil government and the church could not be mixed—that they each served a specific purpose, both fulfilling the plan of God.

As to the civil government, Luther taught that it must be obeyed. Concerning man's spiritual life, his only allegiance was to Jesus Christ and no other. "There is no getting around it, a Christian has to be a secular person of some sort, as regard his own person; according to his life as a Christian, he is in subjection to no one but Christ, without any obligation either to the emperor or to any other man. But at least outwardly, according to his body and property, he is related by subjection and obligation to the emperor, inasmuch as he occupies some office or station in life or has a house and home, a wife and children; because all of these are things that pertain to the emperor. Here he must necessarily do what he is told and what this outward life requires."[1]

[1] *Luther's Works*, Vol. 21, *The Sermon on the Mount and the Magnificat*, ed. Jaroslav Pelikan (St. Louis: Concordia Publishing House).

The seventeenth-century philosopher, John Locke, taught that there was a higher law to which all government, kings, rulers, legislatures, and subjects alike owed their allegiance. Man in his "natural state" was imbued with complete freedom of thought and movement. He was responsible only to himself. In order to create order and to devise protection for himself, man relinquished some of his freedom and privilege to a collective group. This collective group became his society—his nation, town, or state. To administer the common affairs of the group and to protect the collective individuals, the group gave up some of these natural rights to the administration—the government—whether it is called a monarchy, a dictatorship, a democracy, or any other name.

The agreement to relinquish individual rights to the government also required the government, by implication, to protect the individual with fair and just laws. This implied agreement became known as a *social compact*. This social compact provided that:

Legislative supremacy is supremacy within the law and not a power above or beyond the law.

Power in the government can never be arbitrary power.

Not even the majority of the people can vest the government with arbitrary power.

Government is an agent of the people, ruling by consent of the people.

The legislature cannot assume a power to rule by arbitrary pronouncements but is bound to be fair and just.

Laws must be promulgated and must apply to all equally.

The law must be administered by known judges fairly and evenly without fear or favor, applying it the same for rich and poor, favorite and despised.

The law must be general and provide equal protection to all who are subject to it; it may not be applied retroactively and it must be enforced by independent courts, not by the legislature that enacted it.

Legislative power is not judicial power.

The legislature cannot validly delegate its legislative authority because the people have given that authority to the legislature and therefore the legislature cannot pass it on to others.

The people retain a supreme power over the legislature, therefore, the legislature is not the ultimate power in the commonwealth, but the people are.

The Law

From the earliest times until the present, laws continue to change, to be defined and redefined, and to encompass these philosophic ideas into codes of conduct. Although numerous codes and sets of laws have been promulgated over the centuries, some written and some unwritten, the following are examples of the most enduring. The student may observe that they all bear points of similarity, revealing that certain forms of behavior must remain constant if civilization is to survive.

The Commandments

And God spake all these words, saying:

I am the Lord thy God, which have brought thee out of the land of Egypt, out of the house of bondage.

Thou shalt have no other gods before me.

Thou shalt not make unto thee any graven image or any likeness of anything that is in heaven above, or that is in the earth beneath, or that is in the water under the earth:

Thou shalt not bow down thyself to them, nor serve them: for I the Lord thy God am a jealous God, visiting in iniquity of the fathers upon the children unto the third and fourth generation of them that hate me;

And shewing mercy unto thousands of them that love me, and keep my commandments.

Thou shalt not take the name of the Lord thy God in vain, for the Lord will not hold him guiltless that taketh his name in vain.

Remember the sabbath day, to keep it holy.

Six days shalt thou labor, and do all thy work;

But the seventh day is the sabbath of the Lord thy God: in it thou shalt not do any work, thou, nor thy son, nor thy daughter, thy manservant nor thy maidservant, not thy cattle, nor the stranger that is within thy gates;

For in six days the Lord made heaven and earth, the sea, and all that in them is, and rested the seventh day: wherefore the Lord blessed the sabbath day and hallowed it.

Honour thy father and thy mother: that thy days may be long upon the land which the Lord thy God giveth thee.

Thou shalt not kill.

Thou shalt not commit adultery.

Thou shalt not steal.

Thou shalt not bear false witness against thy neighbor.

Thou shalt not covet thy neighbor's house, thou shalt not covet thy neighbor's wife, nor his manservant, nor his maidservant, nor his ox, nor his ass, nor anything that is thy neighbor's. (Exodus 20:1-17)

Code of Hammurabi

The oldest written law that has been thus far discovered is the Code of Hammurabi (king of Babylonia). The law was compiled in approximately 2100 B.C., and it was a harsh one by today's standards. It provided, among other things that:

A person who accuses another of a capital offense and is not able to prove the charge shall himself be put to death.

A witness in a capital case who cannot prove his statement shall be put to death.

A burglar shall be put to death.

A robber shall be put to death.

A man who steals property which belongs to a god or a palace and he who receives that property shall be put to death.[2]

The Magna Carta

In June 1215, the barons of Great Britain confronted the king, and a document hailed as the first great triumph for individual liberty was forged in the heat of that collision. Although the barons were primarily concerned with their own self-interest and protection, the Magna Carta, or Great Charter, containing some 70 clauses, has been broadly interpreted as protecting the rights of *all* of the king's subjects. Much of the

[2] Edward S. Kerstein, *The Milwaukee Journal* (May 1, 1973), quoting from *Treasury of Law,* ed. Richard W. Nice (Totowa, N.J.: Littlefield, 1964).

content of the Magna Carta was of only passing concern. However, it did, for the first time, provide an agreement in which the king conceded that there were laws that protected his subjects which he was obliged to observe. It provided that if the king failed to observe those rights, he could be compelled to do so, by force, if necessary. It provided for *habeas corpus,* jury trials, protection of individual liberty and private property, and freedom of the church and customs of the town.

The opening phrase of the Magna Carta provides: "No man shall be taken or imprisoned or deprived of his freehold or his liberties or free customs, or outlawed, or exiled, or in any manner destroyed, nor shall we send upon him, except by a legal judgment of his peers or by the law of the land."

The Common Law

Over the centuries, as the king's subjects engaged in commerce, religion, navigation, education, agriculture, and the pursuit of every-day activities, they guided their behavior by rules of custom or human experience. Contracts were entered into and broken, marriages occurred, and taxes were paid. The whole human experience was the subject of rules and regulations that developed on the basis of human reason guided by a collective conscience defining right and wrong. This collective experience developed into collective wisdom, which became the symbol of ordered life and disciplined activities. It was self-government based on long usage.

These unwritten and undocumented privileges and obligations became known as the common law because these laws were by and for the masses; they depended upon the people themselves for interpretation and enforcement. Because of its distillation over the centuries, the common law became a form of truth and almost divine wisdom. Its precepts were the collective wisdom of the ages. It transcended acts of the parliament or pronouncements of the monarch.

As disputes arose and the courts of the land were resorted to for interpretation and enforcement of the common law, judges began writing their decisions and the basis for their rulings. In this manner, the wisdom of the common law began to be recorded. Each written decision interpreting and applying the law in a particular manner became precedent for cases that followed. This practice of looking for a case that already has decided a point of law or has interpreted a philosophy of man is referred to as *stare decisis*. The practice is followed to the present in order to give stability and continuity to the law; ordinarily, only the highest court of the land will depart from an established principle of law and, in doing so, will pronounce a new principle that will be precedent for that which follows. Reference is still made to common law rights or privileges in cases where no law covers a particular point.

A generally accepted list is as follows:

Man was created by God and was given certain natural rights.

Man's reason and ability to think separated him from the other creatures on earth.

The natural law that governs all men by their ability to reason results in natural rights for all men.

The natural rights were rights possessed by all men, therefore, all men were equal in the eyes of the law.

The natural law is perfect and, therefore, all men are subservient to it.

For purposes of mutual protection and society, political groups of men have joined together.

These groups are administered by a government that derives its authority from those it governs.

Since the government rules by the will of the people who created it, it has only that authority that is relinquished to it—the remainder is reserved to the people.

The government must remain separate from the religious beliefs of the people—government is temporal, religion is divine.

Law must be truth—fair and just—applicable equally to all.

The government is not supreme over the law.

The law must be administered by the legislature to whom the people have given that authority.

The judiciary must apply the law with justice and reason, without fear or favor.

No man is above the law—and none is beneath the law.

The Declaration of Independence

In Congress, July 4, 1776, the unanimous declaration of the thirteen United States of America was as follows.

When in the Course of human Events, it becomes necessary for one People to dissolve the Political Bands which have connected them with another, and to assume among the Powers of the Earth, the separate and equal Station to which the Laws of Nature and of Nature's God entitle them, a decent Respect to the Opinions of Mankind requires that they should declare the causes which impel them to the Separation.

We hold these Truths to be self-evident, that all Men are created equal, that they are endowed by their Creator with certain inalienable Rights, that among these are Life, Liberty, and the Pursuit of Happiness ————That to secure these Rights, Governments are instituted among Men, deriving their just Powers from the Consent of the Governed, that whenever any Form of Government becomes destructive of these Ends, it is the Right of the People to alter or to abolish it, and to institute new Government, laying its Foundation on such Principles, and organizing its Powers in such Form, as to them shall seem most likely to affect their Safety and Happiness. Prudence, indeed, will dictate that Governments long established should not be changed for light and transient Causes; and accordingly all Experience hath shewn, that Mankind are more disposed to suffer, while Evils are sufferable, than to right themselves by abolishing the Forms to which they are accustomed. But when a long Train of Abuses and Usurpations, pursuing invariably the same Object, evinces a Design to reduce them under absolute Despotism, it is their Right, it is their Duty, to throw off such Government, and to provide new Guards for their future Security. Such has been the patient Sufference of these Colonies; and such is now the Necessity which constrains them to alter their former Systems of Government. The History of the present King of Great Britain is a History of repeated Injuries and Usurpations, all having in direct Object the Establishment of an absolute Tyranny over these States. To prove this, let Facts be submitted to a candid World.

He has refused his Assent to Laws, the most wholesome and necessary for the public Good.

He has forbidden his Governors to pass Laws of immediate and pressing Importance, unless suspended in their Operation till his assent should be obtained; and when so suspended, he has utterly neglected to attend to them.

He has refused to pass other Laws for the Accommodation of large Districts of People, unless those People would relinquish the Right of Representation in the Legislature, a Right inestimable to them, and formidable to Tyranny only.

He has called together Legislative Bodies at Places unusual, uncomfortable, and distant from the Depository of their public Records, for the sole Purpose of fatiguing them into Compliance with his Measures. He has dissolved Representative Houses repeatedly, for opposing with manly Firmness his Invasions on the rights of the People.

He has refused for a long Time, after such Dissolutions, to cause others to be elected; whereby the Legislative Powers, incapable of Annihilation, have returned to the People at large for their exercise; the State remaining in the meantime exposed to all the Dangers of Invasion from without, and Convulsions within.

He has endeavored to prevent the Population of these States; for that Purpose obstructing the Laws for Naturalization of Foreigners; refusing to pass others to encourage their Migrations hither, and raising the Conditions of new Appropriations of Lands.

He has obstructed the Administration of Justice, by refusing his Assent to Laws for establishing Judiciary Powers.

He has made Judges dependent on his Will alone, for the Tenure of their Offices, and the Amount and Payment of their Salaries.

He has erected a Multitude of new Offices, and sent hither Swarms of Officers to harass our People, and eat out their Substance.

He has kept among us, in Times of Peace, Standing Armies without the consent of our Legislatures.

He has affected to render the Military independent of and superior to the Civil Powers.

He has combined with others to subject us to a Jurisdiction foreign to our Constitution, and unacknowledged by our laws; giving his Assent to their Acts of pretended legislation:

For quartering large bodies of armed troops among us;

For protecting them, by a mock Trial, from Punishment for any Murders which they should commit on the Inhabitants of these States;

For cutting off our Trade with all Parts of the World;

For imposing Taxes on us without our Consent;

For depriving us, in many cases, of the Benefits of Trial by Jury;

For transporting us beyond Seas to be tried for pretended Offences;

For abolishing the Free System of English Laws in a neighbouring Province, establishing therein an arbitrary Government, and enlarging its Boundaries, so as to render it at once an Example and fit Instrument for introducing the same absolute Rule in these Colonies:

For taking away our Charters, abolishing our most valuable Laws, and altering fundamentally the Forms of our Governments;

For suspending our own Legislatures, and declaring themselves invested with Power to legislate for us in all cases whatsoever.

He has abdicated Government here, by declaring us out of his Protection and waging War against us.

He has plundered our Seas, ravaged our Coasts, burnt our Towns, and destroyed the Lives of our People.

He is, at this Time, transporting large Armies of foreign Mercenaries to complete the Works of Death, Desolation, and Tyranny, already begun with circumstances of Cruelty and Perfidy, scarcely paralleled in the most barbarous ages, and totally unworthy of the Head of a civilized Nation.

He has constrained our fellow Citizens taken Captive on the high Seas to bear Arms against their Country, to become the Executioners of their friends and Brethren, or to fall themselves by their Hands.

He has excited domestic Insurrections amongst us, and has endeavored to bring on the Inhabitants of our Frontiers, the merciless Indian Savages, whose known Rule of Warfare, is an undistinguished Destruction, of all Ages, Sexes and conditions.

In every stage of these Oppressions we have Petitioned for Redress in the most humble Terms: Our repeated Petitions have been answered only by repeated Injury. A Prince, whose character is thus marked by every act which may define a Tyrant, is unfit to be the Ruler of a free people.

Nor have we been wanting in Attentions to our British Brethren. We have warned them from Time to Time of Attempts by their Legislature to extend an unwarrantable Jurisdiction over us. We have reminded them of the Circumstances of our Emigration and settlement here. We have appealed to their native Justice and Magnanimity, and we have conjured them by the Ties of our common Kindred to disavow these Usurpations, which, would inevitably interrupt our Connections and Correspondence. They too have been deaf to the Voice of Justice and of Consanguinity. We must, therefore, acquiesce in the Necessity, which denounces our Separation, and hold them, as we hold the rest of Mankind. Enemies in War, in Peace, Friends.

We, therefore, the Representatives of the UNITED STATES OF AMERICA, in GENERAL CONGRESS, *Assembled, appealing the Supreme Judge of the World for the Rectitude of our Intentions, do, in the Name and by Authority of the good People of these Colonies, solemnly publish and Declare, That these United Colonies are, and of Right ought to be* FREE AND INDEPENDENT STATES; *that they are absolved from all Allegiance to the British Crown, and that all political Connection between them and the State of Great-Britain, is and ought to be totally dissolved; and that as* FREE AND INDEPENDENT STATES, *they have full Power to levy War, conclude Peace, contract Alliances, establish Commerce, and to do all other Acts and Things which* INDEPENDENT STATES *may of right do. And for the support of this Declaration, with a firm Reliance on the Protection of divine Providence, we mutually pledge to each other our Lives, our Fortunes, and our sacred Honor.*

The Bill of Rights

The first ten Amendments, usually called the Bill of Rights, went into effect December 15, 1791.

AMENDMENT I. Congress shall make no law respecting an establishment of religion, or prohibiting the free exercise thereof; or abridging the freedom of speech or of the press; or the right of the people peaceably to assemble, and to petition the Government for a redress of grievances.

AMENDMENT II. A well regulated militia, being necessary to the security of a free State, the right of the people to keep and bear Arms, shall not be infringed.

AMENDMENT III. No Soldier shall, in time of peace, be quartered in any house, without the consent of the Owner, nor in time of war, but in a manner to be prescribed by law.

AMENDMENT IV. The right of the people to be secure in their persons, houses, papers, and effects, against unreasonable searches and seizures, shall not be violated, and no Warrants shall issue, but upon probable cause, supported by Oath or affirmation, and particularly describing the place to be searched, and the persons or things to be seized.

AMENDMENT V. No person shall be held to answer for a capital, or otherwise infamous crime, unless on a presentment or indictment of a Grand Jury, except in cases arising in the land or naval forces, or in the Militia, when in actual service in time of War or public danger; nor shall any person be subject for the same offence to be twice put in jeopardy of life or limb, nor shall be compelled in any criminal case to be a witness against himself, nor be deprived of life, liberty, or property, without due process of law; nor shall private property be taken for public use, without just compensation.

AMENDMENT VI. In all criminal prosecutions, the accused shall enjoy the right to a speedy and public trial, by an impartial jury of the State and district wherein the crime shall have been committed, which district shall have been previously ascertained by law, and to be informed of the nature and cause of the accusation; to be confronted with the witnesses against him; to have compulsory process for obtaining witnesses in his favor, and to have the Assistance of Counsel for his defence.

AMENDMENT VII. In Suits at common law, where the value in controversy shall exceed twenty dollars, the right of trial by jury shall be preserved, and no fact tried by a jury shall be otherwise re-examined in any Court of the United States, than according to the rules of the common law.

AMENDMENT VIII. Excessive bail shall not be required, nor excessive fines imposed, nor cruel and unusual punishments inflicted.

AMENDMENT IX. The enumeration in the Constitution, of certain rights, shall not be construed to deny or disparage others retained by the people.

AMENDMENT X. The powers not delegated to the United States by the Constitution, nor prohibited by it to the States, are reserved to the states respectively, or to the people.

To Determine the Truth

None of the codes or laws designed for peaceful coexistence by people within a society are self-executing; they cannot enforce themselves. Various methods were developed over the centuries to determine the truth when one was accused of violating the law.

Trial by combat required the accused and the accuser to fight to the death. The survivor was considered to be the one who spoke the truth; thus, justice was done. It is suspected that such "trials" resulted only in determining who was the stronger of the two. When either the accused or the accuser was allowed to hire an advocate or champion to substitute for him, the issue clearly became a test of strength only.

Trial by ordeal resulted in many a person going to his death protesting his innocence. Such trials required the accused to survive intact an ordeal such as walking barefooted through a bed of hot coals or being held or dunked under water for a prescribed period. If the accused escaped alive and unscathed, he was declared not guilty.

Trial by popular acclamation was employed during the French Revolution. The accused was paraded before the populace. If the accused was felt to be an enemy of the people they turned thumbs down. The accused was immediately beheaded.

Remnants of the popular will still remain in the form of the jury system. The 12 jurors represent the community. After hearing the evidence and after receiving instructions from the judge concerning the law, the jury decides the guilt or innocence of the accused.

Conclusion

The police officer's role in this kaleidoscopic evolution of justice is to gather facts and evidence in order to obtain a just result. The officer, reinforced with technicians, tools, weapons, and education, gathers the information and proof necessary to bring the accused before the bar of justice. His honesty and fairness are absolutely vital to the preservation of the integrity of the entire system.

Although our criminal justice system is not perfect and is constantly being improved, it is the best system yet devised. It may be cumbersome, sometimes awkward and expensive, but it is designed for only one purpose—justice. A thin line has been drawn between justice for the community and justice for the accused. That line often shifts dramatically. The officer, like a high-wire walker, is astride that line, walking the delicate balance. His skill, perseverence, and dedication to the high ideals outlined in this chapter make the entire structure operable.

Chief Justice Warren E. Burger, in an address to local and state administrators upon their graduation from the FBI Academy, said in part that:

It is often overlooked that no public officials in the entire range of modern government are given such wide discretion on matters dealing with the daily lives of citizens as are police officers. In the broad terms of public administration, I think it would be a safe assumption that the scope of discretion enlarges as we look upward in the hierarchy of government. In other words, the higher the rank, the greater is the discretion. But this is not true in police work. The policeman on the beat, or in the patrol car, makes more decisions and exercises broader discretion affecting the daily lives of people, every day and to a greater extent, in many respects, than a judge will ordinarily exercise in a week.

. . . No law book, no lawyer, no judge can really tell the policeman on the beat how to exercise this discretion perfectly in every one of the thousands of different situations that can arise in the hour-to-hour work of the policeman. Yet we must recognize that we need not choose between no guidelines at all and perfect guidelines. There must be some guidance by way of basic concepts that will assist the officer in these circumstances.

Basically, as I suggested, it is a matter of common sense and sound judgment, and yet we know that one man's common sense may be another man's mistake. Hence this need for carefully devised basic standards to guide the exercise of this discretion and, second, for careful and comprehensive training of officers before they are thrust into situations that would often baffle the wisest judge.[3]

Student Checklist

1. Are you able to describe the foundation of modern law?
2. Can you show how legal philosophers provide us with a description of a police officer's responsibility?
3. Can you name at least three of the most enduring codes of conduct?
4. Can you write a short essay on why we have police?
5. Can you describe what the U.S. Constitution and the Magna Carta have in common?

[3] American Bar Association Project on Standards for Criminal Justice, *Standards Relating to the Urban Police Function,* Copyright © American Bar Association, 1972, p. 2.

Topics for Discussion

1. Discuss the development of law as we know it today.

2. Discuss why police officers should know legal philosophy.

3. Discuss where the power of the law comes from.

4. Discuss why we need police.

ANNOTATED BIBLIOGRAPHY

The Bible, King James version.

Corwin, Edward S. *The Higher Law Background of American Constitutional Law*. Ithaca, N.Y.: Great Seal Books, 1955. A chronological and historical survey of the philosophical antecedents of the U.S. Constitution and Bill of Rights. It outlines the thoughts and philosophy of history's wisest men, such as Aristotle, Cicero, Demosthenes, John Locke, and others and is used here primarily as source material.

Kerstein, Edward S. *The Milwaukee Journal*, quoting from *Treasury of Law*, ed. Richard W. Nice. Totowa, N.J.: Littlefield, 1964. The article appeared in a supplement of the May 1, 1973 *Milwaukee Journal* that was devoted to the subject of Law Day 1973.

Standards Relating to the Urban Police Function, tentative draft, March 1972. One of a series of tentative reports on a variety of topics that have been prepared by advisory committees of the American Bar Association Project on Standards for Criminal Justice. Recommended by the Advisory Committee on the Police Function, Frank J. Remington, Chairman. Copyright © American Bar Association, 1972.

The study of this chapter will enable you to:

1. Comprehend our changing society and its ethical dilemmas.
2. Describe what a profession is.
3. Write a brief essay describing the recent knowledge and information explosions.
4. Describe how the ethics of police are changing.

2
Our Changing Society and Criminal Justice

The Ethical Dilemma

If a student of law enforcement, a potential policeman, probation officer, or sheriff's deputy were asked to explain the ethical dilemma of criminal justice in today's changing and complex society, he would be hard pressed to improve on the following statement of Justice Louis Brandeis.

Crime is contagious. If the government becomes a lawbreaker, it breeds contempt for law; it invites every man to become a law unto itself; it invites anarchy. To declare that in the administration of the criminal law the end justifies the means—to declare that the government may commit crimes in order to secure the conviction of a private criminal—would bring terrible retribution.

The very selection of a policeman for a community is always something of an ethical gamble. If there is a selection board, it tries as best it can to interview prospective candidates. Thus, when a candidate is finally recommended for hiring, it implies that someone supposedly knows enough about what makes a good policeman to say that the person recommended is a good risk to carry a gun.✓

Societies and civilizations are built upon trust. The ultimate expression of this trust is to be found in the system of justice adopted and developed by society. It is impossible to pick up the newspaper, read a book or magazine, or watch television, and not be overwhelmed to the point of apathetic anger and numbness by the enormity of crimes committed by individuals, corporations, nations, and national leaders. In this seemingly adrift world, one of the few encouraging signs of an anchor to reality is the criminal justice professional. He attempts to function in a society of ever-increasing violence in which the legal, ethical, and moral sinews that bind society together seem to be loosening, if not to be coming apart totally.

In 1967, for example, Americans spent $2 billion on pets, $9.2 billion on alcoholic beverages, and $36.6 billion on automobiles and auto parts. If we add to these dollar amounts what we spend on gambling, cosmetics, and tobacco, we will find that only a comparatively minute amount is spent on the prevention of crime and the maintenance of law and order.[1]

The cost in wasted human lives as a result of drugs, adult and juvenile crime, unbridled hatred and anger, poverty, and child abuse threatens to annihilate the social and moral fiber of our country.

One philosopher has referred to the spirit of the time as "the instrumentalization of the world . . . of man . . . of all values."[2] Man is seen as a toolmaking animal using the world as an ecological toolbox with regard only for power and the fruits of power.

If people are things, and if the material, technical, electronic, and amoral power of man is increasingly paramount, what then is the role and place of the emerging police officer?

We must assume that the public is passing on to the field of law enforcement moral and ethical responsibilities, once held sacred by home, church, and school. Mankind seems unable to live comfortably with individual freedom and personal responsibility. Hounded by compulsive material drives and beset by electronic technology, bemused by rampant pornography, and overwhelmed by a deteriorating environment, mankind seeks the creation of new anchors to painful reality, secured environments in which to grow, live, and create.

A panorama of the past half century depicts depression, the holocaust of Hitler, and a war of massive death and destruction ending in an atomic nightmare in a grave new world. The past decade alone has seen assassinations, gross drug and crime problems, drifting youth, and moral disintegration. This has culminated in ethical and moral pervasion from the street corner to the highest government sources.

The 1970 White House Conference on Children cast further light on the world and the society that the coming generation of police officers would face. Many of the patterns and threads running through the concerns and recommendations of the Conference report included direct, indirect, and implied involvement of criminal justice in all its facets.

For example, it is common knowledge in police practice that

[1] "Children in Trouble," Report to the President, White House Conference on Children, Washington, D.C., Supt. of Documents, 1970/1973.
[2] Abraham J. Heschel, *The Insecurity of Freedom* (New York: Farrar, Strauss, and Giroux, 1966), p. 40 *et passim*.

many officers are killed and wounded while answering marital or domestic quarrels. The criminal justice professional has to be able to look beyond the divorce, separation, and abandonment statistics and realize that new patterns of marriage, family life, and child-rearing are developing. In addition, new factors and patterns involving the mentally ill, the mentally retarded, and drifters in our homes and on the streets will demand law enforcement personnel with new skills. Although statistics can be boring, the White House Conference fact book, *Profiles of Children* (1970), cited the following facts and figures on adolescents relevant to law enforcement problems of today.

An estimated 5 percent of children needing psychiatric care are receiving it.

In 1968, approximately 10 percent of the 50 million school-age children had moderate to severe emotional problems.

One out of three poor children had serious emotional problems that required attention.

Since 1963, juvenile delinquency has been increasing at a rate faster than the population.

In 1968, the reports of juvenile delinquency in urban areas were more than triple the rate in rural areas.

Nearly four times as many boys were referred to juvenile courts as girls.

If present trends continue, 1 out of every 9 youngsters will appear before juvenile court before age 18.

In January of 1970, 5 and one-half million juveniles under age 21 were in families receiving public assistance payments. Among these families, over 80 percent were fatherless, 12 percent had physically handicapped fathers, and 5 percent had fathers who were unemployed or employed only part-time.

The Profession of Criminal Justice

What is a profession? What makes a person a professional? The facets of a profession as they apply to policemen are of great significance.

1. They would include education and training; they would include a body of qualified personnel who are *socially sanctioned*.

2. The practitioners are able to make *ethical professions* in the sense of declarations and claims of high standards of personal and professional conduct.

3. As professionals, they are "sharp" because of combined education, training, and experience.

We traditionally link the term professional with doctors, dentists, and lawyers, yet our coming generation of professional practitioners of criminal justice will be the first to overcome the traditional deep-rooted insecurity and lack of professional status on the part of many law enforcement personnel for a striking reason. Namely, if we can define a professional by the amount of control he has over human life and human destiny, then we must rank the police officer second only to the physician as a professional who requires the best of training and appropriate rewards for competence from society. In turn, this means that the peace officer, precisely because of his control over human life and the destinies of individuals, must have an appropriate code of ethics and an internal set of ethical imperatives within him in order to practice his profession.

We can carry the analogy forward and compare the policeman considering the use of deadly force with a surgeon at the operating table. Both require tremendous coordination of mind, eye, and hand; both demand clearcut, instantaneous decision-making; both hold life and death in the balance of their hands; both are socially sanctioned; and both are under fire by society as individual professionals and as a professional group.

Like the physician, psychologist, and lawyer, the police officer and his colleagues have ethical codes. These behavioral guidelines act as "thermostatic" controls governing the conscience, personal actions, and professional life of the police officer. One generally accepted code, the Law Enforcement Code of Ethics, reads as follows.

> *As a law enforcement officer, my fundamental duty is to serve mankind; to safeguard lives and property; to protect the innocent against deception, the weak against depression or intimidation, and the peaceful against violence or disorder; and to respect the constitutional rights of liberty, equality, justice.*
>
> *I will keep my private life unsullied as an example to all; maintain courageous calm in the face of danger, scorn, or ridicule; develop self-restraint; and be constantly mindful of the welfare of others. Honest in thought and in deed in both my personal and official life, I will be exemplary in obeying the laws of the land and the regulations of the*

department. Whatever I see or hear of a confidential nature or that is confided to me in my official capacity will be kept ever secret unless revelation is necessary in the performance of my duty.

I will never act officiously or permit personal feelings or prejudices, animosities, or friendships to influence my decision. With no compromise and with relentless prosecution of criminals, I will enforce the law courteously and appropriately without fear of favor, malice, or ill will, never employing unnecessary force or violence and never accepting gratuities.

I recognize the badge of my office as the symbol of public faith and I accept the public trust to be held so long as I am true to the ethics of the police service. I will constantly strive to achieve these objectives and ideals, dedicating myself before God and my chosen profession— law enforcement.

Admittedly, ethics and ethical statements make dull reading, yet they have provided, starting with the Ten Commandments, the controls that prevent men from completely behaving as predatory beasts. Yet, considering the "new morality" of today's society, in which society as a whole is hard pressed to set moral and ethical standards to govern the behavior of citizens, let alone observe them, what is the role and ethical obligation of the citizen police officer? Must his rights as a citizen collife with his duties in the field of criminal justice?

Traditionally, obedience to the law, ethical behavior, and moral decisions have been bound and intertwined into an absolute adherence based on extremes of legal versus illegal, good versus bad, and right versus wrong. Situations were black and white. However, since the end of the Second World War, the continuing struggle between heritage and change, between fixed values and no values, and between simple lives and complex living has seen heritage slowly dying. At the same time, man has not been able to adapt as quickly as society and the technology surrounding him. He finds a growing shrinkage of space and time and a negative relationship between the two. He finds the so-called knowledge and information explosions threatening to overwhelm him. He finds that the population explosion is taken almost as a commonplace event, and he finds that the emergence of electronic controls creates what might be called "electronic amorality."

These factors and conditions have led to different views of legal, ethical, and moral behaviors—traditional or absolute, relative, scaled, and situational.

Figure 2-1 . The conflict between heritage and change, between fixed values and no values, has seen the traditional police role slowly dying.

Absolute, or "black or white," approaches have the force of tradition behind them. All aspects of criminal justice have been nurtured by codes for survival of the species. A police officer never questions the law using absolute terminology and methods.

Relative approaches have come into being because of the increasing complexities of living on this planet. Values have become relative to one another and to situations. "Policies" help to "bend" the law and social conditions tend to confuse and confound the search for simple solutions and answers.

The idea of "scaling" values and laws has become more and more popular in recent years. A hierarchy of values replaces the absolute of centuries past. Some values and certain laws are more important than others. The element of bargaining has entered criminal justice and sworn officials may agree to "overlook" or "temper" or "reduce" a charge according to the state of their own moral condition and the dictates of the situation.

It is the concept of the *situation* as governing or controlling the decisions and actions of the criminal justice official that has caught the imagination of the public and certainly the behavior of politicians and public officials in and out of law enforcement. The idea of the criminal justice official as a tool of the state, whether it be at the level of Washington, D.C., the state capital, or the local community, has become a problem in our time. Underlying this is the ethical danger mentioned by Brandeis that the "end will justify the means."

The moral theologian and advocate of "situation ethics," Joseph Fletcher, has stated that there are only three basic approaches to moral decision-making: (1) the legally based; (2) the opposite or lawless approach; and (3) the situational.[3]

Fletcher looks upon what he refers to as the "whole apparatus of prefabricated rules and regulations" as a rigid, torturous, confusing, and hair-splitting system of directives with a centuries-old Judeo-Christian orthodoxy of profound influence on our Western civilization. His concern for our elaborate system of legalisms has a special meaning for people entering all branches of criminal justice. He feels (and with much current justification) that we have really evolved "an elaborate system of exceptions and compromises in the form of rules for breaking the rules."[4]

[3] Joseph Fletcher, *Situation Ethics* (Philadelphia: Westminster, 1966), p. 16.
[4] Ibid., p. 18.

The contradictory rigidity and yet, relativism, of this traditional approach can best be summed up in a paraphrase of a comment by the philosopher Bertrand Russell. Today we have much concern for prostitution, adultery, and pornography, as well as concern for political chicanery. Russell asks why the former have always been considered more wicked than the latter, although a crooked politician can harm and morally confuse many more thousands.

Fletcher's opposite approach needs little comment at a time when anarchy, revolution, and repudiation of all law except love or hate and "one doctrine for all mankind" are growing in popularity. Young people, especially, are exploring lawless, chance-derived superstitions, which might include astrology, witchcraft, and satanic worship.

Fletcher dislikes either polarity. He advocates what he terms "situation ethics." He recommends that decisions concerning any situation be "illuminated" by ethical and moral legality but that individual reason be the "instrument of moral judgment."[5] What is right in a situation may be governed by the circumstances of the situations, by what is fitting or appropriate.

If the student of criminal justice stops to consider this approach to decision-making for one sworn to uphold the law, he may get confused or angered or puzzled by such simplicity. Yet, situational ethics is a child of the last three or more decades.

The advent of dictatorship from Hitler and the genocide of more than 6 million human beings, through the massive upheaval during the Second World War to the reemergence of neodictatorship in the second half of this century, has led to new thinking about any military, paramilitary, or police and police-related forces. This has culminated in the current decade in the so-called Watergate scandals. Any remaining smugness and complacency on the part of law enforcement officials has been shattered by the realization that forms of illegal abuse and shady control of criminal justice agencies are possible when moral and ethical integrity is lacking.

The basic problem derives from the centuries-old dilemma of trusting men; can those fellow citizens who are sworn professionally to protect, defend, and uphold the laws of this country face situations so inhuman that they must rebel against authority, existing laws, and the

[5] Ibid., p. 26.

orders of superiors? Are there unjust laws? Can there be unjust laws? Are there or can there be unjust situations in which it is possible to disobey one's sworn duty in the course of representing the government while trying to protect individual rights in a democracy? Everyday criminal justice enforcement problems—narcotics, race situations, delinquency, marital disputes, pornography, or prostitution—put the law enforcement officer in a decision-making "bind" as to what to do.

Individuals involved in our criminal justice system have to face paradox after paradox: they are very often confronted with situations in which they are "damned if they do and damned if they don't." This paradox is best illustrated by the fact that society is just starting to recognize the contradictions and burdens placed upon the policeman. He is expected to represent heritage in a changing time. He is expected to represent the controls of authority and the controls of tradition, yet he is faced with a hierarchy of ethical decisions in which he often must decide which law he may or may not allow the individual or criminal or the youngster to break or not break. The policeman is faced with the ethical problem of how far one can bend the law before it will break. In keeping with these paradoxical concepts, we find that the policeman is expected to have a definite, if somewhat vague, role in society—a role tainted and tinged by stereotyping, prejudice, and an aura of unreality concerning this stressful profession. Within this framework, in which the policeman is considered to be on the side of our heritage and yet is expected to cope with change, we find that there is not just a "policeman"—a person involved in various aspects of law enforcement.

Rather, we find that there are "policemen" and that there are many emerging roles, styles, and skills involving policemen. These include the policeman as a counselor; the policeman as a human services representative and a member of the human services team; the policeman as a human relations expert; the policeman as a decision-maker; the policeman as an agent for change; and the policeman as a trust-builder between law enforcement on the one hand and the various increasingly hostile segments of society on the other. The policeman is not only expected but is mandated to transmit, carry forward, control, and enforce those aspects of human existence that individuals, society, nations, and civilization have considered worthwhile, and which they have put into a code of laws.

We have seen the very training of policemen change from "police"

to "peace" in focus. Gradually, albeit painfully, criminal practice has
seen the focus change from "head-busting" to a human relations, human
services emphasis. Here again, in criminal justice training, the paradox
of our times holds true. The very emphasis on increased human sensitivity in law enforcement professional training means a more open and
alert combination of maturity and feeling on the part of police officers
toward society in general and the citizenry in particular. This could be
a mixed blessing in terms of ethical behavior. Simply put, if the policeman is to be society's anchor to an increasingly painful and confusing
reality, based on our legal heritage and system in a time of social and
electronic change, then he has to be part of an intertwined cultural
heritage and ethical system.

The idea of ethics stems from the Greek word *ethos*, meaning
"character." Ethics concerns itself with human values, attempting to
put in on the one side the "good" and on the other the "bad," on the
one side the "is" and on the other the "ought," on the one side the
"right" and on the other side the "wrong."[6]

All societies have some sort of working, common-sense code based
on oral and written traditions, stemming in our civilization from a
Judeo-Christian system of ethical beliefs. These are part of an ongoing
system of laws and institutions.

Perhaps it is ironic to students involved in training in the criminal justice professions, let alone in their practice, that even a short scan
of that branch of philosophy called ethics must recognize that ethics in
the classical sense looks to the concept of happiness as the ultimate good.

Nevertheless, this concept is appealing in ultimate value. Our
founding fathers felt that the pursuit of happiness was a legitimate goal
of this nation. But the working police officer or probation officer has to
continually risk his life and ethical integrity in order to pick up the
paradoxical pieces of this ethical commitment.

As wise as the founding fathers were, they could never have envisioned the all-consuming growth of material things and its rape of the
earth. They could not have visualized the emergence of an electronic
technology that has grown from slave to enslaver. They surely did not
equate happiness as their philosophical concern for simple well-being in

[6] *Encyclopaedia Britannica*, Vol. 8, p. 756.

simple times with our current equation that happiness involves fun, pleasure, and "making it,"—in short, an amoral imperative.

For the policeman on the beat, on the street, ethics are at "a gut level." As a human being living in hedonistic times, he may want a piece of the action. But as a trained professional, how do you handle gut ethics?

The Next Generation of Policemen

The philosopher, Max Lerner, commented a few years ago that Americans have always been too intent on solving problems. We have been a nation facing challenges by constantly seeking practical answers and solutions.

These have been admirable traits in past years, but where has it left us? We seem to have degenerated into a problem-solving nation of commissions, study groups, conferences, and committees. It has not been uncommon to find a dozen dedicated (and expensive) commissions charged by public officials to examine education, crime, violence, pornography, drugs, law enforcement, or the like. Cynics claim that when we do not know what to do, we create a learned group to tell us in effect that nothing can be done. In addition, it is often common for a state or national leader to appoint a study commission to solve a problem and then put their findings and recommendations in the office safe because he does not agree with the facts and suggestions.

Lerner's point was that the time has come for us to stop seeking the right answers and to start asking the right questions!

Reports and studies on crime in the streets, violence, drugs, and pornography have accumulated for years. Their conclusions—good, bad, and indifferent—have not always had the agreement, involvement, or cooperation of concerned criminal justice leaders.

Perhaps it is time for criminal justice personnel at all levels, from students and trainees to law enforcement leaders, to ask the appropriate and necessary questions, rather than to be put on the defensive by the public and politicians.

The queries are many, but the basic one facing us now and in the future can be simply put: Will criminal justice personnel serve man or the state?

There are no glib and obvious answers to this question. Traditionally, criminal justice professionals were arms of the state and the community dedicated to serving and protecting the citizenry. But, as this chapter has pointed out, the sum total of conditions has changed. Therefore, criminal justice professionals must change and grow. The public ✓ perception of the fat-gutted, dumb, headbusting "pig" has to be replaced by a perception of the everyday policeman as an intelligent, honest, ethically concerned professional in a high-risk, highly trained, human services specialty—law enforcement.

The very nature of the people he will serve, protect, and be professionally concerned for will require much greater technical and professional training and education than now exists.

Admittedly, it is dangerous to categorize people, but sworn justice personnel must deal with three broad groupings representing the sick and disordered citizens of our society. These fluid, growing groups include the vast army of lonely, drifting schizoid-humanoids; the frightened, suspicious, paranoid-humanoids; and the sociopathic-humanoids; the economic, criminal, and assorted "hustlers" of our time.

Why use the term "humanoid" with its undertones of science fiction? Humanoids are people who are gradually and continually depersonalized and dehumanized by the times, the institutions, and technology of the world we live in. Humanoids are people who are unfulfilled in their striving to be effective people. They are their own executioners, yet they are also very often victims of us all. They live on the torn margins of life, on the moldy edges of existence. No single factor has made them what they are: poverty or riches; broken homes or overindulged homes; school dropout or doctoral dropout. Our country today can be likened to a multifaceted diamond with an increasing number of cracked or damaged facets.

The humanoids in the schizoid facet include the drifters, the alienated, the empty, the unrelated, and the unrelating. This category can include those who seek solace and fulfillment in chemicals and those who are constantly on the run. It can include those who can only stand and stare and those who are unable to leave the safety of infantile sex relationships for the risks and pleasures of adulthood. The policeman and other criminal justice professionals will have to face this vulnerable, defenseless, semifaceless, and unhappy mass of individuals not as strong-armed minions of a heartless state but as enforcers of human services and laws—as agents-for-change able to protect those who may ⌐ really need the most protection from themselves and society's exploitation.

Paranoia and the police is another matter. Experienced police professionals often comment that the two major strains of sickness battling it out in our time involve the pathological-alienated versus the pathological-suspicious. The fanatics in religion, in the military and paramilitary organizations, in politics, education, and other areas of living, are prone to see evil in many of society's institutions. Here we find the cancer of prejudice and bigotry in all too many citizens who have simple, but basically deadly, solutions to mankind's problems. Here we can find some of the biggest enemies of criminal justice and some of its biggest supporters.

People with these paranoid tendencies very often "sense" conspiracies or may band together in their own delusional counterconspiracies. The more the policeman understands the desperately lonely and the desperately suspicious person, the closer we will be to solving the problems of criminal justice.

Sensitive professionals involved in all facets of criminal justice cannot ignore the growing number of alienated, drifting, disordered, and overly suspicious people. The fact that so many unhappy and unfortunate people exist makes it extremely important to improve the police officer's education and training in psychology, social work, and counseling skills.

One broad grouping remains: the sociopathic-personality pattern. This catch-all term can and does include problems of alcoholism, drug abuse, and sexual deviation as well as a garden variety of problem-producing social misfits with poor character structures.

The underlying theme of character disorder has many variations. A thoughtful citizenry, spurred on by the Watergate scandals, recognizes that many democratic values, processes, and institutions may encourage sociopathic behavior in politics, public service (including criminal justice), all professions, and in the business community. Compulsive drives for money, for power, and for success can lead to a decline in moral and ethical standards, can cause values to be distorted, and can result in the use of family, colleagues, employees, and citizens as a means to reach a personal or professional goal. The ethical and professional problems that sociopathic behavior poses for law enforcement personnel are conspicuously dramatized in our magazines and newspapers.

We can "fish" in the sociopathic "pool" and find people who are twisters, who are slick, devious, and lack a conscience, to say nothing of a lack of guilt or remorse for whatever public or private crimes they have committed for their own personal gain.

Law enforcement personnel may be troubled to find sociopathic types who are highly successful in our material, manipulative, free enterprise system. These are very often people who know how to use the shadings of the law and our guaranteed freedom and liberties for their own personal, often materialistic, and sometimes contradictory ends.

Perhaps a word of caution to the student is advisable at this point. At any one time, all of us may have some of the symptoms, behavioral patterns, or characteristics described in the three groupings. In addition, other forms of behavior exist above and beyond what is mentioned here. Therefore, we must maintain a philosophical balance in examining and discussing those aspects of democracy and free enterprise that tend to foster the schizoid, paranoid, or sociopathic behaviors. We must further accept the fact that they blend into one another so that it is hard for a policeman to pinpoint or generalize in any area of criminal justice. Democracy is prone to sicknesses, but social sicknesses and political diseases in the democratic "body" can be self-limiting and self-healing if there is a healthy generation of law enforcement personnel practicing their human services specialty in the best professional manner. In the final analysis, policemen and their colleagues have to have a conscience, a democratic system of values, and a balanced philosophy of criminal justice practice, all based upon a healthy view of democracy and its citizens.

A fourth area might be touched upon, that of the issue of privacy for the individual citizen. Since future generations of policemen will have an amazing variety of electronic devices for invading the privacy of the individual, they will have the electronic means for total depersonalization and possible destruction of the personalities of many people. The physical abuse that law enforcement officials have been accused of may pale before the psychological weapons they will have at hand for dehumanizing otherwise effective people.

Students of criminal justice who are interested in seeing how far we have actually come technically and professionally and yet how little we may have advanced morally and ethically would do well to read the late H. L. Mencken's "Recollections of Notable Cops."[7] Mencken expresses astonishment that a number of college graduates have been appointed to the New York City Police Department in the 1940s, and then goes on to describe the turn-of-the-century policemen with their professional pride because, although badly paid ". . . they carried on their dismal work with unflagging diligence and loved a long, hard chase as much as they loved a quick, brisk clubbing." He then comments, "I well recall the horror of the Baltimore cops when the first board to examine applicants for places on the force was set up. It was a harmless body headed by a political dentist and the hardest question in his first examination paper was, 'What is the plural of ox?' But all the cops in turn predicted that it would quickly contaminate their craft with a great horde of what they called 'professors' and reduce it to a level of letter-carrying or school teaching."[8]

How times have changed! The neighborhood cop on the beat who took pride in the high visibility of his badge and uniform has virtually disappeared. Observers of the human condition of today's world stress the dehumanization of mankind when they heavily criticize criminal justice personnel. They tend to stress the cynicism, brutality, and faceless depersonalization of the police and the public in their relationship with one another; this has led to an unfortunate stereotyping of policemen. On the one hand we have the paranoid, perceptual extreme of policemen as arms of the military with total control over the life and death of the citizenry. We also have the equally unfortunate perception of the police as brutal tools of an unfeeling state.

The severe, stressful conditions of police practice have led the sociologist, Arthur Niederhoffer (a former policeman) to use the term "anomie" to describe this relationship between society and the representatives of law enforcements. He gave the dimensions of anomie as "a morbid condition of society, characterized by the absence of standards, by apathy, frustration, alienation and despair."[9] To paraphrase his general thesis, the challenge for those entering all facets of criminal justice is to overcome the syndrome involving "loss of faith in people,

[7] H. L. Mencken, "Recollections of Notable Cops (1900-1910)" *Happy Days, Newspaper Days, & Heathen Days* (New York: Knopf, 1942), pp. 27 *et passim*.
[8] Ibid., pp. 27, 28.
[9] Arthur Niederhoffer, *Behind the Shield* (New York: Doubleday), p. 90.

of enthusiasm for the high ideals of policework and the pride and integrity.''[10] Niederhoffer points out that the condition of anomie comes about when we find the old .alues of a social system being replaced by a new code or by no code at all.

If this is a time of growing public and private cynicism and immorality, it is particularly challenging for people in law enforcement to avoid attempts to manipulate and distort daily police practice. It is more than ever essential for those sworn to represent and uphold the law to do exactly that. As far as criminal justice practice is concerned, gut level cynicism on the part of the so-called troops on the streets forms the small cancerous cell of anomie for those devoting their professional lives to criminal justice. Niederhoffer encapsules our concern for overcoming this problem when he quotes the late Chief William Parker of the Los Angeles Police Department:

> *But it is also hard for me to believe that our society can continue to violate all the fundamental rules of human conduct and expect to survive. I think that I will have to conclude that this civilization will destroy itself as others have before it. That leaves, then, only one question—when?*

An ancient Hebrew sage was once asked, "Why did God give us two eyes? Why didn't he give us one, or even three eyes?" The sage replied that we were given two eyes, so as to have one with which to look out at the world around us and the other to look inward at the world within us.

If the policeman is to face and cope with the challenging monster called crime, we have seen how facts, figures, psychological groupings, and social interpretations of life in the United States can be looked at with the perceptive outer-searching eye of law and order. But what of the other eye? These selfsame conditions have their potential effect on the policeman as an ethical practitioner and as a human being. The policeman is not immune to the situations he must face. He is an influencer and controller of the situation. Whether he is facing problems of deadly force, problems of mixed ethical decisions, or problems involving the fundamental privacy of individual citizens, it all rubs off on him.

Immorality is a fact of life in our time. The law attempts to define homosexuality, adultery, prostitution, pornography, and other aspects of

[10] Ibid.

crime. Our morbid preoccupation with the mechanics of sex without love has many criminal and quasi-criminal aspects. The exposure of any policeman to the seductive blandishments of immorality poses a deeply personal, ethical, and internal problem for the criminal justice official as a human being. Many a policeman with a fine future in law enforcement has found his career and marriage completely destroyed because in the area of immorality, he was unable to cope as a human being.

The alienation resulting from loneliness, inadequacy, despair, and helplessness found among so many of our citizens is bound to have its effect on the personality and psychological maturity of every policeman. Many policemen sense that they are becoming closed up and distant because of the people they have to face from day to day. There is no greater irony in law enforcement than to find attrition in the ranks of competent policemen as they paraphrase the adage, "We have faced the enemy and he is us."

Peace officers also face the character problems of the "quick buck" artist and the corporate hustler. Criminal justice personnel can be as jealous of material success in a nation obsessed with the acquisition of things as anyone else. Authorities and students of police practice have continually pointed out that the American public is parsimonious when it comes to paying policemen adequately for their professional services, yet quick to preach about the high demands and expectations we have for our professionals in criminal justice. But when the individual has to deal with any and all personnel in criminal justice, whether a policeman, a probation officer, the Federal Bureau of Investigation or a customs officer, we want things settled in a hurry; we want either the easy way out for ourselves or instant arrest and justice for those who have hurt or damaged us or our property. The realities lie somewhere in between. The American public tends to be piously hypocritical where policemen are concerned; with a childlike disbelief that policemen might, themselves, be involved in criminal acts.

Policemen must also face people who are unable to love those close to them. Child abuse, child deprivation, family abandonments, marital homicides, and suicides—all these and more can have a profound and sometimes shattering effect on a policeman as a parent and as a husband.

What is the answer? Is there an answer? The answer lies in *your* ability to keep a part of yourself for yourself and your family. The officer who spends all his spare time still being a cop and hanging around the station house or the office is doomed to an unhappy personal and family life that will eventually catch up with his professional life. The best professional integrity comes from maintaining personal integrity and a good psychological balance as a person.

Some Final Words

This chapter has explored the conflict between heritage and change, the conflict between the policeman as an agent of the state and as a representative of the individual citizen. We have looked at the ethics of the professional peace officer—on the one hand, the so-called gut ethics of everyday police practice and, conversely, the paradoxical problems facing the policeman as he attempts to enforce laws that are formulated by men twice and three times removed from the realities of police action and criminal justice practices on the streets.

Centuries ago, the philosopher, Kant, gave mankind two ethical maxims or imperatives that appear to be totally relevant and appropriate to the ethical needs of criminal justice today. The first stated that we must act so as to treat humanity always as an end and never only as a means. The second stated that we should always act as if the maxim of our actions were to become, by our will, law universal.

Many of the students reading this text will become leaders in criminal justice. As chiefs of police, as directors of national, state, and community programs, or as command personnel at all levels, your own strict adherence to the ethical orders outlined above will ensure that the system of criminal justice and the members of your force or staff will never be manipulated as a means to an end. It will further mean that your men will be so trained and educated that police brutality will minimize, precisely because you follow Kant's second ethical principle and intuitively realize your unethical actions might become disastrous universal law. When a man becomes a means toward an end and when human dignity is forgotten, then we find human beings becoming humanoids once again. We must not forget how easy it is to rationalize our actions, to justify the end result under the title of liberty, democracy, internal security, and related cover-up terms.

Never before have philosophers and peace officers, politicians, and the public been so carefully and sincerely reexamining the dimensions and limits of liberty, freedom, and democracy as living entities.

Some years ago, George Orwell stated:

The point is that the relative freedom which we enjoy depends on public opinion, the law is no protection. The governments make laws, but whether they are carried out, and how the police behave, depends upon the general temper of the country. If large numbers of people are interested in freedom of speech, there will be freedom of speech even if the law forbids it; If public opinion is sluggish, inconvenient minorities will be persecuted, even if laws exist to protect them.[11]

A current philosopher and commentator on man in a democracy, Milton Mayer, in his *Liberty: Man versus State* has commented on the many perceptual facets of liberty: "Plainly, what one man calls justice another man calls expropriation; and one man's security is another man's slavery, one man's liberty is another man's anarchy."[12] Mayer wonders if in our time the rule of law is not becoming the enemy of liberty.

What does it all boil down to? The essence for the coming generation of peace officers involves close adherence to traditionally based ethics; a philosophy that sees liberty and justice clearly and sees them as a fluid dynamic whole in a democratic framework; a humanistic psychological view of mankind; and a stubborn yet flexible sociology of what the United States is all about.

Only then will we move beyond Judge Learned Hand's wry comment: "Liberty is so much latitude as the powerful choose to accord the weak."

Student Checklist

1. Can you briefly outline how our society is changing?
2. Can you describe what a profession is?

[11] George Orwell, *1984* (Harcourt Brace, 1963).
[12] Milton Mayer, *Liberty: Man versus State* (Santa Barbara: The Center for the Study of Democratic Institutions), p. 41.

3. Are you able to write a brief essay explaining the knowledge explosion since World War II?
4. Can you describe changes in police ethics?

Topics for Discussion

1. How is our society changing?
2. Discuss what makes a person a professional.
3. Discuss the knowledge explosion that has occurred since World War II.
4. Discuss whether or not police ethics are changing.

ANNOTATED BIBLIOGRAPHY

Chevigney, Paul. *Police Power*. New York: Pantheon Books, 1969. Patterns of police abuse, using the N.Y.C.P.D. as a role model. The author blames society for giving the police leeway and mandate for ethically and physically abusive behavior.

Cray, Ed. *The Big Blue Line*. New York: Coward-McCann, 1967. An American Civil Liberties Union study of police malpractice and its effect on human rights, the courts, the individual citizen arrested, and accused.

Fletcher, Joseph. *Situation Ethics*. Philadelphia: Westminster Press, 1966. A controversial book based on the glaring assumption that man is capable of handling individual freedom, individual responsibility, and love in a ethical manner based on the demands of the situation, rather than the time-honored moral codes.

Heschel, Abraham J. *The Insecurity of Freedom*. New York: Farrar, Strauss and Giroux, 1966. The late, great philosopher looks at various segmented problems of behavior existence. The prescient chapter on children and youth is especially important for understanding present-day human conditions.

Mayer, Milton. *Man versus State*. The Center for the Study of Democratic Institutions, Santa Barbara, 1969. A fascinating, witty examination of the innate conflicts, paradoxes, and relationships between a remote computer-state and man and his rights. The problem of what is a "just" law is beautifully delineated.

Niederhoffer, Arthur. *Behind the Shield*. New York: Doubleday, 1967. A policeman who turned sociologist examines and discusses the forces that can make a pragmatic policeman able to function and make it on the street. . . . The chapter on *Anomie and Cynicism* is especially significant for the "new entry" peace officer.

White House Conference for Children, *Profiles of Children*, Supt. of Documents, Washington, D.C. 1970. Extremely provocative, sometimes tragic statistics that destroy the assumption that we are a child-loving, child-oriented society.

White House Conference on Children, *Report to the President*, Supt. of Documents, Washington, D.C., 1970. A series of strongly worded proposals to help the president and Congress plan for the next decade concerning children and youth. The president vetoed the Omnibus Bill passed by Congress, designed to implement and put into practice the recommendations outlined in this report. These are tomorrow's citizens and tomorrow's law enforcement personnel, who will meet these "statistics" on the streets.

The study of this chapter will enable you to:

1. Define the term "role" as it applies to a police officer.
2. Write a short essay defining a police officer's role in terms of what he does.
3. Compare police role concepts with juveniles and with adults.
4. Understand why black people see the role of police differently than do white people.
5. List at least five elements involved in behavioral modification.

3
Role Concepts Today

Today's law enforcement officer is often viewed by his public in terms that are as abstract as the definitions of "role" and "role concept." The law enforcement officer does not always experience the luxury of being an individual or even human to his public; instead "he is viewed by subjective impressions rather than by objective reality."[1]

It is the objective of this chapter to identify the disagreements and misunderstandings about what a law enforcement officer is and what he is thought to be. An attempt will be made to account for these differences in a logical manner. Since we will be treading on abstract ground, we must insure that our terms are well defined. For the purpose of clarity, role will be defined as "something a person does as the occupant of a specified position." For example, we can observe the role of "father." If we look at the things that a person holding the specified position of "father" does, we can define his role. As a father, a man does many things, which may include providing financial support for his family, being a model for his son, projecting somewhat of an authoritarian influence over his family, and providing discipline and correction for his children. All of these things are generally done by the father and become part of his role definition.

The Police Officer's Role

The role of the police officer may also be described in this same manner. What does he do as a police officer? Some of the operational functions of the police officer may be controlling traffic, investigating crimes,

---

[1] James W. Sterling, *Changes in Role Concepts of Police Officers* (Gaithersburg, Md.: International Association of Chiefs of Police, 1972), p. 78.

advising citizens, patrolling, administering first aid, and many more functions. They form a spectrum of activity every bit as complex as that of the role of father.

Let us first identify the law enforcement officer's role in terms of what he does. Surprisingly enough, less than 20 percent of the officer's time is spent repressing crime.[2] Most of his time—more than 80 percent —is spent providing various noncriminal services.

> *Police are men charged with the duty of investigating crime and apprehending criminals. To fulfill the duty, they are given authority to invoke the criminal process—to arrest, to prosecute, and seek a conviction. As important as this function is, however, the average police officer spends a relatively small part of his time investigating and prosecuting serious criminal offenses. Most of his day is spent in keeping order, settling disputes, finding missing children, helping drunks, directing traffic, and monitoring parking meters.[3]*

It should also be noted that the size of the community affects the type of activities that occupy the law enforcement officer's time. In larger communities, he spends more time in crime repression; in smaller jurisdictions most of his time is spent in service-type duties.

For example, a study conducted in the Hamilton Township, New Jersey, Police Department (a suburban department serving a population of about 90,000), a list of duties performed by police officers was compiled in the order of their apparent importance:[4]

> Advise, warn, or arrest youngsters
> Preserve evidence
> Stop and question
> Arrest
> Good community relations
> Crowd control
> Search crime scenes
> Interview victims and witnesses
> Issue traffic tickets
> Search and question prisoners

---

[2] Victor G. Strecher, *The Environment of Law Enforcement* (Englewood Cliffs, N.J.: Prentice-Hall, 1971), p. 96.
[3] Hazel B. Kerper, *Introduction to the Criminal Justice System* (St. Paul, Minn.: West, 1972), p. 418.
[4] U. S. Department of Justice, *Police Training and Performance Study* (Washington, D.C.: U.S. Govt. Printing Office, 1970), p. 20.

Make written reports
Testify
Inspect places
First aid
Give information
Mentally disturbed persons
Drunks and alcoholics
Rescue lost persons
Recover property
Control traffic
Assist motorists
Give directions
Guard visitors, property
Refer citizen's complaints
Public nuisances
Election day
Escort parades
School crossings
Check business licenses
Help people who lost keys
Family disputes
Pick up stray dogs

Most citizens believe that the role of a police officer is the "crime fighter" role. Yet, one can see from an inspection of the officer's activity spectrum, that what he actually does often does not fit the role of crime fighter entirely. Although fighting crime, safeguarding life and property, and enforcing the law are a part of the role of the law enforcement officer, there remains the other 80 percent of his role: the 80 percent that is noncriminal in nature. Various groups in society, including law enforcement officers themselves, have different concepts about the law enforcement officer's social service role.

The Role Concept

A role concept can be defined as a set of expectations, held by individuals or groups of individuals, regarding the behavior and attributes of a role incumbent.[5] To express this more simply, we can compare two

[5] Sterling, *Changes in Role Concepts of Police Officers*, p. 9.

Figure 3-1. Police, in their traditional "crime fighter" role.

Figure 3-2. Although fighting crime, safeguarding life and property, and enforcing the law are a part of his role, the other 80 percent is noncriminal in nature. Here, police are assisting in a rescue.

methods of viewing a role. The first method is objective in nature; we remain unbiased in defining the role. This requires the observer to go beyond what he sees and feels personally. The observer must discipline himself to put aside his preconceived notions and pursue the entire spectrum.

The second method of viewing a role is by far the more common. It is a subjective and highly personal view, an individual's *concept* of what he expects the role to be from his personal experience. However, many more factors enter into the formation of a role concept than the individual's immediate experience. Often, the individual observer knows only a few of the total facts. This fragmented picture is then supplemented by personal emotions and attitudes. For example, Arthur Niederhoffer described the citizen's view of the police officer.

> *The policeman is a "Rorschach" in uniform as he patrols his beat. His occupational accouterments—shield, nightstick, gun, and summons book—clothe him in a mantle of symbolism that stimulates fantasy and projection.*[6]

Thus, the individual's role concept of the law enforcement officer is generally formed by perceptions that are pieced together incompletely and inaccurately. There can be little wonder, then, that the *role* of the law enforcement officer differs greatly from the *role concept* of the law enforcement officer.

How are role concepts formed? By definition, role concepts are expectations, and expectations about any given role vary from group to group and from individual to individual. For example, "people in the lower socioeconomic classes have rather distinct expectations of the role of 'child.' To a greater extent than the people in the middle socioeconomic levels, they generally expect children to obey and respect adults and to please them."[7]

Similarly, different groups in society have varying expectations toward the police and the enforcement of the law. These expectations, formed by drawing on past experiences with the police, also depend heavily on the particular needs of an individual or group and the ability of the police to meet these needs. Black people, for example, have historically been subjected to police oppression. Thus, black people today generally anticipate suppressive action by the police.

[6] Arthur Niederhoffer, *Behind the Shield* (Garden City, N.Y.: Doubleday, 1967), p. 1.
[7] Paul F. Secord and Carl W. Backman, *Social Psychology* (New York: McGraw-Hill, 1964), p. 457.

Based upon their present experiences with police, many blacks have the added expectation that "the police can't really do anything for me." This expectation arises from observing their particular community problems and the steps taken by the police to solve them. For example, a black urban neighborhood may have a severe burglary problem. In their efforts to solve these crimes, the police may be ineffective; they may apprehend a few burglars but recover little of the stolen property. Thus, the community residents may conclude that police efforts in reducing burglaries are useless to the community. As a result, if a crime problem does exist, the community has come to expect the police to be of little use, and it avoids community cooperation. As communication further breaks down between the community and the police, the problems are compounded and crime becomes much more difficult to control. These same parallels can be drawn for any group in society. Much can be projected about a group's role concept of police by examining its needs in particular and its experiences relative to the police agency.

Some expectations about the police seem reasonable, and some seem unreasonable. Therefore, some role concepts are a result of unreasonable expectations. For example, an area of a city might be plagued with assaults and robbery. The police in that area may respond by increasing routine patrol, increasing foot patrol in business areas, and generally focusing most of their efforts on that current problem. Manpower shortages may prevent ideal service to other less immediate problems, such as juveniles racing in the streets. The citizen may not be aware of the increased efforts of the police in the assault and robbery areas. When the citizen complains about juveniles racing cars in the streets, he concludes that the police are negligent if they take longer than usual to respond to the call.

When an apparent law enforcement problem arises, the police have an option of either confronting it or avoiding it. If they confront the problem, either they solve it or it remains unsolved. Thus, one of the following three things can happen.

1. The problem is confronted and is solved. In this case, the action of the officer becomes a part of the complainant's role concept. The officer has satisfied the need for service and is expected to do so again, if and when needed. However, it should be noted that the solving of a service function problem may increase the negative aspects of the public's concept of the police role. This becomes especially true in traffic law enforcement because of the American

citizen's inherent belief that traffic laws have been created for the other person and not for him.

2. The problem is confronted and remains unsolved. The problem may remain unsolved because neither the officer nor anyone else can effectively prevent a crime against the person, such as homicide. It may remain unsolved because the officer has no control over the cause, such as domestic arguments. In this case, the officer is viewed as useless, and impotence becomes a part of the citizen's concept of the police role. The citizen unrealistically expects the officer to solve the problem.

3. The problem is not confronted. When this occurs, the officer is called upon to handle situations that seem to be the responsibilities of other agencies. The citizen unrealistically expects the officer to solve all problems, such as trash removal, getting cats out of trees, and so on. The officer's impotence becomes a part of the citizen's perceived concept of his role because the citizen expects the officer to be all powerful when it comes to solving the personal service needs of the citizen.

The manner in which police officers respond to these problems and react to these needs affects the concepts that a group or individuals form of the officer's role. What the group or individuals experience personally and observe through different media also contributes to the formation of the role concept. The individual may have certain preformed attitudes toward law enforcement officers, and when he is confronted with an event that contradicts these attitudes, he will either alter the attitudes to conform with the new experience, or he will screen out the new experience to avoid such a disagreement.[8]

The factors that affect a group or individual role concept of the law enforcement officer can be summarized as follows.

1. The needs and problems peculiar to the group or individual.
2. The personal experiences common to the group or individual with police officers, both past and present.
3. The exposure that police officers receive through various media.

It is important to note that if the expectations are unrealistic, the role concept held by the group or individual is generally unrealistic.

---

[8] Ernest R. Hilgard and Richard C. Atkinson, *Introduction to Psychology* (New York: Harcourt, Brace, & World, 1967), p. 592.

A group or individual may expect too much from the officer; when these expectations are not met repeatedly, the group or individual forms a distorted role concept of officers. This distortion is not common only to citizens. It is also evident in the officer's own concept of his role.

Conflict in the Role Concept

For the police officer, especially the recruit, his role in society is far from being clearly delineated. Relating the advice of a police administrator, Strecher outlines this policy for police officers: "Always know who you are, where you are, and what you are doing there."[9] This may sound as if it were the easiest advice in the world to follow, but a situation that appears relatively uncomplicated on the surface can be quite complex when the various forces pulling the police officer in opposite directions are analyzed. For example, the mere process of "trying up," or, in laymen's terms, checking the security of the doors and windows of commercial establishments, may present a situation to the police officer in which he experiences role conflict. Consider the different directions in which the officer may be pulled.

1. The officer is new and relatively inexperienced. His department has a policy instructing him to frequently check the security of doors and windows of commercial establishments during the hours they are closed. While in training, the officer was instructed to follow this procedure.
2. The experienced patrolman with which the officer works tells him that the practice of "trying up" is a waste of time. The older officers advise "trying up" only if a supervisor is around, or if the particular business is willing to offer the officer inducements for special attention to his business.
3. The young officer is conscientious and hopes to be promoted someday. He questions the ethics of "inducements" to give "special attention" to any business.
4. Since the officer is conscientious, he has been reading various publications, which advise that patrolmen should check the security of business establishments at frequent irregular intervals.
5. In an article in the local newspaper, the Chamber of Commerce has come out strongly in favor of the practice of "trying up" local businesses.

[9] Strecher, *The Environment of Law Enforcement*, p. 92.

6. Citizens groups have reacted negatively to the Chamber of Commerce article that encourages the police to "try up" businesses. Citizens feel that the time should be spent patrolling residential areas. In the opinion of the local residents, the job of protecting businesses should be left to private watchmen.
7. An association representing private watchmen endorses the citizens groups. The association states that the job of protecting private businesses should be their responsibility.[10]

Thus, what the young officer has been taught comes into conflict with the wishes of various individuals and groups, affecting even relatively simple law enforcement duties. The complexity and confusion inherent in the police role are multiplied many times in certain sensitive areas, such as the relationships between police and community groups. How does the police officer, whether he is white, black, Mexican-American, or of any other ethnic origin, view his law enforcement role in the community? What attitudes and prejudices does he bring with

[10] Sterling, *Changes in Role Concepts of Police Officers*, p. 17.

Figure 3-3. How does the police officer, whether he is white, black, Mexican-American, or of any other ethnic origin, view his law enforcement role in the community?

him to his job? Will the individual officer's role be the same in a white community as it is in a community populated by a minority group? The National Commission on the Causes and Prevention of Violence characterized those holding the position of police officer in this way.

> *Police in the United States are for the most part white, upwardly mobile, lower middle class, conservative in ideology, and resistant to change. In most areas of the country, even where segregation has been legally eliminated for long periods, they are likely to have grown up without any significant contact with minority and lower socioeconomic class life styles—and certainly with little or no experience of the realities of ghetto life. They tend to share the attitudes, biases, and prejudices of the larger community, among which is likely to be fear and distrust of Negroes and other minority groups.*

> *Appointed to the police force and brought into day-to-day contact with what is to him an alien way of life, the young police officer experiences what behavioral scientists refer to as 'cultural shock.' His latent negative attitudes are reinforced by the aggressive and militant hostility which greets him even when he is attempting to perform, to the best of his ability, a community service or order maintenance function, or is attempting to apprehend a criminal whose victim has been a member of the minority community.*[11]

In an attempt to assess the new police officer's preparation for dealing with people, James W. Sterling of the International Association of Chiefs of Police conducted a longitudinal study of 113 police officers in four cities, following them from entrance level training through their first year and one-half on the job. Of the background of the entrance level officer, Sterling had this to say.

> *Generally, they had aspired to become a police officer for only a year or two. Very few of them had read anything of substance about the law enforcement profession. By and large, their friends with police backgrounds had been the strongest influence in getting them to enter into law enforcement.*[12]

Concerning the question of how their previous jobs prepared them to work with people, Sterling reports that:

> *Analysis of the subjects' occupational backgrounds showed that 70.4*

---

[11] James S. Campbell et. al., *Law and Order Reconsidered* (New York: Praeger, 1969), pp. 291-292.

[12] James W. Sterling, "Police Community Relations from 'Them and Us' to 'You and Me'" (An address delivered to the National Institute on Police Training and Community Functioning, Miami Beach, Fla., November 1971).

percent of the men had held positions with no significant relationship to people. . . . When you consider this lack of experience in dealing with people, one can hardly feel assured that these men could become prepared to deal with the complex people problems they will confront.[13]

Community Relations

Compounding the individual officer's problems of cultural differences and lack of preparation in dealing with people is the police department's problem of poor community relations. Looking back into the recent history of policing, we can find many practices that were seemingly brutal and abusive, but which had the open or silent approval of most of the members of the community. Even though these practices of misconduct have been eliminated or greatly curtailed, the residents of the community may still have a tendency to view their police as somewhat less than sensitive; unfair, oppressive, and perhaps even unaware of social needs and changes.

A new officer who rids himself of prejudicial attitudes, or masters his personal prejudices so that they do not affect his job, is still perceived by the community as being insensitive, unfair, oppressive, and unaware of social needs and changes. The members of the community respond only to their perceptions of the uniform. As a group, they generally do not consider any officer's professional attributes. Members of the community may therefore act in a hostile manner, regardless of the individual officer's professional behavior. Some community members apparently have been conditioned to the concept that everyone who wears the uniform has certain prejudicial attitudes. Since the new officer is responded to with what he considers to be hostility, he is not given a chance to demonstrate to the community that he is an unbiased professional. Older officers will warn the new officer that his professional considerations are not the appropriate response for dealing with certain groups or individuals in the community, and that "there's only one way to handle those people." The typical ersponse for the new officer is to become more and more like the experienced officers.

[13] Ibid.

The chance the police department had of beginning a new era of excellent community relations is then stifled. The incoming officer is socialized to the standards of the past. Thus, the cycle of poor police–community relations seems to continue unbroken, even when the department has been fortunate enough to recruit an officer who did not bring unfavorable attitudes with him or could control the negative attitudes he did have.

The Black Officer

The discussion thus far has centered primarily on the white police officer and the problems he faces in functioning in his police role. Yet all of these problems are faced by the black officer, who is subject to additional pressures and conflicts.

Nicholas Alex, who conducted an exhaustive study of black police officers in New York City, characterized the special problems of the black officer as follows.

> The Negro who enters into the police role is subject to all the tensions and conflicts that arise from police work. Moreover, the conflict is compounded for the Negro: he is much more than a Negro to his ethnic group because he represents the guardian of white society, yet he is not quite a policeman to his working companions, because he is stereotyped as a member of an "inferior" racial category. He may find it necessary to defend his serving as a police officer and to explain it largely on the basis of economic necessity—that this was one of the best paying jobs that was available to him. But often he feels that he is subject to criticism by his ethnic peers derived from premises inapplicable to his situation—that is, they may consider him a traitor to his race because his race does not benefit from the protection that he offers. Yet he may defend his race because he is a Negro and inextricably bound up in the current struggle for civil rights and the demands of Negroes for social and legal equality. It is difficult for him to play both roles. To be a Negro and a policeman is to be subject to double marginality, and gives rise to some special problems.[14]

Taking these factors into consideration, and carrying the study

---

[14] Nicholas Alex, *Black in Blue: A Study of the Negro Policeman* (New York: Appleton-Century-Crofts, 1969), Copyright © 1969 by Meredith Corporation, pp. 13-14.

further, Alex was able to describe three major ways in which the black officer sees his role.

Type 1. Primary identification with the police role. This is the type of individual who selected the police role because this was what he wanted to be. He has had no difficulty in adjusting to the role because he considers this not only his real life but his definitive life. He outwardly identifies with the role, always sees himself as a policeman first. In order to show that he is a good "cop" he may find it necessary to go out of his way in enforcing the law against Negro violators, especially in the presence of white officers. However, he may see his role as primarily one of instruction— this is the "way up" the mobility ladder, and police work is respectable and pays well. In this way he "fights the white power structure from within."

Type 2. Primary identification as a Negro in the police role. This type of person did not select the role. He perceives his recruitment into the department as having been forced because of lack of job opportunities and discrimination in the market place. He has not adjusted to the role although he considers it an economic fact of life that he cannot take for granted as a Negro. He sees himself as a Negro first and a policeman second. He identifies with the Negro community in its struggle for social and legal equality but not with its deprived life styles. He may attempt to resolve the dilemma of occupying a role he does not like by expressing hostility toward civil service, the police in general, and white policemen in particular. For example, some of his comments might be that if he were white he would not have become a policeman, that civil service is the death of one's ambition, and that cops are basically brutal and ignorant. This type of person develops hate for his official role because that role discredits him in the eyes of the Negro community.

Type 3. The ambivalence in identification. He too did not select the role of policeman. He perceives his recruitment into the department in terms of limited opportunities in other jobs, the police job being the best paying job that was available. He expresses ambivalence regarding his police role and his commitment to his ethnic group. However, he is not at war with the police nor at war with the Negro community, but sees himself as accommodating to the pressures exerted from both sides. He may rationalize his position by saying that he is a bridge linking the Negro community to the police bureaucracy. Thus he develops a political imagination of dual role playing by reduc-

ing the dilemma of extremes to one of practical and realistic accommodation.[15]

A Realistic Role Concept

In discussing the role a police officer plays in his community, a concept that can be described as the "working personality" of an officer, Jerome Skolnick commented:

> *The process by which this "personality" is developed may be summarized: the policeman's role contains two principal variables, danger and authority, which should be interpreted in the light of a "constant" pressure to appear efficient.*[16]

Skolnick's comments are applicable to both white and black officers. We see, then, that the police role concept based on danger, authority, and pressure to produce, needs to be replaced with a police role concept which equally stresses the service function. Whether the officer realizes it or not, 80 percent or more of his time is spent in service-related duties. In order to help the officer serve his community more effectively, view his role in favorable terms, and participate in developing excellent community relations, police departments must develop effective training programs in police role concepts. They must prepare the officer to meet legitimate community expectations and needs.

Education and Training
An education and training program in police role concepts should be guided by the advice and the insight given to us by the nature and history of the law enforcement function. This education and training program should begin with certain assumptions about the general nature of problems at the entrance or in-service levels of training; it must walk the thin line between rigidity and conviction and between open-mindedness and empty-mindedness. Some primary operational assumptions are the following.

---

[15] Ibid., pp. 19-20.
[16] Jerome H. Skolnick, *Justice Without Trial* (New York: Wiley, 1966), p. 44.

1. All attempts should be made to see that the education and training process is lively and creative, an arena where ideologies, ideas, and points of view may clash and compete.
2. Since the problems of behavioral modification are incredibly complex, attention must be given to an enormous range of personal and institutional behavior. Being an effective and professional police officer involves at least:
    a. A sophisticated understanding of the moral, social, political, and legal framework of the society.
    b. An intensive understanding of the community—its values, aspiration, difficulties, needs, and resources.
    c. Considerable personal strength, autonomy, and self-understanding.
    d. The ability to understand, empathize, and communicate with others.
    e. A deep commitment to the basic ideals of justice and freedom within our society.
    f. A deep understanding and knowledge of the policies and practices of law enforcement organization.
3. Programs designed to develop and strengthen all of these attributes should be represented within the behavioral modification function, relative to service-oriented police officers.
4. The standard for any behavioral modification should be excellence. This does not mean that improvement can be of high quality instantaneously. It does mean, however, that behavioral modification should aim high and that it must always resist the pressure to meet short-range needs.
5. Stress should be placed on the development of programs designed to give insight into the personal, social, legal, and cultural context of law enforcement service. The education and training function should be able to develop more sophisticated mechanisms for field training and greater articulation between the classroom and the real world.

Coupled with the above assumptions, it is also important to discuss a positive change theory and learning principles.

Change Theory. Change is an integrated, ongoing process occurring within the individual, enabling him to meet specific aims, fulfill needs and interests, and cope with the living process. Conceptually, the process involves five distinct phases.

1. Unfreezing, in which the individual becomes ready to consider changes in skills, attitudes, information, and behavior.

2. Problem diagnosis, in which the forces supporting the need for change, and the forces working against the changes needed, are identified and assessed.
3. Goal setting, in which the desired changes are stated specifically.
4. New behavior, in which the individual learns and practices.
5. Refreezing, in which the newer learning has been found to be beneficial and is assimilated into the individual's framework of skills, attitudes, information, and behavior.

Learning Principles. There are nine basic learning principles in a sophisticated system of change and behavior modification. These principles are:

1. Change and behavior modification is an experience activated and occurring within the individual. Individuals are not taught; they become motivated to seek newer knowledge, skills, and behavior.
2. Change and behavior modification is the discovery of personal meaning and relevancy. Individuals more readily accept and use concepts that are relevant to their needs and problems.
3. Change and behavior modification is sometimes a painful process. Changing behavior often requires giving up old, comfortable ways of believing, thinking, and acting.
4. Change and behavior modification results from experience. People become independent when they have experienced independence; trusting when they have experienced trust; and responsible when they have experienced responsibility.
5. Change and behavior modification is highly unique and individual. Each individual develops his own way of learning and solving problems. As he becomes exposed to the methods of others, he can refine his own in order to be more effective.
6. Change and behavior modification has its resource in the individual's self. His past experiences provide a rich source of problem-solving and learning tools.
7. Change and behavior modification is both an emotional and an intellectual process; individuals have feelings as well as thoughts. The modification is maximized when individuals say what they think and feel.
8. Change and behavior modification is a cooperative and collaborative process. Helping each other to learn requires a process of interactive interdependence.
9. Change and behavior modification is an evolutionary process. The ability to be understanding, accepting, trusting, confronting, shar-

ing, helping, and evaluating requires a developing, evolving process, which cannot be imposed.

Without reality-based learning and training, little can ever be accomplished. Specific systems in the area of police-community relations and role concepts can be created only when concepts and objectives are soundly based organizationally.

Role Concepts in Police–Community Relations

In too many cases, contacts between law enforcement officers and citizens are abrasive and full of mistrust and misunderstanding. Police administrators have been faced with the problem of attempting to determine what internal programs can be developed to create a sensitivity to and an awareness of police–community relations and law enforcement role concepts.

These objectives can only be accomplished by sound planning, involving the cooperative and total efforts of the entire organization. The steps involved in this process are:

1. An absolute commitment on the part of the organization, reflected in its policy and support. Policy should be formulated with inputs from all members of the organization.
2. A realization that at least 80 percent of police activity is non-criminal and that law enforcement philosophy should reflect this factor.
3. An attempt to redefine and reshape attitudes of existing personnel and new recruits toward a professional service concept.
4. Maintaining a proper balance between the academic and professional aspects of police education and training.
5. A realization that it does not take policemen to teach policemen. There are particular subjects that are best taught by nonpolice personnel, such as the academic areas of sociology, psychology, and criminal law.
6. Developing a system or organizational philosophy based on the behavioral approach to law enforcement goals and objectives in order to modify behavior and attitudes—a system that discusses the emotions of both citizens and police officers. The concepts of stress, fear, anxiety, anger, and humiliation should be openly discussed in order to explore all aspects of police behavior.

7. Developing a system to destroy the myth that all police officers are the same if they are recruited the same way.
8. A realization that concepts such as problem simulation, role playing, and group work are more effective in modifying attitudes and behavior than other typical methods.
9. A realization that change and behavior modification is not just a process for the lower echelons of the organization, but that varying levels of change and behavioral modification take place throughout the organization. Few changes can be realized organizationally if behavior modification is conducted only at the lower levels.

Conclusions

Law enforcement often becomes the object of animosity against the establishment. Because of the policeman's traditional role, this may be a natural sociological or psychological occurrence. It seems clear that if new methods of reducing tensions are not found, an increased polarization in society will take place, which can only lead to more violence and retaliation. In an atmosphere of fear and distrust, the problems themselves lose all proportions. Any attempt to arrive at cooperative solutions becomes impossible.

Law enforcement is generally the reflection of the community. If the community is progressive, law enforcement becomes progressive. If the total community is belligerent, law enforcement becomes belligerent. If a community has racist tendencies or is indifferent to the plight of minority groups, law enforcement will almost always reflect the same tendencies. If the community is apathetic, the law enforcement agency becomes apathetic.

The police must make every effort to understand the needs and aspirations of all members of the community. There is also a great need for the public to understand the proper role to be played not only by enforcement agencies, but by the entire criminal justice system within the community. Such an understanding is impossible to achieve if it is forgotten that the police are essentially a service agency.

If progress is to be made, changes must be sought and initiated by all segments of the community, including the police. The progress of change seems to always begin with small things. Change must be based on an understanding of the community and an appreciation of what the community should be tomorrow and the day after.

The community cannot expect a police officer to be a legal scholar, criminologist, psychologist, urbanologist, and diplomat at one and the same time. The police officer needs the help and understanding of those in his community who have the expertise. More effort on the part of the police must be made to find ways of applying the ideas of the social scientist to the law enforcement function.

It is the community's responsibility to develop a broadened understanding of the police role. The community must also recognize the natural reluctance of the police to accept open criticism, no matter how well intentioned. Thus, it becomes a police responsibility to draw on the intelligence and thoughts of those in the community who can make significant contributions to police efficiency. It is not suggested that the community run the police department. Rather, it is suggested that an effective partnership could be achieved which will enable both groups to progress.

Student Checklist

1. Are you able to define the term "role" as it applies to a police officer?
2. Are you able to write a short essay defining a police officer's role in terms of what he does?
3. Can you describe how juveniles and adults differ in their role concepts of police officers?
4. Do you know the difference between how black people and white people see the police role?
5. Can you list five elements involved in behavioral modification?

Topics for Discussion

1. Discuss the differences between the way juveniles and adults see the police.

2. Discuss the differences between the way black citizens see the police and the way white citizens see the police. Does this differ from the way Chicanos see the role of police?

3. What are the key things to keep in mind when trying to modify behavior?

ANNOTATED BIBLIOGRAPHY

Allport, G. *The Nature of Prejudice*. Reading, Mass.: Addison-Wesley, 1955. pp. 79, 80, 282. This book provides information on "adopting" and "developing" prejudice.

Adorno, T. W., et al. *The Authoritarian Personality*. New York: Harper & Row, 1950. A classic study of authoritarianism, the text also offers a technique for measuring prejudice using a statistical scale.

Barndt, J. *Why Black Power*. New York: Friendship Press, 1968. This work identifies and isolates the positive value of political and economic power for minorities.

Berson, L. E. *Case Study of a Riot: The Philadelphia Story*. New York: Institute of Human Relations Press, 1966. An excellent study of community tension and its consequences.

Bordua, D. J. *The Police*. New York: Wiley, 1967. This work treats the problems of today's police in dealing with a society that seeks both increased civil liberties and increased measures to fight crime.

Brown, C. *Manchild in the Promised Land*. New York: Macmillan, 1965. A sympathetic look at the Negro's psychological problems in American society.

Cleaver, Eldridge. *Soul on Ice*. New York: Dell, 1968. A soul-searching exposition by a black man in white America.

Coffey, Alan, et al. *Human Relations; Law Enforcement in a Changing Community*. Englewood Cliffs, N. J.: Prentice-Hall, 1971. For its size, this work is one of the most comprehensive around. The text treats social problems and their impact on law enforcement.

Cohen, J., and W. S. Murphy. *Burn, Baby, Burn!* New York: E. P. Dutton, 1966. A study into the conditions which led to the Watts riot.

"Corruption Behind Swinging Clubs," *Life.* Vol. 65, No. 23 (Dec. 6, 1968). A discussion of the Democratic Convention demonstrations and an analysis of the contributing factors.

Cross, Theodore L. *Black Capitalism Strategy for Business in the Ghetto.* New York: Antheneum, 1969. Suggests new techniques for an economy that has been deprived of financial leverage.

Derbyshire, R. L. "The Social Control Role of the Police in Changing Urban Communities," *Excerpta Criminologica* Vol. 6, No. 3 (1966).

Devlin, P. A. "The Police in a Changing Society," *Issues of Criminal Law, Criminology, and Police Science* Vol. 57, No. 2 (June 1966). Social change and its effect on traditional law enforcement roles.

Dodd, D. J. "Police Mentality and Behavior," *Issues in Criminology* Vol. 3, No. 1 (Summer 1967), 47–67, School of Criminology University of California, Berkeley. The law enforcement officer's culture and his view of the community in which he works.

Edwards, George. *The Police on the Urban Frontier.* New York: Institute of Human Relations Press, 1968. Written by a former police commissioner of Detroit, this text offers a down-to-earth and valuable discussion of human relations for the law enforcement officer.

Endleman, S., ed. *Violence in the Streets.* Chicago: Quadrangle Books, 1968, p. 471. A study of violence and the response of the police.

Fortas, A. *Concerning Dissent and Civil Disobedience.* New York: New American Library, 1968. Civil disobedience and the "right to dissent."

Freeman, W. *Society on Trial.* Springfield, Ill.: Charles C. Thomas, 1965. A look at changes in today's courts.

Grant, Joanne. *Black Protest.* Greenwich, Conn.: Fawcett Publications, 1968. An interesting and well-documented history of black protest in the U.S.

Grier, W. H., and P. M. Cobbs. *Black Rage.* New York: Basic Books, 1968, p. 231. This book sets forth the psychoanalytical theory of the acquisition of attitudes by minorities. Because many militants espouse this theory, it is felt that police officers should have a knowledge of it.

Heaps, W. A. *Riots, U.S.A. 1765–1965.* New York: Seabury Press, 1966. Covers in depth the thirteen major riots that have occurred in the history of the United States. More contemporary disturbances are treated in the last two chapters.

Johnson, E. H., "A Sociological Interpretation of Police Reaction and Responsibility to Civil Disobedience," *The Journal of Criminal Law, Criminology, and Police Science* Vol. 58, No. 3 (September 1967), 407–11. The dimensions of human dynamics in police problems.

King, M. L., Jr. *Why We Can't Wait.* New York: New American Library, Signet Books, 1964. The frustrations of the Negro in his efforts to participate in American society.

Lomax, L. E. *The Negro Revolt.* New York: Harper & Row, 1964. Explains the history behind freedom riders, sit-ins, prayer marches, and the development and meaning of the racial protest sweeping America today.

Marx, J. *Officer, Tell Your Story: A Guide to Police Public Relations.* Springfield, Ill.: Charles C. Thomas, 1969. A study of police-community relations and the need for public support of police goals.

May, E., "The Disjointed Trio: Poverty, Politics, and Power," *National Conference on Social Welfare: Social Welfare Forum,* 1963, pp. 47–61. An excellent discussion of the relationship of power to poverty through the medium of politics.

Meissner, H., ed. *Poverty in Affluent Society.* New York: Harper & Row, 1966. The effects of poverty in the midst of wealth.

Menninger, Karl. *The Crime of Punishment.* New York: Viking, 1968. A legal, sociological, and philosophical study of crime and corrections.

Momboisse, R. *Community Relations and Riot Prevention.* Springfield, Ill.: Charles C. Thomas, 1969. The text offers a guide to community-relations programming and develops this theme: the only effective way to control a riot is to prevent it.

Oglesby, Carl, ed. *The New Left Reader*. New York: Grove Press, 1969. An anthology on revolution and change whose contributors include Fidel Castro, Malcolm X, Huey Newton, and others.

O. M. Collective. *The Organizer's Manual*. New York: Bantam Books, 1971. Everything one needs to know about organizing a group to take action.

Skolnick, Jerome H. *Justice Without Trial: Law Enforcement in Democratic Society*. New York: Wiley, 1966. An in-depth look at the role of the police officer in today's society.

Skolnick, Jerome H. *The Politics of Protest: Violent Aspects of Protest and Confrontation*. New York: Simon and Schuster, 1969. A report to the National Commission on the Causes and Prevention of Violence.

Stone, Chuck. *Black Power in America*, rev. ed. New York: Dell, 1970. In the words of the *Louisville Times* ". . . a definitive work, well worth reading by black and white alike." One of the best works on the subject, this book makes excellent use of supporting statistical data.

Strecher, Victor G. *The Environment of Law Enforcement; A Community Relations Guide*. Englewood, Cliffs, N.J.: Prentice-Hall, 1971. A particularly valuable study in discussing the variety of settings in which a police officer works: territorial, social, and organizational.

Suttles, Gerald D. *The Social Order of the Slum: Ethnicity and Territory in the Inner City*. Chicago: University of Chicago Press, 1968. Explores how and why slum communities provide their inhabitants with local norms.

"Time Essay, The Police Need Help," *Time* (October 4, 1968), p. 26. The October 4 issue of *Time* truly captures the problem of law enforcement in a changing community.

Tucker, Sterling. *Black Reflections on White Power*. Grand Rapids, Mich.: Eerdmann's, 1969. A black man's view of the white man's system.

Van Den Berghe, P. *Race and Racism: A Comparative Study.* New York: Wiley, 1969. A comprehensive study of the political and social implications of race relationships.

Watson, N. A., ed. *Police and the Changing Community: Selected Readings.* Washington, D.C.: International Association of Chiefs of Police, 1965. An anthology of readings in the area of police-community relations.

Wilson, James Q. *Varieties of Police Behavior.* New York: Atheneum, 1970. Offers particularly interesting studies in the role of the patrolman, the police administrator, and the use of police discretion.

The publications below can be ordered from Superintendent of Documents, Government Printing Office, Washington, D.C. 20402. They are among the most comprehensive studies in their respective fields.

President's Commission on Law Enforcement and Administration of Justice:

> *Commission Report: The Challenge of Crime in a Free Society* ($2.25)
>
> *Task Force Report: The Police* ($1.50)
> *Task Force Report: The Courts* ($1.00)
> *Task Force Report: Corrections* ($1.25)
> *Task Force Report: Juvenile Delinquency and Youth Crime* ($2.00)
> *Task Force Report: Organized Crime* ($0.65)
> *Task Force Report: Science and Technology* ($1.25)
> *Task Force Report: Assessment of Crime* ($1.25)
> *Task Force Report: Narcotics and Drug Abuse* ($1.00)
> *Task Force Report: Drunkenness* ($0.65)
> *Field Surveys I: Report on a Pilot Study in the District of Columbia on Victimization and Attitudes Toward Law Enforcement* ($1.25)
> *Field Surveys II: Criminal Victimization in the U.S., A Report of the National Survey* ($1.00)
> *Field Surveys III: Studies in Crime and Law Enforcement in Major Metropolitan Areas (Volume 1 and Volume 2)* ($3.50 per set)

Field Surveys IV: The Police and the Community (Volume 1 and Volume 2) ($2.75 per set)

Field Surveys V: National Survey of Police and Community Relations ($2.00)

National Advisory Commission on Civil Disorders (Kerner Commission):

Report of the National Advisory Commission on Civil Disorders ($2.00)

Supplemental Studies for the National Advisory Commission on Civil Disorders ($1.50)

National Commission on the Causes and Prevention of Violence (Eisenhower Commission):

Report of the National Commission on the Causes and Prevention of Violence

The study of this chapter will enable you to:

1. Name at least three factors that make it difficult for police officers to cope with change.
2. List steps that have been taken to professionalize police.
3. Identify significant steps recommended to help professionalize police in the future.
4. Write a brief essay on the police as a minority group.
5. List the factors that officers must recognize and deal with on their jobs if they are to avoid becoming bitter.

4
Coping With Change

In two centuries the United States has changed from an agrarian, rural society to one that is primarily industrial, urban, and suburban. This change has confronted our nation with challenges and crises undreamed of by the founding fathers. For the police, in particular, social change has ushered in a series of new and significant problems. Although the police are not responsible for many of the social problems that originate within the community, the public has a tendency to look to the police to solve these problems—or at least to control them. Thus, when the rising crime rate became a public issue in the 1960s, most Americans considered "the crime problem" to be a matter for the police. Now, a decade later, the public is still largely ignorant of the complexities hidden in the phrase, "the crime problem," particularly with regard to causation and prevention. James Q. Wilson noted that:

> The police can do relatively little about preventing most common crimes. . . . A community concerned about lowering its crime rates would be well advised to devote its attention and resources to those parts of the criminal justice system, especially the courts and correctional agencies, which, unlike the police, spend most of their time processing—often in the most perfunctory and ineffective manner— persons who repeatedly perpetrate these crimes.[1]

Nevertheless, most private citizens remain completely unfamiliar with the workings of the criminal justice system, only one portion of which— the police—is visible in its daily operations.

---

[1] James Q. Wilson, *Varieties of Police Behavior* (Cambridge, Mass.: Harvard University Press, 1968), p. 295.

The traditional center of communal living in the United States, the neighborhood, has fallen victim to the increasing suburbanization of our society. Fewer and fewer people are able to regard the neighborhood with any sense of community solidarity or continuity. We are told that eight million Americans change their place of residence each year; the moving van has become the identifying symbol of contemporary American life. Gone is the feeling of solidarity that once bound people together as neighbors in mutual interdependence and protection. Many Americans do not know or even care to know the name of the person living next door. The man in the apartment across the hall is not somebody to whom one can turn for help in an emergency, but rather is a stranger to be looked at with suspicion and fear. The norm of urban impersonality is most shockingly illustrated in the tragic slaying of Kitty Genovese in New York City a few years ago; Miss Genovese was murdered while more than 20 people watched. None of them came to her rescue because none of them wanted to "become involved."

Basic changes in the even more fundamental institution of the family have increased the problems of social sanction and control. Discipline and self-restraint, once considered the principal socializing tasks of the family, have passed by default to a variety of public and private agencies, with the result that children develop into self-oriented, alienated adults. The search among youth for an alternative, humanistic lifestyle as a reaction to the objectionable features of a society dominated by materialistic, exploitative values has been captured by James Michener in his novel, *The Drifters*. According to one of Michener's reviewers:

> *These young people . . . constitute "a new force in history." By and large they reject a world they never made, the parental, the institutional. They see the parental world as characterized by mean-spirited competition and a gray work ethic; by the quasi-enslavement of large groups (women) and smaller ones (racial or sexual minorities); by reliance upon alcohol; by the routine of "adjustment;" by hypocritical worship, in the West, of a dead Judeo-Christianity; and by the real, and probably suicidal, worship of the Juggernaut technology.*
>
> *The world they accept, or are working at creating, is not a mere mutation of the old one. It is, though it borrows much from the history they scorn, "new." It is marked by communal sharing and noncompetitiveness; by the rejection of war (though not all of them reject violence); by cunning compromise with, or outright contempt for, work; by a vague ideal of brotherhood, taking no account of sex*

differences; by reliance upon a whole pharmacopeia of drugs, from pot to heroin; by the quasi-worship of various forms of magic, including sun adoration, amulets and charms, taboo-breaking sex rituals, such nonsense as astrology, tarot and the I Ching, *high-decibel stimulation of the nervous system, and so forth; and by anti-privacy, group-think, and a kind of cheerful rather than an aggressive illiteracy.*[2]

Alienation may lead to attack or retreat, to aggressive militancy in seeking to topple the "establishment," or to a quiet repudiation of a world viewed as horrible and irrelevant. In either case, attack or retreat, the response to alienation is thorough rejection of parental values.

It is not necessary to endorse the values of the counter-culture in order to recognize the profound sickness that afflicts many sectors of our contemporary life. Technological advances and economic achievements have sharpened rather than blunted the tensions within our society and have helped bring about social disorganization in the midst of abundance, with implications that are serious for the police role and functions. Professor Lee P. Brown points out the following.

This urbanized, existential society of conflicting values and interests is also characterized by differential means and opportunities. The American dream is usurped by the social reality of frustration and impotence. Success is promised to all, but the avenues of success are closed to many. Differential opportunities within our . . . complex social structure are conducive to deviate behavior. Thus, into the picture comes the authoritative machinery of the state which imposes controls on man's activities. This authority, established by law, is personified in the form of the policeman. He is the anthropomorphic representative of societal control. In the eyes of certain enclaves of the community, he represents the "thin blue line" between chaos and stability. To others, he is not seen as the protector; rather the oppressor who enforces the dictates of the "establishment."[3]

The police occupy a position between two opposing forces: those who are demanding change and those who seek to preserve the *status quo.* This abnormal position creates pressures that impose a severe strain upon the ability of the individual police officer to adjust. Thus, police

[2] Clifton Fadiman, *"The Drifters:* A Review," *Book-of-the-Month Club News* (May 1971), pp. 1-2.
[3] Lee P. Brown, *Police-Community Relations Evaluation Project* (Washington, D.C.: U.S. Department of Justice, 1971), pp. 3-4.

administrators are confronted with the need to create policies aimed at maintaining the effectiveness, morale, and psychological well-being of law enforcement personnel at all organizational levels.

Although the goals stated above are similar to those sought by the personnel departments of most modern business and industrial organizations, they have become more narrowly identified in recent years with *positive mental health* considerations. The controversial nature of the term mental health as it is used here does not imply any commitment to the pathology or disease models favored by a large number of medical, psychiatric, psychoanalytic, and psychological practitioners in their approach to problem behavior, including the more extreme forms of deviance. Rather, the term refers to the ability of the individual to adapt successfully in order to meet his needs, to deal adequately and effectively with stress, and to see that the means or methods he uses in attaining this state do not themselves become the source of further tension or conflict.

Psychologists who work with criminal justice personnel generally agree that there is probably *less* hospitality toward the mental health viewpoint among law enforcement personnel than in any other sector of the criminal justice system. There are many reasons for this situation, ranging from the low status given to police and police work in mental health professional circles to the antagonism generated by "long-haired liberals" among the socially and politically conservative elements of the law enforcement establishment. There has been more than enough hostility, prejudice, and ill will to go around. On the other hand, many police administrators would welcome any mental health professional who could promise—and deliver—the instruments, techniques, methods, or approaches to help improve the quality of police department personnel and operations.

The mental health specialties have made few, if any, significant contributions thus far to the field of law enforcement. Nevertheless, there is a large potential for contributions to law enforcement by the mental health and behavioral science specialties, both in research and in application. The availability of increased public funding for projects involving aspects of the crime problem and the criminal justice system suggests that it is only a matter of time until mental health and law enforcement professionals discover the mutual advantages of cooperation. As an added incentive, there are many current examples of the benefits of cooperative enterprise in other components of the criminal justice system, most notably in corrections.

We have briefly discussed the conflict-ridden position of the police in our society as a result of rapid, even revolutionary, social change. The National Commission on the Causes and Prevention of Violence did not hesitate to use the popular phrase "revolution of rising expectations" to refer to the current social situation.[4] This so-called revolution contains several elements: unevenly distributed affluence, changes in the law, the ideological thrust of the civil rights movement, a breakdown in traditional social roles and institutional arrangements, and the incalculable impact of space-age technology. The police are obviously not alone in facing a bewildering variety of problems created by the growth of a new type of human relations in our society. But the police are the "cutting edge" of social control, and in this task they are confronted by unique challenges.

Coping with change, the theme of this chapter, involves considerably more than the problems related to mental health, however important these may be. Police efforts to cope with change and the implications of change are best understood from the perspective of increasing self-government through police professionalization. But before we can understand some of the reasons for the success, partial success, or outright failure in the attainment of the objectives involved in the professionalization of law enforcement, it is necessary to examine the peculiar nature of the police role in American society and some of the types of stress that such a role creates for law enforcement personnel.

The Police and The Public

Traditionally, the American policeman has been characterized as poorly educated, poorly trained, and sometimes abusive. It is not difficult to see how the policeman acquired this stereotype. As the Task Force Report of the President's Commission on Law Enforcement and the

[4] *To Establish Justice, To Insure Domestic Tranquility: The Final Report of the National Commission on the Causes and Prevention of Violence*, Introduction by James Reston (New York: Praeger, 1970), p. 35.

Administration of Justice has indicated, "In years gone by it was the attitude among police and public that any man of general ability could learn to police by doing it. Consequently, the then prevailing philosophy was one of providing the recruit with a uniform and badge; arming him with a baton, revolver, and handcuffs; assuring his geographical orientation by issuing him a local street map; and instructing him to 'hit the street' and enforce the Ten Commandments."[5] With background and entrance requirements such as these, it is not surprising that, by 1939, the field had attracted enough maladjusted individuals to prompt sociologist Read Bain to say that three-quarters of the policemen in the United States were mentally unfit for their work. S. L. Kates, after studying the results of psychological tests given to New York policemen, concluded that the more maladjusted policemen tended to be more satisfied with their work than the less maladjusted.[6] In his 1944 book, *The American Dilemma*, Gunnar Myrdal commented: "Almost anyone on the outside of a penitentiary who weighs enough and is not blind or crippled can be considered as a police candidate."[7]

As recently as 1965, an Albany, New York, veteran police officer made the following statement when asked about education and training for police: "You can't apply book training out in the street. You have to rely on men with experience. The training is all right, but you can't take it too seriously."[8] Another senior police officer in Newburgh, New York, when asked about college-level courses for policemen, said, "Police science courses are not necessary. You can't teach a man to be a good policeman: he must have the aptitude naturally."[9] Attitudes of this kind among police find a ready counterpart in public attitudes toward the police, as evidenced by the popularity of abusive terms like "pig," "fuzz," and "the heat."

[5] The President's Commission on Law Enforcement and The Administration of Justice, *Task Force Report: The Police* (Washington, D.C.: U.S. Govt. Printing Office, 1967), p. 137.
[6] S. L. Kates, "Rorschach Responses, Strong Blank Scales and Job Satisfaction Among Police," *Journal of Applied Psychology*, Vol. 34, 1950, pp. 249-254.
[7] Gunnar Myrdal, *The American Dilemma* (New York: Harper & Row, 1944), pp. 538-539.
[8] Wilson, *Varieties of Police Behavior*, p. 152.
[9] Ibid.

What Policing Does to the Police

Jerome Skolnick has presented an analysis of how certain features that he identifies in the policeman's environment interact with the paramilitary structure of the typical police organization to produce what he calls a "working personality."[10] The danger present in the policeman's environment makes him a suspicious person. He must respond to reported assaults against property and persons. As a result of his preoccupation with violence, he develops a stereotyping "perceptual shorthand" to identify "symbolic assailants"; for example, "black equals danger." The individual policeman's suspiciousness does not necessarily result from personal experience, but may develop through identification with fellow policemen who themselves may have been victims of violence in the line of duty. Socially isolated from a community which may, as in the case of ghetto sections of the city, consider them to be similar to occupation troops in an occupied country, the police band together with a solidarity surpassing that found in most occupational groupings.

The authority invested in the policeman's role further isolates him from a public that resents his direction of such activities as traffic and sports events or his regulation of public morality. The policeman is further charged with hypocrisy, because he, himself, is presumed to have taken part in some of the activities he is called upon to suppress, such as drunkenness.

To help explain the "working personality" of the police officer, we can compare the American and British systems of law enforcement. The British policeman is more impersonal in his approach to offenders than his American counterpart because the role of the policeman in British society is more clearly defined and confers authority in a wider range of situations.[11] The American police officer cannot rely solely upon the authority of his badge and must develop effective public relations skills for handling such sticky situations as domestic disputes and the arrest of a public drunk. In addition, the typical English citizen is less likely than his American cousin to challenge the authority of the police. Secure in his role, the Bobby-on-the-beat is much more likely to behave in a respectful manner to a wider range of persons. (No one likes to be

[10] Jerome Skolnick, *Justice Without Trial* (New York: Wiley, 1966), pp. 42-70.
[11] Michael Banton, *The Policeman in the Community* (London: Tavistock, 1964).

given a ticket, however, and even in Russia people grumble over traffic citations.) The American policeman who behaved in an overly respectful way would almost certainly have his motives questioned by a skeptical public. The sociologist, Michael Banton, who compared the respect given to the policeman's role in Britain and America, concluded that the police were a "sacred" (less open to satire and ridicule) sort of institution in Britain. This occurs because the British social system is more integrated and more tradition-oriented than the social system of the United States. British police symbolize the social order to a greater extent than do the American police.

The Policeman as Minority Group Member

The policeman's role in society tends to alienate him from society as a whole. For example, it has been suggested that "the policeman's role is particularly subject to fostering feelings of resentment against society, which flow from a typical source of radical politics—status discrepancies."[12] This refers to the ranking of individuals who are high on one status attribute and low on another. The policeman is given considerable authority by society to protect life and property and to keep public order; he is expected to risk his life if it is necessary to discharge these duties. However, the policeman feels that he receives little prestige for his actions. He gets paid less than other occupational groups who are given comparatively little authority. He is ranked high in authority, but low on a scale of rewards.

This isolation and rejection of the police from society results in a sense of alienation from society. This pressures the police to develop their own subculture with norms that provide them with "a basis for self-respect independent to some degree of civilian attitudes."[13] Thus, many police officers look upon themselves as an oppressed minority, subject to the same kind of prejudice as other minorities.[14]

[12] S. M. Lipset, "Why Cops Hate Liberals and Vice Versa," *Atlantic Monthly* (1969), p. 79.
[13] James Q. Wilson, quoted in Lipset, "Why Cops Hate Liberals and Vice Versa," *Atlantic Monthly* (1969), p. 80.
[14] Ibid.

A minority is a social group whose members experience, at the hands of another social group, various disabilities in the form of prejudice, discrimination, segregation, or persecution (or any combination of these). People tend to exclude police from their circle of friends because of the nature of the law enforcement occupation and its responsibilities. Such social discrimination is illustrated by the comments of a police officer.

> *Several months after I joined the force, my wife and I used to be socially active with a crowd of young people, mostly married, who gave a lot of parties where there was drinking and dancing, and we enjoyed it. I've never forgotten, though, an incident that happened on one Fourth of July party. Everybody had been drinking, there was a lot of talking, people were feeling boisterous, and some kid there—he must have been 20 or 22—threw a firecracker that hit my wife in the leg and burned her. I didn't know exactly what to do—punch the guy in the nose, bawl him out, just forget it. Anyway, I couldn't let it pass, so I walked over to him and told him he ought to be careful. He began to rise up at me, and when he did, somebody yelled, "Better watch out, he's a cop!" I saw everybody standing there, and I could feel they were all against me and for the kid, even though he had thrown the firecracker at my wife. I went over to the host and said it was probably better if my wife and I left because a fight would put a damper on the party. Actually, I'd hoped he would ask the kid to leave, since the kid had thrown the firecracker, but he didn't so we left. After that incident, my wife and I stopped going around with that crowd, and decided that if we were going to go to parties where there was to be drinking and boisterousness, we weren't going to be the only police people there.*[15]

Police are more likely to isolate themselves than be isolated by others. Neighbors and friends never separate the man from the badge. When guests at a party discover there is a policeman present, they typically tell about the "crooked cops" they knew or how unfairly a friend of theirs was handled by a policeman. Most veteran officers grow weary of defending the police and withdraw into close associations with other officers. Given a choice, they would prefer to relax in the company of their fellow officers. In addition, the irregular hours created by shift work makes it difficult for policemen to mesh their off-hours with those of neighbors who have "normal" occupations. A police officer is

[15] Skolnick, *Justice Without Trial*, p. 5.

never "off-duty." Most departments require an officer to carry a gun when he is not working and make arrests in outstanding cases.

Discrimination also affects the policeman's wife and children. The following example illustrates the difficulties faced by the wife of a policeman.

> *Whenever I go downtown shopping I feel like I'm wearing Bill's uniform. When people do special things for you, you're not sure if it's because they like you, or because you're a policeman's wife. It works the other way, too. If I park in the wrong place some people will talk about it. You live in a goldfish bowl.*[16]

The disabilities experienced by minorities are related to special characteristics that its members share, either physical or cultural or both, which the dominant groups holds in low esteem.

To begin with, a policeman is highly visible. His uniform, gun, badge, nightstick, and marked car set him apart. This visibility can add danger or prestige to his position—usually danger. For example, the anthropologist Margaret Mead, writing about policemen, stated, "On millions of television screens, the policeman appears not as an identifiable individual but as one of an impersonal mass of men, helmeted and armed, charging a mass of demonstrators who are yelling derisive obscenities."[17]

As Bayley and Mendelsohn have said:

> *Policemen are anonymous persons. Their uniform, badge, gun, and nightstick distract and hold the eye, obscuring the face and personal characteristics of an officer. In this respect policemen are like members of a minority group: To non-group people they all look alike.*[18]

Policemen are quite aware of their minority status. In one study, for example, 171 police recruits were asked to agree or disagree with the statement: "The respect that citizens have for a patrolman and his position has been steadily increasing over the years." Twelve percent of the recruits agreed with the statement; 72 percent of them disagreed.[19] In another study, only 2 percent of 282 policemen rated the prestige of

---

[16] Jack J. Preiss and Howard J. Ehrlich, *An Examination of Role Theory* (Madison: University of Wisconsin Press, 1966), p. 34.

[17] Margaret Mead, "The Police and the Community," *Redbook* (1969), p. 38.

[18] D. H. Bayley and H. Mendelsohn, *Minorities and the Police* (New York: The Free Press, 1969), p. 1.

[19] D. Bordua, ed., *The Police: Six Sociological Essays* (New York: Wiley, 1967), p. 217.

police work as excellent; 19 percent ranked it as good; and 70 percent ranked it as only fair or poor.[20]

Stress and Its Consequences

One of the consequences of stress is a high suicide rate among policemen. A 1967 study found that the suicide rate in the New York Police Department was 50 percent higher than the rate for all New York City males.[21] In at least one previous period, it had been even higher. A report based on data gathered for the period 1934 to 1940 showed that the police suicide rate in New York City was six and a half times higher than the rate per 100,000 population. The report was prepared at the request of Mayor Fiorello LaGuardia, who was prompted by widespread public alarm over this situation.

Despite its dramatic findings, it is difficult to draw clear conclusions from such a study. For one thing, nearly half of the 93 men who committed suicide had joined the force during a period when recruitment standards were fairly lax; in addition, a combination of political protection and police unwillingness to bring charges against one another had led to the toleration of work abuses and the retention of men whose qualifications were suspect. Moreover, the suicide period coincided with the days of the racket-busting crusade led by Thomas E. Dewey. Dismissals during this reform period jumped from less than one per month to an average of five per month; and men were heard threatening suicide if they were "broken" (dismissed). Cnly about one-third of the men who committed suicide showed outward signs of emotional instability or stress, such as open aggression, poor impulse control, excessive drinking, and marital problems. Marital trouble was significantly involved in a large number of suicides, even those in which the (apparent) precipitating situation was some episode in which demotion or suspension was threatened by a superior officer. It also seems worth noting that at least five of the suicides murdered someone before taking their own life. One man murdered a fellow officer who had refused to drink with him.

[20] Skolnick, *Justice Without Trial*, p. 268.
[21] Arthur Niederhoffer, *Behind the Shield* (Garden City, N.Y.: Doubleday, 1967), pp. 101-102.

Suicide is a complex phenomenon. Its causal relationships are very difficult to establish. The suicide rate among psychiatrists, for example, is the highest of the medical specialties. Does this mean that psychiatrists are subjected to more frequent and intense emotional stresses than are ear, nose, and throat men? Or does it imply that people who have personality characteristics which make them potential suicide risks are drawn in greater numbers to psychiatry as a professional specialty? Until we are able to supply more informed answers to such questions than we can supply at present, we must be cautious in our interpretations of the meaning and significance of suicide rates among occupational or professional groups.

A psychiatrist who served as a policeman in New York City for seven years and later became a psychiatric consultant to the New York Police Department examined 85 policemen between 1962 and 1969 on referral because of some degree of breakdown they had suffered on the job.[22] These breakdowns, however, were exceptions; 85 cases out of a total force of 30,000 people seems to be a small minority, particularly in view of the "emotional hazards" faced by the police in the performance of their duties. Only one of the three cases discussed in detail in the New York Police Department study presents a clear picture of psychosis—specifically paranoia. The second concerns a man worried about cleanliness who could not withstand the stress involved in a week-long stakeout in a filthy cellar. The third case involved a man with a good ten-year work record in the department who developed severe feelings of worthlessness and depression following a departmental investigation into the circumstances surrounding the loss of his shield and gun through theft. This last case emphasizes the importance of "emblems of authority" to most policemen. To have one's shield and gun stolen, as in the case cited above, or to have one's gun temporarily taken away, as is the standard procedure in psychiatric examinations, can be a demoralizing experience. Joining the "rubber gun squad" for any reason involves not only a loss of power and authority, but also a deprivation of departmental confidence.

Obviously, to many of the people in law enforcement, police work is not merely a job—it is a way of life. But it is dangerously simple to overemphasize the importance of emblems of authority to a group

[22] M. Symonds, "Emotional Hazards of Police Work," *American Journal of Psychoanalysis*, Vol. 30, 1970, pp. 155-160.

whose members are frequently accused of harboring a high percentage of "authoritarian personalities." The white coat and title of the physician or the black robes of the judge and the solemn ritual of the courtroom—these are also emblems of authority to the members of these professions, and their deprivation is also accompanied by feelings of self-devaluation and depression. Yet one hesitates to imply that physicians or judges, as a class, have an excess of authoritarianism.

Job Failure and Misconduct

The purpose of the preceding discussion is not to support the proposition that "the policeman's lot is not a happy one." Rather, its purpose is to help us understand the stressful nature of the police role. In recognizing the stressful nature of an occupational role that is at once punitive and supportive in its demands, we must also recognize that these built-in sources of stress have other potential consequences for the police worker in addition to suicide or psychological breakdown.

A study conducted by R. J. Levy attempted to specify some of the variables which might lead to job failure. From the personnel files of 4500 California police officers (including 10 city police departments, three sheriff's offices, and the State Highway Patrol), Levy identified three groups with regard to job tenure during the period 1952–1962: (1) 690 "failures"—officers whose dismissal occurred because of charges brought against them; (2) 643 "nonfailures"—officers who terminated employment for other reasons; and (3) 1333 "currents" who were still employed.[23] Levy then compared the three groups in terms of background information and characteristics. The results of the study were largely disappointing. Out of a total of 140 coded variables, including such variables as marital status, type and extent of military service, stated reason for applying, and whether or not the applicant had ever incurred any debts, very few proved capable of distinguishing the "failures" group. At the time of their appointment, the people in this group were more likely to have been fired from previous jobs, more likely to have been married more than once, and least likely to have been exposed to formal education in police science courses.

[23] R. J. Levy, "Predicting Police Failures," *Journal of Criminal Law, Criminology, and Police Science*, Vol. 58, 1967, pp. 265-276.

By way of contrast, the "currents" appeared to be a less mobile group. They were more likely to have been born or lived for a long period in the city where they applied for police work and were more likely to have held earlier jobs for a reasonably long time. Levy suggests that they appear to be less responsive to environmental stress than the other two groups with which they were compared.

Police misconduct has been attributed to a variety of factors, including poor training, low pay, inadequate screening at the time of recruitment, disillusionment, bitterness over unfair treatment within the department, hostility from members of the community, temptations toward dishonesty that come from merchants and businessmen, and the need to prove oneself to the police fraternity—to "earn your way in" by a willingness to engage in various kinds of criminal conduct. Some of these situational factors are given further emphasis by R. L. Smith in an intriguing article, "Cops as Robbers," based on interviews with two ex-policemen serving time in the state penitentiary for robbery. Both of these convicts explained that illegal activities are extensive among the police—even among policemen who, on a variety of occasions, have shown bravery and dedication in the performance of their duties. They denied that low pay was a direct reason for misconduct and placed the principal blame upon the pressures exerted by both police and citizens alike to conform to a corrupt system. The norm of police solidarity does not permit informing on a fellow officer who engages in misconduct, yet there is no guarantee of support from the "top" if one takes an unpopular stand. They cited the demoralizing effects of learning that proper handling of cases may make enemies for the police officer, while "getting along" and "not rocking the boat" are often the surest path to raises and promotions.

The "police establishment" has been described as a defensive and clannish world that cannot be penetrated by external influences. In some cases, police misconduct—including criminal offenses, excessive use of violence, and racial prejudice—are sanctioned by the conservatism of police departments and policemen who support one another without regard to the nature of the misconduct.[24]

Faced with these characteristics of the job and work, police tend to develop into two polar types of officer: the cynic and the profes-

---

[24] William Turner, *The Police Establishment* (New York: G. P. Putnam's), 1968.

sional.[25] The cynic stands firmly on "an ideological plank deeply entrenched in the ethos of the police world, and it serves equally well for attack or defense. . . . When officers succumb they lose faith in people, society, and eventually in themselves. . . . In their Hobbesian view, the world becomes a jungle in which crime, corruption, and brutality are normal features of the terrain. . . . Such a philosophy, softened by a touch of compassion or a sense of humor, converts men into tolerant observers of the human comedy. . . . Without these saving graces, it leads to misanthropy, pessimism, and resentment—a dangerous combination."[26] The professionals, on the other hand, are an able, dedicated, and growing minority within the ranks of the police, whose importance bears no relationship to its numbers. These people are the source of most of the innovative responses to change. A large part of the continuing effort toward upgrading and self-improvement within law enforcement is represented in the contributions of those police whose objectives, past and present, have involved the development of true police professionalism. As James Q. Wilson puts it, "A thoroughly professional police department—one that is honest, competent, impartial, and ably led—will command the respect and cooperation of citizens and will thus produce in the members of such a department pride and a confidence that they have the support and understanding of the citizens whom they are required to protect."[27] Such a department will also be the best equipped to deal with the problems brought about by social change.

The Origins and Growth of Police Professionalism

In a paper submitted to the President's Commission on Law Enforcement and the Administration of Justice, the following criteria were proposed for professions, in general, and law enforcement, in particular.

    1. Its members are service-oriented, rather than product-oriented.

---

[25] Niederhoffer, *Behind the Shield.*
[26] Ibid.
[27] James Q. Wilson, "Police Morale, Reform, and Citizen Respect: The Chicago Case," Bordua, *The Police: Six Sociological Essays,* p. 143.

2. Its representatives have achieved a high level of competence, based on a mastery of considerable intellectual content.
3. Its representatives are given extensive autonomy and authority in exercising their special competence.
4. There exists in the profession a utilization of scientific knowledge and specialized technique.
5. Its representatives have strong commitments to a career based on their special competence.
6. Its representatives are committed to the spirit of free inquiry, and their loyalties relate more to the profession than to an employing organization. Their values relatives to personal accomplishments relate more to esteem of professional peers than to hierarchical supervisors.
7. They have representatives who are determined to influence change by taking action to eliminate or ostracize all incompetent and immoral members of the organization.

While considering the police to be a profession insofar as they satisfy these criteria, the author of the report noted: "It would seem, to this Commission, that there are many policemen of professional competence and character in the American police service, but that the police service does not meet the standards of a profession to the degree that it should, even though it be a professional activity."[28] Thus, suggestions made to the President's Commission for several levels of police service are an acknowledgment of the fact that true professional recognition may need to be reserved for a highly qualified group within law enforcement.

The Work of August Vollmer

The widely recognized founder of police professionalism is August Vollmer who laid the foundations of the present trend toward police professionalism in 1908. As police marshal of Berkeley, California, he introduced many innovations that were startling for their time and that continue to influence law enforcement all over the world. Under Vollmer's leadership, American law enforcement has been brought to what many consider the brink of full professionalism.

[28] A. C. Germann, "Recruitment, Selection, Promotion and Civil Services," paper presented to the President's Commission on Law Enforcement and the Administration of Justice (Washington, D.C.: U.S. Govt. Printing Office, 1967), p. 192.

Vollmer began his work by establishing the first police training school. In addition, he was instrumental in establishing the School of Criminology at Berkeley. He is also credited with being the father of scientific police investigation. His was the first fully mechanized police patrol system and he pioneered the use of two-way radios for the police. Vollmer also wrote many widely read books on methods of improving police service.

Professionalization after Vollmer

Between Vollmer and the 1930s, there were not many significant steps taken with respect to police professionalization. The 1920s were lean years for police professionalization, especially in the Eastern United States. In addition to the social upheaval known as the "Roaring Twenties," with its many police problems, police departments also had trouble recruiting qualified men. The security offered by civil service benefits attracted many immigrants who had poor educations. The 1930s, however, reversed this trend. The Depression, although it imposed great hardships on the whole country, proved to be a blessing in disguise for the cause of police professionalization. There was now great competition for civil service jobs, and the better educated held an edge in the qualifying examination. Thus, by 1940 more than half of the New York City policemen being hired held college degrees. The same situation occurred, to a much lesser extent, in other American cities. In this same period promotion became much easier for those with high educational attainments. Within 15 years the top ranks of the police service in America were held by the better educated.

World War II also acted as a stimulus toward increasing police professionalization. The war brought many technological advances, such as radar. But it also created problems for law enforcement. Many college-educated young men who otherwise might have entered the police service were drawn into the armed services as officers—a process that did not reverse at the end of the war. The less educated, fearful of mass postwar unemployment, joined the police. Many of the better educated went into industry. Thus, only 5 percent of the men being recruited during this period by the New York Police Department were college educated.

In the postwar years, police professionalization received strong support from the better educated recruits of the 1930s, who now occupied the top ranks in the police service. A new emphasis was placed on education and training and a college-based discipline of "police science" was created. College programs especially designed for law enforcement officers were implemented. College degrees were being recommended as a requirement for supervisory ranks and eventually for all ranks.

Men who joined the police service in the 1930s began to consolidate their gains in the postwar years. Since few men with professional potential were joining the police at this time, much was being done to transform the likely prospects who were recruited into men of a professional caliber. Entrance standards were tightened and pay increases were obtained. There was wide encouragement for the application of science and technology. Thus, the better recruits of the 1930s, now occupying top ranks in police service, generally succeeded in raising police prestige in the middle and late forties.

Despite these advances, the gap between the need for policemen with advanced degrees in education and its realization remains large. In a survey conducted of 6200 officers in 1964, only 30.3 percent had taken one or more college courses and only 7.3 percent possessed a college degree. A 1966 survey of 5700 police officers employed by police agencies in the metropolitan area of Detroit revealed that over 75 percent of these officers had not attended college.

While higher education is necessary to the professionalization of the police, there is another side to this issue. Formal education has been so oversold in this country by its enthusiastic supporters that, until recently at least, it has been regarded as the cure for all ills. It is something of a shock, therefore, to discover that there are people around who view the much-advertised benefits of formal education with a coldly skeptical eye. One such person recently retired as chief of police in a small Southern town. Like many "self-made" men, he takes pride in having acquired his education in the "school of hard knocks" and tends to be *underwhelmed* by college degrees. He has many counterparts among the higher ranks of police administrators who agree with his opinions; neither he nor they can be put off with simple-minded answers to questions concerning the value of formal instruction for law enforcement personnel.

Nevertheless, to a reasonable person, it seems self-evident that the qualities associated with a liberal education—understanding social conditions and human behavior, communication skills, self-discipline, problem-solving ability, and independence of thought and judgment—

are the qualities we are seeking in our law enforcement personnel. The study conducted by Levy among California police officers found that there is greater dissatisfaction and job turnover among the better educated police, but this is a strong argument in favor of reforming the system to better meet their needs, not an excuse for seeking more poorly educated police. At any rate, as the educational base in general continues to rise, police will need more education merely to stay abreast of national trends.

The Current State of Police Professionalization

On the basis of professionalism, American police might be divided into "law officers," "specialists" and "peace officers," or "generalists." Technological change is a major stimulant to professionalization. Within law enforcement, specialization and technological change have produced some groups that seem very close to professionalization, while the generalist remains far from it. FBI agents, because of their education, have the prestige of professionals, as do police laboratory experts, some high-ranking police administrators, professors of police science, and certain other specialty groups.

Despite many obstacles, professionalization of law enforcement has been widely accepted as a goal. Work has already begun on many of the changes that are regarded as necessary in this process. It is encouraging that much progress has been made in many areas, as noted in the following.

Police Science. The theoretical basis for the profession of law enforcement has now been established as "police science." As subject matter, police science treats the following: applications of public administration to police work, criminal law, sociology, psychology, psychiatry, and human relations. Marksmanship and physical education have also been added to this general framework.

Higher Education. Specialized law enforcement programs are now offered by at least hundreds of educational institutions in the United States, most of which are junior colleges or community colleges. The most promising sign in this context is the increasing number of graduates who had not previously been law enforcement officers. However, while a college education is widely regarded as desirable, there is little information available regarding the effectiveness of college-educated patrolmen. There is some evidence to indicate that a college education may actually hinder the performance of certain police tasks, such as the routine duty of issuing parking tickets.

College training can actually create personnel problems for local police forces. Many officers who have completed college quit local police forces for better-paying federal law enforcement positions. Others may drop out of law enforcement altogether to pursue graduate studies. Those who remain may find that their merit increases are resented by other nondegree officers who are working at identical tasks.

Training. The training of police recruits is being upgraded almost everywhere in the United States. Yet it is worth noting that as of 1967, 23 states had laws making such training mandatory.[29]

Professional Organizations. Although there are many organizations of police officers in the United States, most of them bear more resemblance to labor unions than to professional associations. Perhaps the most professional of these is the International Association of Chiefs of Police, founded in 1894.

Code of Ethics. A statement of the canons of the International Association of Chiefs of Police was issued in 1957. However, the statement included no provision for the enforcement of these canons.

Publication. There are approximately 15 national periodicals published for and by police officers. Only two may be considered truly scholarly, *The Journal of Criminal Law and Criminology* and *The Journal of Police Science and Administration.*

Optimism Warranted. Law enforcement appears to have fulfilled to some degree many of the qualifications for professionalization. Some specialists within the occupation seem to have already achieved something akin to preprofessionalism. Recent improvements in standards indicate that the whole occupation may be on the verge of becoming a profession.

---

[29] *Task Force Report: The Police,* The President's Commission on Law Enforcement and the Administration of Justice (Washington, D.C.: U.S. Govt. Printing Office), 1967.

Figure 4-1. Practical, realistic training problems enable the student to apply learned principles to real-life situations. Here, an instructor evaluates the "investigation" by two trainees of a simulated homicide. The presence of a television news cameraman adds to the realism.

Conclusion: The Police, the Public, and the Criminal Justice System

As we noted earlier, Americans discovered the police about the same time they discovered "the crime problem." Academician and layman alike found themselves unacquainted with even the most superficial characteristics of an occupational group whose members numbered nearly a half-million people, whose functions are performed where the going is toughest—on the streets, and whose work is particularly complicated, conspicuous, and important in a time of rising crime, increasing social unrest, and growing public sensitivity. The President's Commission Task Force Report on the Police observes that "it is generally assumed by the public that the police enforce the criminal laws and preserve peace mechanically, simply by arresting anyone who has deviated from legislative norms of acceptable behavior."[30] On the contrary, police work is highly discretionary. First of all, the police do not have the resources to enforce all criminal laws equally. Second, the other agencies in the criminal justice system are unable to cope with all violators. This is evidenced by crowded court calendars, large probation and parole caseloads, and overcrowded prisons. Further, the police are required to enforce many laws that seek to regulate social conduct— laws that are unpopular, ambiguous, often unenforceable, or that can apply to the common activities of ordinary, law-abiding citizens, even though they were intended to apply only to the activities of certain types of criminals, such as.gamblers.

Policemen are expected to act effectively—and do, in fact, live up to such expectations—yet their methods of action are the subject of harsh criticism. This creates frustration and discourages the police in their job performance. A poor job performance has a negative effect upon the public, which in turn reflects its disapproval. The policeman's negative attitudes are further reinforced by such disapproval, with the result that he is trapped within a circle of self-defeating and self-perpetuating behavior.

Finally, it should be noted that the police are responsible for considering the consequences of an arrest. As the Task Force report states, "In light of these inherent limitations, individual police officers must, of necessity, be given considerable latitude in exercising their arrest power. As a result, no task committed to individual judgment is more complex or delicate. A mistake in judgment can precipitate a riot or, on the other hand, culminate in subsequent criminal activity by a person who was erroneously released by an officer."[31] An unjustified arrest can seriously, perhaps permanently, affect the future course of a man's life. The importance of the arrest power and the need for rational exercise of this power cannot be overemphasized.

Yet, it must be our final judgment that the capabilities of American law enforcement for coping with change are substantial and growing. Americans, to paraphrase one of Winston Churchill's observations about the quality of government, are getting a better brand of law enforcement than they deserve. If there are contradictions and inequities within the structure of American law enforcement, these are apt to be—in many cases—a reflection of similar contradictions within our society in general.

[30] The President's Commission on Law Enforcement and the Administration of Justice, *Task Force Report: The Police*, p. 120.
[31] Ibid.

Student Checklist

1. Can you name at least three factors that make it difficult for police officers to cope with change?
2. Can you list steps that have been taken to professionalize police?
3. Can you identify significant steps recommended to help professionalize police in the future?
4. Can you write a brief essay on the police as a minority group?
5. Can you list the factors that officers must recognize and deal with on their jobs if they are to avoid becoming bitter?

Topics for Discussion

1. Discuss what it is that makes some police officers cynical.
2. Discuss what can be done to professionalize police.
3. Discuss what causes police isolation from the community.
4. Discuss what an officer can do to cope with change.

ANNOTATED BIBLIOGRAPHY

Alex, Nicholas. *Black in Blue: A Study of the Negro Policeman.* New York: Appleton-Century-Crofts, 1969. Based on intensive interview of 41 black New York City policeman, this book illuminates the problems, conflicts, and difficulties faced by the minority group member who wears a badge. Although it focuses primarily upon the black policeman—the way he was recruited in the police force, his relations with his white counterparts, and his social isolation from the black community—it provides a thoughtful analysis of broader issues which confront society in law enforcement.

Berkley, George E. *The Democratic Policeman.* Boston: Beacon Press, 1969. Berkley, a sociologist, traveled extensively in Europe, where he attended police classrooms, rode on patrols, and consulted extensively with police administrators and public officials. He has drawn upon his observations of the European law enforcement establishment to make a series of insightful analyses of the contradictions involved in being a policeman in a democratic society.

Niederhoffer, Arthur. *Behind the Shield: The Police in Urban Society.* Garden City, N.Y.: Doubleday, 1967. A comprehensive, at times severely unflattering description of the policeman on the job. Veteran police administrators have taken exception to the validity and generality of some of the author's contentions, but the book makes for lively, informative, and extremely stimulating reading.

Task Force Report: The Police. The President's Commission on Law Enforcement and the Administration of Justice. Washington, D.C.: U.S. Govt. Printing Office, 1967. This is a basic source document for any serious student of law enforcement and criminal justice, this book is a compilation of information and interpretations from experts in many fields regarding the role, tasks, functions, responsibilities, and problems of the police in the United States.

Vollmer, August. *The Police and Modern Society*. Berkeley: University of California Press, 1936. This book is a genuine classic—the summary of examined experience from a lifetime of creative work in law enforcement by a man who was one of the founding fathers of modern police organization. It is necessary, while reading this book, to refer continually to the date: 1936. So many of Vollmer's ideas were ahead of his time that we have still not caught up with most of them.

Wilson, James Q. *Varieties of Police Behavior*. Cambridge, Mass. Harvard University Press, 1968. A thorough, scholarly, and perceptive examination of role models in law enforcement and the socialization of the policeman into the police subculture.

The study of this chapter will enable you to:

1. Define the term "perception."
2. Show how a citizen's perceptions of the police affect the way that the citizen acts toward a police officer.
3. List three factors responsible for differences in perception.
4. Write a short essay explaining some constructive alternatives to help police cope with negative police-community relations.
5. Contrast hostility and aggression.

5

Psychological Factors Affecting Police-Community Relations

The title of this chapter could be misleading at first glance. Psychological factors should not be thought of as fundamental aspects or components of such *groups* of individuals as "the police" or "the community." Rather, psychological factors are *internal* only to the *individual*. But, in our society, individuals do not live by themselves as hermits—people interact with each other in order to survive. Thus, the nature, meaning and consequences of the interactions between and among individual people form the roots of police–community conflict and also hold the key to solving such conflicts. It is within this context that we will discuss psychological factors affecting police-community relations.

We cannot possibly deal with all aspects of the psychological factors affecting police–community relations; volumes could be written on this subject alone. Therefore, our discussion will limit itself to the psychological factors that seem to be most instrumental in determining the nature of police–community relations. Most of the references made in this chapter to "the community" are references to the ghetto situation or the urban neighborhoods of the poor, the socially isolated, and the disenfranchised. This is where most of the police–community relations problems originate. It should be understood, however, that psychological factors are *individual* factors, not *group* factors, and as such, they would apply to individuals across social class and racial lines; only common conditions among individuals can cause these factors to result in predictable group responses.

Our discussion here will deal chiefly with two rather broad phenomena: (1) perception, and (2) aggression and hostility. Finally, we will explore constructive alternatives to improve these psychological factors in order to decrease police-community problems.

Perception

Think about how often you have heard such statements as:

Well, this is the way I see it.

I suppose that is just the way he sees it.

I have to respond the way I see it.

I suppose you have to act in accordance with the way you see it.

The word see in such statements does not usually refer simply to visual sensation. Although the speaker might not understand it at the time that he makes statements such as those above, he is using "see" in a psychologically meaningful sense. He is really using the word see in a manner similar to the way psychologists employ the word perception. Perception does not merely refer to receiving visual stimulation, visually sensing something, or even making visual cues meaningful. Although perception includes sensation in its broadest sense, it also includes much more. Perception is a product. This product consists of experiencing sensations and processing these sensory experiences through a personality. The personality itself has many reference points and is a product of a history of internal stimulation as well as a lifelong accumulation of external sensory experiences, with its own unique pattern of integrating and interpreting these stimulations and sensory experiences.

We might also consider a scientific definition of perception.

The mental process by which the nature of an object is recognized through the association of a memory of its other qualities with the special sense, sight, taste, and so forth, bringing it at the same time to consciousness.[1]

Perhaps even this definition is a bit too technical for our purpose, although it does give us an idea of some of the things that psychologists include in the concept of perception.

To help understand the concept of perception, we will create our own definition. We can think of perception as "the way things (experi-

[1] Leland E. Hinsie and Robert J. Campbell, *Psychiatric Dictionary*, Third Edition (New York: Oxford University Press, 1960), p. 541.

ences) impress and affect us at the moment and the way they lead us to ✓ respond." Thus, thinking of perception as the way one "sees" something is adequate as long as we understand the principles of perception that we have just outlined.

Associated with perception is the concept of behavior. When we use the term perception, we are automatically making certain assumptions about the nature of responses (behaviors) that we expect to be associated with the particular perception. In a functional sense, perception is important because it is instrumental in most of the significant behaviors of human beings.

Since how things affect us is often referred to as "experience" (e.g., "This is the way I experienced it"), perhaps it would aid us in the following discussion to substitute "perceptual experience" for "perception" and to distinguish between "perceptual experience" and "objective experience." To distinguish between them, consider the following example.

> Individual A pulls his van over to the curb and steps out to the sidewalk to ask directions from individual B, who is walking toward him on the sidewalk. Before B finishes giving A the directions he asked for, both men look up simultaneously and see a huge lion approaching them on the sidewalk. "A lion!" screams B, as he turns and runs in the opposite direction down the sidewalk as fast as he can. "Stop!" yells A, but B is soon out of earshot. A then walks to the lion, gently strokes his mane to indicate that all is well, takes the lion to the back of the van, and orders him to leap into the van, which the lion does. A then closes the tailgate of the van, climbs into the driver's seat, and continues on his way, regretting that B did not take time to give him sufficient directions to reach his destination. He would undoubtedly have to stop again and ask directions, which might make him late for his performance at the circus.

In this example the objective experience of the two men was the same, but they had different perceptual experiences. The similar objective experience can be called a "reality" experience; it is the type of experience that can be standardized and agreed upon by most people. Individuals A and B would agree that they saw an animal approach and the animal was a lion. Thus, the lion's appearance on the sidewalk as the two men talked was an objective experience. The perceptual experiences of the two men can be implied by observing their behavior as the ✓ lion approached them. Obviously, B saw the lion as dangerous and a threat to his well-being and, therefore, ran away in fright. Equally as obvious, A did not see the lion as a threat but showed significant affection toward the lion and concern that the lion might be upset. His behavior was to comfort the lion and his most outstanding concern was to get to his destination as soon as possible.

Let us analyze this situation, then, in order to gain some understanding of the factors which tend to influence the nature of perceptual experience. One factor is obviously *knowledge*. Individual A was acquainted with the lion and, since he was the lion's trainer, he knew that the lion was not dangerous and was therefore no threat to either of the two men. Individual B was not blessed with this knowledge and was therefore afraid of the lion. A second factor influencing the nature of a given perceptual experience is *past experience*. Individual A had obviously had experience with this particular lion and perhaps other lions and probably tended to "see" lions in general in a different way than B. B's past experience with lions primarily consisted of indirect experiences, such as seeing lions in the zoo, in movies, and on television; in most of those instances the lions that he had seen were portrayed as being dangerous and threatening. Those in the zoo were locked up and those in the movies and on television were always attacking someone or some other animal. Another factor that is involved in this example, although a little less obvious than the two just mentioned, is that of *need*. The two men had different needs at that point. Individual B had no real outstanding need in relationship to the experiencing of the lion other than the need for survival. He perceived that his need for survival was threatened at that moment; thus, his need for survival was really the motivating factor behind his running. Individual A's most outstanding need in relationship to the situation at hand was related to his desire to put on a good performance at the circus and to reach the circus in time for that performance. Consequently, the temperament of the lion was very important to him so he proceeded to comfort the lion, to load him back into the van, and to drive off as rapidly as he could in the direction of the circus.

It should now be clear that perceptual experiences are unique. The perceptual experiences of any given individual, even in the same objective situation, are probably different from that of any other given individual. The uniqueness of perceptual experience is based, then, upon the fact that *past experiences* are unique, *needs* are unique, and different individuals possess different amounts of *knowledge* about any given situation.

We should now be ready to apply what we have said about perception to some of the problems that exist between the police and certain community groups. In most cases, the policeman on the beat in the inner city perceives the behavior of the typical inner-city dweller differently from the way the inner-city dweller himself perceives his own situation, circumstances, and behavior. It is also true in most cases that the inner-city dweller perceives the police officer, his role, his purpose, and his behavior quite differently from the way the police officer sees himself. The factors responsible for such differences in perception are ✓ the same as we outlined in the discussion about the lion.

1. Differences in past experience.
2. Knowledge.
3. Individual needs relative to the situation in question.

Let us consider another example, one that is more closely related to our discussion of police-community relations. John is a white middle-class citizen, age 25, and has lived all of his life in a suburban area near a large American city. Roy is a black citizen, also age 25, but has lived all of his life in the inner-city ghetto of that same large American city. John and Roy are walking down a sidewalk within the inner-city area together when they see a police officer, on foot, approaching them. As the officer draws nearer he nods his head in greeting and smiles. John responds, "Good morning officer" and returns his smile. As the officer passes on down the sidewalk, John becomes aware that Roy looks uncomfortable. He recalls that Roy at first did not look at the officer. But after he had said, "Good morning," Roy had looked up at the officer with a tremendous frown on his face and a look of contempt in his eyes. Roy neither spoke to the officer nor returned his smile. John is puzzled; he cannot understand Roy's reaction. To John, the officer was obviously trying to be pleasant. He did not offend John or Roy, and he showed no indication of ill-will toward them. Yet Roy finds it very difficult to understand John's behavior because just as Roy was beginning to trust John as a white person, John really put his foot in it. John demonstrated to Roy in that instance that he was inclined to be friendly with police officers. John feels that Roy now believes John is "just like all other whites"; when the chips are down, John is on the side of the white cop.

Is John's perception of Roy in this instance "true"? Or is Roy's perception of John "true"? Whether these perceptions are true or not, the perceptual experiences of the two men in this instance are nevertheless quite real, and capable of affecting their attitudes toward each other, their ability to trust each other, and their method of behaving toward each other in the future.

Another question to be asked is why did they react differently toward the same objective experience: the approaching of a police officer who greeted them with a friendly smile? First of all, although the police officer was looking at both of the men when he gave his nod of greeting and smiled, Roy perceived that he was not smiling at him at all. He felt that the officer was smiling at John because John is a white man and was an unusual but welcome sight for the white police officer in his dreaded day-to-day experience of walking the beat in the black ghetto. Throughout his life Roy's only relationships with police officers have been negative ones. Roy has learned through experience to avoid police officers at all costs. He has learned that "the main purpose of the police is to control blacks and not to protect them." Roy perceives that what the police mean by control is to "keep blacks in their place," "prevent them from expressing themselves," "depriving them of most of the nicer things in life," and so forth. Roy's past experiences with police officers have included their frequent questioning of him about crimes committed—crimes which he knew nothing about. In fact, Roy has never committed a crime in his life. In the past, however, police officers have taken him down to the precinct station and applied pressure to get him to "finger" friends who have been accused of crimes. And, on several occasions, when Roy indicated to them that he knew nothing about whether or not the person involved had committed a crime, he was told that if he did not cooperate, little or no mercy would be shown to him by the police when they caught him in a crime (which they seemed to feel was inevitable).

Moreover, Roy has never heard any of his friends indicate that they had ever been protected by police officers. His friends always talked about the police as the "enemy." Roy is often afraid as he walks down a ghetto street after leaving the movies. He is afraid of other ghetto dwellers who are in the habit of robbing and otherwise taking advantage of persons caught walking alone on the street late at night. Roy has caught himself on many occasions wishing that there was a police department which would protect him from such hoodlums. Yet, he has never felt that any police officer saw this as his role in the ghetto. Through his own experiences and conversations with his friends, Roy has come to view the police as the most definitive instrument of an oppressing society, deployed not only to protect the rest of society *from* him but to keep him *down* in every way. In contrast to Roy's past experiences with the police, John had always been taught that the policeman was his friend. John read about the helpful policeman in story books; police officers came to his schools, and even one of his father's best friends was a police lieutenant who lived in the area. John remembers the time when his family returned from a vacation at their lake cottage and discovered that their house had been burglarized. They called the police and, after the house had been searched, it was discovered that the only missing item was $50, which John's mother had placed in an envelope and left on the coffee table before leaving. After the police had talked to John's parents, one of the officers said, "Don't worry, Mr. and Mrs. Jones, we got sufficient evidence and we will get the thief and your $50 will be returned." As John grew up, he became friends with a few police officers, who went out of their way to be nice to him. On occasions, he had been stopped by police officers for speeding or committing some minor traffic violation. But he seldom received a ticket, only a warning which usually ended in, "Sir, I'm going to let you go this time, but be careful, we want you to get wherever you are going safely." In general, John has always thought of the police officer as his friend and that the chief role of the policeman in the community was to protect citizens.

Because of these past experiences, John and Roy responded differently to the smiling policeman as he approached them on the sidewalk. Their differential behavior was obviously based upon their differential perception. Their differential perception was in turn based upon the differences between them in terms of past experiences with the police, knowledge of the situation that they were in at the moment, and personal needs.

We have already described how John's and Roy's *past experiences* with the police were different. As far as *knowledge* is concerned, John did not know or understand the style of police activity in the ghetto. Perhaps the police officer was speaking to John rather than speaking to Roy. John could not perceive this possibility because he never experienced differential treatment by police officers.

John and Roy were both reacting to reality as it impinged upon them. For the individual, his perceptual experience *is* his reality. It is his *learned* pattern of "seeing" things, a pattern which is learned because of the *need* to be prepared to respond in a manner consistent with his own best interest. Since perceptual experience is not altogether a conscious phenomenon, the individual would be at a loss if you were to ask him to explain why he "sees" things the way he does. In the case of our smiling police officer, Roy could not have readily explained to John why his perception of the officer's behavior was negative. Similarly, John could not have readily explained to Roy why he perceived the officer's behavior to be positive.

As a general summary of our previous discussion, it would be wise to acknowledge one basic reality with respect to perceptions as they affect police-community relations. There are many different perceptions of the police function, whether we are referring to the ghetto, the middle- and upper middle-class suburbs, the political arena, or the total society. Some people see the police as their *personal* instruments for ending or reducing crime on the street to assure their personal safety. Others see police as an *instrument of society* with the somewhat broader aim of maintaining a degree of harmony, consistency, and peace (whatever the latter has come to mean in today's world). Some people have a more restricted view of the police, seeing them as an agency to suppress underprivileged and minority segments of society. Still others perceive the police as an agency by which white society confines and reinforces the boundaries of black ghettos and/or ghettos of other minority groups. The police are also viewed as being so helplessly caught between social class, racial, and political factions that they are utterly stymied in their work but yet they are made the scapegoat for the ills that are inevitable in a society torn by such conflict. It is doubtful that any two individuals selected at random on the street would have the same complete role perception of the typical police officer or the police function. They would agree on some points, but they would definitely disagree on others.

Part of this confusion is due to our inability to adequately define crime in some functional, nonarbitrary, and meaningful sense. It seems that our concept of crime tends to change as majority practices change, and there is always a lag in updating the criminal code to keep pace with the shifting of majority practices. Yet, if we could define crime at any given point in time in a meaningful (in terms of the human being, the act, and societal demands), consistent, and equitable sense, many of the destructive differential *perceptions* of the role of the police officer in the community would decrease.

Distorted Perception

Perception cannot be thought of as true or false, but it can be correctly labeled distorted when an individual's perception is significantly different from what most people consider to be a reality of the moment. Distorted perception, regardless of its level of severity, always stems from internal psychological conflict.

The most severe types of distorted perception—hallucinations and delusions—are seen in the symptoms of psychotic patients.

A hallucination is the "apparent perception of an external object when no such object is present."[2] Hallucinations may be visual or auditory. The objects seen or the sounds heard are very real to the individual perceiving them. For example, a psychotic prison inmate told the prison doctor that the Devil was visiting him every night and he wanted to change cells so the Devil would be unable to find him. The doctor persuaded prison officials to humor this inmate by permitting him to change cells. But after a few days the inmate reported that the Devil found him again. According to the inmate, Satan had mistakenly left his "fork" in the new cell during his first visit. The inmate carefully hid the fork and Satan, apparently thinking that he was helpless without his fork and assuming that the inmate would use the fork on him, never bothered the inmate again. This hallucination was not restricted to seeing an object (the Devil) that didn't really exist (from the standpoint of the perception of the vast majority of the population), but the inmate also heard Satan's voice speaking threateningly to him. The inmate's distorted perception, then, not only caused him to be extremely fearful but also to risk punishment from prison authorities by insisting that he be allowed to change cells.

Delusions are false beliefs that are maintained by the individual despite objective contradictory evidence. There are two main types of delusions: (1) delusions of grandeur ("I am a superior individual"), and (2) delusions of persecution ("People are out to get me"). For example, a psychiatrist was asked to examine an individual who thought that he had a direct relationship with God. This perceived relationship included the specific stipulation that it was impossible for the individual to be harmed within a certain period of time. To prove the authenticity of his claim (a delusion), the individual drove his automobile off an expressway at a high rate of speed into a ditch. Miraculously escaping

[2] Ibid., p. 328.

from this ordeal without major physical injury, he immediately took further steps to convince a pleading friend of his invulnerability by walking through a blazing brush fire. Still convinced of his invulnerability, he vehemently denied the existence of the second-degree burns sustained as he walked through the fire. Although this man is now confined in a mental hospital, his delusions of grandeur still exist.

A second case illustrates delusions of persecution. Some years ago, a prison doctor was called to a cell block to intervene when a hospital aide was being chased by a psychotic inmate. The chase began during a routine conversation when the inmate suddenly said to the aide, "You are the person who has been out to get me for years." At this point, the inmate reached across the desk for the aide, who jumped up and started running. In actuality, this particular inmate had been seriously persecuted about 20 years back by a rather sadistic prison guard. What would have been a normal reaction if the hospital aide had actually been that guard was indeed an abnormal reaction, based upon distorted perception in this instance. The hospital aide did not, in any objective sense, resemble the prison guard who had persecuted the inmate 20 years ago. Indeed, the inmate had, during the intervening years, accused a number of men with whom he came into contact of being his persecutor. He had acted similarly on the basis of this distorted perception and, in several cases, he had actually fired shots at his perceived persecutor.

The delusions of persecution we see in psychotics are simply an exaggeration of the *projection* mechanism that often is used as a psychological defense in so-called normal individuals, based upon the extent and intensity of their internal psychological conflict. Because projection is motivated by internal psychological conflict, it is a form of distorted perception. Since we feel that projection is the major form of distorted perception negatively affecting the relationship between the police and ghetto dwellers, it will be given special consideration here.

Projection as an Instance of Distorted Perception

Two medical definitions will help us understand why people tend to project.

In projection, the individual attributes his own feelings and wishes to another person, because his ego is unable to assume the responsibility for these feelings or tolerate the painful affects they evoke.[3]

As used by psychiatrists (projection) means the process of throwing out upon another the ideas or impulses that belong to oneself. It is the act of giving objective or seeming reality to what is subjective. The expression implies that what is cast upon another is considered undesirable to the one who projects. The person who blames another for his own mistakes is using the projection mechanism.[4]

The first requirement for projection is that there is something which we regard as negative about ourselves. It is this that we project onto others. However, this does not mean that we actually have conscious insight into these negative aspects of ourselves. On the contrary, if we did have complete insight, we would tend to correct these negative aspects of ourselves and would have no need to project them. This brings us to the second requirement for projection; that is, incomplete insight. The third requirement is that there must be an object to project upon. Further, unless the individual in question is psychotic (like our inmate friend), the person doing the projecting must be able to rationalize his projection to the extent that at least a significant number of people might think that his statement about the object of his projection is justified. Another way of saying this is that we tend to project upon others the shortcomings we see in ourselves, but are unable to deal with in ourselves. This would also imply that we are not satisfied with merely projecting the shortcomings upon others, but we must then deal with those others as if they did indeed have such shortcomings. For example, when the police officer, because of insufficient insight, projects his aggressive tendencies upon the ghetto dweller, he does indeed perceive this other person as threatening, and he takes steps to cope with what he perceives as aggression in this other person. Perhaps the real reason why a police officer might be reluctant to permit a "normal" expression of aggression by the ghetto dweller is that, subconsciously, the police officer is afraid the ghetto dweller might have the same negative aggressive tendencies as he has himself. Such a police officer relieves

[3] Alfred M. Freedman, M.D., and Harold N. Kaplan, M.D., *Comprehensive Textbook of Psychiatry* (Baltimore: The William & Wilkins Company, 1967), p. 298.
[4] Hinsie, *Psychiatric Dictionary*, Third Edition, p. 579.

himself of the responsibility for coping with his own aggressive tendencies because he has projected them onto other people. Thus, he sees the aggression in them, not in himself. He can use his projected aggression (which he actually sees in the other individual) as a justification for an open display of hostility on his part. This gets to be a vicious circle and the ultimate loser, from the standpoint of wholesome personal development, is really the police officer himself. Such a vicious circle reinforces itself and prevents the development of real insight. Without real insight, it is difficult for the police officer to correct the negative aspects of his personality.

Many psychologists and psychiatrists over the years have maintained that the major source of projection is the negative side of our personalities, and that we all have such negative sides. We can minimize our tendency to project to the extent that we are able to accept the positive *and* negative aspects of our personalities. Sigmund Freud believed that a tendency to reject and not cope with "id impulses" (the negative aspects or darker side of personality) is responsible for projection. A few years later a follower of Freud's, Carl Jung, conceptionalized "the shadow" as the darker side of man's personality and termed it the "projection-making factor" in personality. Again, it is Jung's contention that to the extent we are able to accept "the shadow" as a real part of our personalities, we are able to bring it under the control of our total personality; therefore, the need for projection is tremendously decreased. A contemporary psychologist, Rollo May, has used the term daemonic to conceptualize the notion that man is both good and bad, and he is necessarily so. Otherwise, according to May, human striving would cease. However, if an individual is not willing to accept the "bad" that is in him, such nonconstructive activities as projection are inevitable.

Extreme destructive consequences of projection—oppression and persecution—are discussed by Thomas Szasz, who maintains that historically the scapegoat has been an indispensable part of societies. Human beings are social animals and as such are always members of some group. To maintain and strengthen group membership, nongroup members must be attacked. Individuals who are not members of the major-culture group may at any time be labeled deviant either because they have broken some rule or because respected authorities cast them in this role. Individuals may be singled out and persecuted for their real or imagined deviance and become scapegoats. In distinguishing between ourselves and some others who are "deviant," we imply that these others are "alien" and therefore not like us "normal people" who belong to and constitute the group. Once the issue of whether or not the other is really human "like the rest of us" is questioned, any behavior directed toward the other can be rationalized; thus oppression of the other is not condemned because it is not as if they were "people like you or me."[5]

What are some of the reasons for not accepting the darker parts of our personalities, for projecting them outside instead? The most obvious reason is that we do not sufficiently trust ourselves to take a deep look at ourselves; we fear what we might see. However, some people are able to achieve the objective of introspection to a greater degree than other people. There is also social reinforcement of the tendency to project. For example, I might be driven by internal conflict, a lack of self-acceptance, or a tendency to reject the darker side of my personality to project upon black ghetto dwellers that it is they who are inherently lazy, disrespectful of the rights of others and of human life, and capable of responding only to force. If I am alone in this perception and I am not psychotic, I probably would abstain from expressing these perceptions or behaving in direct accordance with these perceptions. However, if I am a member of a police force and I am aware that the vast majority of my co-workers perceive the ghetto dweller the same way (although they, too, might well be projecting), my tendency to project in this fashion is reinforced. Thus, I begin believing that my projected perception is real, which justifies my own negative behavior in relationship to these people. If a majority of the members of the larger society perceive the situation similarly, my perception and behavior become even more legitimate from my frame of reference and I would be less inclined to assume that something is wrong with me, or that I am in need of self-examination. Of course, if the majority of the nonghetto members of society shares my perception based upon projection along this line, laws will be passed on the basis of assumptions that these perceptions are true. Thus, the projection has become institutionalized.

Projection has a negative impact upon police–community relations from several perspectives. First, having projected his shortcomings outwardly onto someone else, the individual, whether he is the police or the policed, is then prevented from seeing, understanding, and coping with his own shortcomings. Thus, personal development is hindered.

[5] Thomas Szasz, *The Manufacture of Madness* (New York: Harper & Row, 1970).

Second, projection lends itself to the support of individuals of one group who are pathologically hostile toward individuals in another group and, consequently, it encourages inhuman treatment. Finally, since the individual doing the projecting cannot face the negative aspects of himself (and this is indeed why he projects them onto someone else), he certainly cannot face these projected negative aspects in the other person (the object of his projection). Therefore, the likelihood of his establishing a real relationship with this other person is just about nil.

The Self-Concept: A Personalized Form of Perception

Social scientists have long recognized that the nature of a person's self-concept (the extent to which it is healthy or unhealthy) and level of self-regard is influenced, to a large extent, by how other people relate to him. In 1934, George Herbert Mead advanced his "looking-glass" theory of the self. His reasoning was as follows: At first, not being conscious of who or what he is, the individual is incapable of experiencing the self. However, he can and does experience others. These others react to him and he experiences their reactions. As a result of experiencing these reactions, the individual learns to think of himself as having certain qualities and, by the same method, he learns what values to associate with these qualities. He learns to have feelings and attitudes about himself. In the final analysis, an individual responds to himself as others respond to him. His self-concept (the way he sees himself) is a reflection of the way others "act as if" they "see" him.

Most present-day "self" theorists do not feel that the human individual is quite as pliable or quite as much a slave, psychologically speaking, to "what others think of him," as this theory suggests. However, the most modern "self" theorists agree that attitudes of others do influence the nature of the self-concept and the level of self-regard. The most outstanding present-day "self" theorist, Carl Rogers, maintains that the avenue by which others have influence on the self-concept and level of self-regard of a given individual is the extent to which they show unconditional regard for, and acceptance of, the individual as he is. By so doing, the individual is encouraged (and psychologically permitted) to accept himself as a total person with value and worth. To the extent that he accepts his total self ("good" and "bad"), he is capable of knowing, directing, and controlling himself. He feels more positive about himself. His self-regard is increased. As he becomes more inclined to accept himself, he is less inclined to project his negative feelings onto others. He loses his fear of seeing others as they really are. He becomes more willing to accept others as total persons. His regard for others is increased. As Rogers explains:

> When an individual perceives and accepts into one consistent and integrated system all of his sensory and visceral experiences, then he is necessarily more understanding of others and is more accepting of others as separate individuals.[6]

The psychologists Hall and Lindzey further explain Rogers' theory as follows.

> A person who is defensive is inclined to feel hostile towards other people whose behavior, in his eyes, represents his own denied feelings. When a person feels threatened by sexual impulses, he may tend to criticize others whom he perceives as behaving in sexual ways. On the other hand, if he accepts his own sexual and hostile feelings, he will be more tolerant of their expression by others. Consequently, his social relationships will improve and the incidents of social conflicts will decrease.[7]

The Self-Concept and Police–Community Relations

Professor Louis Radelet, in his book, *Police and the Community*, has observed that:

> It is commonly assumed that brutality is the principal complaint of minorities against the police. Several studies, including the Michigan State University Survey for the President's Crime Commission in 1966, debunk this assumption. The most frequent complaint is permissive and differential law enforcement in areas which black and other minorities predominately reside. The chief grievance is inadequate police protection and services in inner-city neighborhoods. It is regarded by minorities as the worst form of racial discrimination.[8]

Not being "equally protected by the law" is psychologically interpreted by many inner-city dwellers as an indication that they are not

[6] Carl R. Rogers, *Client-Centered Therapy; Its Current Practice, Implications and Theory* (Boston: Houghton Mifflin, 1951), p. 520.

[7] Calvin S. Hall and Gardner Lindzey, *Theories of Personality* (New York: Wiley, 1957), p. 487.

[8] Louis A. Radelet, *Police and the Community*, Vol. I, Chapter 6 (Beverly Hills, Calif.: The Glencoe Press, 1973).

worthy of such protection, that they are not "as good" as those who are protected, and, when they are "good," it doesn't make any difference anyway. Such a psychological attitude has a tremendous negative impact upon wholesome self-concept development.

Wholesome self-concept development also depends upon an individual being treated as an individual and rewarded and punished according to his own acts, not by the perceived acts of the group to which he belongs. Some people in our society have come to believe that the shortest step to individual self-confidence is the development of a sense of group solidarity; once the group is solidified, they then strive to ensure that the group is respected. This theory is meaningless when we consider that in the inner city, for example, the individual does not necessarily choose to be a part of the group. He is forced into the group and is told to believe that his significance lies with the fact that he is a part of the group. He may not necessarily believe this himself, but the idea of group solidarity leads the police and the rest of society to perceive it this way. Consequently, how can the individual be proud of something that he did not choose himself? He did not necessarily choose his identification with the group—it was forced upon him. Consider the following quotation.

> In general, police and blacks are obsessed with the need to instill respect in each other. For both, the demand for respect is for recognition on the basis of group membership rather than for a positive reaction to personal qualities . . . for each group, the other symbolizes threats that lurk on every corner of the ghetto.[9]

Group solidarity does not necessarily give rise to a healthy or positive self-concept. If groupism is forced upon the individual, it most definitely has a negative impact upon his self-concept. To develop a healthy self-concept, individuals must be permitted to think of themselves as being relatively independent and capable enough to assume responsibility for themselves. The individual who is most inclined to have a positive self-concept is the individual who has the following characteristics.

> He is authentic (real). This means that he knows himself rather well; he accepts himself for what he is, and he is open to his inner feelings regardless of what they may be.

> He is integrated as a functioning person (he is self-consistent, whole, and has a sense of personal unity).

[9] Ibid.

He is autonomous; his perception of self and sense of self-hood are not blurred or distorted by deficiency needs which tend to lead to either unproductive dependency on others, systems, causes, groups, and so forth or the exploitation of others.

He is spontaneous: in the words of Erich Fromm, "It is possible to arrive at an understanding of the essential quality of spontaneous activity by means of contrast. Spontaneous activity is not compulsive activity, to which the individual is driven by his isolation and powerlessness; it is not the activity of the automaton, which is the uncritical adoption of patterns suggested from the outside. Spontaneous activity is free activity of the self and implies, psychologically, what the Latin root of the word, spont e *means literally: of one's free will."*[10]

Any activities on the part of the police that would make it necessary for the individual to be cunning, to lie, and to deceive would tend to interfere with his development of a sense of authenticity and would interfere with his being real, open, and truthful to his own experiences and feelings. When the police treat the individual in accordance with stereotypes concerning the group of which the individual is perceived to be a member, the individual is not being granted the freedom to be autonomous. This freedom to be considered as an independent person is necessary to the development of a wholesome self-concept. Whatever interferes with the individual's capacity to assume responsibility for his own acts and to act spontaneously according to his own values also interferes with his development of a wholesome self-concept. Finally, when the individual cannot make sense out of his isolated experiences or when he is expected to play contradictory roles, he cannot function as an integrated person; and because of this, it is difficult for him to develop a realistic self-image.

The police officer who honestly tries to serve a society of people who seemingly cannot make up their own minds what they really want him to do finds it difficult to have an integrated, and therefore a positive, perception of himself. Professor James Q. Wilson discussed this issue some years ago. He recognized that there is no single explanation for the problem of police morale. Many forces tend to bear upon the problem. Professor Radelet summarized Wilson's point as follows.

---

[10] Erich Fromm, *Escape From Freedom* (New York: Rehearst Corporation, 1969), pp. 284-285.

The crucial concern of the individual police officer is in finding some consistent, satisfying basis for his self-conception to be able to live with himself in reasonable tranquility. The gravity of this concern, of course, varies with individual officers and departments. . . . The problem of morale or self-respect results from two aspects of the policeman's role. First, he often deals with his clients as adversary. Secondly, the policeman is frequently under pressure to serve incompatible ends.[11]

Aggression and Hostility

It is important to talk about aggression as we discuss the psychological factors influencing police–community relations. Aggression, although it is an essential ingredient of the human personality, is considered to be undesirable by a very large percentage of our population, especially when it is seen in others. This is especially true when the police officer views what he considers to be the "aggressive lawbreaker" or even aggression among inner-city dwellers or minority group members in general. Normally, the police officer, from the standpoint of his perception, is in no position to recognize and appreciate the fact that aggression is a very necessary element of the personalities of all people. Aggression is indeed necessary for wholesome development—the development of a sense of self-worth, self-importance, and the tendency to be self-assertive in the positive sense. Like Freud's "id impulses," Jung's "shadow," and May's "daemonic,"[12] it is quite necessary for the individual to learn to express, direct, and control his aggressive tendencies. If he is not allowed to adequately express his aggressive tendencies, they will become distorted and will interfere with his own development as well as his later adjustment to the demands of society.

It has been observed for some time now that an inability to express anger seems to be related to psychoneurotic depression. Aaron T. Beck, in his book on depression, has this to say about anger.

[11] Radelet, *Police and Community*, Vol. I, Chapter 6.
[12] These constructs, briefly discussed under the topic of projection, were proposed by Freud, Jung, and May to describe the coexistence of positive and negative forces within a person and the conflict inherent.

The relative absence of anger among the more severely depressed patient, particularly in situations that uniformly arouse anger in other people, may be attributed to their tendency to conceptualize situations in terms of their own supposed inadequacies. One currently popular explanation for the relative absence of overt anger in depression is that this affect is present and, in fact, intensified in depression but is repressed or inverted. . . . The theme of the dominant schemas is that the depressed patient is deficient or blameworthy. Proceeding from this assumption, the patient is forced to the conclusion that insults, abuse, and deprivation are justifiable because of his own supposed shortcomings or mistakes. Remorse, rather than anger, stems from these conceptualizations.[13]

When the individual is permitted to express his aggressive tendencies and therefore to become aware of them, they become a part of his active personality (his willful expression of himself and his needs) and are subjected to his willful control. Aggression thus becomes an active expression of the individual, an activity which the individual engages in as a result of considered thought. He is permitted to think about such behavior because he has permitted such behavior to reach a point of conscious awareness. On the other hand, *hostility*, one of the most negative psychological reactions of people, is a *passive* response. The individual does not initiate hostility as a *willful*, *active* response; he becomes a victim of hostility when he is not in control of his aggressive tendencies or when he is not permitted to be responsible for his aggressive tendencies. When someone else attempts to continuously prevent him from normally expressing aggression, then hostility becomes inevitable. Aggression can be aimed at realistic, constructive objectives, while hostility is never *consciously* aimed at anything. Aggression is an *action* in the psychological sense, while hostility is always a *reaction*. We can speak to, relate to, and deal with the aggressive individual in the positive sense because he is aware of his aggression and the reason for his aggression. But we cannot constructively relate to, deal with, or reason with the hostile individual because he has not owned up to his aggressive tendencies and is probably unaware of the real reasons for his hostility. For example, the following incident demonstrates the negative consequences of unexpressed aggression and how these consequences are relieved by the appropriate expression of aggression.

[13] Aaron T. Beck, *Depression* (New York: Harper & Row, 1967), p. 288.

Jim Brown, a young man with a nine-to-five job, found himself stranded in the service department of an automobile dealership where he had recently purchased his new car. The automobile had given him a lot of trouble during the three months in which he had owned it. He had to take it back to the service department several times for repairs, resulting in a significant amount of time lost from his job. On this particular occasion, fearing that his job might be in jeopardy if he had to wait several hours for his car to be repaired, Jim asked the service manager if he could use the telephone to call a friend who would pick him up and take him to the job, leaving the car to be repaired. The service manager hesitated, but finally gave Jim permission to use the phone. Jim made the call and was told that his friend was at another number. He then picked up a scrap of paper from the service manager's desk to jot down the number so he could call his friend there. The service manager angrily snatched the scrap of paper from his hand and shouted, "Don't write on that!" Jim, concerned about his job and the problems with the car, ignored the service manager's reaction. However, as he returned to the job, he began to think about what the service manager had said and became extremely angry, first with the service manager and then with himself for not having spoken up and "put the service manager in his place." After all, he thought, "I spent my money for the car, it's not working and I am supposed to be the one to get angry. He (the service manager) is there to serve me and he really should have had someone take me to my job in the first place." As he thought about the matter, Jim became angrier and angrier. His unexpressed aggression, which would have been normal for the situation, was converted into hostility, which is itself negative both personally and socially. From a personal standpoint, Jim hated himself for not having spoken up at the moment the stimulus for aggressive behavior presented itself. His unexpressed aggression was negative from a social standpoint because he generalized his hostile feelings and swore to never buy another car from this particular dealership and to advise all of his friends of the treatment he received there, hoping that they, too, would not buy cars from that dealer.

Fortunately, Jim was not satisfied with his hostile reaction and he took further steps to cope with his frustration. The next morning, (a Saturday, so he was off work), Jim went to the dealership, looked up the service manager, and literally "told him off." He told the service manager just what he had thought when he was alone on the job the afternoon before. He told him that he saw him as a servant and it was his responsibility not only to let him use the telephone, but to transport *him to his job if his car had to be left for lengthy repairs. He told the service manager that it was he, Jim, who should be upset because it was he who had been inconvenienced by an automobile for which he had paid a lot of money. He then told the service manager that he was going to talk with the owner of the dealership and tell him about the episode. Jim followed through on this threat. He walked into the owner's office and asked the secretary if he could speak with the owner. He was permitted to talk to the owner, who was surprised at the attitude of his service manager. The owner immediately called the service manager into the office and, in Jim's presence, verbally reprimanded him for his actions and told him that if he wanted to keep his job he would have to sincerely apologize to Jim at that moment and thereafter see that Jim was transported to his home or his job if it was necessary for him to leave his car for repairs.*

The decision to return to the dealership that Saturday morning was an aggressive act on Jim's part. It was goal directed and it expressed his true feelings openly and directly. As a result, Jim's hostility disappeared and his negative feeling toward himself subsided. Jim no longer felt the need to discourage his friends from patronizing this particular dealership.

From this example we can see that the appropriate expression of aggression serves a healthy, constructive, and vital function. Many police officers, however, feel that their role requires them to stifle all aggressive responses of select individuals. The police officer's perception that he needs to prevent people from expressing aggressive tendencies (because he views these people as potential lawbreakers) is based upon at least two of the factors that we have already said were responsible for distorted perceptions: (1) the nature of the police officer's own needs in relationship to aggression, and (2) a lack of knowledge concerning the need of others to aggressively assert themselves and the consequences that result when people are prevented from "normally" expressing their aggressive feelings. If a person is afraid of his own aggressive tendencies, he is inclined to *project* his fears upon the people with whom he deals, and he therefore becomes afraid of aggression in other people. We have already discussed the mechanism of projection in this connection. In terms of the police officer's lack of knowledge concerning the expression of aggression by others, this may be due to the fact that we do not give our police officers adequate psychological training before putting them on the beat. For example, consider the following quotation from the book, *Psychology Today—An Introduction.*

*Aggression, to most people, means murder, assault, or rape and many
are convinced that our society is being made the victim of increasing
violence. Yet, a careful review of violent crimes statistics suggests that
relatively speaking, there has been no substantial increase in aggressive
crimes during recent years. It is true that robbery and forcible rape
rates show moderate increases. Aggravated assault rates have increased
the most but are far below the rate of increase for property or nonviolent crime. In fact, it is quite likely that changing the form in which
crime is reported is what has created a paper crime wave of staggering
proportions. If simple categories assault and robbery, (for example)
are reported with no information about the degree of severity of the
crime, then an assault is an assault with no clear indication that we
are or are not becoming more savage as a nation.*[14]

In terms of the ill effects of not being permitted to express normal
aggressive tendencies, this source further states that:

*Aggression directed inward, with the self as a target, is an even more
difficult theoretical tangle to unravel. Because it is not possible to
study those who succeed in killing themselves, we must rely in specu-
lative reconstruction of what led to the act. . . . Suicide is, of course,
the most violent form of aggression directed to the self, but it is only
one of many forms of self-punishment. . . . In the United States, suicide
rates vary with status in society. . . . City residents kill themselves more
often than do rural dwellers and those living in the most crowded areas
do so with higher frequency.*[15]

Suicide, then, is the most extreme form of unexpressed aggression
or aggression turned inwardly. The significant role of aggression in
psychological health is stressed in the *Encyclopedia of Aberrations.*

*The gratification of adequate justified aggression is essential for mental
health. Many neurotic features could be eliminated if people were
taught to develop a sound self-assertion, to feel neither guilty about
their aggressions nor to suppress them to an unnecessarily great degree.
. . . The development of aggressiveness is one of man's normal reactions to the disappointments and the opposition he encounters in the
course of his life. If, for some reason, he cannot develop this aggression, anxiety sets in. Then it seems as if the energy which would otherwise be felt as an emotional quality is added to the energy content*

[14] *Psychology Today—An Introduction* (Del Mar, Calif.: Communications/
Research/Machines, Inc., 1970), p. 93.
[15] Ibid.

which is an essential part of the accompanying physical symptoms. Many people find it easier to endure pain that comes from physical rather than psychological sources.[16]

Aggression is indeed basic to the biological as well as the psychological essence of the human being. Aggressive impulses are biologically determined and, when sublimated, serve to foster progressive and constructive forms of adaptation.[17] The word "sublimated" refers to aggression that has been translated into some positive form by the active, conscious individual himself. Aggression cannot be sublimated by outside control; it can only be sublimated by the individual himself. Sublimation, then, is the ability of the individual to recognize his own aggressive tendencies and the sources of his aggression to a large extent; and to direct his reactional tendencies to his aggressive feelings in a fashion that would promote his own well-being in a socially constructive way. The ambitious person in our society may be said to be an aggressive individual. The principled politician who is steadfast in his views and who struggles to see that "right wins out," is indeed an aggressive individual who has sublimated his aggressive tendencies. The individual who feels the active responsibility for supporting his family and will stand up for his right to receive fair employment is a constructively aggressive individual. The individual who decides that he is an important person within his own right and that he is not going to let anyone take advantage of him is a constructively aggressive individual. These examples show that aggression is often a socially acceptable quality. Therefore, we must ask ourselves why we cannot permit other people to be aggressive. Part of the answer is that those of us who find it most difficult to permit other people to be aggressive have been unable to handle our own aggressive tendencies. Thus, we are afraid that others cannot handle their aggressive tendencies.

Another part of the answer may be that the individual is not always able to control his own hostility. Thus, hostility always seeks justification outside of the logical control system of the individual. It seeks its justification in generalizations about people, not in individual persons as they actually live, act, and react. It also seeks its justifications in clichés, which are detached from actual interpersonal involvement

---

[16] Edward Podolsky, *Encyclopedia of Aberrations* (New York: Philosophical Library, 1953).

[17] Hinsie, *Psychiatric Dictionary*, Third Edition.

and in circumstances and conditions that the hostile individual obviously cannot personally direct or control. In other words, the individual's tendency to establish outside justification for his hostile acts and feelings psychologically relieves him of the responsibility for a "product" of himself—a reaction that comes from within his personality and which affects his relationships with others, his hostility. This amounts to disowning a part of his natural "self" (no matter how distorted this expression of self might be) and, consequently, a part of his self becomes alien to him. Because it is alien to the rest of the self, it becomes threatening to the entire personality. Thus, a vicious circle sets in and justification for the hostility becomes even more urgent.

It is not hostility, but aggression, that is an essential aspect of all normal personalities and which is always in need of expression. If aggression is permitted normal avenues of expression at the time that the aggressive need arises, then, as a rule, the expression of aggression is constructive from two standpoints: (1) It immediately relieves frustration and, consequently, prevents the development of hostility which might eventually become detached from the stimulus situation. Thus, by not being bound up in prolonged anger and frustration, more energies are available on the part of the individual to permit considered thinking and the use of his other resources which might be relevant to the situation at hand. (2) It lets the other individual (or individuals) who might have been responsible for that aggressive stimulus (or instrumental in its onset) know where the offended individual stands, what he is feeling, thinking, and why. An opportunity is then provided for corrections to be made, misunderstandings to be cleared up, and the negative effect upon the relationship to be eased.

As an example of the need to express aggression in a psychologically healthy manner, consider the following story told by the chief psychologist in a prison intake and diagnostic unit.

It was my responsibility to give all incoming inmates a battery of psychological tests and an intensive psychological interview to aid in the recommendation of training and treatments programs for each inmate during his stay in prison. Having a rather small staff of professionally trained psychologists, I had to resort to training inmate clerks to do most of the group testing and some of the individual testing.

One morning a very muscular inmate rushed into my office (which was in the intake cell block) and declared in a loud, angry voice, "I told that damned con (referring to one of the inmate clerks who had just attempted to give him a test) that I wasn't going to take any of your g—— d—— tests and he said that I had to see you about it. I just came in to tell you where you can shove your tests. You are nothing but social parasites, all of you, making your living on us cons." By this time, the inmate clerk who had attempted to give him the test had rushed into my office to assist me if our loud friend became physically abusive. The prison officer who routinely sat outside the testing room also saw the angry inmate rush into my office and he appeared simultaneously at the door of my office with the inmate clerk. I immediately asked them why they walked into my office while I was in conference. I said to them, "Both of you know better and please close the door as you leave."

With the appearance of the two men at my office door and after my remarks to them, the angry inmate's face took on an entirely different appearance. He stopped talking for a moment and simply stared at me. Then he said, "You don't know who I am do you? My name is Tom Jones. I am the one who escaped from that other joint. I have been in and out of this joint a number of times and I have never gone through this B.S. of taking tests." I replied that I knew very well who he was, although I had never met him before, and added, "Yes, to save the time required to tell me about it, I also know that you have a reputation for fighting, violating prison rules, and you have been in the hole (solitary confinement in prison) a countless number of times. Does that about size it up? It certainly took a lot of getting steamed up for you to simply tell me that you do not wish to go through the testing procedures. Okay, you may leave, you don't have to take the test."

After these remarks he rushed out of my office to his cell. Within 10 minutes he was back in my office asking, "What are you going to do, send me to the hole? Why didn't you let the screw (the prison officer) take me to the hole when he came in?"

I was ready to laugh at his concern of the moment and asked, "Is that what you wanted? Were you trying to get sent to the hole? Why should I accommodate you by sending you to the hole? That's neither my duty nor is it my bag in any way. Furthermore, why should you be forced to take the tests if you don't want to take them? The only reason for giving anyone any of the tests is to facilitate the efforts on their part to improve themselves while they are here if they desire to do so. Obviously you don't feel that the tests can help you in any way and you certainly are not the only person who feels that way about these procedures."

The inmate left but returned to my office the next day and said that he would like to take the tests after all. I told him that I didn't feel he should take them because he felt that they did not have any meaning for him, and that the results would probably be invalid since he had a poor attitude. I added, however, that if he insisted he could take the tests. He elected not to take them, but what happened afterwards was quite revealing in terms of how desperately hostility needs reinforcement to "stay alive" and how a failure to reinforce it can change a person's entire perspective along positive lines.

We talked every day for several days to follow. At some point in our conversation, he said, "What are you trying to prove? Why didn't you really send me to the hole the other day? How can a man let a con talk that way to him and do nothing about it? I don't know what you are trying to pull, but I am nobody's guinea pig." I then said to him, "I take it that you didn't like the way I acted. If I am so weird and odd, why do you keep coming back?" He then said to me, "You are the guinea pig, you are the odd one as you say, I suppose I am trying to figure you out."

"When you do," I told him, "please let me know what you come up with; I have spent quite a few years, too, trying to figure me out." It was then that he said, "I really don't believe that you didn't get angry. Why didn't you get angry? I have been in and out of these joints most of my life and I have never seen anyone in authority fail to get angry when a con puts him down, and they do much more than get angry."

"Now I finally see why," I began, "you don't understand my reaction, and I don't understand why you are so surprised at my reaction. Our perceptions of what happened, and really what was in back of what happened, are quite different. Evidently you perceived that you put me down and therefore I should have been angry. You have apparently had a lot of experience coping with anger in this connection, but when I didn't show anger you didn't have any ready-made response. You kept coming back almost begging me to be angry with you because somehow that would have validated your impression of prison officials. You felt that I robbed you of your chance to validate what you want to believe about all people who work in prisons and who can go home after the day is over. That's why you became even more angry with me. But now that you have finally accepted the fact that I really didn't feel angry about your rather childish and, I suspect, embarrassing now that you look back on it, tirade, you are simply confused. Now *let me tell you how I perceived the situation. Really, rather simply, it is impossible for you to really put me down, that is, given your circumstances at the present time. I feel no threat from you. Whereas you felt that I had some control over your destiny, I didn't feel that you had any significant control over my life or destiny. I know that I could leave the prison when the day was over and never really return if I so desired. I know you couldn't do the same. I expected you to be angry because, although I may not have acted as childish as you did, I am sure, in your shoes, I would have been angry, too. If you had been in a position to really threaten my well-being, say if you had been my boss, I'm sure my perception of your behavior would have been different and I would have, in all likelihood, acted quite differently." I added, "I hope it doesn't injure your feelings, but the simple fact is, you are not in the position to really put me down in the sense that I would really feel it."*

A lot happened after that in my relationship with this particular inmate, but the most important thing is that he went on to become my chief clerk and worked with me for several years until his release from prison. After he was released from prison until he moved from the area, we remained friends with much mutual respect for each other.

The implications of this story, in light of the present discussion, should be obvious to most readers. In a nutshell, the essential lessons to be learned are as follows.

1. Resulting from the inmate's need system, influenced by years of negative, impersonal, hostile treatment in prison situations (and in other confining situations), he was generally angry and hostile, but was especially hostile toward prison officials.
2. He considered the tests to be at best "crap" and at worst, exploitative, because he had seldom met a person or encountered a situation who or which was really intent upon helping him as a person, as an end within his own right.
3. All of his coping devices (despite the fact that they were distorted) including toughness, which he had learned as a necessity for psychological survival, were to no avail when he encountered the prison psychologist's attitude. As a result, he became temporarily disoriented; he lost his composure, and was exposed directly to his inner fears and anxieties.
4. Such recognition of anxiety, fears, and real feelings of personal inadequacies was possible only after his usual defense (generalized hostility) failed.

5. His hostility, as a defense, failed only because the prison psychologist did not reinforce it in this situation by meeting his hostility with hostility.
6. As he recognized his anxieties, fears, and feelings of inadequacy, he was able to cope with these. This he did in the month that followed.
7. The prison psychologist's failure to return his hostility, although very disconcerting at first, caused him to soon see the psychologist as nonthreatening, creating the basis for a healthy and productive relationship.

Clearly then, expression of aggression can be constructive and beneficial not only to the individual venting his feelings, but to the relationship between him and the other individual who was responsible for the aggressive stimulus.

Constructive Alternatives

To cope with some of the psychological factors that tend to negatively influence police–community relations, especially in the ghetto situation, there are certain steps that can reasonably be taken. At the top of this list is the need to improve the recruitment and training of police officers. Recruitment methods should be designed to screen out individuals who have a need to aggress on others in defense of their own egos, those who are oriented toward stereotypes rather than toward individuals, those who tend to be lacking in self-knowledge and are not inclined to accept themselves as a total personality (both the positive and negative aspects of themselves), or individuals who are simply looking for a job. This would, of course, require increased pay rates for police officers. This would also mean that police officers would generally have to have a higher level of formal education.

As a part of this screening procedure, all potential officers should be exposed to intensive psychological testing. Such testing should reveal whether or not the prospective police officer is interested, in general, in helping people or whether he is interested in oppressing people. The type of person who is ordinarily interested in one of the helping professions probably would, in the long run, make the best policeman. This would be a person who is really sensitive to the needs of other people, a person who "likes people," and a person who is not enslaved to self-centered attitudes.

There should be intensive and ongoing psychological training for police officers. Such training should include both personal encounter experiences (with emphasis upon understanding themselves) and experiences oriented toward the understanding of those to be policed by them.

Each police officer should be given some opportunity to be helpful to ghetto dwellers in a very meaningful way. The police officer should be given an opportunity to study, along with community residents, the needs of the community in relation to police efforts. This could be a rotating situation where each police officer would have this kind of experience with a number of people in the community. This combined police-community group could be deployed to assist other people within the total community (including the police department) to understand the problems involved in police-community relations and to work toward their solutions. Thus, a different concept of community actually emerges.

Modifying Disharmonious Perceptions (an Exercise)
From the standpoint of the individual, perception is always "real." However, when viewed outside of the frame of reference of the individual perceiver, perception can be said to be either harmonious or disharmonious. Perception is disharmonious to the extent that it gives rise to destructive behavior. It is harmonious to the extent that it is instrumental in bringing forth constructive behavior. By definition, then, projection is always disharmonious perception; it is never constructive. In general, perception can be said to be disharmonious when it has the following effects.

Psychological reactions of the individual
1. Causes the individual to feel alone and alienated.
2. Causes the individual to feel powerless (unable to influence his own life in the direction of personal goals and objectives, or to take charge of his own destiny).
3. Causes the individual to feel less "altogether," less integrated as a personality.

4. Causes the individual to be less independent, less autonomous, and less responsible for himself.

5. Interferes with the development of self-knowledge and self-acceptance, and causes the individual to be less open to experience and to his real feelings.

Group reactions

6. Conditions negative feelings on the part of the members of one group toward members of another group.

7. Causes the assumption that value gaps between groups cannot be bridged and the feeling that value differences between groups exist where they really do not.

8. Causes members of one group to think that they are either better or worse, as a whole, than members of another group.

9. Causes people in one group to want to harm people in another group.

These reactions are repeated in the material that follows with possible perceptions associated with them. In each case, first assume that these perceptions are the perceptions of the ghetto dweller, and then devise procedures or programs for modifying each perception in a fashion that would make it more harmonious. Next, assume that these perceptions, in each case, are the perceptions of the police officer, and again formulate procedures or programs for modifying each perception to make it more harmonious.

Psychological reaction of the individual

1. Psychological reaction: the individual feels alone and alienated from others.

   Possible perceptions associated with this reaction:
   I belong to nothing and to no one;
   I stand alone in a society which is completely insensitive to my needs and relatively insensitive to my existence;
   I am not really related to anyone or anything in a significant way.

2. Psychological reaction: the individual feels powerless (unable to influence his own life in the direction of personal goals and objectives, or to take charge of his own destiny).

Possible perceptions associated with this reaction:
> I am a passive victim of my conditions;
> I have no real say in my life;
> I am helpless to improve my life.

3. Psychological reaction: the individual feels less "altogether," less integrated as a personality.

Possible perceptions associated with this reaction:
> Because of probable consequences, it is best not to express certain of my feelings, attitudes, and yearnings;
> My feelings are wrong, especially my aggressive feelings;
> My gentle feelings would be abused if expressed;
> There is neither sufficient time and opportunity nor sufficient "pay-off" for personal intellectual development;
> People would become suspicious if I show that I care and am concerned about the needs of others;
> I have to keep up a tough front here in the ghetto at all costs.

4. Psychological reaction: the individual is less independent, less autonomous, less responsible for himself.

Possible perceptions associated with this reaction:
> I am not complete within myself in any significant way;
> I don't have any significance in and of myself;
> My significance lies with my status as a group member and what other people think about the group, they also think the same about me;
> The group sets the limitation of what I can do.

5. Psychological reaction: the development of self-knowledge and self-acceptance by the individual is interfered with; the individual is less open to experience and to his real feelings.

Possible perceptions associated with this reaction:
> I am so busy striving to figure out what you think I am and what you want me to be that I don't have time to figure out what I really am;
> I must strive to be what others want me to be, although I am confused as to what they really do want me to be;
> I don't possess feelings which are not consistent with what others think I should feel.

Group reactions

6. Psychological reaction: negative feelings develop on the part of the members of one group toward members of another group.

Possible perceptions associated with this reaction:
> They (ghetto dwellers) are lazy, dirty, and dishonest;
> They are destructive and they don't have much in a positive way to offer society;
> They (police) are aggressive, sadistic, and cruel;
> They are only out to control and not to protect me;
> They do not have my interest at heart.

7. Psychological reaction: it is assumed that value gaps between groups cannot be bridged, and felt that value differences between groups exist where they really do not.

Possible perceptions associated with this reaction:
> They are different from me in fundamental ways;
> Since value differences are responsible for the conflict between the two groups, the conflict is inevitable.

8. Psychological reaction: members of one group think that they are either better or worse, as a whole, than members of another group.

Possible perceptions associated with this reaction:
> The group of which I am a member is better than the other group;
> The group of which I am a member is worse than the group of which I am not a member.

9. Psychological reaction: people in one group want to harm people in another group.

Possible perceptions associated with this reaction:
> We had better attack them before we are attacked by them;
> It is necessary for our own survival to engage them in combat;
> Your group represents a threat to me and my well-being and I must militantly oppose your group.

Student Checklist

1. Are you able to define the term "perception?"
2. Can you show how a citizen's perceptions of the police affect the way that the citizen acts to a police officer?
3. Can you list three factors responsible for differences in perception?

4. Are you able to write a short essay explaining some constructive alternatives to help police cope with negative police–community relations?
5. Do you know the difference between hostility and aggression?

Topics for Discussion

1. Discuss what we mean by the term "perception."
2. Discuss how a citizen's perception of the police affect the way that the citizen acts toward a police officer.
3. Discuss some constructive suggestions to help police cope with negative police–community relations.

ANNOTATED BIBLIOGRAPHY

Beck, Aaron T. *Depression*. New York: Rehearst Corporation, 1969. This book is a broad survey of systematic studies relevant to all aspects of depression. It includes a critical analysis of causes, symptoms, diagnosis, and treatment.

Elizer, A. "Content Analysis of the Rorschach with Regard to Anxiety and Hostility," *Rorschach Research Exchange and Journal of Projective Techniques*, 1949. This is a treatment of the meaning of the content of Rorschach responses as they indicate the manifestation and causation of anxiety and hostility.

Freedman, Alfred M., and Harold N. Kaplan. *Comprehensive Textbook of Psychiatry*. Baltimore: The William & Wilkins Company, 1967. This is a compendium of theories and research findings in the area of psychiatry, tracing its developmental history. It describes current thinking pertaining to psychopathology and its treatment.

Fromm, Erich. *Escape From Freedom*. New York: Rehearst Corporation, 1969. This is Fromm's most comprehensive presentation of his social psychological approach to the understanding of persons and the treatment of psychiatric conditions. Fromm elaborates on his concepts pertaining to the essential conditions of man, the nature of his response to these conditions, the pathological and positive aspects of these responses, and the problems and blessings associated with psychological freedom.

Hall, Calvin S., and Gardner Lindzey. *Theories of Personality.* New York: Wiley, 1957. A survey of classical and contemporary personality theories presented by means of a comparative approach with respect to perception of the nature of man, the nature of personality, and the sources of psychological conflicts and strengths.

Hinsie, Leland E., and Robert J. Campbell. *Psychiatric Dictionary*, Third Edition. New York: Oxford University Press, 1960. A dictionary of all the important terms or concepts used in psychiatry from Hippocrates to the present.

Podolsky, Edward. *Encyclopedia of Aberrations.* New York: Philosophical Library, 1953. A compendium listing brief definitions of unfamiliar terms in psychiatry, including short articles representing summaries of various psychiatric subjects and illustrations of normally obscure concepts.

Psychology Today—An Introduction. Del Mar, Calif.: Communications/Research/Machines, Inc., 1970. A well-illustrated contemporary volume including contributions from some 40 psychologists who examine the history and current status of the science of psychology.

Radelet, Louis A. *Police and the Community*, Vol. I, Chapter 6. Beverly Hills, Calif.: The Glencoe Press, 1973. An extensive treatment of the many current facets of law enforcement, crime suppression, social service, and the maintenance of order in the United States. The volume deals with the attitude of the police and all the constituents of the community as they relate to both problems and solutions in the areas of police–community conflicts.

Report of the National Advisory Commission on Civil Disorders. New York: Bantam, 1968. This volume presents the findings of the Commission relating to the causes of civil disorder, with extensive suggestions of methods and procedures for coping with the problem.

Rogers, Carl R. *Client-Centered Therapy; Its Current Practice, Implications and Theory*. Boston: Houghton Mifflin, 1951. The author's classical presentation of his innovative approach to psychotherapy. He breaks away from the tradition of the therapist's personality dominating the psychotherapeutic situation and expounds rather elaborate theory to support the notion that the client is the important entity in therapy, and that the growth and improvement of the client lies essentially with the permissive and accepting nature of the client-therapist relationship.

Szasz, Thomas. *The Manufacture of Madness*. New York: Harper & Row, 1970. The author draws parallels between certain current psychiatric practices and methods used during the Inquisition to indict witches.

The study of this chapter will enable you to:

1. List and describe the three levels of communication.
2. Diagram the communication process.
3. Write a brief essay describing what we mean by "cues."
4. Describe body language.
5. Tell why nonjudgmental learning is an important skill for police.

6

The Communication Process

Colin Turnbull has written a much discussed book, *The Mountain People*, concerning the Ik tribe of East Africa. The members of the tribe cheerfully abandon their children and put their old out of the tribe to die. The thesis? "Supposedly human qualities that we prize so highly—like love, generosity, and consideration for others—are not basic aspects of human nature. These may be social qualities; they are not biological."[1] As a veteran criminal justice employee or as a newcomer to the profession, you have "talked" all of your life. Therefore, do you need to read this chapter? Is effective communication "a basic aspect of human nature"? A great measure of the "new" policeman's success will depend upon his ability to relate to human beings in increasingly difficult situations. This implies what every successfully married couple learns early—good communication takes work and thought—it is not something you were born with.

This chapter will attempt to do two things. First of all, it is designed to help you think about the quality of your communication and offers some suggestions that you might find helpful in learning to improve it. Second, the chapter asks you to consider citizens as individuals, not as a large mass to be dealt with. Both of these topics suggest that if you can handle communication well and honestly, your job will become easier.

[1] Leslie Cross, "The Ik Gave Him a Jolt," *The Milwaukee Journal*, Book Section, Part 5 (Sunday, May 6, 1973), p. 6.

The Levels of Communication

Communication is a process that operates at three levels: *intrapersonal*, *interpersonal*, and *person-to-group*. Intrapersonal communication goes on within yourself. A good example is the thought processes you have when about to throw a bowling ball or to ski down a hill. We talk to ourselves all the time. This chapter touches upon intrapersonal communication, particularly in the segment on listening. The academic community has just begun to wonder about the intrapersonal communication of criminal justice professionals. What happens to the thinking processes of the new recruit? Some suppose that the stresses of the occupation may distort the intrapersonal process, resulting in cynical, tough patrolmen, high divorce rates, and even illness.

Feeling a sense of alienation, which Alvin Toffler attributes to the huge amounts and immense speeds at which information reaches us, society's choice of reading materials reflects interest in intrapersonal communication. Several of these books, including Eric Berne's, *Games People Play* and Tom Harris' best-seller, *I'm O.K., You're O.K.*, show interest in this area. Witness also the beginning of encounter sessions and advancing knowledge about Gestalt psychology.

Person-to-group communication implies a fairly formal situation. For example, during your career you may address a group of school children and appear in courtrooms. There are many fine texts available on preparing specifically for these public presentations, some of which are listed in the Annotated Bibliography. Although undoubtedly some of the material in this chapter may help you with such assignments, its concern does not rest in formal situations.

Interpersonal communication requires the involvement of another human in the process, usually in a semiformal setting. This communication process will be the major focus of our chapter. The section will examine interpersonal communication in three areas: verbal, nonverbal, and the art of effective listening.

Communication is a *process*. Figure 6-1 should give you a concrete idea of this process which occupies much of your waking time.

The ultimate *Source* of communication is the brain, where your *Message*, the idea you wish to transmit, is *Encoded*. One encodes in many ways—we speak, write, or direct traffic, via gesture. Your message is *Decoded* by a *Receiver*. You possess several human decoders, notably your own brain, eyes, and ears. These enable us to receive messages.

Figure 6-1.

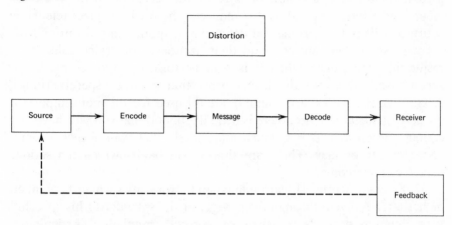

If you speak a different language, your receiver cannot decode your message. *Feedback* is the systematic or spontaneous response to a message. When it is nearing time for class to end, you give your instructor systematic feedback by closing books, putting on your jacket, and examining your watch. Your instructor knows it's systematic, but you will pretend that these actions are spontaneous. Men experiencing the separate world of the armed forces tend to return home with encoding devices, including, "Pass the !#%ing butter." Many mothers experience great *Distortion* in decoding such messages. Profanity is a chief message-distorter, and this topic will be examined again. Distortion is at the top of the model, because it may occur within any of the figure areas. If your original message is poorly thought out before you send it, distortion begins as the words leave your mouth.

Thus far we have examined communication in an almost abstract manner, pondering three levels at which it operates and a communication model. Let's now consider specific ways to improve encoding and decoding.

Verbal Cues

Victor Strecher notes, "A special category within the second mode of presentation is that of police conduct on the telephone. . . . Voice, diction, reaction to the citizen's call, approach to the problem, and basic etiquette are the criteria of judgment. Here again, negative evaluations cannot be reversed. The police telephone response can easily predispose a complainant to a favorable or unfavorable reception of the radio car officers who later respond to this request. These who neglect telephone courtesy will not overcome the deficiency in police image through the correctness of their uniform and their approach to service calls. As a result the work, even when it is well performed, becomes harder to accomplish."[2] Because the mechanisms that produce speech (lungs, larynx, vocal cavities, articulators) are all used for the more important purpose of sustaining life, there is little likelihood that you will have any serious speech defect. It is much more likely that your speech is careless, slovenly or lazy. These are simply bad habits which the serious person can overcome.

Emerson wrote, "I learn immediately from any speaker how much he has already lived, through the poverty or the splendor of his speech." Pronunciation depends primarily on correct articulation. Articulators are the teeth, tongue, lips and hard palate. Sounds to pay particular attention to are f, p, b, and v. These sounds are hard to pronounce correctly. As our society becomes more educated, the policeman begins to deal with a larger population possessing a certain standard of pronunciation. Each of us lapses into an occasional "yeah." There may be situations where you might wish to deliberately apply a more casual diction or word usage.

However, as a norm, sloppy articulation can be annoying, and it is extremely unprofessional. Do you use "kinda," "jist," "gonna," "cause," or "dere"? Or are your sentences filled with "you know," "and uh," or "sorta"? This type of habit is simply corrected if you are aware of it. As students in a captive audience, we notice these defects in an instructor, but it is difficult to turn the table and objectively examine our own speech habits, proceeding to change them.

Careful articulation is difficult enough without a wad of chewing gum. Veteran police officers viewing the documentary, "Super Cop," snickered as a group of rookies, polished in new uniforms, met community leaders in Chinatown while chewing away at gum. The gum was humorously inconsistent with the professional image that the rookies were trying to achieve.

Two other major areas of vocal characteristics are volume and

---

[2] Victor Strecher, *The Environment of Law Enforcement* (Englewood Cliffs, N.J.: Prentice-Hall, 1971), p. 104.

rate. Everyone has an "Aunt Maude." When she calls, you hold the telephone six inches from your ear, and every word is still clearly audible. Coupled with the military uniform, a loud voice is going to prolong the "red-neck cop" stereotype. What is your reaction to a raised voice? You raise your own, right? But with a client you have the power to declare *his* raised voice disorderly conduct. What if you begin a transaction with a louder tone than normally used socially, and thus things escalate? Is the citizen really at fault?

Our society equates fast speech with excitement. Fight narratives delivered in a staccato nonstop rate add excitement to even a dull match. For the policeman, consideration of this fact makes the rate of his speech all-important. As an example, consider what happened at a hit-and-run accident. The victim's motorcycle was all but demolished, and he lay sprawled in the middle of rush-hour traffic, bleeding profusely from the head. Despite the obvious necessity for speed, the veteran sergeant on scene communicated slowly with witnesses before radioing a report. Therefore, he did not heighten an already excited situation. He slowed down the witnesses' rate of speaking, and increased the intelligibility of the communication he was receiving. Although too rapid a rate of speaking increases the chances for distortion, there is another problem which is just as bad—drawling your words, making them sound disconnected. The listener will lose both interest and the trend of your thoughts.

A popular greeting card carries this message, "Sorry, but that is the way I am ... I was like this in the beginning, am now, and ever shall be ..." This is a handy motto to have around if you do not want to grow up. However agonizing, an effective experience is listening to one's voice over a tape recorder. This is effective feedback for analyzing your voice. The ability to objectively self-criticize is difficult, but just as you check your uniform, a periodic evaluation of voice is equally important. It's a matter of training the ear to hear what is wrong.

Another valuable voice training device is the phone company's tele-trainer unit, available in most cities. The equipment allows you to monitor your voice over the phone. Assuming in general that male criminal justice personnel will not be as good on the telephone as wives or girlfriends, let us review a few basic rules for speaking with this instrument.

1. Be courteous at all times, *especially* when things are a mess.
2. Avoid slang, bearing in mind our discussion of diction.

3. Be brief, but clear and concise. Use complete sentences. Try organizing your thoughts in advance, particularly if you are initiating the call.
4. Speak clearly in as relaxed a voice as possible, directly into the mouthpiece. The distance may vary, due to some of the new phone equipment that is more sensitive to pick-up, but one-half inch to an inch is generally an accepted rule.
5. Making a phone call to a client, or receiving one, is not the time to take a coffee or snack break.
6. Try to picture the person at the other end of the line sympathetically. Talk to that person, not that telephone.
7. Keep the receiver close to your ear.
8. If you must consult with someone, put the client on hold if such equipment is available. Nothing is more aggravating, nor presents a more unprofessional image, than monitoring a shouted conversation.
9. Letters and numbers will obviously play a crucial part of police phone communication. Take care when pronouncing them, thus avoiding incorrect spelling, misunderstanding, and repetition. Effective enunciation requires that every sound be given its proper value.
10. As much as humanly possible, refrain from interrupting the other person; allow people to finish what they want to say. (A discussion of nonjudgmental listening appears later in the chapter.) However, emergency phone calls which involve agitated citizens may require firmer guidance to get the proper information.

The telephone voice characterized as bad is expressionless, mechanical, indifferent, impatient, and inattentive. While you may come across as "tough" in the station, the receiver of the communication may, in turn, come across as a bristly, hostile citizen the next time he encounters a patrolman. Why send the citizen away from the phone with this feeling? The policeman phoning for information might find citizens more receptive to providing it, if these people felt they were dealing with a human being, not an automaton.

As well as encoding through the voice, our brains possess the almost unconscious ability to turn thoughts into words. Still, subconsciously we control which words will emerge. Within the criminal justice field, particularly as the police role changes, society's attitude will be to consider policemen professionals. In the transitional period, there is a lot to be gained from using the language your education is contributing. Don't pull yourself up short, attempting to cut these words out. You don't need to overwhelm citizens with jargon; instead, use your vocabulary as a civilized tool.

Our previous discussion of encoding devices noted that profanity was a common language distorter. A personnel journal reported that the use of profanity as a regular on-the-job pattern in a factory contributed to the eventual decision in a matter up for arbitration. An angry employee suggested that his foreman "perform an act of indignity upon himself," causing the supervisor to seek his dismissal. The union took the matter to arbitration on the grounds that the use of profane language was customary in the plant, accepted by the company, and indulged in by the foreman. Upholding the company, the arbitrator said, "There was abundant testimony of the use of these terms, but little of instances where these words were spoken in anger. When the speaker is mad and uses such terms, he intends them to be degrading and it is an insult to the recipient."[3] Irving Rein's delightful book, *Rudy's Red Wagon: Communication Strategies for a Contemporary Society*, points out obscenity's three functions: it gains attention; it supposedly exposes the hypocrisies of a contemporary society; and it is the ultimate expression of aggressive vocal hostility. Rein's conclusion is that this language has a limited value—it may momentarily attract attention, but in the final analysis it reduces or destroys the user's capability to negotiate and locks him out of power. Charles Rossiter has also conducted a study on profanity; one of his major points is that the less we use a particular word, the greater power it possesses to upset. A secondary point brought out by the study is Western man's tendency to reject his body, thus giving certain words a taboo character, particularly for parts of the body not visible.

Words can also be distorted interculturally. Before the decision to drop the first atomic bomb on Japan was made, a message was sent to their government warning them. The answer they sent back to American leaders contained the word, "migugostu," which can be interpreted two ways: it can be either an abrupt dismissal phrase, *OR* may mean, "we will take it under advisement, and consider it." The American interpreter read the phrase as the rebuff, perhaps wrongly, with

[3] Fred Joiner, "When You Call Me That, Smile," *Personnel Administration*, May-June 1960, p. 45.

tragic consequences for the inhabitants of Hiroshima and Nagasaki. Possibilities for language distortion interculturally are very likely.

Another problem to watch out for is the tone of voice. In situations where communication is repetitive, it is easy to present a bored, monotonous tone. This insulates the speaker from other people and produces a feeling of coldness. Clergymen repeating the same ritual each Sabbath encounter this, as do actors in the long run of a play. Communication theory defines this as "paralanguage,"—it is not what you say, it is how you say it. Long observation of Jack Webb's performance on "Dragnet" and attendance at police-oriented movies show that there are many tones of voice for delivering the Miranda Warning. The police dispatcher sighing, "Yesss, lady," into the telephone communicates to her in a definite way.

Some days you may be feeling low, angry at the world, or even "hung over." Our voice patterns will reflect this in our inflection and intonation of words. While no one is eternally patient, a professional police officer deals with a captive clientele. Generally, the client has no choice in his relationships with you—he must relate. How often do you find yourself reacting sarcastically to a citizen? You may say nothing which can be reported to superiors, but you may say a great deal, and saying a great deal *more* enough of the time can mean extensive damage to the police department's image in the community. There is a poem about woman's usage of the word "nothing." When you ask her what's wrong and she replies, "Oh, nothing," you may be very sure there is "something," and the wise husband will find out what it is.

Nonverbal Cues

Correct interpretation by police officers of nonverbal cues offered by suspects has saved many police lives, and stopped many crimes. A major police function—directing traffic—is accomplished by nonverbal cue. We see, then, that nonverbal communicative behaviors relate to interpersonal communication. But how is this done?

Best-seller lists have featured several new books on body language. These books primarily concentrate on the concepts of body position as a communication device, use of personal space, and the influence of certain clothing. Science is beginning to seriously examine these various areas of nonverbal behavior, and major concepts are emerging which are valid for the criminal justice professional. Julius Fast, author of *Body Language,* notes that sometimes our body cues reinforce our words, and at other times they may contradict one another. Jurgen Ruesch, in his textbook on nonverbal communication, discusses the relationship between words and movements.

> *The relationship between verbal and nonverbal codifications can best be conceptualized through the notion of metacommunication. Any message may be regarded as having two aspects: the statement proper, and the explanation pertaining to its interpretation. The nature of interpersonal communication necessitates that these coincide in time. . . . Thus, when a statement is phrased verbally, instructions tend to be given nonverbally. The effect is similar to an arrangement of a musical composition for two instruments, where the voices in one sense move independently and in another change and supplement each other but nonetheless are integrated into an organic and functional unity.*[5]

Nonverbal cues are probably displayed most prominently in Western man's usage of personal space. People tend to establish their own territory. Robert Ardrey's book, *The Territorial Imperative,* traces this concept to biological inheritance, examining how animals establish certain territories. Fast relates a delightful anecdote in his book in which he experiments with a friend in a restaurant by moving his silverware and dishes, piece by piece, as if inadvertently, into the other man's table space. His friend became noticeably upset. This is also illustrated by the behavior of students in the classroom: After high school, the "assigned-seat-alphabetical-order" arrangements cease, but notice how students tend to occupy the same territory in college classrooms. You may find yourself slightly irritated when someone occupies "your space." Another example of the "territorial imperative" occurs when police officers jealously guard their squad cars.

A local shopping center had a display of squad cars from various suburban police departments, which children and adults were allowed to examine at close range. Standing at the top of the mall, one could observe the policemen handling this demonstration. They displayed covert symptoms of territoriality over the cars. True, some of the things could have been dangerous to young children or damaged by them, but the feeling that the squad car was a "territory" was overwhelming.

---

[5] Jurgen Ruesch and Weldon Kees, *Nonverbal Communication* (Los Angeles, Calif.: University of California Press, 1969), p. 192.

These officers were reacting to an intrusion into their territories, even though in this case the intrusions were proper and even sanctioned.

Another way to prevent effective communication is by using physical obstacles. The authority figure sitting behind a desk places an obstacle between himself and the client that is unnecessary and hampers effective communication. In effect, this use of territory says, "You must obey me. I am your superior." This obstacle probably arouses feelings of defensiveness in the receiver. As Fast observed: "We learn certain tricks of domination to control a situation. We can arrange to be higher than our subordinates, or we can allow our boss to be higher than we are. We can be aware that we dominate our children when we hover over them. . . ."[6] For example, the act of stopping a vehicle is structured to place the policeman in an authoritative position. The citizen remains seated in his car, while the policeman occupies "territory" over him.

Movement across social distances in our culture also distorts communication and causes feelings of anxiety. Huseman and McCurley, in a study of police communication behaviors, found that policemen experience most of their problems in communicating with minority groups.

The nonverbal cues you send and receive may also be misleading. From birth we attach great importance to these cues. Not only can more than one emotion be displayed at the same time. The following anecdote illustrates correct reading of nonverbal cues, and emphasizes the difficulty cross-culturally.

> I recall very well a scene of some years ago, just as daylight was breaking, on the island of Wake, in the mid-Pacific. The commercial passenger plane on which I was flying from Tokyo to San Francisco had put down to refuel, and we passengers were shepherded into the restaurant at the terminal building to have breakfast. All of us were sleepy, disheveled, and tired after a night-long flight. As a consequence, we did not feel particularly sociable. I took my seat at a small table along with two other American men, who appeared to be businessmen, and a middle-aged Japanese, who proved to be a college professor barely able to speak a few words of English. None of us paid any attention to any of the others, until I noticed the Japanese was regarding his American companions with rather obvious distaste. Then I smiled at him, and handed him the salt cellar for his eggs, holding it

[6] Julius Fast, "Can You Influence People Through 'Body Language'?" *Family Circle*, November 1970, p. 90.

toward him in my right hand, with the fingers of the left hand lightly touching the base of my right hand palm—a typical Japanese gesture of respect. For a moment he looked unbelievingly at the unexpected behavior of this strange foreigner. Then his face broke into a broad smile of sheer relief and I could almost hear him say to himself, "Perhaps they are not barbarians after all." It was quite a lot to accomplish by so simple a device as knowing how to hold one's hands.[7]

An excellent experiment for skeptical communication students is the "trust walk," in which one student is blindfolded and, without any cues except touch, leads another for 15 minutes. Here are some comments from student paragraphs.

In the blind-leading experiment we depended entirely on nonverbal communication, especially tactile and body movements. A person's sensitivity was really tested in that he had to perceive the attitudes of the person leading him to decide how far he could trust him.

Comparatively speaking, the use of nonverbal cues is less obvious in everyday messages. My failure to properly lead my partner to an intended destination without the aid of verbal signals hindered a simple process.

A favorite exercise in marriage counseling sessions is to instruct a wife to lean from an upright position into her husband's arms for a given amount of time. The couple then discusses the concept of trust and the feelings that this simple nonverbal exercise produces.

To illustrate how nonverbal communication can be distorted by inferences made from observations, many universities present "staged" fights within the classroom. Most criminal justice majors participate in at least one of these incidents. After the disruption, students are asked to comment accurately on *exactly* what occurred. In one school, the only black student in an otherwise white class approached his instructor about staging such an "experiment." The instructor agreed, but cautioned him not to expect much, since students were familiar with this learning device. On the designated morning, two black men dressed in bright colors, wearing large Panama hats, were having a noisy discussion with the student experimenter as the class entered the room. After the session began, the men came in, attempting to remove the black student. Rather than sitting with blasé smirks on their faces, the white students

[7] C. Arnold et al., *The Speaker's Resource Book*, from Robert Oliver's speech, "Culture and Communication" (New York: Scott Foresman, 1966), p. 125.

left their seats; the men jumped into the fray while one girl ran for the campus police. After immediately stopping the experiment, the instructor, somewhat shaken, introduced the "abductors." The first was a graduate student in sociology, and the other, who had an Afro hair-do and a beard, was the assistant dean of admissions. The class was asked: Why did you believe this was real? (One class member had witnessed three such stagings that semester alone, and he was one of the first to react.) The answer? Blacks dressed "that way" behave that way. Thus, this had to be real. Then, why did they defend the only black in the classroom? Their answer was: "Because he dressed conservatively."

Hans Tech's article, "Cops and Blacks: Warring Minorities," notes the following:

> The men involved feel that their interpersonal skills and their qualities as human beings are insufficient to the problem of coping with the enemy. Each man comes to feel that he must rely on his group identification—badge or color—as a substitute for answers he cannot find in himself. . . . Neither party need conclude that it has to make the delicate judgments implicit in personal encounters: the matter is prejudged; two men approach each other not as human beings, but as uniformed members of military forces engaged in a doomed truce in a no-man's land.[8]

A veteran officer in a police–community relations class remarked, "If I approach a citizen to give a ticket, and push my hat back on my head, hook my thumb in my belt buckle and smile, I'm in for trouble." Some departments are beginning to experiment with dressing their policemen in blazers, thus softening their image. Researchers still must scientifically test and evaluate the effects of this change upon citizens and police alike, but the uniform, or more particularly the nonverbal cues given off in wearing it, send definite signals to sources. Awareness of this factor is a major step toward improving communication.

Training manuals for airline personnel, as well as hijacking profiles, emphasize nonverbal cues, picturing passengers in different body positions, with various expressions on their faces, wearing different clothing. "Most everyone agrees the picking and choosing process consists of surface observations," commented one career woman. Selling yourself nonverbally means heightened awareness of body positions,

---

[8] Gerald Leinwand, ed., *The Police* (New York: Pocket Books, 1972), p. 200.

usage of personal space, and the influence of certain clothing on potential receivers.

The Listening Process

On October 30, 1938 Orson Welles' Mercury Theatre presented a radio play entitled "The War of the Worlds." Of the six million listeners in the audience, one million thought that the United States had been attacked by an alien planet. The reactions of people varied tremendously: "I looked out of the window and nothing looked unusual. I thought, it hasn't reached our section yet." "We looked out at the street and Wyoming Avenue was black with cars. People were running away, we figured." "My husband said, 'If it were true it would be on all of the radio stations,' he turned the radio dial, and got music; 'Nero fiddled while Rome burned,' I retorted."

In Minnesota 20 families banded together, put wet handkerchiefs over their faces, and left the city, heading for the country. In Chicago a woman burst into a prayer meeting and announced, "The end of the world is here." In New York a man who had been confined to a wheelchair for 20 years, leaped from his chair, got into his automobile and drove away. "War of the Worlds" is a prime example of distorted communication. Despite advance publicity, announcements at beginning and end, with the required station breaks, this play terrorized one million people because they did not listen to the complete message.

Hearing is the act or power of perceiving sound. In contrast, while hearing with normal ears is an automatic process, listening is a mental exercise. Radio and television broadcasters are continually concerned with how many people are hearing their programs. However, the question, "Does anybody listen?" seems immaterial to them, and yet this is a radically different thing.

Let us distinguish three levels of listening. The lowest level is being able to hear; the second is being able to repeat back, and the third is the level of listening in which one actively participates and is involved in the communication pattern. Only when thoughtful consideration has been given to the message can we claim that we have actually listened.

Paul Rankin, in a pioneer listening study, estimated that we spend 9 percent of our time writing; 16 percent reading; 30 percent speaking, and 45 percent listening. This is one-third of the average lifetime, and yet how effectively do we employ this 45 percent?

Americans are not good listeners. In general they talk more than they listen. As one theorist states, "It is really not difficult to learn to listen—just unusual." Many of us, while ostensibly listening, are actually preparing a statement to "stun" the company when we gain the floor. You need a good relationship of listener and speaker in a conversation—in fact, an effective *listener* leads the conversation. John F. Kennedy was famous for the incisive questions he asked and the way he listened to replies. Robert Saudek, who conferred with him at the White House while producing *Profiles in Courage* for television, later told friends, "He made you think he had nothing else to do except ask you questions and listen—with extraordinary concentration—to your answers. You knew that for the time being he had blotted out both the past and the future. More than anyone else I have ever met, President Kennedy seemed to understand the importance of *now*." We all crave good listeners. Sporadic or half-attentive listening are easily detected through nonverbal cues received by the source.

Recent literature in this field of communication centers around the concept of nonjudgmental listening. Carl Rogers outlined the idea in his book, *On Becoming a Person*: "I would like to propose, as an hypothesis for consideration, that the major barrier to mutual interpersonal communication is our very natural tendency to judge, evaluate, to approve or disapprove the statement of the other person or the other group."[9] Rogers goes on to state that real communication occurs when one listens with understanding, trying to place himself in the other person's position. This is most difficult in highly emotional situations—the kinds of situations criminal justice personnel often deal with. When a police officer encounters similar situations, such as quarrels in the same family over and over again, he may have a strong desire to "tune out." That behavior is exactly what is ineffective.

In many Wisconsin communities, surburban police departments employ a "court officer," who serves as liaison between the district attorney and his department. One such officer encountered continued friction with a fellow officer over the matter of ticket dismissals. "The law is the law," the second officer adamantly stated. It did not matter to

[9] Carl Rogers, *On Becoming A Person* (Boston: Houghton Mifflin, 1961), p. 328.

him whether or not the defendant had good reason for clemency from the judge; he wouldn't listen to explanations, but merely delivered lengthy tirades. Suddenly the duty roster rotated the men, and this officer became—you guessed it— the court officer. In a few weeks his entire attitude changed completely. He learned to listen to complete explanations. Not only can you evaluate too quickly, but you may selectively perceive to hear whatever you want to.

Weaver summarizes, "All this really means is that in order to understand a verbal message well, you must understand the talker to some degree. This makes communicating with a total stranger somewhat difficult when you get above the level of asking or giving directions or talking about the weather."[10] In *Future Shock*, Alvin Toffler speaks of the increasing number of short-duration relationships, particularly in service occupations. He points up the difficulty of a professional attempting to listen and communicate with increasingly large numbers of people. We will discuss this concept later, but we must first recognize the difficulties in application of nonjudgmental listening.

Tests on listening show repeatedly that people have an average listening efficiency of only 25 percent. (This varies—some people can retain up to 70 percent and others only up to 10 percent.) Listening is not an easy, passive process. It is hard work, characterized by faster heart action, quicker circulation of the blood, and a small rise in bodily temperature.

Most people talk at a speed of about 125 words a minute. There is good evidence that if thought were measured in words per minute, most of us could think easily at about four times that rate. It's extremely difficult to slow down thinking time; thus we normally have about 400 words of thinking time to spare during every minute a person talks to us. What do we do with that excess thinking time while someone is speaking?

In interpersonal relationships we too often prepare our next comment; in formal situations, as the speaker bores us, we become impatient and turn our thoughts to something else. Soon the side thought trips become too enticing, and when attempting to return to the speaker, we're lost. The good listener uses his thought speed for advantage, not

---

[10] Carl Weaver, *Human Listening: Processes and Behavior* (New York: The Bobbs-Merrill Series in Speech Communication, 1972), p. 88.

side trips. He constantly applies his spare thinking time to what is being said. Ralph Nichols has put forth several suggestions for what he calls a "thought pattern" in listening:

1. Try to anticipate what a person is going to talk about, what point he is trying to get at.
2. Weigh a speaker's evidence by mentally questioning it. As he presents facts, ask yourself, "Are they accurate?" "Do they come from an unprejudiced source?" Be sure, however, to allow the speaker to finish presenting his evidence.
3. Listen between the lines for nonverbal cues, facial expressions, gestures, and body movements. The changing tones and volume of a voice may add meaning as previously noted.
4. Judge the content of what someone is saying, not the delivery. Lincoln was a terrible speaker from a technical standpoint. He had a high-pitched, squeaky voice—he was tall, gangling, and ugly, but the Gettysburg Address has content.
5. Avoid defensiveness. A listener wastes thought time, calculating what hurt is being done to his pet ideas, plotting mentally an embarrassing question to ask. Whenever we listen to someone else's ideas, we open ourselves to the possibility that we are wrong.
6. Try to find common areas of interest. G. K. Chesterton once said, "There is no such thing as an uninteresting subject; there are only uninteresting people." Bad listeners dismiss a speaker after the first few sentences without asking what ideas that person is presenting.
7. Resist distractions. Poor listeners tend to tolerate bad listening conditions and in some instances even create them. Fight these by some direct action—close the door, or move from behind the desk where you're tempted to fiddle with papers.
8. Exercise your mind. Poor listeners are inexperienced in hearing difficult expository material. The poor listener has for years sought light recreational material for listening, something our media caters to. Wilson Mizner, the late American dramatist, summed it up when he said, "A good listener is not only popular everywhere, but after awhile he knows something."

Listening is one type of personal improvement that can be accomplished alone; it is not related to intelligence. The responsibility for listening is shared between receiver and source, where formerly the source bore the burden. If he wasn't worth listening to, one didn't. During early American theatricals, you carried tomatoes and rotten eggs to the performance—you did not have to listen. A former police chief, now involved in teaching, often says to his students, "Now I hear what you're saying, but I'm not getting it all. Play it back again." The easy way out is the "teacher bluff": an instructor does not really try to understand the idea the student is offering. Don't take the easy way.

The Final Communication Quality

The squad car is repeatedly cited as the great insulator in police work, as are heavy caseloads for probation and parole officers. Organizational systems theory, notably that advocated by Warren Bennis, says that in the organization of the future a group of people will come together, perform a task, and disband. Many corporations are already operating that way. Given the policeman in the squad, the changing nature of neighborhoods, and the sheer numbers of people dealt with in human relations occupations, people in these professions will need to develop high degrees of trust quickly, as will society. In reply to a questionnaire, one policeman answered, "I do my work impartially and without emotion." One simply cannot deal with that many human beings over an extended time without emotion.

Agreed, it is easier to wall one's self off, presenting the militaristic picture. You will be fair, but will you be effective? Other professions struggle with the same problem. Consider yourself in the hospital. Do you like the nurse entering with a pat, "Good-morning-how-are-we-feeling-today?" She does not want an answer; she wants no trouble.

People entering the criminal justice profession need to possess a final communication quality. Unlike the development of voice, or listening abilities, this concept has a rather vague quality to it. It is called empathy, and theorists maintain that those entering people-oriented professions need to have large amounts of it. It is the ability to understand another, or to comprehend his feelings, attitudes, or sentiments. Dr. Derek Miller, a University of Michigan psychiatrist, recently completed a study which enables him to predict that some teenagers with no criminal record will eventually become murderers. The key to this prediction is dehumanization of that person through parental mistreatment. Miller states: "Dehumanization means an individual loses the capacity for human empathy. He is simply not capable of recognizing how others feel."[11] Empathic response is a mental-physical reaction. One tends to react as one receives cues. If I am hostile, you respond in kind. (Remember previous discussion of louder voices, encouraging louder voices?)

Frank Manella's article, "Humanism in Police Training," contains a credo for this recognition of others, which is appropriate for an occupation in which 60 percent of the employees maintain they entered the field because they enjoyed working with people.

> *I believe . . . in the essential dignity of every human being no matter what their status or state in life are. The test of this belief in human dignity depends upon my not becoming disillusioned or bitterly cynical toward people who exhibit weakness and inadequacy.*
>
> *I believe . . . that people can change. If I accept this assumption about human nature then I can avoid the fallacy of personality fixation which tends to classify people as "good" or "bad" and incapable of changing behavior once a certain age level is reached.*
>
> *I believe . . . people change people! Humans change only through the help of other humans. All police officers can become a force for purposeful human change—a force prepared to help man cope more effectively with his limitations, inadequacies, and strengths.*
>
> *I believe . . . in the essential goodness of all men who, if given a chance, can attain that level of human potential with which they have been endowed.*[12]

Law enforcers possess broad discretionary powers, yet far too little is done to train employees in the day-to-day usage of discretionary judgment, although this is rapidly changing. The occupation carries with it the power to initiate communication; the power to control it; the power to send messages of distaste and disgust. Everyone knows there are ways to give tickets, and then there are *ways*. Research shows that if one member of the organization consistently misuses his power, it will be at the expense of the entire organization. Thus, criminal justice groups cannot resist the bad impact of even small amounts of negative communication. An unknown philosopher said:

[11] Derek Miller, "Test Can Predict Young Slayers Doctor Says," *The Milwaukee Journal*, Section 1 (Sunday, May 6, 1973), p. 12.
[12] Frank Manella, "Humanism in Police Training," *The Police Chief*, Vol. 38, No. 2, February 1971, p. 28.

It is a law of human life, as certain as gravity: To live fully, we must learn to use things and love people . . . not love things and use people.

Student Checklist

1. Can you list the three levels of communication and describe each?
2. Can you diagram the communication process?
3. Can you write a brief essay describing what we mean by "cues?"
4. What is body language?
5. Why is nonjudgmental learning an important skill for police?

Topics for Discussion

1. Discuss how the communication process takes place in an individual.
2. Give illustrations of different types of "cues."
3. How does body language assist or interfere with communication?
4. Discuss the importance of nonjudgmental learning as a skill for men and women in the police role.

ANNOTATED BIBLIOGRAPHY

Berne, Eric. *Games People Play*. New York: Grove Press, 1964. A classic description of the interpersonal games we play in everyday life and the communication behaviors related to them.

Coffey, Alan, et al. *Human Relations: Law Enforcement in a Changing Community*. Englewood Cliffs, N.J.: Prentice-Hall, 1971, Chapters 10 and 11. These later chapters apply the humanistic approach to communication directly to criminal justice.

Fabun, Don. *Communications: The Transfer of Meaning*, Kaiser Aluminum & Chemical Corporation. Toronto, Canada: The Glencoe

Press, 1965. A pictorial booklet, which graphically presents the aspects of the communication process in a colorful, easy-to-understand fashion.

Fast, Julius. *Body Language*. New York: Pocket Books, 1971. A recent best-seller, describing man's use of body language to communicate messages, both intentional and unintentional.

Goffman, Irving. *The Presentation of Self in Everyday Life*. Garden City, N.Y.: Doubleday, 1959. An analysis of man's roles in everyday life, and how he plays and uses them.

Huseman, Richard, and Stephen McCurley. "Police Attitudes Toward Communication With the Public," *The Police Chief*. Vol. 39, December 1972. A solid research study in this area that is well documented and interestingly presented. Worth looking up in the library.

Jouard, Sidney. *The Transparent Self*. New York: Van Nostrand Reinhold Company, 1971. A simply written, but solidly researched book about intrapersonal communication.

Knapp, Mark L. *Nonverbal Communication in Human Interaction*. New York: Holt, Rinehart and Winston, 1972. A good paperback for the student interested in learning more on the topic.

McCroskey, James, et al. *An Introduction to Interpersonal Communication*. Englewood Cliffs, N.J.: Prentice-Hall, 1971. This is fine introductory material for the student interested in the communication process, nonverbal and organizational communication. A good place to begin.

Nichols, Ralph G., and L. A. Stevens. *Are You Listening?* New York: McGraw-Hill, 1957. While somewhat dated, this book is a fine citizen-oriented treatment of the subject. The primary author is a long-term expert in the field of listening.

Powell, John S. J. *Why Am I Afraid to Tell You Who I Am?* Chicago: Argus Communications, 1969. Short, snappy, colorful paperback, with useful insights on self-awareness and interpersonal communication.

Rein, Irving J. *Rudy's Red Wagon: Communication Strategies in a Contemporary Society*. Glenview, Ill.: Scott, Foresman, 1972. Brilliantly witty application of communication theory to real life.

Filled with collage and cartoon, the book makes theoretical points, right and left, effortlessly.

Rogers, Carl. *On Becoming a Person*. Boston: Houghton Mifflin, 1961. A classic, beautifully written guide to personal growth and creativity. The section on nonjudgmental listening might be particularly appropriate for criminal justice students.

Ross, Alec. *Talking is Speech*. New York: Macmillan, 1968. A good paperback, useful both in formal speech preparation and in providing a guide for voice training.

Rossiter, Charles M., and Robert Bostrom. "Profanity, Justification, and Source Credibility." Presented to the National Society for the Study of Communication, Cleveland, Ohio, April 1969. Rossiter is presently affiliated with The Department of Communication, Merrill Hall, The University of Wisconsin–Milwaukee, Milwaukee, Wisconsin. Copies are available by writing.

Strecher, Victor. *The Environment of Law Enforcement*. Englewood Cliffs, N.J.: Prentice-Hall, 1971. A well-written, theoretical treatment of the policeman's role in society. The last two chapters of the book are particularly relevant to interpersonal communication.

Tiger, Lionel. *Men in Groups*. New York: Random House, 1969. An excellent analysis of communication behaviors in male settings. Interestingly written.

Toffler, Alvin. *Future Shock*. New York: Random House, July 1970. A particularly effective book on society's pace, when coupled with Strecher's book. (See previous citation.)

Weaver, Carl H. *Human Listening: Processes and Behavior*. New York: The Bobbs-Merrill Series in Speech Communication, 1972. Although theoretical in sections, most of the book is easy reading and contains many helpful suggestions for improvement.

The study of this chapter will enable you to:

1. List the blocks to effective communication frequently encountered in police–community relations.
2. Identify three police programs aimed at removing blocks to communication with citizens.
3. Compare a police department with both a military and a nonmilitary model; list the advantages and disadvantages of each.
4. Describe the difference between active bias and simple preference.

7
Blocks to Effective Communication

This chapter will examine effective communication—the aspect of police service that ultimately decides whether the police organization is successful or inefficient. There are five blocks to effective communication: (1) community distrust, (2) the police view of the community, (3) poor training of police, (4) the organizational structure of the police department, and (5) scapegoating.

Communication Blocks

Community Distrust
If the citizens do not trust the police, they will not talk to them: they will avoid police contact. Therefore, if distrust causes avoidance and failure to communicate, the implications for the police organization are really very dramatic. Citizens will not report crime; they will not give statements to officers who are investigating crimes; and they will not testify in court. The result is inefficiency and an unsafe community.

The Police View of the Community
If the police organization views the community it has sworn to protect as a dangerous place full of people who are criminals and who are hostile to them, it is to be expected that the police will react in a negative way: they will not feel free to communicate with the community. The police will be guarded and careful when they have contact with the citizens they are protecting. As a result, the police themselves will contribute to widening the gap between the police and the com-

munity because their belief system will be reinforced by negative community contacts. Eventually the police will become afraid of and hostile to the very people they are supposed to be protecting and serving.

Poor Training

Many current studies clearly demonstrate that the training of American police is deficient. Most police academies have a training curriculum consisting of less than 400 classroom hours. And there are many communities that still simply issue a young man a gun, put him on the street with an oldtimer for training, and expect him to perform the complex job of providing police service to a dynamic, demanding society. Even when an academy is well structured, consisting of 400 or more hours of training, the curriculum concentrates on the law enforcement task, which occupies only 20 percent of the police officer's time.[1] Eighty percent of the officer's time is devoted to service activities, yet training in the service function is, for the most part, ignored in the police academies. Thus, dedicated and responsible officers are put on the street unprepared for the tasks they will face. They do not have a real perspective of the true attitude of the community they are policing (rich or poor) and they do not have an appreciation of the historical factors that shaped the community and created whatever fears or prejudices exist within it. They are not equipped with the techniques necessary to defuse dangerous situations with finesse. Unfortunately, they are too often taught to respond to threats or hostility with force.

This lack of training in such subjects as introduction to social theory, basic psychology, minority history, constitutional law, ethnic studies, interpersonal relations, and communication skills allows communication blocks to remain intact. In many cases this training deficiency builds new deterrents to effective communication.

Organizational Structure

The majority of America's police departments are paramilitary organizations. There are "chains of command," defined areas of responsibilities, volumes of rules and regulations, and a clear hierarchy of memberships. Police organizations have chiefs, deputy chiefs, captains, sergeants, and

[1] Report of the President's Commission on Law Enforcement and Administration of Justice: *The Challenge of Crime in a Free Society*, Nicholas deB. Katzenback (Washington, D.C.: U. S. Govt. Printing Office, 1967).

patrolmen, and many large organizations carry the military tradition even further; here we see the ranks of colonel, major, and corporal in the organizational structure.

The results of the paramilitary structure being used for a police service organization are well described by Egon Bittner.

> *Another complex of mischievous consequences arising out of the military bureaucracy relates to the paradoxical fact that while this kind of discipline ordinarily strengthens command authority, it has the opposite effect in police departments. This effect is insidious rather than apparent. Because police supervisors do not direct the activity of officers in any important sense, they are perceived as mere disciplinarians.*
>
> *Contrary to the army officer who is expected to lead his men into battle—even though he may never have a chance to do it—the analogously ranked police official is someone who can only do a great deal to his subordinates and very little for them. For this reason, supervisory personnel are often viewed by the line personnel with distrust and even with contempt.[2]*

An even more important consideration is that the paramilitary organizational structure not only blocks effective communication within the organization because of the superior/subordinate relationship, but the same working relationship inevitably is transferred to contacts between patrol officers and citizens.

The reason for this phenomena becomes clear when the paramilitary structure is understood to be a network of parent/child relationships. The first "parent" in the organization is the chief. He assumes the "father" role and, although he may be an intelligent, benevolent, and kind chief, he does not expect or want to be challenged. He gives orders and directions and he expects them to be carried out without question. If the chief gives the order to a deputy chief, in that particular interaction the "child" is the deputy chief.

In the next communication between the deputy chief and the captain or major, the deputy chief becomes the father and the lower ranking officer, the child. He takes the orders and direction from acknowledged authority without question.

Thus the organization's method of problem-solving is an institutionalized parent/child model. If patrol officers are a product of such a

[2] Egon Bittner, *The Functions of the Police in Modern Society* (Bethesda, Md.: National Institute of Mental Health, 1970), p. 59.

model, it is only natural that they will attempt to use the model in their interaction with the public. This is the crux of the communication block. Citizens do not want to be treated like children—they do not appreciate the authoritarian role of the beat officer. When the officer treats them like children, they react in many ways, such as actual verbal or physical attack, expressed resentment, refusal to cooperate, and withholding vital information.

The following example is illustrative of the result of a parent/child message to a citizen and an adult/adult message to a citizen.

In the case of an automobile intersection accident, the investigating officer finds physical evidence that one of the drivers involved in a two-car accident ran an arterial stop sign, hitting a second vehicle that clearly had the right-of-way. He was able to establish this by examination of the skid marks and by determining the point of impact in the intersection. What he needs most at this point is an unbiased witness to give him a statement that will support his conclusion based on a reconstructed accident scene. The authoritarian officer would attempt to get a witness by saying to bystanders, "Anyone who witnessed this accident step forward, I will need a statement." The tone of voice and the implications of the word "statement" all carry overtones of judicial process, subpoena, and eventually court. On the other hand, the officer who addresses a crowd of onlookers at an accident and says, "I need some help, can anyone assist me in finding out what happened here" will probably be more successful.

Scapegoating

Gordon W. Allport defines scapegoating as ". . . a phenomenon wherein some of the aggressive energies of a person or a group are focused upon another individual, group or object; the amount of aggression and blame being either partly or wholly unwarranted."[3]

In more specific terms, police have often focused their attention on particular groups or individuals when such attention was really unwarranted.

There are a number of steps that precede scapegoating. If we are aware of the progression, we will be able to spot the danger signs and

[3] Gordon W. Allport, *The Nature of Prejudice* (New York: Doubleday, 1954).

take action before a serious problem occurs. These steps are (1) simple preferences, (2) active biases, (3) prejudice, (4) discrimination, and (5) full-fledged scapegoating.

Simple Preferences. We all have preferences—we like people who agree with us, who have similar backgrounds, and who share our value system. Our socialization process in many overt and subtle ways teaches us to prefer spaghetti to curry, gefilte fish to soul food, blondes to brunettes, or Cadillacs to Fords. This simple preference for one food or one type of person to another is both natural and inevitable. A technical term for this simple preference is predilection.

Active Biases. Here the simple preference turns stronger. People state their preference in negative terms, instead of saying I prefer spaghetti to curry. The statement might be "I don't like curry," or "I don't like Jewish food." An active bias is the stepping-off point toward a closed mind, an ineffective person, and an uninformed person. It immediately precedes a full-blown prejudice.

Prejudice. Many people have prejudices, which means that they have a tendency to prejudge certain groups, persons, or events. It is a prejudgment that is rigid and inflexible. Although a prejudice does no great social harm as long as it is not acted out, in the case of people involved in public service, it is extremely difficult not to let a prejudice affect judgment.

Discrimination. This is an act of exclusion prompted by prejudice. The most common example is the discrimination against blacks by the white society. This discrimination manifests itself in many different ways; employment, housing, and social institutions are examples. It is one of America's most pressing social problems. It is also a problem that profoundly affects American police and their level of professionalism. Consider the fact that blacks have been systematically excluded from police service and from promotional appointments if they are fortunate enough to get into a police organization.[4] Since this condition has existed in our

---

[4] *The Task Force Report on the Causes and Prevention of Violence* clearly supports this statement with empirical data. [The National Commission on the Causes and Prevention of Violence, *Task Force Report on the Causes and Prevention of Violence* (Washington, D.C.: U.S. Govt. Printing Office, 1969).]

police forces for so many years, it is not surprising that many policemen will look upon blacks and other minorities who have been similarly excluded, as being unworthy, unwanted, and unacceptable as human beings.

Full-Fledged Scapegoating. Scapegoating manifests itself after all the preceding steps are fulfilled. It consists of concentrated aggression in both word and deed. The victim is abused both physically and verbally. The persons or group being scapegoated are often given credit for astounding power and evil, as in the following examples: "The Jews are ruining America"; "Ship all blacks back to Africa and crime will stop"; "Wetbacks (Mexicans) are responsible for all of California's labor problems"; and "All blacks are inherently lazy." When such statements are seen in print they are easily identified by anyone with average intelligence as simplistic statements. Yet many people use these statements day after day and, unfortunately, they believe what they are saying.

Why Scapegoating Occurs

Allport identifies a number of reasons for the phenomena of scapegoating. Among them are: "tabloid thinking," self-enhancement, peer pressure and conformity, fear and anxiety, and displaced aggression. Some of these are discussed more fully on the following pages.

Tabloid Thinking. This is the process in which people simplify a problem by blaming a group or class of people. For example, some people blame crime on illegal drug abuse; they feel that most crime is caused by addicts trying to get money to feed their habit. Although addicts do commit crime, in reality they are responsible only for a small percentage of the crime rate. Thus this tabloid-thinking process allows people to overlook real issues while they focus on the wrong object.

Consider the following statistics issued in 1973 by the National Council on Alcoholism.

> *There are an estimated 94 million consumers of alcohol in the United States. Of these, one in ten has developed the disease of alcoholism and adversely affects the lives of an average of five others intimately related to him. Those 94 million who are directly affected and the 45 million affected by relationship are subjected to personal injury and illness and disruption of their lives in the following ways, among others.*

1. *A third of all suicides committed are by alcoholics.*
2. *Forty percent of juvenile delinquency is related to parental alcoholism, and 40 percent of cases brought before a family court for divorce were attributed to alcoholism in the home.*
3. *Fifty percent of all fatal auto accidents involve alcohol, and 50 percent of those involve alcoholics. In one year over 4 million people were also seriously injured or maimed.*
4. *Alcohol abuse is on the rise and drug abuse declining among teenagers.*
5. *One in every 10 employees is a problem drinker. The annual loss to the economy through alcoholism is estimated at $16 billion because of absenteeism, accidents, termination of trained personnel, mismanagement, and related causes.*
6. *Over 80 percent of misdemeanor and felony offenses are alcohol-related. Alcohol is our "hardest" drug in terms of crime, violence, mental disturbance, and social disability. It accounts for 59 percent of all mental health cases and 37 percent of welfare recipients and is the leading cause of death either directly or as a contributing factor or complication in other illnesses or disorders and accidents.*
7. *Alcohol is a mind-affecting drug, just as are marijuana, heroin, cocaine, amphetamines, and barbiturates, and its serious effects are more extensive and damaging than all the others combined.*

Efforts against the crime, injury, and death caused by alcohol are very limited in the United States. We spend most of our resources fighting illegal drug use. Although all drug abuse should be fought, tabloid thinking nevertheless leads the fight against crime into the wrong battle.

As a final offering of proof of the danger of tabloid thinking, consider the expenditures of moneys in New York City to fight alcoholism, the problem involved in 80 percent of our misdemeanors and felonies. New York City spends $1 million a year on rehabilitation programs for its 1 million alcoholics. Conversely, the city spends $40 million a year to rehabilitate its 250,000 drug addicts. Yet 6 out of 10 drug addicts participating in a methadone treatment program have to be discharged for unmanageable alcoholism!

Self-Enhancement. Some people have inferiority complexes. People who are experienced in interviewing police applicants often discover men who want to join the police department because they feel that having a badge and a gun will make them something they are not; that is, strong, more respected, or allowed to exercise control or authority over other people. Such applicants are serious liabilities to the police profession if they slip through the screening process. They will cause many communication blocks with the community through their scapegoating of others to cover their own inferiority. This type of person is also dangerous because he is often afraid; this personal fear often causes him to use excessive force. The use of such force when it is not warranted leads to a breakdown in communication between the police and the community.

Peer Pressure and Conformity. The need to belong to a group or organization is very strong in most people.[5] A new officer who joins an organization that engages in scapegoating will find himself joining with his fellow officers just so he can be part of the group. This is particularly evident when a new officer is coupled with an "old-timer." Too often the officer ends up acting like his trainer.

Fear and Anxiety. Some people scapegoat because they have fears or anxieties about a group or a person. One of the first blocks to communication identified in this chapter was a false perception of the community. Although some individuals will be unable to communicate or respond to the community effectively because they are anxious or afraid, the scapegoater will become overtly brutal, both physically and verbally. Thus, he will perpetuate and increase the gap between the citizen and the police officer.

Suggested Programs

The communication problems we have identified are complex in nature. Although there are no easy answers, communication blocks can be overcome. This requires work, thought, and effort. If American police are to accomplish their mission of preserving the peace, protecting the innocent, and improving the quality of life in our communities, they must establish positive interaction with the community.

[5] For further insight into what motivates human behavior, see Abraham H. Maslow, *The Farther Reaches of Human Nature* (New York: The Viking Press, 1971).

The following programs are suggested as a means of bringing both the image and the reality of a situation into focus. Not every program is relevant to every organization. Each is offered as an idea that has worked for another police department trying to meet the demands of contemporary society. Some of these programs are expensive and most take time, but there are no fast answers.

Humanistic Training

The Los Angeles County Sheriff's Office designed and implemented a stress training program for police recruits, which they used for a number of years. This sheriff's department in many ways symbolizes what is needed in a modern police organization; the department is willing to question established procedures and to change if necessary.

Dr. Howard Earl, the under-sheriff, compared the effects of stress training (which involves a military command/reaction curriculum in the police academy) to a second type of academy training—the "humanistic" approach. The new curriculum involved using a problem-solving approach in the training of new cadets. Dr. Earl then carefully tracked the careers of those recruits who graduated from the stress and the nonstress training programs. The evidence after several years clearly supported the nonstress academy.

The graduates of the more humanistic environment were better problem solvers, had better overall records, and had fewer conflicts with citizens. They were, in fact, clearly superior officers.

Educational Liaison

In 1968 the University of Cincinnati and the Cincinnati Police Division carried out a joint project to study the attitudes of junior high school students toward police. The study found that a lack of knowledge about the mission and function of law enforcement was a primary contributing factor in poor student attitudes toward police. The study also found that police officers lacked knowledge about the nature of early adolescence and about special procedures that might be used in handling teenagers.

A police–community relations program was designed to bring about improvement in police–juvenile relations on a mass scale. The program consisted of three parts: (1) a pretest to determine student attitudes toward police; (2) an in-school educational program; and

(3) a posttest to determine if attitudes had changed. The program was conducted on an experimental basis in certain schools and in the police academy. Analysis of the results revealed that the classroom presentations produced a significant shift in attitudes among white students of both sexes, a lesser shift among black girls, and no significant differences among black male junior high school students.

The Cincinnati project was a milestone in the area of police–community relations. It represented the first direct, systematic effort to change existing attitudes through education. It also led to an improvement in communication efforts between the police and the youths participating in the study.

Ride-Alongs

As part of its overall effort toward developing improved relations with the community, the Menlo Park, California, Police Department has, for some time, invited citizens to ride in a patrol vehicle with a police officer as he performs his regular patrol duties. For the most part, these efforts in the Belle Haven community of Menlo Park have been successful. It was known, however, that the prevailing attitudes toward police among the young people of this area were highly unfavorable—so much so that the department had been unsuccessful in initiating any sort of "neutral ground" contact with this particular group of youths. The youths of Belle Haven were simply not willing to be coaxed into any sort of alliance with "the man."

Belle Haven has approximately 1300 homes and apartments in an area of about 10 square blocks. Ninety-five percent of the residents are black. Of the 1300 households, 524 are known to have an income of less than $7500 a year; 154 of these have less than $5000; 115 less than $3000; and 78 less than $2000 annual income. The median age is 19 years.

In the fall of 1971, the department decided to establish a ride-along program with the youths in Belle Haven. The first task was to determine why the youths were declining to participate. After talking with many of the black youths, school officials, parents, and the police officers themselves, the reasons for the reluctance to participate in the program became clear. A black youth riding in a police vehicle meant only one of two things: either that youth had been arrested and was being involuntarily detained, or he had "sold out" and was acting as a "snitch," or informant, on his peers. Such a social stigma and its consequent effect were too strong to permit any of the youths to volunteer for any sort of a contact with a police officer.

To reduce the stigma related to being seen in the company of a police officer, the department decided to implement changes in the program. First, instead of having only one youth in the patrol vehicle at a time, it was decided to group the youths in numbers of three. This method has two advantages: (1) the youths feel more comfortable through mutual support from within the vehicle; and (2) to the rest of the community, it would not appear to be a "bust."

It was also decided that the first ride-along experience should be with a black police officer because it was felt that the black youths might have a greater trust in a black officer. Then, after it became evident that both parties survived the experience with no ill effects, future ride-along experiences for that group were to be scheduled with other officers in the department.

Fortunately, these adjustments in the overall ride-along program had the desired effect. In October 1971, the department was successful in initiating a small spark of interest in the ride-along experience among the black youths, and was able to coax a few small groups of three youngsters each to accompany an officer during his regular patrol. By December 1971, favorable word had spread throughout Belle Haven, and many youths were spontaneously requesting participation in the program. This was an encouraging development, since neutral ground alliances are practically unknown in today's typical police–minority citizen contact.

The ride-along program in Menlo Park and the efforts to make it a successful one in Belle Haven were based upon the following subjective feelings.

1. That members of the community, especially those of minority races, have had limited or indirect access to information about the police department, its officers, and their function in the community. This biased information is often based on rumor, or it results from the negative past experiences of family or friends.

2. That this information is based upon a situation in which the police were likely to have been viewed in a negative context; that is, conflict with the law resulting in the overall effect of the police being viewed only as the "enforcers"—the police are to be feared or hated as a consequence.

3. That providing a suitable opportunity for a black youth to experience the functions of the police in a direct manner and in a positive situation will permit the individual to form his own impressions and opinions of the police officers, independent of second-hand and indirect information.
4. That personal contact with a police officer while riding along in his patrol vehicle will improve communication between the minority youth and the police officer.

By January 1972, it was clearly evident that the Belle Haven ride-along program was working and was becoming an ongoing community-relations effort. After consulting with the community resource officer and the patrol officers already involved in the ride-along program, the department decided to conduct a research project to determine what effect, if any, the program was having upon the attitudes of minority group youths towards police officers in the community.

At the outset of the research study, the central hypothesis was that the ride-along experience would produce a measurable and significant change in attitude toward police officers among those youths who participated. Further, it was hypothesized that this change would be in a positive or favorable direction.

The study included an experimental group of 50 youths and a control group consisting of 86 youths.

When a youth from the Belle Haven population appeared or volunteered for the ride-along program, he was immediately furnished with a waiver of responsibility form that had to be signed by his parents or guardian. This was essential because of the potentially hazardous nature of the experimental procedure. In addition, immediately prior to an initial ride-along experience, each youth was asked to take the Attitude Toward Police Scale. The ATP is a brief 20-item questionnaire (devised by Robert Fortune) that takes about 10 minutes to administer.

After the initial ride-along with a black officer, each youth was then rotated across three additional officers for the remainder of the experience. The youth was nearly always in the company of two peers; however, the composition of the ride-along group did not necessarily remain consistent throughout the twelve-hour experience.

During the period when the youths and police officers were in contact, considerable emphasis was placed on facilitating communications between them. The officer generally encouraged the youths to ask questions about whatever took place during the course of the ride-alongs, which varied in terms of activities encountered. For example, some three-hour periods were quiet with respect to out-of-the car activities; this would permit a good deal of interaction to take place between the officers and youths. On many other occasions, however, little time for verbal interaction existed because the officer had to respond to emergency situations. During one ride-along, the officer responded to a shooting and the ride-along subjects were exposed to the fatal result. Hence, the experience was nearly always different for each youth and could vary from casual conversation to a highly stressful, intense, and emotionally charged situation.

After the fourth ride-along experience, each youth was again administered the Attitude Toward Police Scale. Two months later each youth was mailed a follow-up Attitude Toward Police questionnaire. The experimental time span for each subject in the study was approximately 12 weeks—four of which were spent in the ride-along program itself; and an eight-week interval prior to the administration of the follow-up questionnaire.

A control group of youths was chosen from seventh and eighth grade students at Menlo Oaks School in Menlo Park. There were 50 experimental group students, ranging in age from 9 to 18 years, with a mean of 12.2 years. There were 27 males and 23 females in the experimental sample; all were black. The control group youths consisted of 86 students between the ages of 12 and 15. Most of the participants in the experimental group were peers of the control group; the control group was also black.

On the basis of the statistical analysis of the main effects of the experimental design, the following statements were inferred.

1. There was no significant difference in initial attitudes toward police between those subjects who volunteered for the ride-along and those who did not.
2. A significant shift in attitudes toward police, as reflected by mean ATP scores, followed the ride-along experience. This change in attitude was in the favorable direction of more positive attitudes towards the police.
3. The attitudinal shift did not diminish significantly over a period of two months.
4. Subjects who did not participate in the ride-along program experienced no significant shifts in their attitudes toward the police.

Data also showed that the person who might be expected to

show the greatest gains in favorable attitudes towards police as a consequence of the ride-along experience, would be a 12-year-old male who tends to have unfavorable initial attitudes toward police.

It is apparent that the program provided an opportunity for meaningful communication to develop between the police officer and the black youths. It created a "neutral ground" setting in which the law enforcement officer and the teenager were able to exchange information about each other. With this newly acquired information, the minority youth modified his perceptions of the police officer and what he saw as that officer's role in law enforcement activities.

Practically all of the youths who participated in the program acknowledged that they not only felt the police were more friendly with them after the experience, but that they themselves felt more friendly and could communicate better with the officers.

The favorable shift in attitude that followed the ride-along experience was able to withstand the passage of time. The findings of the study strongly suggest that the ride-along experience serves as a sort of "social inoculation" in terms of the citizen's ongoing perception of the law enforcement officer over a period of time. In contrast, the attitudes toward police among minority group youths who had not participated in the program were remarkably negative and stable over a period of time.

The research in Menlo Park provides considerable support for the hypothesis that a police ride-along program will produce significant favorable shifts in attitudes toward police among minority group youths. This change in attitude toward the police appears to survive with the passage of time. It occurs across a wide range in age of those youths participating, in both sexes, and across a wide range of initial attitudes toward police.

The dramatic change in the negative attitudes of black youths to positive attitudes about their police department indicates that a ride-along program can be a big part of the complex answer to having a community say *our* police, not *the* police.[6]

---

[6] The more complete report on the Menlo Park Ride-Along experiment appeared in the March 1973 issue of the *Police Chief Magazine*. Coauthors were Dr. Carlton W. Purviance and Victor I. Cizanckas.

Community Survey

In the sections on Community Distrust and Police View of the Community, the implications of the police and the community distrusting each other were discussed. One way to overcome these blocks in communication is to find out what people *really* think and believe.

It has been the experience of many cities that the loud and profane voice is most often heard and responded to. The beat officer develops negative attitudes toward an entire community based on the speeches of a few vocal dissidents. The officer feels unwanted, unappreciated, and disliked by the total community.

Particularly disturbing to police officers is the voice of the militant calling for withdrawal of police patrols and advocating community policing. The same militant groups generally threaten the police agency and the individual police officer with violence.

In 1969, the Menlo Park, California, Police Department decided to challenge the profane voice; to go to its black community and find out what the truth was. The questionnaire on page 170 (Figure 7-1) was designed specifically to be uncomplicated and easily administered.

The questionnaire was administered by survey teams working on two successive Sunday mornings. The teams consisted of officers, dispatchers, detectives, the chief of police, and reserve officers and matrons. Persons in 385 homes were contacted; 209 males and 246 females, with a median age of 39.6, were interviewed using the questionnaire.

On question #1, only 49 residents rated the police department as poor. Over 50 percent of these persons stated that they would give the department a higher rating if it increased traffic enforcement and made more juvenile arrests. One hundred thirty persons rated the department as fair; again, many stated the rating would be higher if the police placed more emphasis on neighborhood traffic enforcement. One hundred eighty-six rated the department as good and 39 rated it as excellent. Only 29 persons wanted *less* patrol service; 202 wanted more, and 183 were satisfied with present services.

In an era that has produced citizens unwilling to become involved, question #4 (Would you be willing to assist the police department during a community crisis?) was of particular interest. The response was overwhelmingly favorable. Two hundred and fifty black Americans said they would assist their police department during a crisis. This represents approximately 60 percent of the persons surveyed. Forty persons signed up for the police reserve and 13 asked for career information.

There are many lessons to be learned from this survey, which covered 30 percent of the homes in a community that has experienced disorder. Black Americans want quality patrol service just as white Americans do; their safety complaints (traffic) are similar to those of white Americans, and they are committed to their city government to

QUESTIONNAIRE
MENLO PARK POLICE DEPARTMENT
COMMUNITY SURVEY

Date: _____

Address _____
Sex _____
Age _____
Race _____

1. Would you rate the Menlo Park Police Department as:
   a. _____ Poor   b. _____ Fair
   c. _____ Good   d. _____ Excellent

2. Regarding patrol service—would you recommend:
   a. _____ More   b. _____ Less   c. _____ Same

3. How can we improve our service to you?

_____

4. Would you be willing to assist the police department during a community crisis?
   Yes _____ or No _____ (If yes—name and phone number)

5. Would you or anyone in your family be interested in joining the police reserve? (If yes—obtain name and mailing address)

6. Would you or anyone in your family be interested in a police career?
   Yes _____ or No _____ or Don't know

7. Do you have any questions of other city departments?
   Yes _____ or No _____ (If yes we will be glad to contact them)

Figure 7-1. A community survey.

the extent of volunteering assistance when needed. An even larger portion would have been surveyed had not the surveyors been invited into homes, asked questions, and offered refreshments; all pleasurable, but time-consuming. The survey team members developed different attitudes and a new sense of commitment to the black community. The community, in turn, had a better feeling toward the police because of its concern for their feelings. The beat officers, who received the results of the survey, know that their efforts and risk-taking are appreciated and wanted. The community and the police are communicating.[7]

Social Service Action

There are many police/citizen contacts that do not result in any criminal charges. This can occur because the police officer feels that the case does not merit prosecution, the parties do not bring charges, or the matters are not criminal. Often such contacts merely reflect a broader underlying social problem; in such cases, the appropriate response to achieve a long-term solution can best be provided by social workers, counselors, and other social service personnel. The police officer can provide only a short-term solution to the particular incident—a solution that lasts until the next call for assistance by the same parties or until matters deteriorate enough so that criminal action is necessary.

Police are often called to handle such problems and, because their time and resources are limited, they merely restore order for a short time, often leaving the person unhappy because they were unable to provide a solution of some duration.

Still, in the course of handling such cases, police officers, particularly the community relations officers, consume an enormous amount of time performing social work functions. These tasks can be better performed by trained social workers. In addition, the cost of such efforts more appropriately should be borne by the county or city governments, rather than by the police departments.

It is clear from reviewing various presidential advisory commission reports that police organizations must shift their philosophy of policing and place a greater emphasis on programs that are *proactive*

---

[7] A more complete analysis of this survey appeared in *The Police Chief Magazine*, April 1970, pp. 45-49.

rather than reactive insofar as social problems are concerned. One proactive program is described in the following pages.[8]

Social Service Action Program

A. Procedure

The suggested procedure for the social service action program is as follows.

1. Whenever a police officer encounters a problem that might be dealt with by the social service agencies, he makes note of the case and refers it to county service representatives (CSR).
2. The CSR makes a call-back with the officer if necessary, to interview the person in order to determine whether the case ought to be referred to an agency, and whether the person is receptive to the referral.
3. The CSR then refers the case and makes periodic follow-ups to assess the progress of the individual and the success of the program.

B. Suggested Categories

Some of the categories of contacts that appear appropriate for this program include, but are not limited to:

1. Family disturbances
2. Child abuse cases
3. Alcoholics
4. Rape victims
5. Juvenile matters, including:
   a. Runaways
   b. Drug abuse
   c. Chronic truancy
   d. Expulsion-prone students
   e. Some juvenile offenders
6. Lonely senior citizens

C. Benefits

One of the chief benefits of the program is that it channels cases that previously were given short-term treatment into mechanisms for longer-term solutions. At the same time:

---

[8] The Program was designed for use by San Francisco Bay Area Departments by Betsy Cohen, a Stanford University law student, while she was involved in a special research program to improve police services in April 1973.

1. It provides a service to the community and establishes positive communication.
2. It relieves the department of cases where officers are called upon many times to handle the same problems with the same people.
3. It serves a crime prevention function by treating problems before they escalate into physical violence or other more serious antisocial behavior.
4. It provides one more channel through which the citizens of the county who need the county's services are informed of and referred to these services.
5. It assists the police officers (particularly the community resource officers) in social work tasks and relieves the city (and the department) of bearing the cost of what the county theoretically ought to provide; it shifts these tasks to those who are trained to handle them.

Community Communication Net

Figure 7–2 (page 174) is a working model that depicts a network of community resources which should be tied together either wholly or in part when there are community problems.

The idea is a simple one. The police agency prepares a model similar to Figure 7-2, based on the resources and interest groups in its community; appended to which diagram are the telephone numbers of key people in each organization.

In the event of community crisis, rumor problems, or a simple misunderstanding regarding a police action, the police managers responsible for solving the particular problem would refer to the diagram, decide which agencies should be contacted, and then set the machinery in motion.

The communication net systematizes what many police organizations are now doing in a haphazard way. It has proven to be an effective resource tool for some departments and it serves as a ready checklist to ensure that communications are complete.

Organizational Development

To answer the problem posed in the section on organizational structure —the Menlo Park, California, Police Department instituted a program

MODELS

COMMUNITY COMMUNICATION NET

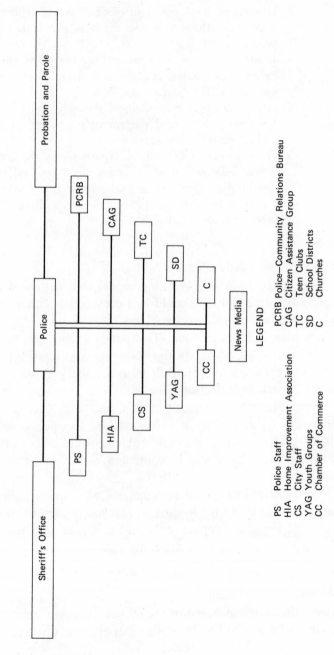

Figure 7-2. A community communication net.

in 1968 which, in contemporary management terms, is called organizational development.

Organizational development has been the subject of many management articles and books in recent years; usually discussed in connection with profit-making organizations, but rarely associated with public service agencies. Organizational development, or "OD," within a police department is almost unknown.

OD is more than an effort to manage all of a company's resources, including its management style and behavior in relationship to each other. In many ways it is finding one's self. It is admitting that work is not only rewarding and challenging, but is also fun. It is also the realization that not all people can adjust to a management style that calls for self-direction, little supervision, and freedom to participate and express one's own ideas. Organizational development is also unpleasant. It produces trauma, uncertainty, and discomfort while you are building, changing, and waiting for results. It also takes time! You cannot decide to try organizational development for a month or two and see if it works: the real rewards and dividends take years.

The Menlo Park Police Department's four-and-a-half year program resulted in many statistical successes in crime reduction and service production. It also brought about a philosophical change, new working relationships, and new ideas about the structure of a police department and the job roles of the people in the organization.[9]

Menlo Park began its organizational development by establishing new promotional requirements in September 1968. At that time the city personnel board set January 1, 1972, as an effective date for requiring sergeants to have an associate of arts (AA) degree prior to promotion; lieutenants are required to have a bachelors degree or a State of California Advanced Police Officer Standards and Training certificate.

Next, the department changed its work schedule to one of rotating days off, giving officers two consecutive three-day weekends out of every five-week period. Shift rotation was accomplished twice a year and coincided with area college semester breaks. There was no seniority preference in shift rotation. For those officers taking advantage of new

---

[9] See "Uniform Experiment and Organization Development," *POLICE Magazine*, September 1971, pp. 45-49, for additional reading.

work schedule procedures to attend college, the city of Menlo Park paid tuition and cost of books up to nine units each semester.

The department also decided to conduct in-service training programs every Friday, requiring all officers to report one-half hour early for work. The first Friday of the month consisted of shooting practice on the department's range. At the end of the shooting practice, an International Association of Chiefs of Police Training Key was given to each officer for review during the week. On the second Friday, the first Training Key was reviewed with the shift supervisor, and a second Training Key was distributed. On the third Friday, a videotape presentation was made on the subject matter of the Training Keys. These videotapes were prepared by department personnel assigned on the basis of expertise and interest in a given field. On the fourth Friday, officers were tested on the subject matters of the month.

The department enrolled all staff officers in various supervisory and management programs at California State College, Long Beach; the University of California, Santa Cruz; San Jose State University; and the University of Santa Clara Graduate School Seminar Series on Municipal Management.

The department deliberately decentralized its management. Participatory management became a department goal. The agendas and minutes for staff meetings were published and anyone in the department could place an item on the agenda. A patrol officer who was president of the Police Officers Association participated in all monthly staff meetings. The Officers Association was formed at the suggestion of the chief of police and the participation of the Association's president in staff meetings was by invitation, not a directive. Staff meetings were in fact problem-solving sessions, and not simply meetings to receive directives from the chief.

In the fall of 1969 the department published and posted a "Theory Y" policy statement, that read: We believe that:

1. *The expenditure of physical and mental effort in work is as natural as play or rest.*
2. *External control and the threat of punishment are not the only means for bringing about effort toward organizational objectives. Man will exercise self-direction and self-control in the service of objectives to which he is committed.*
3. *Commitment to objectives is a function of the rewards associated with their achievement.*

4. *The average human being learns under proper conditions, not only to accept but to seek responsibility.*
5. *The capacity to exercise a relatively high degree of imagination, ingenuity, and creativity in the solution of organizational problems is widely, not narrowly, distributed in the population.*
6. *Under the conditions of modern industrial life, the intellectual potentialities of the average human being are only partially utilized.*[10]

This drastic change from the paramilitary model was not accomplished easily. It required constant attention from a dedicated staff and a lot of psychological adjustment on everyone's part. Some men rejected the management change and left the department. After two and one-half years of OD the department stabilized and was at full strength, with a large list of applications.

When stabilization was achieved, the department decided to formalize what had been accomplished. A three-day seminar was held at the State of California Conference Center in Pacific Grove, California, in January 1971. The participants included the chief of police, two lieutenants, six sergeants, the traffic inspector, a community resource officer, a patrol officer, and the president of the Police Officers' Association. The city manager also participated during the second day of the conference. With the exception of the traffic inspector, all of the participants had been involved in formal management training programs during the two-and-one-half year development period. All participants decided they could not proceed without a basic philosophy to guide them. This is what developed.

Menlo Park Police Philosophy

The Menlo Park Police Department is a municipal multiservice organization, designed to provide better living and safety for citizens.

Recognizing it must relate and respond to community needs that are dynamic and constantly changing, the department is pledged to recruiting talented personnel who are committed to their fellow man and are free from color and economic bias.

While rejecting an authoritarian approach to problem solving, the

---

[10] Douglas McGregor, *The Human Side of Enterprise* (New York: McGraw-Hill, 1960), pp. 33-45.

department is continually involved in enforcement, prevention and education programs designed to control and reduce crime and traffic accidents.

The department commits itself to its employees and will make every effort to provide a work atmosphere conducive to personal and career development.

Ultimately, we hope to provide quality police service at minimum cost to the citizens we serve.

As conference participants examined existing working relationships and job roles, it became apparent that the officers were, in fact, team policing. They defined a team as a problem-solving police unit that utilized available skills and expertise in a coordinated effort to meet organizational objectives. They also acknowledged a *group* responsibility for all police services and activities. The result of the conference was a "change" organization designed to meet the demands of the future. The paramilitary model is obsolete in Menlo Park. Figure 7-3 represents the present working structure of the department.

Conference participants decided to eliminate the titles of sergeant and lieutenant, replacing them with "police operations manager" and "operations director." The following job descriptions were developed.

1. *Operations director.* Plans, directs, and coordinates the activities of a police service division. Innovates and generates programs designed to meet organization objectives. Is an advisor to the chief of police and may act in that capacity in his absence.

2. *Police operations manager.* Develops, trains, and coordinates a police service team to provide community protection and services. Conducts surveys and researches special needs of the community. Generates programs that will accomplish organizational goals. Exercises budget control and as a member of a management team, continually analyzes department philosophies, objectives, and programs, and makes recommendations for change.

3. *Crime specialist.* Conducts burglary prevention programs and investigations, acts as resource to a police service team, providing training and investigative expertise. Acts as a member of a major case investigation team.

4. *Community resource officer.* As a member of staff services, he coordinates efforts to establish a working relationship between the community and police service teams. Provides information and programs to citizen's groups and schools. Develops and implements

Figure 7-3.   A police organization and operating schematic.

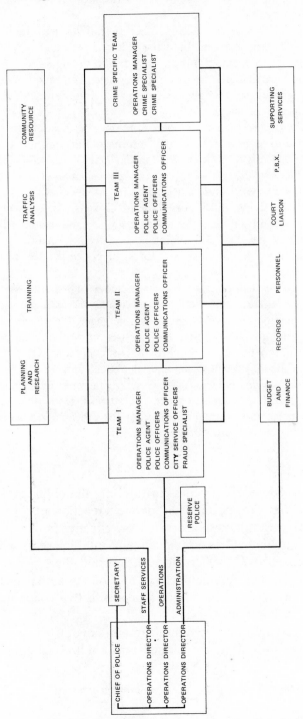

community relations groups. Evaluates overall department community relations efforts.

5. *Traffic inspector.* As a member of staff services, he is a resource to police service teams and the office of the chief of police. He is an ex-officio member of the city traffic commission. He coordinates and participates in major injury accident investigations. Also, he prepares monthly accident data and citation ratios for use of police operations managers.

6. *Police agent.* As a member of a police service team, provides expertise to team members, assists in accomplishing objectives, and acts in capacity of police operations manager in his absence.

7. *Police officer.* As a member of a police service team, he protects life and property and assists the city in an overall effort to provide better living and security for its citizens. Answers calls for assistance and service. Conducts criminal and general investigations. Helps develop and maintain positive interaction with the community. Maintains an awareness of police service needs and developments.

8. *Communication officer.* As a member of a police service team, he coordinates team activity and makes assignments at the general direction of a police operations manager. Operates various types of communication equipment. Assists in communication training of department personnel. Provides information and assistance to the public through personal and telephone contact.

9. *City service officer.* As a nonsworn member of a police service, he conducts residence checks for citizens who are vacationing and reports city ordinance violations for processing. He also does radio and parking control relief work.

Uniform Change

In assessing police effectiveness in fulfilling the obligations of the profession, we have to examine the public's reaction to the man in blue (or any color traditional uniform). How effective is this officer in dealing with a public that has an immediate mental image of what he is and what he represents? There is no question that the range of reaction is wide: fear, distrust, contempt, hate, awe of the authority figure, silent respect. Many of these responses hinder effective communication with the people we are trying to serve.

Professional police administrators have tried to improve the police image by selling the "blue" uniform through public relations programs and efforts in public education. This is extremely expensive and time-consuming; the achievements are often offset by uncomplimentary television programs.

There are other factors that must be considered if we are going to attain the professional status we keep talking about. If national polls are correct, America likes its police, thinks the police are doing a fair job, yet places them very low in professional status (54th) out of 90 professions—equal to playground directors. The police officer is placed higher on the occupational ladder when he is a detective. The patrol officer's image suffers badly from historical police practices, political appointment, minimal educational requirements, and low pay.[11]

Contemporary mass communication often compounds the image problem by projecting the beat officer as an incompetent with subnormal intelligence ("Car 54—Where Are You?"). An automobile commercial showing a Southern officer as overweight, arrogant, and cigar-chomping is another example of attitude programming. In addition, the media often projects a picture of an officer who is continually involved with violence when, in fact, only 20 percent of the officer's time is spent in crime related duties in most jurisdictions.

If the beat officer is a product of a society that places him low on the occupational scale, he will either consciously or subconsciously place himself in the same position. Thus, along with its organizational change, the Menlo Park Police Department also changed uniforms in order to give the beat officer a new role identity and increase his competence and job role satisfaction. This uniform change is particularly important now that many police departments are recruiting men with college educations. If we do not fulfill this higher caliber officer's needs for satisfaction in the police profession, we will lose him to other professions. Part of the answer to this problem is redesigning the job role of the beat officer, giving him more responsibility and allowing him greater discretion in decision-making. The uniform change is a logical part of such a new concept.

One final hypothesis was the feeling that the uniform change would reduce assaults on police officers. Menlo Park hoped that the

[11] Nicholas deB. Katzenbach, Chairman, *The Police: Report of the President's Commission on Law Enforcement and Administration of Justice* (Washington, D.C.: U.S. Govt. Printing Office, 1967), pp. 13, 121.

officer in a business suit will be looked upon as a resource person to solve problems and not as a scapegoat. The statistical data collected over a four-year period supports the experiment and it has been institutionalized in Menlo Park.[12]

Considering the problems addressed in this chapter, the following experience of two Menlo Park officers is worth reflecting upon.

The two officers were dressed in neat green blazers that bore a pocket emblem with the symbol of a tree and the word Police across the top. They were sitting in the rear of a restaurant having breakfast when a black family consisting of two adults and three children left their table, walked out of their way to the rear of the restaurant, and stopped by the officer's table. Their comment? "Thank you for changing uniforms, we feel we can talk to you now."

Student Checklist

1. Are you able to list the blocks to effective communication most frequently encountered in police community relations?
2. Can you identify three programs aimed at removing blocks to police–citizen communications?
3. Can you compare a police department with a military model? With a nonmilitary model?
4. Can you list the advantages and disadvantages of each model?
5. Do you know how to describe the difference between active bias and simple preference?

[12] See "Interim Uniform Report," *Police Chief Magazine*, April 1970, pp. 28-29.

Topics for Discussion

1. Discuss the common blocks to effective communication between police and citizens.
2. Discuss three types of police programs aimed at removing blocks to effective communication.
3. Discuss the difference between active bias and simple preference.
4. Discuss the advantages and disadvantages of a nonmilitary police image.

ANNOTATED BIBLIOGRAPHY

American Behavioral Scientist, XIII, Nos. 5 & 6 (May, June, July, and August 1970). This issue is devoted to a study of police and society. There are several excellent papers on police perceptions of blacks and community relations.

Berkeley, George. The *Democratic Policeman*. Boston: Beacon Press, 1969. Mr. Berkeley presents a fine examination of American and European police systems. A very readable author, he gives directions for the future and defines present problems.

Chevigny, Paul. *Police Power*. New York: Pantheon Press, 1969. A stark and somewhat shocking report of police abusing their authority. It is an interesting side of police work that can destroy public confidence in government systems.

Clark, Ramsey. *Crime in America*. New York: Simon & Schuster, 1971. Mr. Clark presents a balanced view of crime in America and draws the image of crime and its reality into focus.

Conot, Robert. *Rivers of Blood, Years of Darkness*. New York: Bantam Books, 1967. This provides an excellent analysis of the Watts, California, riots and the sociological conditions that contributed to the civil disorder. It has interesting documented incidents that point out the need for reform in police operations.

Earle, Howard H. *Police–Community Relations, Crisis in our Times*. Springfield, Ill.: Charles C. Thomas. Dr. Howard Earle, an experienced law enforcement officer, does an excellent analysis.

Geary, David. "Police Fad or Future?" *The Police Chief*. April 1969. This provides a rationale for examining new uniform styles by police.

Geary, David. "College-Educated Cops—Three Years Later." *The Police Chief*. August 1970. A description of the experience of the first medium-sized city police department using college-educated officers.

Maslow, Abraham. *The Farther Reaches of Human Nature*. New York: The Viking Press, 1971. An excellent reference for the serious student of human nature. It will give a police officer another dimension to draw from in his dealings with people.

Niederhoffer, Arthur. *Behind the Shield: The Police in Urban Society.* Garden City, N.Y.: Doubleday, 1967. This book gives an insight into the authoritarian personality and into many of the underlying problems in police organizations that eventually effect the public.

Watson, Nelson A. *Police–Community Relations.* International Association of Chiefs of Police, 1966. This should be required reading for every student of police–community relations.

The study of this chapter will enable you to:

1. Describe the percentage of crime news in the average daily paper in the United States.
2. List some reasons why the media may actually increase crime by reporting it.
3. List some reasons for a code of conduct for the press.
4. Contrast the responsibility of the press with the responsibility of the police.

8

Police-Press Relations

The principal links between local law enforcement personnel and the community are the mass media. Except for the relatively few persons who become directly involved with the police, private citizens learn of police activity, of crime prevention, of the pursuit and apprehension of criminals, and their disposition in the courts by what they read in their newspapers and see and hear on television and radio. Thus, the image that a police department has in a community, favorable or otherwise, will depend almost exclusively upon what the typical citizen reads, hears, and observes in the local media.

The crucial importance of the media to local police departments can, most simply, be emphasized by some basic statistics that indicate the massive impact of the media on the citizens of this country. The state of Wisconsin is a typical example. In that state, which contains one-fiftieth of the nation's population, there are 36 daily newspapers, whose total circulation is greater than the number of households in the state. In addition, there are 116 commercial radio stations and more radio receivers than people. The signals of the state's 17 television stations reach every community in the state, in which almost 99 percent of the people have at least one television set. There are also more than 250 community (usually published weekly) newspapers, with a combined readership of over 600,000.

Multiply these figures by 50, and you have the total number of mass media outlets in this country—more than enough to provide every citizen, even the most apathetic, with substantial access to the news of his community, his state, the nation, and the world.

These statistics would be of little interest, either to the police or the community, if it were not for the fact that the media, from which our citizens receive virtually all their news about crime, are so committed to the coverage of crime. There is some difference of opinion as to how much news about murder, robbery, rape, and larceny the public really wants or demands. But there can be no doubt that, with or without public demand, the media are determined to offer maximum coverage of crime. Estimates from various surveys in recent years have placed the proportion of crime news at from 3 to 10 percent of the total space in daily newspapers across America. The New York *Daily News* has devoted as much as 33.5 percent of a single issue to violent crime.

But these figures do not tell the whole story. Papers can emphasize crime (grossly overemphasize, the critics of the press argue) by the placement of stories on page one, by large, black, and often lurid headlines, and by other attention-getting devices. "In weighing the effect on justice," John Lofton, author of *Justice and the Press*, has written, "The play and the slant of crime news are even more important than the amount of space allotted to the subject. . . . The large and dramatic headline on the front page gets more attention from readers than a small, unprovocative item buried on the back pages." In large city newspapers in particular, sensational crimes are often given more space than significant news of national and international events. The story of a $15 robbery in a small community often occupies more space in the local newspaper than the expenditure by the local government of hundreds of thousands of dollars.

There is the rare newspaper which deliberately restricts its crime coverage. One such paper is the La Salle (Ill.) *Post-Tribune* which, as a matter of policy, keeps crime news off its front page, although not out of the paper altogether. That paper's publisher, Curtis H. Clay, explained that:

> *The intelligent criminal enters his career deliberately, with eyes open to chances of beating the law. He believes he is smarter than the police. Publicity encourages him; he likes to see his name in the headlines. He laughs at the "dumb cops" and continues his outlawry, glorying in his notoriety. If and when he gets caught, he is ready to face the music. Wasn't his name on the front page for weeks, months? . . . Publicity can't stop him. It will not injure his reputation. It will enhance it.*[1]

---

[1] Curtis D. MacDougall, *The Press and its Problems* (Dubuque: William C. Brown, 1964), p. 389.

There are, however, far more defenders than there are critics of heavy crime coverage. One such man, who disagrees with Publisher Clay's theory, is Thomas S. Rice, a close student of the press. Rice believes that even the sensationalizing of crime can be a powerful aid in fighting crime:

> ... It is far, far better for the safety of our citizens and their families that we should have too much crime news instead of too little. ... Every improvement in police administration and methods have followed newspapers playing up crime. Constant harping on Al Capone, with the definite object of bringing him to book, was not making a hero out of him. The Chicago newspapers which led the fight against that contamination of their city had the definite purpose of causing his fall. ... Capone and other lawbreakers have come to grief from systematic sensationalizing of their personalities as well as of their deeds until the public rose in revolt.[2]

Rice claimed that what he called "systematic sensationalizing" led not only to Capone's downfall but to the creation of the Chicago Crime Commission, which helped improve the administration of criminal justice in that city. Similar "sensationalizing" by newspapers, Rice said, led to the creation of similar commissions in Cleveland, Baltimore, and Philadelphia.

Whatever one thinks of the relative merits of the conflicting arguments of Clay and Rice, it is the latter's views that are followed and practiced by virtually all publishers, editors, and reporters of the daily newspapers of America. Newspaper coverage that followed the 1946 arrest of a 17-year-old Chicago youth, William Heirens, for several brutal murders was reasonably typical: the five Chicago newspapers gave, in total, much more coverage to the Heirens case, from arrest to sentencing, than to critical national events. A study of 85 issues of Chicago newspapers during that period revealed 62 banner headlines for the Heirens case, 11 to the operations of the Office of Price Administration (which affected the pocketbooks of virtually every person in America), and only 4 to atomic bomb tests.

Whether or not the readers of American newspapers share this preoccupation, the favorite topic of the media, newspapers in particular, is violent crime. And while the degree of sensationalizing in American newspapers has diminished in the last 50 years, there is more than

[2] Ibid., p. 391.

enough evidence that the press is fascinated—morbidly so, its critics say—with crime. There is also evidence to suggest that some newspapers exploit what they claim to be public interest in crime in order to sell their newspapers. Ed Murray, managing editor of the Los Angeles *Mirror*, wrote of the Marilyn Sheppard murder case: "This case has mystery, society, sex, and glamour," thus explaining the massive coverage American papers gave to an event that was really a rather ordinary homicide.[3] Herbert H. Krauch, editor of the Los Angeles *Herald and Express* (2000 miles from the murder and trial site) said of the trial of Sam Sheppard: "It's been a long time since there's been a murder trial this good."[4]

There are other editors who, like Murray and Krauch, are convinced that crime news sells newspapers. And there is evidence to support them. In 1956, for example, two sisters were raped and murdered and the resultant stories boosted total circulation of the city's daily newspapers by 50,000 copies. One year later when a rapist ran wild in San Francisco, that city's four newspapers had a field day. The *Chronicle* called the attacker the "Torture Kit Rapist" (the victims had been manacled and tortured by the rapist who had used a knife, adhesive tape, manacles, and scissors). The *News* called the murderer the "Fang Fiend" (because he had been described by one would-be victim as having "canine teeth, which protruded fang-like over his lower lip"). A 23-year-old warehouse clerk was arrested as the rapist-murderer; when another man confessed, the press abandoned the case. But the coverage had been profitable, for during each day of the almost two-week coverage of the case, each San Francisco newspaper sold about 15,000 more copies than normal.

From the point of view of the police, overcoverage and sensationalizing of crime may not in themselves produce law enforcement problems. Occasionally, however, the press works at cross purposes with the police, and law enforcement is hindered. This is particularly true in kidnapping cases, where the relationship between press and police is the most critical; the safety of the victim often depends upon the cooperation given by the press to the police. Former FBI Director J. Edgar Hoover once compiled a list of cases in which he claimed the media

[3] John Lofton, *Justice and the Press* (Boston: Beacon, 1966), p. 182.
[4] Peter C. Sandman, et al., *Media: An Introductory Analysis of American Mass Communications* (Englewood Cliffs, N.J.: Prentice-Hall, 1972), p. 369.

had seriously hindered the work of his agency. One such case cited by Hoover was the Mattson kidnapping. Newspapermen prevented contact with the kidnappers of young Charles Mattson by refusing to leave the neighborhood of the Mattson home in Seattle. The boy's father received a letter from the kidnappers containing a newspaper picture of reporters around the house and said there would be no contact until they left. The Mattson boy was later found dead, obviously murdered by the kidnappers. In another case, the Peter Levine kidnapping, a reporter, trying to verify rumors that the boy was missing, phoned the boy's father who, caught off guard, admitted that his child was missing and said that he was willing to pay ransom. Warned by the kidnapper to prevent publicity, the father tried to persuade the newspapers to suppress the story, but the papers refused. Later, the headless body of the kidnapped boy was found floating in Long Island Sound.

But, in other cases, the press has shown restraint and cooperation with the police. In the Lindbergh kidnapping case, the press voluntarily suppressed the contents of the original ransom note and the fact that the Treasury Department had sent the serial numbers of the bank notes used as ransom to banks across the country. The press also refrained from following Lindbergh on his futile trips to meet the kidnapper and deliberately misled the kidnapper by publishing false information about police activity. Such cooperation did not save the Lindbergh infant, but it did eventually lead to the capture, trial, and execution of Bruno Richard Hauptmann for the kidnapping and murder of young Lindbergh.

In recent years, newspapers have been more restrained in kidnapping cases. In 1954, a 60-hour "conspiracy of silence" by all San Francisco newspapers, wire services, and broadcasters was credited with saving the life of a kidnapped real estate operator. However, a year later, the New York *Daily News* was widely, and properly, condemned by police and others for failing to go along with other New York area newspapers that had refrained from publishing accounts of the kidnapping of one-month-old Peter Weinberger.[5] Frightened by the crowd at the site selected for the transfer of the ransom money, which had been reported in the *Daily News*, the kidnapper killed the baby.

The press has occasionally thwarted police work in nonkidnapping cases as well. By reporting detailed clues discovered by the police

[5] MacDougall, *The Press and its Problems*, p. 395.

or announcing the time and place of a planned investigation, the press can—and in some cases actually does—tip off the criminal, who may destroy the evidence and avoid capture. But again, the record of the press is mixed, for persistent, imaginative reporters have helped the police to solve crimes and, in some cases, have solved the crimes themselves. The brutal murder of Bobby Franks in Chicago in 1923 was solved by the detective work of two reporters of the Chicago *Daily News*, whose suspicions led to the arrest and conviction of Nathan Leopold and Richard Loeb. In 1930, the Kansas City *Star* solved the murder of Mrs. A. D. Payne by her husband. Ku Klux Klan leader D. C. Stephenson went to prison for the murder of Madge Oberhalzer as a result of the investigative efforts of the Indianapolis *Times* and the Vincennes *Commercial*. The Chicago *Daily News* won a Pulitzer Prize for uncovering the stealing of millions of dollars from the Illinois State Treasury by the state auditor, Orville Hodge. The complete list of similar newspaper exposés of crime is long indeed, evidence that the press and the police are not necessarily natural adversaries.

The press has not only uncovered crime and criminals, but it can point to a long record of exonerating men already convicted of crime. In 1932, Joe Majczek was sent to prison for life for a murder he insisted he had not committed. Twelve years later, a series of articles in the Chicago *Times* revealed that he had been convicted largely on the testimony of a witness who had been threatened with prosecution for violating the Prohibition law unless she identified Majczek as the murderer. Majczek thereupon was freed from prison, fully pardoned, and compensated by the state for his 12 years in prison. The same year that Majczek was freed, a young, inarticulate Negro, Willie Calloway, was sentenced to life imprisonment for murder. His case came to the attention of reporter Ken McCormack of the Detroit *Free Press*, who wrote a series of articles that helped to exonerate Calloway. Calloway was then released after eight years in prison for a crime he did not commit.

The Need for Guidelines

The conflict between the media and the police can be eased by compromise but not eliminated altogether, for the function of each is basically dissimilar. The task of the police is to prevent crime, to maintain law and order in the community, to protect the citizens of a community, and to apprehend and to bring lawbreakers to justice. The obligation of the press in a free society is to seek out and report the truth, even though such truth may occasionally embarrass or even hinder the police. On one hand, the First Amendment guarantees an absolute right to print virtually anything, free of legal restraint. Yet, under the Sixth Amendment, every person has the right to a fair trial, which means a trial by a jury of his peers who have not been influenced by prejudicial publicity before and during trial. The police are often caught in the cross fire of these competing rights.

Before 1935, there was comparatively little concern for the rights of suspects and defendants, some of whom were badly treated by the police or the press, or by both. Then came the trial of Bruno Hauptmann for the kidnap-murder of the Lindbergh infant. The press, which had shown such commendable restraint before Hauptmann's capture, treated the trial at Flemington, New Jersey, as a combination circus and passion play, as did the prosecution, the defense, and the public itself. The prosecutor told a reporter that he "would wrap the kidnap ladder around Hauptmann's neck," a threat that was duly carried in the newspapers of the day. The defense counsel ordered stationary for Hauptmann to answer his "fan mail"; the letterhead carried a facsimile of the kidnap ladder. The press allied itself with the prosecution, charging once that the defendant was making "senseless denials" and, on another occasion, with being "a thing lacking in human characteristics." Although photographs had been forbidden in the courtroom, not only still pictures, but motion pictures as well, were taken and displayed to the public.

It was the Hauptmann trial that first compelled the organized bar to consider the need for a code of conduct that might prevent the improprieties and excesses of that trial. An 18-member committee of newspapermen, broadcasters, editors, publishers, and lawyers agreed on a general code of conduct to guide prosecutors, defense counsel, and the press in future criminal trials. The code drawn up by this committee was accepted by the American Bar Association but, except for Canon 35 (which prohibited photographs in the courtroom), the guidelines were generally ignored until two events many years later—the assassination of President John F. Kennedy and the Supreme Court decision in the Sam Sheppard case.

The aftermath of the Kennedy assassination did more than anything since the Hauptmann trial to spur new remedies for the injustices of pretrial publicity. "From the moment of his arrest until his murder two days later," the American Civil Liberties Union concluded, "Lee Harvey Oswald was tried and convicted many times over in the newspapers, on the radio, and over television by the public statements of the Dallas law enforcement officials. Time and time again, high-ranking police and prosecution officials stated their complete satisfaction that Oswald was the assassin. As their investigation uncovered one piece of evidence after the other, the results were broadcast to the public."[6] The Warren Commission reached similar conclusions in its 1964 report, and also criticized District Attorney Henry Wade and Police Chief Jesse E. Curry for their statements to the press which, the Commission believed, were potentially harmful to both the prosecution and the defense. The Commission criticized, too, the press for its lack of self-discipline, which created general disorder in the police and court buildings in Dallas. The events in Dallas that weekend, the Commission said, "are a dramatic affirmation of the need for steps to bring about a proper balance between the right of the public to be informed and the right of an individual to a fair and impartial trial."[7]

But the need for definitive guidelines did not become critical until 1966 when the Supreme Court, in the Sheppard decision, told the bench, the bar, the police, and the press that every defendant in a criminal case was entitled to a trial unpolluted by prejudicial pretrial publicity. It is widely held that the 1955 trial of Dr. Sheppard is one of the most flagrant examples of irresponsible behavior, not only by the news media, but by the judiciary and law enforcement officials as well. The Supreme Court, in reversing Sheppard's conviction, agreed.

In its Sheppard decision, the Court offered explicit guidance on how trial courts and police should seek to preserve the defendant's right to a fair and impartial trial, preventing interference by the press. Many of these strictures were incorporated into guidelines that were later drawn up by joint bench-bar-press committees in various states, although many of the Supreme Court "rules" were already contained in such guidelines established prior to 1966.

Among the many guidelines—or statements of principles, as they are called in some states—are those in Oregon (a Bar-Press-Broadcasters

[6] Lofton, *Justice and the Press*, p. 130.
[7] Ibid., p. xii.

Joint Statement of Principles); in Massachusetts (a Guide for Bar and News Media); in Kentucky (a Press Association Statement of Principles for Pretrial Reporting); in New York (a Code on Fair Trial and Free Press of the New York County Lawyers Association); and in Philadelphia (a Statement of Policy of the Philadelphia Bar Association). In 1965, the Department of Justice adopted rules, later to be known as the Katzenbach (after the then Attorney General) Guidelines, regarding release of information relating to criminal proceedings by law enforcement personnel of the Department and its agencies, such as the Federal Bureau of Investigation.

These guidelines, particularly as they apply to police, are basically similar. One such set of guidelines was drafted in 1968 by the Wisconsin Advisory Commission on Pretrial Publicity, which included a local police chief, a county sheriff, a district attorney, both newspapermen and broadcasters, several academicians, and a trial judge. Because the product of this group is relatively typical of such guidelines, it is summarized in the following pages.

The Wisconsin Guidelines

There was, first, an acknowledgment that the release of certain information prior to criminal trials involves, perhaps inevitably, a conflict between the defendant's right to a fair trial and the public's right to know. Since law enforcement officials should not have to carry the total burden of making difficult decisions on what information should and should not be released, there ought to be a code to guide the police.

The police and the press must agree upon the underlying principle that the news media have the right and the responsibility to publish, and the public has the right to have, the truth about the administration of criminal justice. Both those rights must be balanced against the rights of defendants and the state to a fair trial.

What information should police release to the press, and thus to the public? The police, after arrest, may make available to the public the text or substance of the charge; the name of the investigative and arresting agency; the length of the investigation; and the defendant's name, address, age, employment, and marital status. If the defendant in a criminal case is a juvenile, most states have statutory restrictions on the release of information that may include the name of the defendant. Police officers are advised to examine such statutes.

During the investigation of a crime, certain information may be released if it is necessary to that investigation or to the apprehension of a suspect. It is considered permissible, for example, to make available to the press photographs of the suspect or "wanted" posters, to publicize the issuance of a warrant, or to warn the public that a fugitive may be armed and dangerous. Richard Speck, who was later convicted of the mass murder of eight nurses in Chicago, was caught after his "Wanted" picture was published in Chicago newspapers.

There is certain information that the Wisconsin Commission advises should *not* be released. Occasionally, a suspect or defendant in police custody confesses to a crime (usually, though not always, the one for which he is being held), or he makes an admission that seemingly points to guilt. A suspect, for example, may deny having committed a murder but may admit to having been near the scene of the murder. The guidelines are virtually unanimous on this issue, and the statement of the Wisconsin Commission is typical: "Police officials must never disclose that a person in custody, whether formally charged or not, has confessed or made an admission or an incriminating statement. The police must not release the text or details of such a confession or admission . . . or even make public the fact that a person has refused to make a statement, or has made any statement bearing on his guilt or innocence."

Other information that must not be released, since it would clearly prejudice potential jurors, includes the results of investigative procedures, such as polygraph examinations, ballistics, or other laboratory tests, or fingerprint identifications. This information should not be released whether the results of such tests point to guilt or innocence. Police should not make any statements on the identity or the credibility, and certainly not on the expected testimony, of prospective witnesses. At no time, before or after arrest or the issuance of a complaint, should the police make any statements or furnish any information to influence the outcome of a defendant's trial. Nor should they release any information that might have that effect. This prohibition includes, according to the Wisconsin Commission, police theories or interpretations about evidence, statements about the character of the accused, and statements of opinion about the guilt or innocence of the accused.

There are more difficult questions. What if the defendant requests an interview with the press or the press with the defendant? Under the Wisconsin Commission guidelines (and most others), the police may permit such interviews only if the person in custody requests it and only after he has been advised of his right to counsel. If the person already has an attorney, that attorney must be advised of the request for an interview. Unless all these conditions are met, the police should not permit any interviews.

Another difficult decision for the police arises when the news media request or demand pictures of the suspect (or defendant) while he is in jail or being transported in custody. The guideline suggested by the Wisconsin Commission provides that the police should not encourage the news media in such photographing or televising, but neither should such picture-taking be "discouraged." The police certainly should not allow or require the deliberate posing of a person in custody. The police may, however, give the press a current photograph of a person under arrest.

There is some difference of opinion among commissions like Wisconsin's on whether police ought to release information to the press about the circumstances of an arrest. Suppose, for example, that five minutes after a bank robbery and two blocks from the bank, a man is captured with a gun and a satchel of cash in his possession. Should these facts be made available to the press and thus to the public? The Wisconsin Commission answered this question in the affirmative: "It is appropriate for police officials to make a factual, unadorned statement of the arrest and the surrounding circumstances of a person charged with a crime, including the defendant's resistance to arrest, or the fact that the defendant possessed or used weapons, or that contraband was in his possession at the time of arrest." While pretrial guidelines suggest that such information is too prejudicial to the defendant and thus should be withheld, most opt for release of such information. But, like the Philadelphia Bar Association, they add a cautionary note: "The police should not display or comment on weapons or 'loot' or other physical articles found on the defendant."

Finally, there is the problem of the prior criminal record of a suspect or defendant. That prior record might not be admissible in a trial, but a juror might have read in the press, for example, that a man on trial for manslaughter had been convicted previously of second-degree murder. That knowledge might influence the jurior's decision. Release of a prior record is, therefore, clearly prejudicial to a defendant, even though that record is a public record available to the press. The Wisconsin Commission, as well as most other commissions, have resolved this dilemma with a compromise: "The police shall not *volunteer* information concerning a defendant's prior record. However, since (such) records are ordinarily matters of public record, they . . . may be made available *upon specific inquiry*. (Emphasis added)

The Oregon Bar-Press-Broadcasters Code has a provision missing from other codes but which, most police and undoubtedly most citizens would agree, is a valuable addition to any set of publicity guidelines: "Good taste should prevail in the selection, printing, and broadcasting of news. Morbid or sensational details of criminal behavior should not be employed."

Police Operational Responsibilities

We have dealt thus far with what information should or should not be released to the press. Almost as critical to the police is the question of *who* in the police hierarchy ought to make those decisions. It is preferable, although not always possible, that statements relating to crime be made by the ranking officer in the department or, if he is absent, by someone he has designated to do so. If the chief of police or his designee are not available, the policeman on the scene of the crime should be entitled to make available to the press, in the words of the Wisconsin Commission, "basic and unelaborated information" about the crime, but no more. Although most guidelines are silent on this point, police officers who are uncertain about releasing or withholding information, ought to resolve all doubts in favor of withholding information. If the decision to withhold information was wrong, it can be corrected by a later release. If, however, information that should have been withheld was released, the damage has been done.

Voluntary guidelines, such as those in Wisconsin, Kentucky, and Philadelphia, are not binding on the press. Several months after the adoption of the Philadelphia guidelines, to which the local press subscribed, there was a particularly brutal multiple murder in that city. The Philadelphia newspapers ignored the guidelines, releasing a text of a suspect's confession. Police authorities felt no more compelled to be bound by the guidelines than did the newspapers; both the police chief and the mayor held a press conference to announce that there was no doubt that the suspect in custody was the guilty man. The press of Philadelphia was not punished nor, in fact, could it be under the Supreme Court's interpretation of the First Amendment. Nor were the police held legally accountable for their release of highly prejudicial publicity, simply because the guidelines were not binding.

But there is nothing to prevent a local law enforcement agency from formally adopting its own guidelines or from making joint bench-bar-press-police guidelines mandatory for members of that agency. The Katzenbach Guidelines did just that by forbidding Justice Department employees from releasing certain information; the employee who violates these rules is subject to suspension or dismissal. In November 1964, the New Jersey Supreme Court ordered a ban on "potentially prejudicial statements" by prosecutors and defense lawyers and suggested that similar statements by police officers should be dealt with by superior officers as "conduct unbecoming." But local police departments need not wait for court orders or for the adoption of state statutes that would permit or require discipline of police officers who release "potentially prejudicial" information. They can adopt and apply the rules themselves.

From the point of view of the police, guidelines on the release of information relating to criminal trials have substantial advantages. With guidelines, it is simpler for the policeman on the beat, or the chief back in the station house, to withstand the pressure of the press or the public for information that should not be released. If a joint press-bar-police guideline has been adopted in a community or a state, the police officer, when faced with a demand for information, can point to that guideline and say, "Look, we've agreed, and so did you, that this kind of information should be withheld. We are sticking to that agreement." If the police have adopted their own guidelines or rules, the police officer can say: "I can't give you that information; our rules don't permit it. You wouldn't want me to be fired, would you?" The police officer's decision is then removed from a personal basis, for he is guided or bound by rules.

Crisis Situations

The advent of militancy in the 1960s, the urban guerilla warfare, student unrest and demonstrations, the civil rights protests, the riots and the fire bombings brought new problems to the police. It became imperative that they develop effective working arrangements with the mass media.

One commentator said: "Nothing, but nothing, ever happens the same way after you put a television or movie camera on it." Television, with its capacity for instantaneous reporting, has often incited violence, usually unintentionally, by attracting those who seek attention. Both rioters and police have been known to perform for the media. And occasionally the media have manufactured the news. During the riots in Newark, New Jersey, for example, a newspaper photographer from a New York newspaper was seen urging, and finally convincing, a young black boy to throw a rock for the benefit of the cameras. In Chicago in the late 1960s, a television camera crew was seen leading two "hippie" girls into an area filled with National Guardsmen. As the cameras started rolling, one of the girls cried on cue: "Don't beat me, don't beat me!" Virtually all of the media outlets have their own rules against this sort of staging, but occasionally the rules tend to be forgotten during a major upheaval.

A less violent confrontation was described by an observer in the 1960s after a three-man television crew arrived at a labor picket line. Although the crew chief was disappointed because, from a pictorial standpoint, it wasn't much of a demonstration, he decided to film it anyway ("We may as well get it."). As the observer related: "The light man held up his 30-foot lamp and laid a 4-foot beam of light across the picket line. Instantly, the marchers' heads snapped up, their eyes flashed. They threw up their arms in the clenched Communist fist. Some made a 'V' with their fingers, and they held up their banners for the cameras." The event was transformed into something substantially different than it would have been had not the television crew arrived to record it.

Immense damage can result during a civil disturbance as a result of a lack of restraint by press or police, by inaccurate reporting, by journalistic sensationalizing, by police overreaction, or by a breakdown in communication between the press and the police. A false rumor that police had killed a black cab driver in Newark, New Jersey, and an unfounded report of the killing of a seven-year-old boy in Plainfield, New Jersey, fanned major disturbances in those cities. In Tampa, Florida, a deputy sheriff died in the early stages of a riot that intensified after both the Associated Press and United Press International reported that he had been killed by rioters when, in actuality, he had suffered a heart attack.

Although television coverage does provide incentive to violence, police ought to realize that coverage can also have the opposite effect.

No one, including demonstrators, wants his unlawful acts recorded on camera. The presence of cameras can also have a restraining influence on overzealous police authorities; during the late 1950s and early 1960s, the Justice Department encouraged media coverage of civil rights demonstrations in the belief that it would inhibit violence by unsympathetic police in the Southern states.

Except in the rare instance when police intend to engage in improper conduct, it is in their best interest to have reporters present. In Chicago in the 1960s, comedian Dick Gregory complained that police had been "brutal" in arresting him. Station WMAQ-TV carried Gregory's statement without comment, then reran the film showing Gregory being arrested, a film that did not bear out his claim. The Chicago police were grateful.

Media representatives have long been aware of their grave responsibilities during riot situations. As far back as June 1963, in anticipation of confrontations at Selma, Alabama, Richard Salant, president of CBS News, sent a memorandum to his news personnel at Selma. He warned of "the unsettling effect on a stimulated crowd that the TV camera has," and requested that personnel and equipment be as unobtrusive as possible, and that cameras be turned away or covered when there was any danger that their presence might aggravate tensions.

Because of the growing evidence that the presence of news media, particularly television, at the scenes of disorders often encourages or even produces violence, the National Advisory Commission on Civil Disorders in 1968 urged news organizations to discuss among themselves the special problems involved in covering riots and to formulate directives to guide such coverage. Out of those recommendations came some detailed guidelines adopted by the three networks—ABC, CBS, and NBC (some of these self-imposed "rules" predated 1968, however).

While the network guidelines were basically similar, CBS seemed to go the furthest. Police should be aware of such guidelines so that they might, when necessary, insist that the networks abide by their own self-imposed limitations. It is important for police to study the checklist of "do's" and "do nots" because so many of them refer to the police:

1. Use unmarked or camouflaged cars and equipment (CBS and NBC).
2. Use caution in characterizing or estimating the size and intensity of the crowd; balance all statements by rioters with statements by responsible officials (CBS and NBC).

Figure 8-1. Television coverage of scenes of potential disorder has an ambivalent role. It may provide an inventive to violence; yet it may also deter it, since neither demonstrators nor police would wish to have unlawful acts recorded on camera.

3. Avoid giving the exact location of the riot or specifics about weaponry. "Cap" cameras if they are contributing to the disorders (all three networks).

4. Do not reenact, simulate, stage, or aid demonstrations (ABC and NBC).

5. Do not provide "live" coverage (ABC and CBS).

6. Avoid interviews with participants or self-appointed riot leaders (NBC).

The networks have agreed that extreme care should be taken in the use of inflammatory descriptions or catchwords (such as "police brutality" or "angry mob"), that disturbances should not be called a "riot" or "racial" until officially so designated, and that extra care should be taken to avoid blinding officers with klieg lights and flashbulbs. The networks agree, too, that their reporters and technicians should request police escorts or protection when needed and that the police are entitled to ask for special credentials from newsmen. And, perhaps most important, the networks agree that the more experienced newsmen be put in charge of covering riot situations and that they establish liaison with the police.

There are, however, several basic differences in network guidelines. ABC and CBS have prohibited "live" coverage of civil disturbances, but NBC has not. CBS recommends that their personnel and their local affiliates obey all police instructions, NBC coverage may be in opposition to police wishes, and ABC has no policy on this issue.

Local affiliates of the networks have their own policies, which are usually in conformity with the networks to which they belong. But police ought to check to make certain since there may be some differences. Police should also check network policies, which are subject to change. Local television stations occasionally go beyond the caution of their networks. For example, Radio Station WOL in Washington, D.C., during the riots there in April 1968, broadcast gospel music in the hope of quieting the black community. And Station WEYN in Wichita, Kansas, during civil disorders, stayed on the air beyond its usual sign-off time to play music, using black announcers. During the entire evening, the station carried no news of the riots in the city nor, in fact, of any news events at all. That there is danger in such a news blackout, however, was shown during the riots in Detroit. The first person killed in those riots was a woman who was shot as she drove through the riot area, unaware of the disorder because Detroit radio and television stations kept news of the conflict off the air until many hours after the trouble erupted.

A committee of the Northern California Chapter of the Radio and TV News Directors Association has drafted a set of guidelines that fills in some of the gaps in the network codes:

1. Competition between broadcasters should continue, but the focus should be changed from dynamic impact to calm reporting of vital information to the public, with maximum assistance in reestablishing of control as the primary goal.
2. Law enforcement authorities should take necessary steps to ensure that adequately informed staff members will be on duty at command posts and be available to supply properly identified broadcast newsmen with pertinent information about the disorder.
3. Reports should be calm and objective and should present the overall picture. They should be devoid of sensationalism, speculation, and rumors which could incite or further extend disturbances or stir news breaks.

Although their interests are sometimes competing, the press and the police have common goals in riot situations—to restore order as quickly as possible. Full, fast reporting by the media can help, as can efficient police reaction. But the media must have the cooperation of the police in getting the facts; and the police must have the cooperation and the voluntary restraint of the media. The press and the police should not wait until a full-scale riot is upon them. Contingency plans, especially when there is reason to anticipate disorder, should be drawn up.

Strategies for the Future

The simplest way to maintain effective communication between the police and the media is to schedule periodic meetings at regular intervals. It might be preferable, from a psychological point of view, to alternate the meetings between police headquarters and the local radio or television station or newspaper. Since the various media outlets in local communities are almost always competitive, it will usually be necessary to meet separately with each station or paper.

These meetings can help clear up misunderstandings and explore common goals before a crisis, such as a local riot, develops, or before relations between police and the media became so strained that they may go beyond healing. Local police departments would be well advised, if they have not already done so, to appoint a public information officer, whose function it would be not only to represent the police at such meetings but to serve as a permanent source of information for the press and public.

A Press Council

A more formal liaison between police and media that ought to be considered is the establishment of a local press council.

The press councils (patterned after such councils in Great Britain) were relatively scarce in this country until 1967 when the Mellett Fund subsidized several advisory groups in California, Oregon, and Illinois. These councils, whose purpose is to establish a communication link between the press and the public, have been operating with varied success in such diverse communities as Honolulu, Hawaii; Bend, Oregon; and Redwood City, California. The councils (in some localities called mass media councils, community-media councils, or communications councils) are generally made up of working journalists and public members. Much of the work of a council involves reviewing complaints submitted by noncouncil members as well as by council members themselves. In Bend, Oregon, for example, many of the public inquiries concern press coverage of police activities and crime; the publisher of the local newspaper, the Bend *Bulletin*, was able to educate the council, and through the council the public, as to the *Bulletin's* role in reporting crime. Occasionally, suggestions made to or by the council have led to changes in newspaper coverage of crime. Often, the criticisms are rejected, usually for good reason, by the press members of the council.

Local press councils have not been formed for the sole purpose of establishing liaison between the police and the media. But there is no reason why the police should not cooperate if a proposal for a local press council is seriously considered in a community; the police might even volunteer a representative to serve as a council member. The police might, if the circumstances suggested, initiate the establishment of a council in their city—or even in their state. The first statewide council was established in Minnesota in 1971, largely through the efforts of the Minnesota Newspaper Association.

A more specialized press council—solely concerned with crime news—might be considered. It might consist of 11 persons—5 from the media (perhaps three from the management or editor's level and two reporters); an attorney or a judge; a police official; and 4 members of the public.

Experience with existing press councils suggests that the public members ought to come from among the professional or academic community, with at least one person who represents the working class. The chairman should be a public member rather than a representative of the media. Such a council could be financed by a state media association, but the cost would be small; most of the expenditures would be used for travel expenses of members conducting investigations.

Although the council could occasionally focus on community problems (and the press coverage or lack of coverage of them), most of its work would involve receiving complaints against media handling of crime news, the investigation of such complaints, and the issuing of public reports on its findings. The council findings on a particular complaint would be published and sent to all news media and agencies of the state, including the offending media. The council would not, and under the restrictions of the federal and state constitutions, could not have any other powers—certainly not the power to punish. Its only sanction would be publicity.

The Newspaper Ombudsman

Another link between the media and the public, and one which police might profitably make use of, is the newspaper ombudsman. The term is derived from that Swedish official who deals with citizen complaints against agencies of government.

John Herchenroeder, the Louisville *Courier-Journal*'s first ombudsman, handled 900 complaints in the first two years after his position was created in 1967. In some cases, the complaints resulted in corrections, changes in news policies, and expanded coverage in some areas. In many cases, the readers were told that they were in error. Other newspapers trying the ombudsman approach include the Lafayette, Indiana, *Journal & Courier*; the St. Petersburg, Florida, *Times* and *Evening Independent*; the Utica, New York, *Observer-Dispatch*; the Rockford, Illinois, *Morning Star and Register*; the Milwaukee, Wisconsin, *Journal*; and the Washington *Post*. More recently, local radio and television stations, such as WFAA-TV in Dallas and WISN-TV in Milwaukee, have offered the same kind of service to their listeners.

Many of these complaints against local media outlets involve grievances by citizens who feel that accounts of particular crimes have been badly reported, sensationalized, exaggerated or, in a few instances, underreported. There is no reason why local police cannot take advantage of the existence of an ombudsman at a newspaper or radio-television station to register their own complaints, as long they believe their complaints to be well founded, and are made with an awareness of the different functions of the police and the media.

Mutual Education

The most vital approach to improved relations between the police and the media is mutual education.

Not many years ago, Norman E. Isaacs, then the managing editor of the Louisville *Times*, told an audience at Northwestern University that crime reporting was basically "the same kind of job that was being done 25 or 30 years before, and it was a rotten job then." Justice Wiley Rutledge, in a Supreme Court decision, wrote that, with notable exceptions, "There is perhaps no area of news more inaccurately reported factually, on the whole . . . than legal news."[8] But in the years since 1950, newspapers have become increasingly aware of the need for specialists in the reporting of crime news. More and more papers are using trained experts; for example, the New York *Times* has used former lawyers and, in one case, a former assistant United States attorney, to report crime news. The Medill School of Journalism subsidizes a three-month seminar for newspapermen to further their education. Stanford University has spent over one million dollars for mid-career educational programs for experienced jornalists. Much of this education and training is in the area of legal and crime reporting.

What is obviously needed is the same kind of mid-career training and education for police personnel in the techniques, methods, and operations of the mass media. Such education might be provided by the often-proposed national police academy. It might come from a subsidy by a local newspaper, which might conduct such a course in the media for police officers or cooperate with a local university in offering such training. The university might offer, through its journalism or mass communication departments, media courses especially designed for police personnel.

One worthwhile innovation was undertaken in 1973 when law enforcement officers in the city and county of Sumter, South Carolina, completed a college-credit course, perhaps the first in the nation, in press law and press relations. The courses were given by the journalism faculty of the University of South Carolina, and the class of 15 included the Sumter police chief, the county sheriff, and the police chief of nearby Manning. During the semester, the executive editor of the Sumter *Daily Item* addressed the class on the newsman's position in police-press relations. It was felt that the police officers ended the courses with a much greater perception of the mass media than when they began the courses.

Because the press's relations with the mass media are so crucial

[8] Lofton, *Justice and the Press*, p. 279.

to effective law enforcement, police education in the ways of the media is vital. A police officer should understand the theory of the press; how the local press functions, its techniques and personnel. He must understand the relationship between the editors and the reporters (whose influence on newspapers are vastly underrated), the problems of deadlines and mechanical limitations, and how decisions are made on the placement and emphasis of news stories, particularly those involving crime. He should understand the laws of libel as they affect the reporting of crime news. He should know how and when to go "off the record" (or speak without attribution), when to give the press what it wants and when to refuse, and how to refuse with tact and diplomacy. The police officer ought to study the newspaper, the radio, and the television stations in his community and then put that knowledge to effective use in the interest of better law enforcement.

Student Checklist

1. Can you describe the percentage of crime news contained in the average daily newspaper in the United States?
2. Do you know why the treatment the media give to crime news is so important?
3. Do you know how the media can increase crime?
4. Can you compare the responsibility of the press with responsibility of the police?

Topics for Discussion

1. Discuss how the media may actually increase crime.
2. Discuss some of the reasons for a code of conduct for the media.
3. Discuss the police responsibility and the press responsibility.
4. Discuss those things the police should not volunteer to the media about a crime.

ANNOTATED BIBLIOGRAPHY

Lofton, John. *Justice and the Press.* Boston: Beacon Press, 1966. A valuable history of the conflict between the demands of a free press and the right to a fair trial, delineating the responsibilities of both the press and the bench-bar-law enforcement personnel. Good summaries of American cases that excited wide interest: Sacco-Vanzetti, the Lindbergh kidnapping, Billie Sol Estes, and Dr. Sam Sheppard, among others. In the appendix are various guidelines for press and bar, adopted in cities and states across the country, and the landmark Sheppard decision.

Lange, Baker, and Ball. *Mass Media and Violence*, Vol. XI. A Report to the National Commission on the Causes and Prevention of Violence. Washington, D.C.: Library of Congress, 1969. This comprehensive report contains helpful accounts of civil disturbances of the 1960s, and the media coverage of them, coverage that either inflamed or quieted down the disturbances. There are descriptions of instances of cooperation between the media and the police and discussions of what happens when such cooperation is lacking. The appendix carries discussions of the need for guidelines for media and police and includes specific guidelines adopted by the networks, TV stations, radio stations, and newspapers.

MacDougall, Curtis D. *The Press and its Problems.* Dubuque, Iowa: Wm. C. Brown Company, 1964. This book contains an analysis of the press's attitude toward coverage of crime and how, in practice over the years, this practice has changed, with examples of coverage of various criminal cases. Among the problems explored are whether coverage of crime glorifies lawbreakers, whether newspapers interfere with the administration of justice, and what effect newspapers should strive for in the handling of crime news.

Rivers, Blankenburg, Starck, and Reeves. *Back-Talk (Press Councils in America).* San Francisco: Canfield Press, 1972. This book, written by those who established and operated several local press councils, describes how these councils worked (and, in some cases, did not work). It tells why the press councils are needed, how they are formed, and what effect they have on the mass media. The growth of state and regional councils is also discussed.

The study of this chapter will enable you to:

1. Describe the origination of police–community relations as a separate operational concept.
2. Write a short essay describing the difference between police–public relations and police–community relations.
3. Describe the major purpose of community relations activity by a police department.
4. List weaknesses in the public relations concept.
5. List six examples of police public relations programs.

9

The Difference Between Public Relations and Police-Community Relations

During the short history of police–community relations, there has been little agreement on what it actually is. This lack of agreement among law enforcement professionals has resulted in the development of programs and approaches to community relations that reflect the personal views of local administrators more than they reflect any widely accepted body of knowledge. As a result, there has been considerable confusion about what community relations efforts should accomplish, and how.

It is generally accepted that police–community relations as a separate operational concept originated in the St. Louis Police Department in 1957. Since that time, the community relations concept has experienced sporadic growth throughout the nation. While the need for community relations is widely accepted today as a crucial part of police administration, its current prominence is of short duration. For example, a recent study conducted by the California Attorney General's Office indicated that of 69 California police agencies having community relations units or officers, over 60 percent were established since 1969; the earliest was established in 1962.[1]

The rapid growth of community relations programs resulted from the violent confrontations of the mid- to late sixties. In larger cities and urban centers, law enforcement administrators realized that they were confronting problems that traditional police tactics were not capable of solving. Administrators in smaller cities, usually on the urban fringes, recognized the possibility that violence might spill over into their communities. In both cases, the creation of specialized units, or the assign-

[1] Attorney General's Advisory Commission on Community–Police Relations, *The Police in the California Community* (Sacramento: State of California, 1973).

211

ment of so-called community relations duties to specific officers, was the response. It was widely felt that such specialized responsibilities could help improve communications between increasingly activist minority groups and the police. In fact, the primary goal of such units at the outset was usually to serve as go-betweens; interpreting the attitudes, desires, and intentions of minority citizens and police agencies to each other.

Over the years, additional duties have been assigned to the community relations specialty. Thus, the community relations function has been variously described as a problem-avoidance methodology,[2] an "art" which is embodied in police administrative philosophy,[3] a way of integrating police operations with community needs and desires,[4] and a way of accommodating the reality that the police are part of the political system.[5] These views have resulted in police involvement in remedial education projects, employment counseling, encounter groups, intensive training in human relations, teaching school, inspecting residences for antiburglary campaigns, and dozens of other activities.

This dispersion of effort both reflects and intensifies the lack of agreement on just what community relations is. However, most theoreticians and practitioners agree on one point: what community relations should not be. The President's Commission on Law Enforcement and the Administration of Justice stated that community relations is:

> ... not a public relations program to "sell the police image" to the people. It is not a set of expedients whose purpose is to tranquilize for a time an angry neighborhood by, for example, suddenly promoting a few Negro officers in the wake of a racial disturbance.[6]

Despite this warning, and despite the fact that most professionals recognize that community relations must go further than mere image improvement on the part of law enforcement, there is considerable con-

[2] International City Manager's Association, *Police Community Relations Programs* (Washington, D.C., 1967).

[3] Howard H. Earle, *Police-Community Relations: Crisis in our Time.* Second Edition (Springfield, Ill.: Charles C. Thomas, 1970).

[4] Lee P. Brown, "Police–Community Relations Evaluation Project" (unpublished, undated manuscript).

[5] Attorney General's Advisory Commission, *The Police in the California Community.*

[6] President's Commission on Law Enforcement and the Administration of Justice, *The Challenge of Crime in a Free Society* (Washington, D.C.: U.S. Govt. Printing Office, 1967).

fusion between the concepts of public relations and community relations. Too often the tendency is to regard community relations as:

> . . . public relations, in the traditional sense, i.e., the development of a favorable public impression of a given product—often called "imagery"[7]

There is a definite relationship between community relations and public relations. It is important, however, to recognize their differences and to practice both concepts in a way that will meet the needs of the contemporary police agency most effectively. Doing so requires: (1) developing an acceptable definition of each, and (2) developing an analytical framework within which they can be examined.

We have already noted the problems involved in defining community relations. However, for purposes of the following discussion, it is necessary to construct a definition that includes the most significant characteristics of those definitions discussed earlier. We also need a definition that can be generally applied to a wide range of police efforts. The following definition is suggested.

> Community-police relations is a philosophy of administering and providing police services, which embodies all activities within a given jurisdiction aimed at involving members of the community and the police in the determination of: (1) what police services will be provided; (2) how they will be provided; and (3) how the police and members of the community will resolve common problems.[8]

The key element in this definition is that community relations is a philosophy of police administration that basically involves integrating police operations with community needs in an ongoing fashion.

Admittedly, the preceding definition is not too specific. It must be as broad as it is, however, to include the many activities which make up community relations. Any definition of public relations is also broad. It, too, must include the wide variety of operations carried out in its name. For example, Webster defines public relations as:

> The promotion of rapport and goodwill between a person, firm, or institution and other persons, special publics, or the community at

---

[7] George D. Eastman and Esther M. Eastman, *Municipal Police Administration*, Sixth Edition (Washington, D.C.: International City Management Association, 1969).

[8] Attorney General's Advisory Commission, *The Police in the California Community*.

large through the distribution of interpretative material, the develop-
ment of neighborly interchange, and the assessment of public reaction.[9]

A review of various texts on public relations reveals a variety of definitions. They all have one element in common: each holds that public relations includes those activities that attempt to explain agency goals and operations to the public and to gain public support for those goals and operations.

These two definitions should not lead to the conclusion that either community relations or public relations can be isolated or explained easily. Neither concept is as simple as a basic definition might imply. Rather, the two are complex and can only be understood when several of their individual characteristics are examined.

A Common Framework for Analyzing Community Relations and Public Relations

Since community relations and public relations are related, and since they are both properly part of police administration, it is important to understand their differences. In the final analysis, it is not a question of whether criminal justice agencies should practice the tactics of either; rather, it is a question of balance and emphasis.

A useful analytical framework for these two elusive concepts focuses on three characteristics of their activities:

1. The purpose of the activity.
2. The processes involved in the activity.
3. The extent of citizen involvement.

Purpose of the Activity

Perhaps the most confusing element of police operations is their purpose. While it might initially seem simple to explain why the police do what they do, careful study indicates otherwise. This is true for almost all police activities, not just for those related to community relations. For

---

[9] *Webster's Third New International Dictionary of the English Language Un-abridged* (Springfield, Mass.: G. & C. Merriam Company, 1971).

example, it can be stated that the purpose of police patrol is to prevent crime from occurring, to minimize response time to calls for service, to provide opportunities for contacts between citizens and police officers, and to identify conditions that encourage criminal activity. It is difficult to pinpoint which of these purposes is paramount at a given time; they all are applicable and might be merged into a general purpose, such as the provision of crime-related services to the public.

It is also important to note that stated purposes often conflict with what is actually being done. Purposes generally embody values which the police agency is attempting to secure. In practice, however, other values than those set forth in writing may motivate action. For example, the California studies discussed earlier indicated that often "there is little clear and definitive correlation between stated goals and current programming efforts."[10] Data provided by responding California law enforcement agencies reflected that their tenth ranked goal was to "improve youth," yet young people were the most frequently identified target group for community relations programs. Additionally, fewer than 7 percent of the agency goals were to "improve the police image" or "make the field officer's job easier," yet some 25.1 percent of all programs described by the agencies fell into a public information category in which most public relations or image-enhancement activities are contained. Careful consideration must always be given to what is being done, to determine whether or not it agrees with stated values and purposes.

One common purpose of public relations activities is to develop and maintain a good environment in which to operate. Since the majority of bureaucratic organizations, including the police, are basically open systems, they rely upon other agencies for support. The police must rely upon the general public for a minimum level of support or noninterference to accomplish their mission; they must ask legislative bodies for budgetary funds; and they depend on other elements of the criminal justice system to process the persons they introduce into that system. It is important, therefore, that they influence, as much as possible, the attitudes that these various institutions hold toward them.

[10] Attorney General's Advisory Commission, *The Police in the California Community.*

To attain a desirable operating environment, the police use a public relations concept which works toward this unifying theme. They inform the various significant publics about the police mission and its priorities to enhance their positive image, to minimize obstacles to policies and procedures, and to encourage support for their policies and operations.

Public information is perhaps the most routine and widely applied public relations activity in which the police, and most other organizations, engage. It is a strongly held value in our culture that the informed and educated citizen is the best participant in democratic government. This has often led to the belief that if people understand why certain agencies of government, such as the police, perform as they do, then they will be supportive of that performance. There is, however, a tremendous amount of misinformation about the police among the members of the general public. This misinformation is fostered in part by the popular entertainment media, which portray the police as glamorous, crime-fighters most of the time. It is further promoted by the fact that most news coverage of police activities focuses upon their crime-related duties, because these are the most newsworthy. Although these emphases are understandable, they seriously misrepresent the totality of the police job, which consists, for the most part, of noncriminal responsibilities. Still, it is not uncommon for police public information campaigns to build upon such misperceptions by largely confining themselves to criminal themes.

Image enhancement is a logical extension of the public information effort. The police realize that community-wide respect and cooperation are difficult goals since there are so many negative aspects of the role that society has assigned to them, and because they are charged with making large numbers of people adhere to unpopular standards. It is important that they promote a positive image of themselves whenever possible. In most cases, this takes the form of stressing the "helping" and "emergency" attributes of the police role. Public information campaigns that focus upon the police officer rescuing lost children, shooting it out with armed robbers, and providing first aid at the scene of an automobile accident serve the image enhancement purpose well.

Other purposes of public relations efforts are to minimize obstacles to police policies and procedures, and to encourage support for police policies and operations. Overcoming obstacles implies conscious opposition. Support, on the other hand, can range from passive to active behavior—from not consciously opposing the police to consciously promoting and supporting them. For example, as long as the vast majority of the citizens do not object to certain police operations, the administrator can assume some degree of acceptance. Such passive support may not be particularly helpful to the police department, but it need not be harmful. In certain areas, such as a campaign to burglar-proof residences, public support and cooperation of an active nature are necessary.

It is obvious that the separation of the purposes of public relations into specific categories is artificial, for they are interrelated and overlapping. A single police public relations project may include elements of several or all of the purposes described. Yet these purposes provide a basis for analyzing a project and they reflect its inherent values.

Community relations programs can, and often do, have many of the same purposes as those listed for public relations. Their own goals go beyond public relations values. Community relations programs strive to integrate community forces and law enforcement agencies into active partnerships for dealing with the many social and criminal problems assigned to the police. In this context, the primary purposes of community relations activities are: (1) to determine the appropriate range of services that the police will provide to the community; (2) to determine how these services will be provided (in the sense of appropriate tactics and procedures); and (3) to establish ongoing mechanisms for resolving problems of mutual interest to both the police and the various segments of the community.

These broad purposes encompass a wide range of activities and objectives. Yet their philosophy is simply that of providing police services that stress the interrelationships and dependencies of law enforcement practitioners and citizens. The police must depend upon the community as a source of legitimacy: the community must depend upon the police to provide services essential to maintaining an atmosphere of stability. The ultimate purpose of community relations activities is to create and maintain mutually supportive relationships between police and citizens.

Processes Involved in the Activity

The processes include those services provided in conjunction with particular programs: the direction of information flow; the hierarchical level of police agency involvement; and the breadth of agency involvement. Since these activities are conducted to accomplish agency purposes such as image enhancement and the gaining of public support, it is administratively advantageous to make them as simple and controllable as possible to facilitate their repetition and not divert energies from other, more highly valued tasks. An excellent example of such routinization is the agency-initiated press release. By developing standardized forms, regular distribution channels, and central review, the agency assures prompt, uniform, and administratively sanctioned promulgation of its stories.

Closely related to the routinization and standardization of public relations activities is the fact that they include a range of services designed primarily to serve agency needs. Public relations strives to make the agency's job easier. Thus, it is to be expected that even those activities performed as services to persons or organizations outside the agency are primarily designed to benefit the agency. Again, the agency-initiated press release is a good example. Although such releases serve the news media by providing newsworthy information in a readily digestible format, the selection of material and its initial presentation are structured to maximize their image-building or support-gathering potential for the agency.

The press release also illustrates another characteristic of the public relations activity; namely, a one-way flow of information: most information flows *out* from the agency. Although information enters the agency via questions or comments made by newsmen, this is minimal and not a major element of the activity. This outward flow pattern reflects the belief that if the various publics in the agency's operating environment are adequately "informed" about police operations, they will be more supportive of them.

The final two descriptive characteristics to be examined in our analysis of public relations efforts involve organizational responsibility for, and participation in, such efforts. Since virtually all police agencies are hierarchical in nature, it is relatively easy to pinpoint management responsibility. However, it is not possible to generalize about the level of responsibility for public relations activities; this responsibility varies dramatically among departments. It is important, however, to identify responsibility when analyzing programs, for this is a good indicator of the importance attached to the activities by the department's administration. Generally, if a program is considered to be of major significance, it will be conducted by a relatively high-ranking member.

It is easier to generalize about the breadth of agency involvement. Since the public relations thrust is essentially to gain support, and since it is usually structured to be routine and standardized, it does not often involve significant commitments of energy from all elements of the department. Rather, public relations efforts tend to be narrowly assigned, usually to supportive elements such as administrative units. Public relations is a tool of police management, not an essential component of operating philosophy. Thus, it is easily compartmentalized.

The processes that comprise community relations activities are often significantly different than those just discussed for public relations. In the first instance, the components do not lend themselves to standardization and routinization, if they are properly performed. Since community relations activities are designed to perform an integrative function—linking the police agency to a wide array of publics and interests in the community—their functions must be flexible and capable of rapid change. The situations that demand quick attention from police administrators are not often compatible with routine, standard operating procedures; they are often a reaction to the insensitivity inherent in those very procedures. However, elements of community relations may also become routine.

In the area of services, community relations departs radically from public relations. It was noted that public relations services are primarily agency-oriented. The services performed as part of the community relations process, in contrast, should manifest a significant tendency toward the needs of clients, other institutions with which the police agency works, and pertinent publics in the community. The integrative, problem-solving nature of community relations requires that it provide services that are identified as important to the publics served. For example, a police storefront center in an urban neighborhood can serve the police by providing information on criminal activity, by acting as a complaint center, and by improving communication with citizens. If it is truly a community relations activity, it will also provide citizens with services that they identify as crucial, such as liaison with other government agencies, assistance in domestic crises, and counseling services. There is an intentional balance of self-serving and citizen-serving processes.

This balance includes reciprocal information flow. The communication process in community relations services not only to broadcast the police point of view, but also to stimulate useful discussion of issues and to solicit feedback from appropriate sources in the community. This has been one of the major stated values of community relations since its inception, although, in practice, there is a common tendency to emphasize the outward flowing messages.

As in the case of public relations, the hierarchical setting of responsibility for community relations activities is so varied that it defies generalization. If community relations activities are specialized, their responsibility should undoubtedly be that of a ranking agency person. But if the activities are expected to pervade the entire organization or involve only specific, line-level units, responsibility might be assigned to lower levels. Each instance must be evaluated independently.

The breadth of agency involvement is a different matter. While certain aspects of community relations may be assigned to specific departmental units, involvement generally crosses divisional boundaries. This requires a distinction between specialized programs, which may have relevance only to a certain geographical or functional unit, and general practices aimed at accomplishing community relations objectives department- and communitywide. The former are likely to be successful on a long-term basis only if the latter are part of the department's operating philosophy.

Citizen Involvement

In our analysis of public relations and community relations efforts, we must also consider the extent of citizen involvement in these activities. Although the police have either assumed or have been assigned responsibility for dealing with many of our more complex social problems, it is folly to think that they alone can solve any of them. In reality, the police are only able to provide limited specialized attention to the most crucial problems, usually in a crisis reactive fashion. Real solutions require much broader efforts by many segments of the community. Even effective crisis reactions often require the involvement of nonpolice resources.

In most public relations activities, citizen involvement is kept to a minimum. It is generally passive; the citizens receive information dispensed by the law enforcement agency or consume services that primarily serve agency purposes. In most cases, citizens are reasons for, but not participants in, the activity.

In contrast, community relations activities often rely heavily upon citizen involvement. The citizen is, by definition, an active participant. The police agency does not relinquish responsibility for administering agency programs or practices relating to community relations. It does, however, ensure that citizen resources are properly accommodated, both to provide assistance in accomplishing police goals and to stimulate feedback on issues and problems.

Weaknesses in the Public Relations Concept

The preceding discussion has described characteristics of those activities that commonly comprise public relations and community relations, in accordance with the earlier definitions of each. There is some danger in making such generalizations; obviously, not every activity in either category will possess all of the qualities associated with it here. These generalizations do serve, however, as useful tools in making judgments about the real thrust of activities carried out in the name of either of the concepts.

Given the earlier definition of community–police relations, it is apparent that public relations activities are quite different from those of community relations. Public relations activities are certainly a part of a properly applied program of community relations, but they are not an adequate substitute for such a program. Table 9-1 indicates that public relations activities are commonly characterized by a thrust toward image enhancement, a one-way communication flow, a highly centralized organizational arrangement, and a failure to respond to resources and needs represented by the communities served.

The confusion of the principles of public relations with that of community relations results in a number of problems. First, public relations techniques fail to provide true problem-avoidance and problem-solving mechanisms, which are at the heart of the community relations concept. The public relations program is too often concerned with defending and preserving the department's current operations and image than with coping with problems in the operating environment. An active

TABLE 9-1. **Characteristics of Public Relations as Compared to Community Relations**

	Public Relations	Community Relations
Purpose	Attain-maintain good environment Inform public Enhance image Minimize obstacles Stimulate support	Develop police–community partnership Integrate community needs with police practices
Process	Routinized functions comprise activities Agency-oriented services One-way (outward) information flow Responsibility compartmentalized	Flexible and adaptable functions comprise activities Community-oriented services Two-way information flow Responsibility dispersed throughout agency
Citizen Involvement	Consciously kept to a minimum	Actively sought and stimulated

community relations philosophy, in contrast, makes it a point to identify such developing problems and to stimulate alternative responses that can then be tested by proper agency authorities and significant community forces to determine their applicability.

Second, public relations-oriented efforts often reach the wrong targets. Since they are concerned with maintaining the department's image, they often aim at solving problems through intermediaries. For example, the provision of public speakers is a common public relations device. The department thoughtfully provides knowledgeable officers to speak to civic groups, clubs, schools, and business concerns. It is basically an educational effort, but it generally reaches those citizens who are not really police problems and who are likely to be supportive of the department. The speaker talks "at" his audience, answers a few questions, and returns to headquarters. In most instances, everyone is pleased. There has been no dialogue, however, and the citizens have rarely been stimulated to take an active part in solving any police-community problems. Rather, the department has used another organization as an intermediary in getting its message out, hopeful that by building support among such people, future problems might be averted.

Third, the public relations thrust can actually alienate many concerned citizens. When it becomes apparent that the thrust of an agency's community-oriented efforts is to maintain its current position with no real concern for soliciting or using outside assistance, most persons sincerely interested in helping will become disillusioned and either withdraw or become vocally critical. Additionally, many of the intermediaries upon which the public relations-oriented department relies to get its message out can become disenchanted with their roles. The community newspaper, for example, which receives only superficial news releases that fail to discuss significant issues of concern, will soon refuse to print them. Only so much descriptive material about training courses, medal of valor awards, and numbers of arrests made during a month will be printed if real problems of rising crime rates, citizen dissatisfaction with police performance, or similar issues are being ignored.

Fourth, public relations efforts often are ineptly applied to deal with crucial issues. By their nature, public relations tactics are able to deal with these problems only in a superficial fashion; they lack any real ability to induce internal change or to mobilize external resources in an active problem-solving partnership with the department. The purpose of public relations is not to solve problems by dealing with their substance. Rather, it is to change perceptions of the problem among significant publics. Thus, when any bureaucratic organization attempts to solve major operating problems through a primarily public relations apparatus, the superficiality of the approach is more likely to aggravate matters.

Finally, public relations is always regarded as a secondary element of police management. Its compartmentalization puts it in a disadvantageous position to influence decisions on policy or procedures. Its utility to the agency lies not in participating in making such decisions, but in assuring their acceptance once they are made. This relegation to secondary decision-making status identifies (to all careful students of agency operations) the lack of influence that public relations activities really have.

Strengths of the Public Relations Concept

The public relations concept has a distinct and valuable place in agency operations as an element of an overall community relations program when the latter is truly part of administrative philosophy. There are at least five functions that are essentially public relations in thrust but which complement community relations efforts.

First, the public relations purpose of informing the public can be valuable to both the law enforcer and the citizen if it extends to critical issues. The "whys" of police policies and procedures can be explained to the public. The alternatives to current practice, as seen by the agency, can be explained and any trade-offs outlined. But such explanations must be straightforward; this is the point at which the public relations effort supports the community relations effort. These explanations must honestly portray the police position to inform, not to sell the status quo. Proper performance of police tasks, not public relations techniques, must do the selling.

The second function that can be properly served by public relations efforts is the development of community support. In keeping with a community relations philosophy of stimulating a broadly based partnership in combating crime, the generation of support must be only a part of the overall mission, and it must be done with scrupulous honesty. The agency should emphasize the stimulation of active support, including the involvement of citizens in crime prevention and control activities. The agency should be wary of the passive, lip-service kind of support that characterizes the purely public relations approach. Stimulating citizen involvement represents the greatest kind of support any criminal justice agency can promote.

This leads to the third use of public relations activities as part of a balanced, community relations philosophy: the supplementing of agency operations and specialized programs. Once again, this use relates to the value of informing the public about what the police are trying to accomplish. In this sense, public relations is appropriately used to initiate discussion about an agency program and to encourage feedback from concerned citizens. It is also appropriately used to explain in some detail the "whys" of an activity. It should not be used to overshadow shortcomings with success stories or to refute criticism without careful consideration of its accuracy.

The fourth, and perhaps the most important function that public relations activities can perform as part of an overall community relations effort, is to integrate the many diverse undertakings of the department into a coherent whole for the public. The contemporary police agency performs a confusing variety of tasks, ranging from catching criminals to providing on-site assistance in the most serious of man's emotional crises. To perform these tasks, we have devised numerous specialized programs, activities, and techniques. True public understanding of the police role and mission requires that they be exposed to the police operation in its entirety. It falls to the police organization to construct and present a balanced and accurate picture of its mission for public study and reaction. This implies emphasizing both the mundane and the sensational, the dull and the controversial—and how they relate to one another.

Finally, public relations can continue to perform many of its traditional functions even when operating in a community relations mode, but these functions become subordinated to the principles of the broader concept. For example, it is unrealistic to ask any bureaucratic organization to abandon its efforts to achieve support for its programs. The realities of competing for scarce operating resources—money, men and material—preclude such simplistic proposals. Nevertheless, the achievement of support, including image enhancement, must be accomplished in accordance with a strict set of guidelines requiring honesty and integrity in the tactics used. Building the agency's image should be a conscientiously controlled means of providing better service, not the ultimate goal of the agency's community relations program.

Examples of Public Relations Programs

Thus far, this chapter has focused on the differences between the concepts of public relations and community relations as they are commonly applied by the contemporary law enforcement agency. In this final section, attention will turn to examining several public relations programs. There are few "pure" public relations programs, just as there are few agencies that embody only the characteristics associated with the concept in the preceding pages. Any evaluation of an agency's orientation must be made by examining the total structure of its operations. Some representative examples of community outreach efforts are described in the following pages.

Speakers Bureau. One of the most common public relations programs is that of the speakers bureau. Most law enforcement agencies will provide speakers to local civic or business organizations upon request. Typically, these speakers provide a short informative talk on such topics as drug abuse, shoplifting, traffic safety, or burglary protection. Occasionally they provide informational brochures for the audience.

Ride-Along. Another common program is the citizen ride-along. This program allows members of the general public to accompany a police officer on routine patrol. While some jurisdictions place few restrictions on the ride-along program, many require that the rider be free of a criminal record or meet requirements of age, occupation, or other significant conditions. The ride-along program does have elements of mutual education for both citizen and police officer, but its primary purpose is to help the citizen "understand" the difficulties of modern police work. See Chapter 7 for a fuller description of a ride-along program.

Police Station Tours. Like the provision of speakers, the guided tour of the police station has become standard fare for many schools and civic organizations. Depending upon the size and sophistication of the agency, such tours include visiting the jail, crime lab, line-up room, communications center, records center, and various operating bureaus or divisions. Tours are often arranged in conjunction with police week ceremonies.

Awareness-Alert Programs. The issuance of bulletins about particular crime problems occurring in the community are also illustrative of the public relations program in the sense that they are primarily informative. During the holiday season, many police agencies will issue circulars to businessmen pointing out various shoplifting techniques. Some agencies also insert burglary prevention messages in public utility billing statements or bank statements. Although these awareness notices often call upon the citizen to help the police by making it hard for the criminal to consummate his unlawful act, they seldom follow up on such requests, nor do they provide any realistic means for helping the citizen to do so.

Citizen Recognition. Many agencies give awards to citizens who provide particularly helpful services to the police. Such awards may be given for bravery or merely for reporting a suspicious person who turns out to be a burglar or armed robber. In either case, the agency makes a formal presentation of a plaque or some other suitable award to show its appreciation for an informed and involved citizenry.

Figure 9-1. The precinct tour is at the simplest level of public relations programs. Yet the goodwill and mutual understanding that it engenders are strong proof of its values.

Dual Programs

The preceding activities are predominantly public relations-oriented. They seldom go beyond the purposes of informing the public and enhancing the police image. There is another category of activities, however, which includes both the elements of public relations and community relations. The ultimate impact of these dual programs depends upon the emphasis placed on the various elements and upon the context in which they are applied. Examples of such activities are described in the following pages.

Citizen Watch. The many varieties of citizen watch programs range from those in which residents of a neighborhood are asked to keep an eye on their neighbors' homes for strange activities, to those in which citizens are mobilized into committees to work with local police units in identifying local problems and developing responses to them. In the first instance, the police ask citizens to report any suspicious activities occurring in the neighborhood. The citizen merely becomes an extension of the police patrol apparatus. In the latter instance, the police officer on the beat and the citizen endeavor to perfect their partnership responsibilities in identifying those problems that can be ultimately corrected by police intervention.

Rumor Control. The rumor control program reached its zenith during the days of violent street confrontations, generally between the police and residents of racial and ethnic minority neighborhoods. It basically involves developing information-gathering and promulgation networks for identifying unfounded or exaggerated rumors and for counteracting them with the facts before they can precipitate trouble. Usually, local leaders, such as teachers, ministers, and others, are used to counteract the rumors. In many communities, the rumor control operation never went beyond providing information. In others, however, the rumor control network has developed into a useful forum for discussing common police problems in minority neighborhoods.

Storefront Centers. The establishment of storefront centers, primarily in disadvantaged neighborhoods, has received considerable attention in recent years. Billed as a means of bringing the police officer closer to the people, the storefront puts police representatives in commercial buildings in the neighborhoods they serve. The centers serve as complaint reception locations, mini-precinct houses, meeting places, and numerous other purposes. Ideally, the storefront center can provide a useful bridge between the community and the police. Its effectiveness, however, depends upon the extent to which it embodies principles of public relations (e.g., one-way information flow and providing a means for selling the police viewpoint) or principles of community relations (e.g., providing a forum for mutual problem-solving).

Conclusion

It must once again be stressed that the difference between public relations and community relations is not always clear-cut. The guideposts developed in this chapter can help the student make some informed judgments about certain police activities, but such judgments must always be tempered by the context in which the activities occur. The contemporary police agency embodies a complex set of interrelationships. The needs of community service must always be met within the constraints of the prevailing sociopolitical environment. This will always require that the agency rely upon public relations tactics to help assure its position in relation to other forces at work in the community. The extent to which such primarily self-serving devices influence the agency's receptivity to community input is the ultimate determinant of whether the agency is operating under a philosophy of community relations or public relations.

Student Checklist

1. Can you describe the difference between police–community relations and police–public relations?
2. Can you list six examples of police public relations programs?
3. Can you describe how police–community relations originated as a separate operational concept?
4. What is the major purpose of police community relations activity?

Topics for Discussion

1. Discuss the difference between police–public relations and police community relations.
2. Discuss the major purpose of police–community relations activity.
3. Discuss what prompted the origination of police–community relations activity.
4. Discuss the major purpose of police–public relations.

ANNOTATED BIBLIOGRAPHY

Attorney General's Advisory Commission on Community-Police Relations. *The Police in the California Community*. Sacramento: State of California, 1973. Reports on a comprehensive study of police–community relations in California, including analyses of police role development, minority recruitment and retention problems, significant forces influencing the development of attitudes toward the police, and the qualitative nature of community relations programs conducted by California police agencies.

Black, Sam. *Practical Public Relations*. London: Pitman Publishing, 1970. Examines public relations as concept and practice in Great Britain. Its applicability to the American scene lies mainly in its coverage of public relations methodologies, all of which have application in this country. The first section examines objects and aims of public relations. The second section goes into detailed consideration of press relations, use of the printed word, photography, exhibits, radio and television, and the spoken word.

Blumenthal, L. Roy. *The Practice of Public Relations*. New York: Macmillan, 1972. Analyzes and describes public relations from a business perspective. Provides supplemental reading lists on each major topic covered.

Brandstatter, A. F., and Louis A. Radelet. *Police and Community Relations: A Sourcebook*. Beverly Hills, Calif.: The Glencoe Press, 1968. This book of readings covers a wide range of subjects relevant to police–community relations. Of particular interest is Section 5, which describes principles underlying contemporary programs in community relations.

Coffey, Alan; Edward Eldefonso; and Walter Hartinger. *Human Relations: Law Enforcement in a Changing Community*. Englewood Cliffs, N.J.: Prentice-Hall, 1971. This book sets a foundation for examining the subject of police–community relations through the medium of the social problems assigned to the police for mediation or resolution. It proceeds to examine prejudice and attitude formulation and concludes with an examination of police–community relations programs.

Earle, Howard H. *Police–Community Relations: Crisis in our Time.* Springfield, Ill.: Charles C. Thomas, 1970. From the perspective of an executive of a major county police agency, Earle details the essential elements of a community relations program as he views it. The book is excellent for its consideration of the wide array of activities commonly undertaken as community relations oriented.

Myren, Richard A. *Decentralization and Citizen Participation in Criminal Justice Systems.* Public Administration Review. Vol. XXXII, Special Issue, October 1972. This article, part of a symposium, examines citizen participation in the process of criminal justice. It examines particularly the ways in which citizens can participate in the provision of police services and the extent to which such participation is practiced.

Robinson, Edward J. *Communication and Public Relations.* Columbus, Ohio: Charles E. Merrill, 1966. This book uses the medium of case studies to examine public relations as a communication process between institutions and publics. The communicative element is stressed throughout the presentation and serves as the theoretical underpinning for the entire presentation.

The study of this chapter will enable you to:

1. Describe how scientific management has operated as a negative factor in police–community relations.
2. List the advantages and disadvantages of decentralization of the police.
3. Describe why the use of police discretion is necessary.
4. Write a short essay showing how the use of police discretion may appear to be injustice.
5. Compare police priorities in apprehending bank robbers and vandals.
6. List some police practices that destroy good relations with the community.

10

Destructive Police Practices

In recent years the law enforcement profession has been severely criticized for its practices and methods of operations. As a result, thorough examinations have been conducted to assess the degree of alienation that exists between the police and society, and attempts have been made to bridge the gap between the police and the citizen. One of these attempts at bridging the gap is the establishment of community relations programs to inform the citizens of the problems facing the police. This communication is felt to be necessary because of the social isolation that has developed between the police and the community.

Jerome Skolnick suggests that there is a mutual social rejection between police and society.[1] According to Skolnick, this social rejection results from three factors: (1) social isolation, (2) police solidarity, and (3) danger. Therefore, current community relations efforts are all designed to combat the alienation that results from this lack of communication between the police and the citizens.

One often hears police officers say that the community does not understand them or the police role. But why does this misunderstanding exist? Some commentators blame the police; they argue that the police themselves fail to understand the police role or how they interrelate with the community. This view originates in the historical concept of the police role. In the past, the police considered themselves to be purely ministerial officers, enforcing the law evenly and without the

[1] Jerome H. Skolnick, *Justice Without Trial: Law Enforcement in Democratic Society* (New York: Wiley, 1966).

233

use of discretion. Modern concepts of police administration recognize that discretion is an important part of the police role, yet the historical viewpoint that the police must be impartial in the enforcement of the law still carries the most weight. As a result, the police officer, himself, is confused about his exact role. This confusion alienates him from the citizenry because he cannot explain why he believes he should enforce the law impartially when, in actuality, he is practicing discretionary enforcement.

Any organization has a strong sense of the norms and values that have developed during its life, which influence its contemporary actions. Some commentators argue that the police professional has failed to examine the historical development of the police organization and the effects that police history have upon citizen alienation. For example, police resistance to the demands of community control and of decentralized operations reflects the historical influence on the current norms and values. These citizen demands contradict police practices of the past quarter-century; the modern police manager seeks centralization as a way to achieve efficiency and effectiveness. One would suspect, however, that the contemporary police manager has forgotten the original motivation for this effort. If we were to return to the latter part of the nineteenth century, we would find that the practice of centralized control developed to help the chief of police gain control of the organization and eliminate corruption. While this was the major motivation behind centralization, it could not be formally stated. Rather, the demand for organizational efficiency was used as a justification.

Historical Development

We cannot examine the development of police organizational and management concepts without also considering historical developments in the management field. The drive for the improvement of police services occurred at the same time that there was a general demand for improvement in both business and government. It was a time of muckrakers and reformers. Society was growing more complex: reforms were required, not only in the United States but in Europe as well.

Many tend to view political reform as being separate from managerial reforms. Perhaps we would be more successful in tracing the current position of law enforcement if we would use the David Easton concept of systems analysis.[2] Easton would consider the law enforcement organization as one existing in a total environment that would be exercising demands upon the organization. Using his concept of scientific management, the system would have to reorder its priorities, at least minimally, to meet the demands for reform and efficiency. This concept of scientific management, while being responsive to the demands of the day, has led to many of the destructive police practices currently existing.

It is not the intent of this chapter to detail the history of this movement, yet a basic knowledge of its precepts is necessary for an understanding of contemporary problems. The scientific management movement resulted from the Industrial Revolution. If mass production was to be achieved, there had to be some uniformity and efficiency.

The early leaders in scientific management were Fredrick Taylor, (USA), Henri Fayol (France), and Max Weber (Germany). Their goals were to deal with the manner in which a job was performed and with the way things were organized. Their common theme was: (1) there was one best way to complete a task; and (2) there was a single organizational model that could be used uniformly, regardless of size or other conditions.

This theme was accepted by society: people could relate this approach to developments in science, in which absolute methods had to be followed. The efficiency criteria would be met by the use of scientific measurement devices. The fact that all processes would be scientifically evaluated and measured would remove the "people" element from management considerations. This would lessen political influence and remove corruption from governmental services.

These ideas were further refined by what might be called the second generation of management leaders. Lyndall Erwick and Luther Garlick had perhaps a greater direct effect on public administration and police services than those who preceded them. They formalized such concepts as "unity of command" and "span of control." They also developed a symbolic word, "POSDCORB," which, if followed, provided the manager with the elements of success.[3] This acronym stood for:

[2] David Easton, *Systems Analysis of Political Life* (New York: Wiley, 1965).

P–Planning
O–Organizing
S–Staffing
D–Directing
CO–Coordinating
R–Reporting
B–Budgeting

The influence that Erwick and Garlick had on the law enforcement field becomes evident when the works of the early leaders of police administration are examined. The International City Managers Association, O. W. Wilson, V. A. Leonard, and Bruce Smith reveal a search for the all-encompassing method and model organization.

These authorities were faced with the same difficulties encountered by their contemporaries in other areas of administrative thought. In their efforts to achieve efficiency, they neglected to consider social costs, the political environment, community culture, and citizen values. These exclusions were a continuous source of frustration. But instead of acknowledging the importance of these factors, they explained their frustrations in another way. Their refuge was to insist that they were on the right track, but that the means to achieve their goals had not yet been refined.

If we are to consider the destructive practices of the police, we must understand their origins. In most instances, if not all, they are the direct result of a striving to develop tests for efficiency. These are reflected in measurement criteria, centralization, and organizational models.

Systems and Community Values

The police occupy a strategic position in any society since they are charged with the responsibility of enforcing the norms of society. In order to perform this role, they must interact with the members of society. The importance of this interaction and cooperation varies with

[3] Bertram M. Gross, *The Managing of Organizations: The Administrative Struggle*, Vol. 1 (New York: The Free Press of Glencoe, 1964), p. 144.

the nature of the total society. In a strictly regulated society, the conflict in values becomes less important because the individual values tend to be less important. In societies where the individual himself is considered to be important, value conflicts become vital to the systems maintenance of the community, and the law enforcement value system must accommodate community values to a greater degree.

This value system has two principal elements. The first deals with the goal of efficiency; the second with a reward system to individual officers when they perform certain activities that are thought to be more important. This second element will be discussed in greater detail later.

How can the police goal of efficiency create conflict between themselves and the community? For most of us it is difficult to conceive of anyone objecting to an act based upon improving service and reducing cost. Yet this is exactly what is happening today.

An excellent example of this enigma is the issue of centralization versus decentralization of the police service. As an element of citizen control of the police, many community organizations are demanding that the police be decentralized. Those who advocate this concept believe centralization has made the police unresponsive to community problems. On the other hand, these people believe decentralization will bring the police and the citizens closer together. This is illustrated by the demand to get the police back on the beat.

The police response, supported by others in government, has been to resist such demands in most instances. If one examines their protestations, it becomes evident that police resistance to decentralization is rooted in the arguments put forward by the scientific management movement.

Although the police couch their arguments in terms of efficiency, response time, and need for command control, they fail to identify another element in their resistance to decentralization. James Q. Wilson, in describing this fear, has stated:

> Precinct commanders in a decentralized department would have greater freedom of action and more control over their patrolmen; precinct commanders in a dispersed department would surrender that control to whatever constellation of political forces the neighborhood might produce.[4]

[4] James Q. Wilson, *Varieties of Police Behavior* (Cambridge, Mass.: Harvard University Press, 1968), p. 290.

Thus, we have the two motivating factors for the scientific management movement influencing the decision-makers.

However, a counter-argument has been developed by Alan A. Altshuler, an advocate of community control.

> ... *community control advocates contend that the central issue in the ghettos at the present is legitimacy, not efficiency. . . . If a choice had to be made, it would be justifiable . . . to trade off some efficiency, and even some honesty, for an alleviation of social tensions.*[5]

In this case the advocates of decentralization are stressing social benefits versus efficiency and costs.

It is true that social costs are difficult to evaluate. The police administrator finds it impossible to include such items in his criteria of efficiency. As Altshuler has indicated, citizens may well be prepared to accept increased costs and reduced efficiency in order to have community-based police services.

This was exactly the decision made by the citizens of San Francisco in 1972. The police had recommended that the city administration close two precinct stations on the grounds of better utilization of police resources and increased efficiency. Despite much community opposition, the city administration approved the closure. The community reacted by circulating a petition to have the matter submitted to a vote of the people, and sufficient signatures were obtained to place the issue on the ballot. The people voted to reverse the closure and the two stations have since been reopened. The city administration and the police had misjudged the will of the people, because the people saw a social cost benefit not perceived by the professionals.

Police Discretion

Enforcement patterns may be another cause of conflict between the citizens and the police. The police have traditionally maintained that they are purely ministerial and have no discretion in enforcing the law. This would give one the impression that all laws are equally and uniformly enforced.

---

[5] Leonard Ruchelman, *Who Rules the Police* (New York: New York University Press, 1973), p. 78.

The use and abuse of police discretion can be a destructive police practice since the police decide the levels of enforcement that are to be applied in a community. The level of enforcement can range from no enforcement at all to total enforcement of the laws. In addition, the police can decide to have different levels of enforcement in different segments of the community. This can be done through policy decisions that reflect the value system of the police. For example, the Los Angeles Police Department discovered after the Watts riots that their policy of issuing citations instead of warnings for mechanical violations on automobiles was a source of irritation to the poorer individual who had to take a day off from work to go to court. He was required to show proof that the violation had been corrected. Although no fine was imposed he had lost a day's wages. This economic loss was more damaging to him than to the more affluent person. The police, using their discretion, changed this policy and reduced the irritant.

Police Value Systems

Promotion, assignment, and recognition are based on an internal value system, which may be in conflict with the values and needs of the community. Paul Jacobs touched upon this issue when he stated:

> In the tradition of modern police work, most patrol work is viewed as only a steppingstone to a better police job and not the most important police function. The reward to a "good" patrolman in a patrol division is transfer to a "felony car," where he does not have to wear a uniform on duty, or promotion to plainclothes detective status.[6]

This attitude reflects the emphasis that the police system places upon certain classifications of crime. There is a higher status associated with the apprehension of a suspect charged with a felony than one charged with a minor misdemeanor. This higher status is also reflected in the promotion and pay assigned to detectives. In the detective bureau itself, there is an allocation of higher status to those assigned to the investigation of the more serious crimes.

Yet, as Jacobs indicates, this takes the best officers from the

[6] Paul Jacobs, *Prelude to Riot* (New York: Vantage Books, 1967), p. 55.

street confrontation.[7] The newer, inexperienced officer tends to be the contact point with the community, which may cause increased misunderstandings and citizen alienation.

Another problem results from conflicting evaluations by the police concerning the definitions of "serious" crimes. In some cases, crimes which the police consider to be "less serious" are those most visible to citizens. For example, in allotting resources, many more man-hours will be devoted to the apprehension of a bank robber than to the apprehension of a vandal. Yet, in a recent poll of citizen concerns conducted in the preparation of this book, the primary concern was neighborhood vandalism. Thus, it is evident that much of the alienation between police and citizens results from differences in priorities.

Policy decisions made by police administrators also alienate the police and the citizens. For example, in many large cities the police have adopted the practice of taking telephone complaints and do not assign a patrol unit to conduct a follow-up investigation. The citizen may view this as lack of concern for his problem. Thus, there is a need for a review of such policies because of their social costs in terms of community support.

Police Operational Measurement

In the first section of this chapter we examined the influence the scientific management movement had upon the police organization and administrator, emphasizing efficiency. However, we have not yet considered the practical effects of such efforts.

How does one measure efficiency? This is a real problem for the police administrator. As James Q. Wilson has described the situation:

> ... the police chief has only the most rudimentary knowledge of how well his patrolmen are preventing crime, apprehending criminals, and maintaining order.[8]

Yet, the administrator is required to evaluate his efforts. When he prepares his budget, the administrator has to justify additional manpower

[7] Ibid., p. 56.
[8] Wilson, *Varieties of Police Behavior*, p. 58.

requests by backing up his requirements with measurable criteria. The municipal budgetary process has traditionally justified manpower requests on the basis of production costs per unit. City and county managers are accustomed to allocating resources based upon cost per unit. While it is relatively easy to determine the costs for paving a mile of roadway, it is far more difficult to analyze the unit costs of police activities. Jacobs describes one police lieutenant's efforts to evaluate efficiency.

> ... he issued "report cards" each month ... (on the card) the individual officer's record was kept: if he exceeded the monthly averages, the figures were written in blue; if he went under, they were written in red.[9]

The use of this method is subjective and does not measure either efficiency or effectiveness. The lieutenant may believe he is measuring efficiency, but in reality he is only using a divisional average as his key.

The basic question remains—can we be efficient, but not effective? This concept is a difficult one to comprehend and should be considered along with a second concept: can efficiency be counterproductive of obtaining community support?

Efficiency vs. Effectiveness

The question of efficiency versus effectiveness is central to the issue of destructive police practices. Let us consider the question of efficiency. The test of efficiency has usually been the number of units produced in specific time periods at a *pro rata* cost. Are we also willing to accept this as a test of the effectiveness of an organization?

What is meant by the term "effectiveness" and what is its effect upon the decision-making of the police administrator? In order to discuss this element, we should identify to some extent the police role. If the police role is to maintain a tranquil society, then all of its activities must be tested against this criterion. To put it another way, does the specific activity relate to the accomplishment of this objective?

This is followed by yet another question that should be answered by the police administrator: should he opt for efficiency or effectiveness?

[9] Jacobs, *Prelude to Riot*, p. 57.

As a commanding officer of the Los Angeles Police Department argues, he should have both, but if he had to make one choice, he would choose effectiveness.[10] The example he used was the issuance of traffic citations at a poorly designated intersection. Although motorists violate this stop sign, no accidents have resulted. Is the issuance of a large number of citations at this location efficient or effective?

Commander Vernon's position is that it may be efficient, but it certainly is not effective if the department's goal is to improve highway safety. The officer writing the traffic citation may be efficient since he observes a violation and issues a citation, yet he is not furthering the basic objective of the police in traffic safety. To be truly effective, the police should have taken steps to have the intersection redesigned by the traffic engineer.

From the standpoint of resource allocation, the officer's time was spent in counterproductive activities. Had he patrolled the highway, he might have been responsible for a reduction in the number of traffic accidents. The problem for the officer is how to justify patrol activities to his supervisor.

Field Interrogation Reports

A common practice of most police departments is the use of field interrogation reports (F.I.). The use of such reports are justified by law enforcement personnel as being necessary to report the activities of suspicious persons. However, the F.I.s have become a measure of productivity of the patrol officer in most departments. They have become part of the "report card" by which efficiency is judged.

A veteran police officer once stated, "Don't they realize F.I.s are meaningless?" When pressed for a reason, he explained that any experienced officer can get names and addresses out of telephone books. It was his belief that the purpose of F.I.s had been lost and their use had just become part of a numbers game. And if they are questionable from a

---

[10] Address, May 1973, by Commander Robert Vernon, Los Angeles Police Department, to a Police Community Relations Leadership Institute, San Jose State University.

police standpoint, what effect can they have on the community? From this viewpoint we would have to consider who in the community is usually contacted by the police. Seldom are white, middle-class citizens ever checked; it is usually the poor or minority members who are interrogated. These citizens, because of constant field interrogations, become suspicious of the police, which leads to a mutual alienation.

The police have failed to communicate to the community the necessity for these field interrogations: they fail to identify the objectives of such efforts. The "shotgun" approach of indiscriminate F.I.s are neither necessary nor desirable.

Vagrancy

Vagrancy laws were brought to the United States by the colonists. Enacted in 1349 in England, they were established to control the labor force.

William Chambliss has described the current status of vagrancy statutes in the United States today.

> Their main purpose, however, is clearly no longer the control of laborers but rather the control of the undesirable, the criminal, and the nuisance.[11]

Although these laws are not "efficient" as we have been using the term in earlier sections, they are, however, an efficient tool in disposing of those who fail to meet community norms.

We should consider each of the groups Chambliss identifies for us. First, there is the control of the criminal element. The police have, in the past, arrested a suspected criminal on the grounds of vagrancy because he did not have employment. The court would render a suspended sentence on the condition that he leave town. This use of vagrancy laws has been declared unconstitutional for a number of years.

In both the North and the South, civil rights workers were arrested under catch-all sections of vagrancy laws. Later these same laws were used to control those involved in other protest movements and

---

[11] William J. Chambliss, *Crime and the Legal Process* (New York: McGraw-Hill, 1969), p. 61.

hippies. Vagrancy laws were also used against those who could not give a satisfactory (to the police) account of themselves, generally the poor and members of minority groups. In many instances their only real crime was that they failed to meet the values of the white police officer.

The use of these laws as a control mechanism is a practice that demeans the basic objectives of law enforcement. If we identify the role of the police as that of just enforcing the laws, such actions might be justifiable. But, if we reject the earlier view, that of the traditional manager, such actions are inappropriate.

Summary

We have examined some examples of destructive police practices: there are countless others we might have considered. Our concern should be directed to how the organization might have allowed these destructive police practices to develop. We saw that the police organization developed in an era that was rejecting corruption and incompetence. This was a time when managers were looking for a new direction—the scientific management movement appeared to be their salvation.

It was a simplistic time in our history. The questions and answers were simple and there was little awareness of the complex issues of society. This approach is inadequate for the current period. We must develop new management styles and techniques by which we must test all police practices.

The first step in this effort is to identify both the police role and objectives. If we develop the objectives of the police, then we can examine police practices to determine if these practices are furthering the objectives. In addition, the police administrator must address himself to the issue of effectiveness versus efficiency. He must develop new methods of measuring efficiency since the traditional measurement devices of counting arrests, citations, and field interrogations have created some of the destructive practices we have discussed.

The frame of reference of the police administrator must turn from the suppression of crime to its prevention. And if our current practices have produced alienation between the community and the police, new methods must be devised to gain community support. It has often been demonstrated that the poor and members of minority groups want better police protection. We must convert this desire into a crime prevention partnership, which is essential if law enforcement is to meet its objectives. No police department has the manpower to perform the job alone. For this reason, community participation is vital.

Student Checklist

1. Are you able to describe how scientific management has operated on a negative factor in police–community relations?
2. Can you list the advantages and disadvantages of decentralization of the police?
3. Are you able to tell why the use of police discretion is necessary?
4. Can you write a short essay showing how the use of police discretion may appear to be an injustice?
5. Can you compare police priorities in apprehending bank robbers and vandals? Can you state how this affects police–community relations?

Topics for Discussion

1. Discuss the conflict between the scientific management of police departments and police–community relations.
2. Discuss the advantages and disadvantages of centralization of the police.
3. Discuss the need for police discretion.
4. Discuss how the use of police discretion may appear unjust.
5. Discuss how police priorities in apprehending bank robbers and vandals can affect police–community relations.

ANNOTATED BIBLIOGRAPHY

Chambliss, William J. *Crime and the Legal Process.* New York: Mc-Graw-Hill, 1969. This book covers the sociology of the criminal law, the emergence of legal norms, the administration of criminal law, and the impact of legal sanctions. Included are good discussions of the arrest process, prosecution, and sentencing.

Gardner, John A. *Traffic and the Police: Variation in Law-Enforcement Policy.* Cambridge, Mass.: Harvard University Press, 1969. Describes the role of various state and local agencies in setting traffic enforcement policy. Analyzes in depth the traffic activities of four Massachusetts cities.

Gross, Bertram. *The Managing of Organizations: The Administrative Struggle.* New York: The Free Press of Glencoe, 1964. Covers the development of management thought. Part II has an excellent description of the evolution of managerial theory. Part III discusses the problems and reorientation of earlier concepts.

Jacobs, Paul. *Prelude to Riot*. New York: Vantage Books, 1966. Section I discusses the police with particular attention to the Los Angeles Police Department. Section VII reviews the findings of the McCone Commission and the Watts riots.

Ruchelman, Leonard. *Who Rules the Police*. New York: New York University Press, 1973. Attempts to gauge police behavior from the perspective of civil accountability and control. Section I deals with accountability and control; Section II, discretion and the criminal justice system; Section III, police abuse.

Wilson, James Q. *Varieties of Police Behavior*. Cambridge, Mass.: Harvard University Press, 1968. The study considers how the uniformed officer in eight communities deals with common offenses. Section IV has an excellent discussion of police discretion. Sections V, VI, and VII deal with different management styles.

The study of this chapter will enable you to:

1. Explain the reasons given for the use of selective enforcement and discriminatory application of laws.
2. Define the legal authority for discriminatory and selective enforcement.
3. Describe some of the administrative problems created with this practice.
4. Describe why some police administrators refuse to acknowledge the existence of selective and discriminatory aspects of law enforcement.

11

Selective and Discriminatory Enforcement of Laws

Against a backdrop of traditions of government by laws and equality of all persons under the law, one of the most perplexing problems confronting the administration of justice is that of selective and discriminatory enforcement of laws. Many times during the working day a police officer will make a decision that will, in effect, suspend or modify statutory laws. Moreover, police administrators, legislators, prosecutors, and judges are aware that police officers commonly make this kind of judgment. Traditionally, both police administrators and the other criminal justice agencies (such as the judiciary) that check police actions, have avoided formal discussion of the question of discretionary enforcement of laws. A simple explanation, which may be an accurate one, is that other criminal justice functions depend quite heavily on the willingness of the police to accept responsibility for discretionary enforcement of laws. These other agencies delegate this authority to the police even though they may be giving up some of their own rights and responsibilities in the process.

Although the decisions of a police officer to allow a speeder to go on his way with only a warning, or to overlook penny gambling by senior citizens engaged in a card game, initially may appear to be harmless, many citizens are becoming more aware that the laws are applied differently in communities that are supposed to be governed by the same statutes. And, since our burgeoning urban population centers are composed of so many different types of people, the process by which a police officer tries to match his selective law enforcement decisions with priorities for the enforcement of laws becomes increasingly complex.

The average citizen's most frequent contacts with government are likely to be through law enforcement personnel. The nature of the citizen's contacts with the police is likely to form the basis for his attitudes, not only about the criminal justice system, but about government in general. In building and maintaining good government–community relationships, it is important to maintain a high level of public confidence in local government. It is essential that the public has confidence in the integrity of its law enforcement agencies if these agencies are to have full community support. The question that must be confronted is whether selective, or, discretionary, law enforcement is in conflict with the idea of equality and fairness under law, potentially undermining public confidence. To answer this question, we must examine the following:

1. The nature of selective and discriminatory law enforcement.
2. The commonly given explanations for the selective enforcement and discriminatory application of laws.
3. The legal authority for discriminatory and selective law enforcement.
4. The administrative problems created by the practice.
5. The basis for police administrators' refusal to acknowledge selective and discriminatory aspects of law enforcement.

The Nature of Selective and Discriminatory Law Enforcement

The practices that we shall discuss represent only that part of the police assignment calling for the use of judgment by police administrators and individual police officers. As a law enforcer, the patrolman or detective is constantly faced with the question of whether observed circumstances permit official police action. Is there "probable cause" to make an arrest? Do the observed circumstances permit the officer to stop a citizen and ask him about his identity or business? Is the observed conduct a violation of the law?

The police officer's judgment on the question of whether or not a violation of the law has taken place is not within the scope of our discussion. The kind of activity that concerns us is related to the situation where the officer believes that he does, in fact, have sufficient grounds to arrest or otherwise invoke the criminal processes. Therefore, our discussion will focus on the choice not to enforce laws when a violation clearly exists. This choice may occur at both the administrative and operational levels of a police department.

The Administrative Choice

It is most unusual for a police organization to express its policies for either the selective or discriminatory enforcement of laws. Through informal, compelling means, any of the levels of command in a police department may develop policy for less than full and uniform enforcement of laws. James Q. Wilson, in his book, *Varieties of Police Behavior*, describes the development of departmental policies through the weighing of the idea of "strict enforcement" against accommodations that will serve other values. He suggests that at times a department may have to sacrifice strict application of laws to achieve the values of "order" and "service giving," which are also part of the police mission.[1]

The police officer who chooses full enforcement, as opposed to following the unstated selective enforcement decisions that have been made by either his department or supervisor, may not be subjected to direct disciplinary action, but he may be severely penalized in terms of promotional ratings or in work shift or unit assignments. His production of cases that may relate to violations of the law, but which are not consistent with the selective enforcement policies of the department, may be viewed as counter-productive to departmental goals. The fact that informal, unstated policies can have a substantial effect on actual enforcement activities is illustrated in John Gardiner's book, *Traffic and the Police*.[2] Gardiner's study concerned patterns of traffic law enforcement activities in comparable cities located in the same state and subject to the same laws. The data that he collected on the demographic character of the communities, their arrest and conviction statistics, and information obtained from interviews with police personnel, clearly show that unstated enforcement policies actually produced different patterns in the application of laws in each of the cities studied.

[1] James Q. Wilson, *Varieties of Police Behavior* (Cambridge, Mass.: Harvard University Press, 1968).
[2] John Gardiner, *Traffic and the Police* (Cambridge, Mass.: Harvard University Press, 1969).

Operational Level Choices

When there is a police-citizen contact, the choice not to enforce the law is frequently made by the patrolman. His decision may have very little visibility and is not likely to be reviewed by a supervisor. When he makes this type of decision, the officer may also be making legislative, prosecutorial, and judicial decisions. As a legislator, he makes specific choices to clarify what the enacting legislature stated in general language. He also establishes classes of exceptions that are not specifically provided for in the statutory laws. The police officer also plays the role of a prosecutor, but, unlike the prosecutor, he does not have statutory authority. The police officer, without any authority for doing so, may decide not to proceed against a suspected perpetrator of a crime in exchange for the suspect's cooperation, which may have a value to law enforcement.[3] As a judge, the officer may determine from the facts of the case that the offender should be given a suspended sentence (release with a warning) or subjected to on-the-spot sanctions of the police officer's own design. Examples of this may be the confiscation of contraband, requiring the offender to participate in a social program or charitable act, or to make restitution in exchange for not being processed through the formal criminal justice system. But, unlike most of the decisions made in the official capacities of legislator, prosecutor, or judge,

[3] In most jurisdictions there are immunity statutes that the prosecutor may invoke. The effect of these statutes is to allow a citizen to testify before an investigative body without subjecting himself to the peril of having the information that he divulges subsequently used against him in a criminal proceeding. A grant of immunity almost always requires judicial approval. An example of such a statute is the Federal Immunity Act, which provides that a U.S. Attorney may move for immunity on behalf of anyone he wishes to call as a witness, but who he believes will refuse to provide information under his privilege against self-incrimination (Section 6000-3, Title 18, U.S. Code).

It should be noted that the prosecutor may also have power to terminate a pending matter through the plea of *nolle prosequi*. This procedure is also usually subject to the approval of the courts (see Rule 48, Federal Rules of Criminal Procedure).

There are many situations, however, where the prosecutor is in a position to use his discretion not to proceed in an arbitrary manner. See *Challenge of Crime in a Free Society*, President's Commission on Law Enforcement and the Administration of Justice, U.S. Govt. Printing Office, 1967, p. 133. But I would argue that, in an operational sense, the extent of the prosecutor's discretion is not nearly as great as that of the patrolman.

the police officer's exercise of discretion is not recorded or otherwise subjected to any systematic form of public audit or review.

The police department itself is not in a position to either measure or control most of the discretionary decisions made by its officers. When there is no record of a contact, the reviewing supervisor does not have much to work with. Unlike soldiers, with whom police officers are frequently compared, police officers perform much of their work out of the direct view of supervisory personnel. A patrolman or a detective generally works alone or with a partner who is at the same level of authority and is unlikely to file a report on his partner's otherwise unreported activities, except in clearly abusive instances. The object of the police activity—the suspect—is not likely to report the fact that an officer has treated him with leniency. It is almost as unlikely that a complainant will proceed independently against a police officer who has failed to act on his complaint.[4]

Explanations for Selective Enforcement

At the Administrative Level
A police administrator may find himself overcharged with responsibilities. Considering the quantity and breadth of laws that he is charged with enforcing, he may quite reasonably conclude that he will not be able to meet the challenge with available resources. The administrator with limited budget and manpower allocations must make decisions as to their "best" application. Since most police administrators do not have enough resources for full enforcement of *all* laws, some alternatives that might be considered are discussed in the following paragraphs.

He can attempt to enforce all laws strictly on a first-come, first-served basis. He can consider each law and each violation of a law to be equally important. Conceivably, a department following this method of operation would require a patrolman to proceed in the pursuit of a speeding motorist, passing by an armed robbery in progress. It is unlikely that a police department attempting a rigid, legalistic approach to enforcement activities would be able to maintain its policies in the face

[4] Albert J. Reiss, Jr., *Police and the Public* (New Haven, Conn.: Yale University Press, 1971), p. 190.

of community pressures for priorities. As discussed previously, most communities do have a sense of priorities regarding law enforcement activities. Conversely, the police administrator can decide that different offenses and circumstances present different weights in terms of operational priorities. In his opinion, virtually no effort should be made to enforce some laws, while the enforcement of other laws should be limited to only a small portion of the incidents covered by the relevant statutes. His ordering of priorities might be based on his own judgments concerning the relative importance of laws and of their enforcement in given kinds of situations. Another possible basis for his establishment of priorities would be his estimation of the extent of public support for given patterns of selective law enforcement. As Wilson noted:

> The administrator becomes attuned to complaints. What constitutes a "significant" citizen demand will, of course, vary from city to city. In some places, a political party will tell the police whom to take seriously and whom to ignore; in other places, organized community groups will amplify some demands and drown out others; voices to heed and how to heed them. Whatever the filtering mechanism, the police administrator ignores at his peril those demands that are passed through.[5]

It usually becomes clear to the sensitive police administrator that strong community support for nonenforcement of laws makes enforcement operationally difficult. As the strength of public opposition to a given law increases, the cost of any specified level of enforcement is bound to increase. Given this relationship, the police administrator knows that some laws will require substantially more effort to enforce than others. In addition, the effect of strong enforcement efforts against the preferences of some sectors of the community may be very costly in terms of a loss of cooperation from those sectors in other law enforcement efforts.[6]

This is not to say that an administrator will always choose the policy that produces the greatest amount of successful law enforcement effort at the lowest unit cost. His judgment may cause him to determine that the costs of losing support of some community groups because of police efforts may be compensated for by the value of enforcement to

[5] Wilson, *Varieties of Police Behavior*, p. 70.
[6] Reiss, *Police and the Public*, pp. 68-102.

the larger community. An example of this might be a strong enforcement campaign directed against drug dealers, which might alienate the community of drug users and be much more expensive to maintain than an intensified effort against parking ticket scofflaws. On the other hand, the value to the larger community in terms of the reduction in property crimes as a result of the reduction in drug activities would most likely outweigh the cost of enforcement.

The politically powerful residents of the community may not want selective enforcement of laws, but instead prefer that the laws be applied only in limited situations. Thus, parking laws may be strictly enforced in some areas, but during holiday shopping seasons, the police may adopt a policy of "forgiveness" in areas surrounding shopping centers. Selective enforcement also occurs in the application of laws against prostitution. For example, police arrests of prostitutes and their clients may cause business conventions to avoid some cities. When convention business is lost due to strict enforcement of vice laws, members of the business community may exert considerable pressure on police officials to relax enforcement of these laws. At the same time, the police administrator may recognize that there is strong support in the community as a whole for laws against prostitution; if this were otherwise, the legislature would have changed the law. The result of these opposite pressures upon the police administrator may lead him to adopt law enforcement policies that limit prostitution to a controlled level of practice. Prostitution flourishes, but it becomes hidden from the public view. Therefore, it is not likely to cause mobilization of citizens who would favor full suppression. The police administrator's objective in adopting a selective enforcement policy would be to strike a bargain with the citizens who support limited prostitution in exchange for their support of "more important" law enforcement objectives.

There is a hidden danger to law enforcement in this kind of balancing act. That danger is loss of integrity in the public eye. General public knowledge of selective and discriminatory patterns of law enforcement will produce, at the very least, the attitude that justice can be negotiated.

The kinds of selective judgments that can be made at the command levels of policing may be duplicated at every level of authority in a department. The extent to which an individual officer can serve his own biases is dependent upon his level of command authority. This is not to say, however, that the greatest freedom to serve the individual bias is at the top command level of a police department. In some areas of enforcement, an operational level decision-maker has greater freedom; when he implements decisions, fewer people need to be drawn into his confidence and the visibility of the actions he takes or omits may be very low.

As previously noted, the administrator seldom issues orders or makes public statements listing the criteria for selective law enforcement policies. The administrator expects his subordinates to develop the "right" kinds of priorities without specific direction from him. This method of operation is undoubtedly reinforced by the fact that legislators, courts, and prosecutors rely on the police to use discretion when applying laws. These assumptions, although never formally stated, bear an important relationship to the laws that will actually be enforced in the community.

There have been notable exceptions to the administrative level "rule of silence" on selective enforcement policies. In 1963, for example, Superintendent Orlando Wilson of the Chicago Police Department issued a memorandum instructing his officers not to enforce an ordinance applying to a vehicle that had only one operative headlight, if, in the opinion of the arresting officer, the driver intended to have the inoperative light repaired immediately.[7] More recently, and in a more sensitive area, Connecticut State Police Commissioner Cleveland Fuessenich announced a policy that would allow his officers to use discretion in determining whether an arrest should be made in cases involving the possession of small quantities of marijuana. The more conventional *public* law enforcement position is to be found in the statements of other Connecticut police chiefs who were interviewed about their reaction to the Fuessenich announcement: "The law says a crime has been committed. . . . Who is to say which law will be enforced? ". . . it is the court system which has the discretion over cases brought before it . . . the system should remain that way." ". . . it is not the job of the law enforcement agency to pick out which laws shall be enforced and for which people."[8]

[7] Herman Goldstein, "Police Discretion: The Ideal vs. The Real," *Public Administration Review,* Vol. 23 (1963), pp. 140, 147.
[8] New Haven, Connecticut, *Register* (December 2, 1971), p. 1.

At the Operational Level

The patrolman is charged with responding directly to the citizens' requests for service and to public safety and order situations on the streets of the community. In most cases, he alone must decide what action to take. He may observe an event, consider several alternative courses of action, and make a decision without recording it or doing anything that anyone else could report. For example, a police officer can observe a motorist drive through a red traffic signal and decide not to give chase. In this sort of situation, not even the citizen knows that he has been the focus of law enforcement discretion. This kind of decision is among the least visible of the criminal justice processes.

When he is being observed by a suspect, a complainant, a fellow police officer, or a supervisor, the officer is aware of the responses he can expect to the various alternative courses of action he may be considering. Thus, an awareness of these responses most likely will determine what he does. As a result, the literal interpretation of the law to the situation might only be of secondary importance.

The operational level decision-maker's judgments are governed by the same kinds of influences that effect the decisions of the higher level administrator. But, since the patrolman operates within a much smaller political sphere, he finds his relationships with the more limited community potentially more intense. The reciprocal impact of both the officer and the community becomes clearer. It is easier to "bargain" within these more intimate relationships.[9]

If a policeman were forced to explain his selective or discriminatory law enforcement decisions, he might give some of the reasons discussed on the following pages.

Strict Enforcement of the Law Could Result in Injustice.

1. The legislature did not intend for some laws to be applied literally; the law was intended to apply only to the situation where wrong is being done. The officer may feel that an event is not within the coverage of a statute, even when it is clear that the statute, taken literally, would

---

[9] One police officer interviewed during the course of the Wilson study reported that when he was instructed to tell the priests in his area that they would have to close down their bingo and carnival concessions, he was fearful of being excommunicated. Wilson, *Varieties of Police Behavior*, p. 107.

apply to the event. The police officer's interpretation of the event may be that the "perpetrator" has not really done anything wrong. His decision may be influenced by the view that the legislature assumes that its enactments will be applied with a certain amount of judgment. After all, if the legislature included in each law examples of *every* kind of situation or exceptional circumstance that it wished the law to apply or make exception to, the laws would become extremely complex and almost impossible to work with.[10]

The officer could conclude that the legislature has made assumptions about the kind of men who enforce laws, and trusts that they will act sensibly in interpreting the statute. The police officer then views an act in terms of his own sense of right or wrong; a sense of right or wrong that is derived from his own experiences. He then would find it difficult to enforce a law against conduct that he believes is "right," even though the conduct would be "criminal" if the statute were strictly applied.

2. The statute in question is out of date; to apply it to a contemporary situation would work an injustice. Most states have been in existence for more than 100 years, during which time they have accumulated laws that no longer relate to contemporary needs. The legislatures may have intended that these laws be strictly enforced at the time that they were enacted. But many years have passed since their enactment and, since legislatures do not review all existing law each time they convene, they have probably lost sight of some laws. Consequently, it is not unusual to find examples in any state's body of law which, when read in terms of modern life, appear both questionable and laughable. A search for such

---

[10] The problem that faces legislators in writing laws so that they are usable was discussed by Justice Frankfurter in his dissenting opinion in Winters v. U.S., 333 U.S. 520 (1948) at 514-15: "Unlike the abstract stuff of mathematics, or the quantitatively ascertainable elements of much of natural science, legislation is greatly concerned with the multiform psychological complexities of individual and social conduct. Accordingly, the demands upon legislation and its responses are multiform. That which may appear too vague and even meaningless as to one subject matter may be as definite as another subject matter permits, if the legislative power to deal with such a subject is not to be altogether denied. . . . If a law is framed with narrow particularity, too easy opportunities are afforded to nullify the purposes of the legislation. If the legislation is drafted in terms so vague that no ascertainable line is drawn in advance between innocent and condemned conduct, the purpose of the legislation cannot be enforced because no purpose is defined."

statutes uncovered laws against swearing, kiteflying, entertaining on Sunday evenings, depicting felonies in movies, candy cigarettes, and engaging in sports other than baseball on Sunday![11]

Although these laws are literally applicable to many observed situations every day, most police officers would not consider enforcing them. Some legal scholars argue that a pattern of nonenforcement of statutes, combined with common violations of these laws and legislative inaction, constitutes a form of repeal.[12] This position has never been adopted by a major court system, however.

3. *Given that observed behavior violates the law, the officer may believe that if the perpetrator is arrested, the official system will not handle the matter justly.* The effect of an arrest on the citizen may be more detrimental than justice requires. Since the effect of an arrest may be a criminal conviction, a police officer in a specific case may feel that criminalization is too serious a consequence for the perpetrator's acts. His sense of empathy leads the officer, especially when he is dealing with juveniles or persons who are situationally vulnerable, to feel that he himself, a friend, or a relative could have easily been involved in a similar situation. Because he personalizes the crime, the officer may conclude that he is not dealing with a real "criminal." Therefore, he may feel that the first step of the stigmatization process—the arrest—should not be taken. This kind of decision-making by the police officer may result from his lack of confidence in the judgments made at other levels in the criminal justice system. The officer may believe that the decision-makers at other levels of the system may not be able to distinguish, as he can, between the offender and real criminals. His judgment will also be influenced by the knowledge that as the case moves further along through the system, his control over the disposition will be lessened and eventually excluded. While he may hesitate about making an arrest, the officer might also believe that *some* sanctions should be applied to people he is unwilling to process through the formal criminal justice system. Thus, he may develop a series of informal alternative sanctions that can

[11] Arthur E. Bonfield, "The Abrogation of Penal Statutes by Nonenforcement," *49 Iowa Law Review*, 389 (1964).
[12] A good treatment of the doctrine of desuetude (laws that are no longer practiced), as it relates to discriminatory law enforcement, can be found in Bonfield, ibid.

be applied to the "noncriminal" law violator on-the-spot. These alternatives may consist of reprimands, informal arrangements for participation in community social treatment programs, or mild punishments. The citizen may be instructed to contact a clergyman or counselor, or arrange for some form of restitution. For example, the neighborhood youths caught stealing fruit and candy from a grocery store might, with the cooperation of the store owner, be "let off" if they agree to make restitution or help sweep out the store on a number of occasions. These options are subject to the officer's desire to make adjustments as well as to the responses that he can expect from citizens—not only the violator, but victims and observers as well. The more hidden the decision is from the public view, the more latitude the officer has in the kinds of decisions he can make.

It might be useful to point out the impact that citizens can have on the enforcement decisions of a police officer. A 1968 Michigan study of police encounters disclosed that "Police did not file an official report in a single instance where the complainant expressed a preference for unofficial handling of a felony or misdemeanor. When the complainant expressed a preference for official action by the police, officers tended to follow the preference."[13] The study also found that citizen preference to charge is most likely to be persuasive in the handling of felonies. In many misdemeanor cases the officers were likely to view the matters as being really civil in nature or the product of the momentary indignation of the complainant.

If an Arrest Is Made, the Official System Will Not Treat the Offense Seriously Enough. A police officer may believe that the law violator will not receive the punishment he deserves if he is arrested and handled through official channels. The officer may believe that the rules of evidence, court procedures, and the attitude of the courts may not adequately support the enforcement of some laws. He may feel that courts are "soft" on burglars, drug users, and demonstrators. Accordingly, the officer may feel that on-the-spot punishments inflicted through repeated aggressive stops, the taking of contraband, and other forms of harassment are much more effective ways to implement the law than are the official processes. The officer may assume that even if a stop or taking of prop-

---

[13] Reiss, *Police and the Public*, p. 83.

erty is illegal in a technical sense, the citizen will not be likely to complain. When an individual has been caught "with the goods," even if he has been handled inappropriately by an enforcement agency, he is not likely to initiate independent proceedings against the law enforcer if no formal process has been initiated against him. To discourage this type of activity, the U.S. Supreme Court in two important decisions (*Mapp* v. *Ohio*, 367 U.S. 643, and *Miranda* v. *Arizona*, 384 U.S. 436) imposed an exclusionary rule on state criminal proceedings. This rule was imposed not because the evidence in question was unreliable, but because the Court had no other way to control unlawful conduct by the law enforcement agencies that obtained the evidence. The Court said it felt that questions about the misconduct of police could be more easily handled as side issues in a criminal proceeding brought against a victim of such improper conduct, than through complaint procedures brought independently against a police officer.

The Community Does Not Support Enforcement of the Law in Some Cases. A police officer who wants to gain the greatest acceptance and approval possible from the community may attempt to determine the kind of enforcement that is wanted and deliver it. The police officer may believe that the neighborhood that he serves has a greater tolerance for certain types of conduct than does the urban area at large. As long as this behavior is limited to a neighborhood that he feels accepts this conduct, he will not initiate formal action against it. He may believe that the community will not tolerate the criminalization of members who are respectable by its standards.

For example, an officer may believe that assaults between black citizens residing in a ghetto area are both common and acceptable forms of social contacts within that community. He may also believe that the assault complaint that the ghetto wife makes against her husband is similar to the complaint that the more affluent wife takes to a family counselor. Consequently, the police officer may overlook an assault case that would almost certainly result in an arrest in a middle-class area.

This type of assumption by police officers may be dangerous, and it may be the source of disharmony between a community and a law enforcement agency. A survey conducted by the U.S. National Advisory Committee on Criminal Justice found that black ghetto communities are not satisfied with the level of service they are receiving from law enforcement. It was reported that many people in these communities feel that

"... the police maintain a much less rigorous standard of law enforcement in the ghetto, tolerating illegal activities like drug addiction and prostitution and street violence that they would not tolerate elsewhere."[14]

In another kind of situation, which also deals with a police officer's own interpretation of community norms, an officer may feel that he will be harshly judged if he raids a "social" poker game taking place in the basement of a citizen's home. The officer's assumptions about the moral values of a community, warranted or not, may cause him to conclude that:

1. The prevalence of the activity in question is great.
2. The community does view the activity as wrong.
3. The community would view enforcement of the law in relation to the viewed activity as wrong. Enforcement may elicit negative responses from the community in the form of: political pressure to cause the officer to be either reprimanded or transferred; social ostracism from the community and treatment with great incivility; lack of cooperation in other aspects of the police mission; and physical threats to his well-being.
4. The value of enforcement against the observed activity may be outweighed by the general loss of the officer's effectiveness to render law enforcement services in higher priority areas; this loss of effectiveness results when the community withdraws its support.

The Community May Want Laws To Be Applied Discriminatorily Against "Objectionable" Persons Whose General Conduct and Presence Are Not Illegal. Occasionally, infrequently invoked laws and the nonuse of commonly enforced laws may produce objectives that have not been legislated. A specific community may have a low tolerance for certain social or racial types; a politically influential sector may be strongly opposed to certain businesses or activities. Differential enforcement or nonenforcement of laws can be used to enforce a community bias. The threat of enforcement of obscure laws can be used to deliver the message that an individual or activity is not welcome in the area. The law enforcer can also deliver the same kind of message by overlooking violations of law committed by members of the community against people and activities viewed as "undesirable."

[14] Report of U.S. National Advisory Committee on Civil Disorders (Washington, D.C.: U.S. Govt. Printing Office, 1968), p. 61.

Other Parts of the Criminal Justice System Have Suspended the Operation of Some Laws. Attempts to enforce some laws have been greeted by a supervisor's criticism rather than commendation. The patrolman who has spent most of the afternoon arresting and processing seven members of the local octogenarian club who were caught wagering nickels in a domino game in the park may be criticized by his sergeant because several burglaries were occurring on his beat. The patrolman soon learns that he must place his priorities in the proper order.

In addition, it is possible that law enforcement efforts in some areas may be deemed inappropriate or a nuisance by prosecutors and judges. For example, during Wilson's study, a judge was asked to react to the observation that over 59 percent of the gambling cases brought to court in his jurisdiction were thrown out. The judge answered, ". . . above all, I don't believe gambling constitutes a serious crime. The judge has to reflect community attitudes. What else can he do? He's a human being. . . . Seventy-five percent of the public gambles. . . . I know the police chief here is death on gambling, but I can't understand why. . . . It's not a great sin in my eyes. I simply cannot get too excited about it."[15]

Not all communities would place gambling at the low level of importance as Wilson's judge; nevertheless, a common complaint of prosecutors and judges is the overwhelming volume of cases they have to handle on the system's inability to render justice within a reasonable period of time. Thus, the courts turn to law enforcement agencies and press for careful selection of cases rather than full enforcement of laws.

There May Be a "Trading" Advantage of Law Enforcement Value in the Decision Not To Enforce the Law. The use of informants by the police is well known. The police–informant relationship need not be organized as a regular series of transactions. In many cases the individual police officer is in a position to bargain with the "caught" offender. The caught offender, in return for not being arrested, or for lenient handling, may give the officer information that will help solve a much more important case or catch a much more serious offender. Jerome Skolnick's study of criminal investigators found that burglary detectives often permitted

---

[15] Wilson, *Varieties of Police Behavior*, p. 106.

informants to commit narcotics offenses, while narcotics detectives allowed informants to steal.[16]

It May Be Inconvenient To Enforce the Law. Would processing the case require the officer to work overtime? Would an arrest cause a day off to be spent in court? Will a meal be lost or substantially delayed by a decision to enforce? Considerations such as these may very well have an impact on what an officer may do in a given situation. This is especially true when he is given little or no boundaries to govern how choices are to be made.

The nature of the patrolman's job is such that no amount of structure will totally limit his ability to personalize each contact that he makes. Therefore, the development of priorities and the ability to make judgmental decisions are an appropriate part of the policeman's job. If not recognized, then no focus can be brought to bear on the kinds of values that are important in decision-making and the kinds of controls that are necessary to permit the system to function with integrity.

Legal Authority for Discriminatory and Selective Law Enforcement

Statutory law speaks directly to a police officer's duty when he is confronted with what he believes to be a violation of the law. For example, Section 82, Chapter 125 of the 1971 Revised Statutes of Illinois states:

> *It shall be the duty of every sheriff, coroner, and every marshal, policeman, or other officer of any incorporated city, town, or village having the power of sheriff, when any criminal offense or breach of the peace is committed or attempted in his presence, forthwith to apprehend the offender and bring him before some judge or magistrate to be dealt with according to law.*

The Illinois statute is representative of most state statutes that prescribe a peace officer's duty. The officer is not given any authority to discriminate between cases that appear to fall under the literal terms of a statute. An exception to this rule would be where an officer has knowledge of a court decision holding a portion of a statute or ordinance to

---

[16] Jerome Skolnick, *Justice Without Trial* (New York: Wiley, 1966), p. 129.

be unconstitutional or in some other way limiting its literal application. If the law allows for tempering its application with mercy or with any other quality, it does not appear that statutory law provides the police officer with the authority to do it. The New Mexico statute is an exception to this rule, however. Section 1, Article 1, Chapter 39, Statutes of New Mexico, 1970 appears to direct peace officers to use judgment to discriminate between apparent violations of the law.

> It is hereby declared to be the duty of every sheriff, deputy sheriff, constable, and every other peace officer to investigate all violations of the criminal laws of the state of New Mexico which are called to the attention of any such officer or of which he is aware, and it is also declared the duty of every such officer to diligently file a complaint or information, if the circumstances are such as to indicate to a reasonably prudent person that such action should be taken.

Acknowledging that discretion is exercised is a most important first step, but it is only the first one necessary for the rational reform of selective enforcement decision-making policies. Even though the legal duties of police are clearly stated, there are numerous documentable instances of selective law enforcement at both the administrative and operational levels of policing. Furthermore, the courts have carefully avoided responding to any reference to these kinds of practices. A defendant is not ordinarily allowed to raise, in his defense in a criminal prosecution, the fact that authorities knowingly ignore hundreds of similar violations. The issue, if raised, is usually treated as being irrelevant to the question of the defendant's guilt. Clearly, the question of whether or not the defendant committed certain acts is not answered by the assertion that other persons may have done the same thing.

In relation to fact-finding in the individual case, it would appear that the court's treatment of such matters is reasonable. But important issues are avoided. Does the "law," as it is applied in a given community, appear to single out particular people and not their acts? And does this method of applying laws result in unequal protection of citizens, in violation of the Constitution? Setting the legal issues aside, it would seem fundamentally unfair for any agency to reserve statutes for application only to unlucky people who fall into a special, but not legally defined, class. The U.S. Supreme Court has attempted to deal with the issue of unequal protection under the law raised by discriminatory law enforcement. The case of *Yick Wo* v. *Hopkins* (118 U.S. 356, 1886) is the most frequently cited case in this area. It dealt with the situation of Chinese laundry operators who were subjected to regulations that apparently were never enforced against Caucasian businessmen. The regulations in question did not provide for differentiation by race, but patterns of enforcement over a period of several years made the discrimination obvious. The Court said:

> Though the law itself be fair on its face and impartial in appearance, yet, if it is applied and administered by public authority with an evil eye and unequal hand, so as practically to make unjust and illegal discrimination between persons in similar circumstances, material to their rights, the denial of equal justice is still within the protection of the Constitution.

Although the *Yick Wo* case would appear to provide a remedy for the victim of discriminatory law enforcement, it has been used in the courts in a very narrow manner. *Yick Wo* is generally held to be applicable only to situations where a contending party can show that there has been a systematic program of discrimination focused specifically on him or persons easily identifiable with him as members of the same class. This is an almost impossible fact for a defendant to prove in most cases and it would not apply to the many discriminatory law enforcement decisions that are made by individual police officers every day. In a more recent case, the Supreme Court avoided dealing with the issue of discriminatory enforcement of a vagrancy ordinance against the defendant when there were many other violators present at the time of his arrest. The defendant alleged that he was arrested not so much for vagrancy but because his previous public statements were unpopular with the police officers present.[17]

In addition to defendants in criminal cases, other citizens may also be concerned with the problem of selective law enforcement. The only way they can correct selective law enforcement policies they do not like is through the political system. Some effort to use *writs of mandamus* have been made. *Mandamus* is available by statute in most American jurisdictions. It is an action that can be brought against a public official to compel him to perform specified ministerial acts that are directed by statute. Since *mandamus* is generally held applicable to ministerial acts that do not involve the use of judgment by the part that it is directed to, courts have been unwilling to use the remedy to tell police departments

---

[17] Edelman v. California, 344 U.S. 357 (1953).

how to conduct their business. The courts will not involve themselves in supervising the operation of the function of policing, which requires continuous attention and the exercise of judgment.

Other attempts have been made to seek court orders compelling police to do their duty. These efforts have, for the most part, failed because the courts are unwilling, except in the most abusive cases, to substitute their judgment for that of an agency under the executive branch of the government.

Administrative Problems Created by the Practice

The present situation is not a healthy one. Police administrators make secret policies and individual officers are called upon to tailor justice on a daily basis. The officer, for lack of clear policy, can only guess what his supervisor would have him do. In most instances, he improvises.

If the selective law enforcement policies of police work were officially recognized, several important advantages could be gained. First, the selection, training, and supervision of police could reflect this important dimension of the job. It is absurd to think that a practice that represents a major portion of police work must be excluded from police training programs because the institutions will not recognize that the practice exists.

Second, the working police officer is in a very ambivalent situation; he must have guidelines to help him make the correct decisions. He knows that full enforcement of laws may be objectionable, but he has no resources or counsel available to help him make decisions. When the officer makes a selective enforcement decision, his confidence in his own integrity may be undermined by the feeling that he is part of an illicit conspiracy. Believing that he should make exceptions in the application of laws, he is unable to act openly because the special accommodation is not supposed to be made. The necessity that all must be unspoken taints the contact of the officer with the citizen and even with his fellow officer. This conspiracy of silence presents a negative image of the entire system. In addition, the refusal of police administrators to control a major portion of police work because they are interested in keeping selective enforcement policies secret, hurts their ability to deal with substantial questions of corruption and the abuse of citizens.

The alternative is to produce guidelines on selective law enforcement policies. These guidelines would relieve both officer and citizen anxieties regarding the legitimacy of dispositions and would probably produce more effective police–citizen communications. The supervisor could require and expect truthful reports of dispositions without fear that he may be told something he does not want to hear. Resources could be developed to assist officers in their decision-making. Open forums on selective enforcement practices and the development of information bureaus would help guide officers in considering available referral and consulting resources for different kinds of cases. Selective decisions would be made on a less arbitrary and more informed basis.

A third advantage of open policy formulation for selective and discriminatory law enforcement is the candor that it might improve in police handling of citizen complaints. Frequently, an agency will be evasive and thus undermine its credibility, instead of offering an explanation of what might very well be a defensible selective law enforcement policy. The citizen might not agree with the policy of the precinct not to ticket illegally parked cars in a particular area, while his own automobile was cited only a block away. But the establishment of a high level of credibility with the citizen may have a positive value far greater than the negative feelings caused by a policy disagreement.

Why Police Administrators Refuse to Acknowledge Selective Enforcement Practices

Police administrators who want to keep selective and discriminatory law enforcement policies secret often use five arguments.
1. If policies of nonenforcement or special enforcement were stated, the administrator would have to defend the quality of his decisions.
2. Acknowledgment of such decisions would cause the police administrator to lose his image of impartiality.
3. Statutory law prohibits the development of such policies.
4. Discretion breeds corruption.
5. There is a danger that stated policy, rather than statutory enactment, would become the limit of the law.

With reference to the first argument, the responsible administrator of one of the most essential and pervasive of public services owes the community an explanation for decisions that will directly affect the conduct and quality of life. If there is no defensible basis for establishing a policy or an exception, the administrator should revoke it.

Second, there is little value in perpetuating an image of impartiality. When selective enforcement takes place at the operational level of the department, citizens think that the police chief knows and has approved it. The police administrator should not attempt to delude the public any more than he should refuse to acknowledge and explain his department's operational policies.

The argument that selective law enforcement may be illegal is perhaps the most substantial of the arguments made. However, the legality of selective enforcement decisions is not determined by whether or not they are secret. Public policies that discriminate illegally do not become legally sanctioned when they become secret. The only effect of secrecy is the loss of public credibility with a resulting undermining of citizen confidence in the system. As previously noted, the legislatures and courts depend on law enforcement agencies to make selective decisions. If a police administrator were to clearly state his policies and the reasons for them, and provide controls for their implementation, it is quite likely that the legislative and judicial branches of government would stretch to accommodate them. In addition, at the very least, other functions of government would be forced to share the knotty problems presented by the strict enforcement question.

As to whether discretion breeds corruption—if this is true it would be true whether the use of discretion is open or secret. But the effect of officially developed and publicly defended policies—together with structures created to review and control the use of discretion—would be to illuminate the situation so well that corruption would not have its present opportunity to flourish.

It may be true that if policies of selective law enforcement were made public, citizens might argue that the law is suspended by the existence of the policy. As will be suggested in the following section, this should not be a defense for the citizen in the individual case, unless he can show that the violation of policy resulted in an obvious injustice; if he can show this, the argument would be totally justified, whether policies of exception are expressed or informal.

A Proposal

In 1972 the American Bar Association published its *Standards Relating to the Urban Police Function*. The *Standards* urged that legislatures recognize police use of discretion in formulating selective law enforcement decisions. They also emphasized the importance of developing an orderly and open method of police policy formulation and the control of its use in the area of discretionary enforcement.[18]

The use of discretion in law enforcement today is highly suspect and subject to considerable abuse. Wilson suggests that a most important first step in police organizational reform is the official recognition of selective law enforcement.[19] There is virtually nothing that can be done to deal constructively with this omnipresent aspect of police work until we recognize that it does exist. The general public is aware of selective law enforcement and it is time for professionals to admit that they use it.

The police are not the only governmental employees who have been hesitant to admit that they use discretion. Professor Kenneth Culp Davis, whose views are based on years of scholarly study of administrative agencies and the use of discretion, draws a frightening picture of the dangers lurking in the unreviewable and uncontrolled use of discretion in important public functions. The gains in credibility that would be obtained through official recognition of the use of discretionary decision-making in police work will more than offset the inconvenience and costs involved.

In order to facilitate official recognition of the use of discretion in the police profession, Professor Stephen A. Schiller of the University of Illinois suggests that police departments establish enforcement policy boards.[20] The chairman of each board should be the chief of police. The purpose of the board would be to review law enforcement policies and, if it is found that there is a need for special selective policies, statements of these policies ought to be made, together with an explanation of the

[18] American Bar Association, *The Urban Police Function* (New York: Institute of Judicial Administration, 1972), pp. 13, 116-144.
[19] Wilson, *Varieties of Police Behavior*, pp. 83-88.
[20] Stephen A. Schiller, "More Light on a Low Visibility Function," *Police Law Quarterly*, Vol. 6 (1972).

reasons for their adoption.[21] These statements should be made public and given to line personnel along with their training materials.

Schiller does not suggest that the board include civic or community representatives. Rather, he leaves this decision to the chief of police. There should be some procedures established for citizen inputs to the board, however. This is not to say that the board should judge individual citizen complaints: that is not its job. Individual citizen complaints and testimony should be used by the board only for the purpose of helping it arrive at sound law enforcement policy and to review operations under existing policies.

As part of its structure, the board should have a policy implementation unit that should systematically collect data on the use of policy at the operational level. The unit should keep records on inquiries by police officers and report the officers' difficulties in understanding policies in operational settings. It should also be available to field personnel, to offer guidance on policy interpretation in particular cases. The data collected by the policy implementation unit should be periodically reviewed by the board, together with citizen and police inputs.

As stated previously, the board would not review an individual citizen complaint of arbitrary or discriminatory treatment. The citizen would be encouraged to take his complaint either to the regular police internal affairs unit or to the courts.

---

[21] At this point many would argue that such an undertaking by a police agency, even given express direction by the legislature to form a board to develop policy for selective law enforcement, would constitute either an usurpation or an illegal delegation of legislative authority. As a practical matter, the so-called nondelegation doctrine is no longer workable. The courts have recognized that the complexities of regulatory needs make such a doctrine totally unfeasible. K. C. Davis in his *Administrative Law Treatise—1970 Supplement*, in sections 200-200-4, demonstrates through decided cases that the doctrine has lacked vitality from the time of its inception. A rule of nondelegation cannot be operationally implemented without tremendous cost in the quality of public regulation. Davis, in section 200-5 of his *Treatise*, suggests that the focus should not be on nondelegation but on controls and safeguards against abuses of delegations. Also see K. C. Davis, *Discretionary Justice* (Baton Rouge, La.: Louisiana State University Press, 1969), p. 44.

The Courts

If a citizen is charged under a statute that is the subject of an articulated selective law enforcement policy, the court should decide whether the application of the statute to the defendant conforms with the policy. One of the costs of the right to develop policy is the obligation to conform to it. If the defendant's conduct falls within an area of exclusion, the burden should be placed on the prosecution to show that the application of the law to the defendant should be excused.

When the defendant raises the existence of a selective policy in relation to the offense he has been charged with, the court should determine whether the policy itself, although correctly applied in a given case, is arbitrary on its face. A court determination that a selective law enforcement policy is arbitrary should not have the effect of discharging a defendant, but should result in nullification of the policy itself. When a court finds an enforcement policy to be void, the department responsible for the policy should have the ability to appeal the question to a reviewing court. This would, of course, make it necessary for the policy board to have the support of legal counsel.

Internal Review

When a citizen who is not a defendant in a criminal prosecution has a complaint, either with reference to nonenforcement or unequal enforcement of laws, a police department's internal affairs unit should be able to answer his questions. Where appropriate, these cases should be referred to the policy implementation unit, which should determine whether the complaint indicates a violation of departmental policy. If such a finding is made, the policy implementation unit should have the power to order corrective action. At the very least, the citizen complainant can be fully informed of the reasons for the policy.

The data produced by all reported incidents should be collected and used to provide information for review of policies. If the policy implementation unit believes that operational procedures under a particular policy are not meeting the expectations of the policy board, it should recommend that the board initiate a special review of the policy.

Once selective law enforcement policies are stated by the department, legislators will have a chance to act on them. If the stated policies, together with the assumptions upon which they are based, go beyond what the legislature is willing to tolerate as possible options under its enactments, the legislature can clarify any misunderstandings through committee proceedings or more definitive statutes. If the legislature specifically rejects the interpretation given a statute by a law enforcement agency, the agency will have to follow the legislative direction. However, issues between the legislature and the police will be clearly developed for review by the electorate.

Conclusions

The President's Commission on Law Enforcement and the Administration of Justice and several distinguished scholars have pointed out the need for official police recognition of selective law enforcement policies. They do not agree as to where corrective action ought to be directed, but they all feel that there is an immediate need to do something other than support the continued avoidance of the issues presented. While police administrators agree that there is a need for selective law enforcement policies, there have been no significant efforts by these administrators to establish and clarify these policies. Perhaps this has occurred because most recommendations in this area have been too vague. Therefore, the following projects are suggested.

1. Statutory revision, adding to existing statutes that describe the peace officer's duty to arrest "... if the circumstances are such as to indicate to a reasonably prudent person that such action should be taken."
2. Develop within police departments structures for policy articulation and policy implementation. Both programs should be open, and should be publicly reporting functions of the police department.
3. Police selection, training, and supervision models should reflect a consciousness of selective law enforcement as an aspect of police work.

The inability of police administrators to openly discuss their needs has resulted in a continuous narrowing of law enforcement discretion. Refusal to acknowledge discretionary judgments about operational policies leads to increased friction between citizens and police and between operational level personnel and their administrators. Increased disharmony between the agencies in the criminal justice system also occurs.

The claim to professionalism that law enforcement makes requires an assumption of the obligations of a profession. Reiss says that an attribute of a profession is "the making of decisions that involve technical and moral judgments affecting the fate of people."[22] Police make these kinds of decision but refuse to acknowledge them because of a general unwillingness to defend the assumptions upon which these decisions are made. As Reiss suggests, if the police do not compromise, it is almost certain that external controls will be developed to govern the police use of discretion.

Law enforcement personnel and prosecutors have shown an amazing determination to be secretive and indecisive in dealing with issues of widespread public concern. The extension of the federal exclusionary rules to the states, for example, represents a recognition by the Supreme Court that police and prosecutors showed themselves to be consistently evasive in dealing with those problems. Most scholars would agree that the exclusionary rule is not constitutionally required, but was used because the Court believed that it was the only way a reasonable amount of protection could be offered for important constitutional rights and protections.

When the issue of custodial interrogation was brought before the Court in *Miranda* v. *Arizona* (384 U.S. 436), the Court as well as law enforcement personnel were conscious of a history of abuses related to the practice of interrogation. From the Wickersham Commission Report in 1931 to cases docketed in the Court in 1965, were found numerous verified instances of abusive and unlawful behavior on the part of "law enforcers." There had been a succession of cases dealing with interrogation, each of which had been determined by the Court on the circumstances of the individual case, but each decision contained an announced concern for the lack of controls against abusive police practices.

The law enforcement profession did not want to develop guidelines to limit custodial interrogation to the small number of cases where they may be an essential tool in the solution of a crime. Nor did they want to develop controls that would limit the possibilities of abuse in the cases where interrogation is used. Rather, law enforcement's spokesmen firmly held onto the unsupportable position that the uncontrolled use of interrogation is essential to effective law enforcement in all cases. They did not reflect any concern at all for the development of the internal

[22] Reiss, *Police and the Public*, p. 123.

mechanism that would eliminate the kinds of police abuse described in the records before the Court.

Recognizing that the law enforcement profession was unresponsive to the needs that it had pointed to again and again over a period of 10 years, the Court found itself forced to impose a rule that would, in essence, eliminate the need to depend on the judgment of law enforcers. The Court, finding a lack of credibility in law enforcement's position, looked to the records of the many successful prosecutions that had not depended upon the use of confessions and to the experiences of jurisdictions that had reduced the importance of interrogation in their criminal processes. The Court stated, "Although confessions may play an important role in some convictions, the cases before us present graphic examples of the overstatement of the need for confessions."

Had law enforcement shown the capacity to be selective and willing to state the reasoning for its decisions and to provide controls to eliminate abuses, it is likely that the Court's decision might have been to continue to decide individual cases on their merits, anticipating a substantial reduction in the number of reports of abuses due to the responsible action of law enforcement agencies. Thus, the law enforcement profession learned that it must meet important policy issues within its own sphere of operations, in a straightforward manner. If law enforcement professionals do not assume these responsibilities, other agencies will make the decisions for them.

Student Checklist

1. Can you explain the reasons given for the use of selective enforcement and discriminatory application of laws?
2. What is the legal authority for discriminatory and selective enforcement?
3. Can you describe some of the administrative problems created with this practice?
4. Could you also describe why some police administrators refuse to acknowledge the existence of selective and discriminatory aspects of law enforcement?

Topics for Discussion

1. Discuss the reasons for the use of selective and discriminatory law enforcement.
2. Discuss the legal authority for this practice.
3. Discuss some of the administrative problems created with selective enforcement and discriminatory application of laws.
4. Discuss why some police administrators refuse to acknowledge this practice.

ANNOTATED BIBLIOGRAPHY

American Bar Association. *Standards Relating to the Urban Police Function*, 99, 116–144 (1972). The Bar Association work on the urban police function consists of a series of standards formulated over a period of several years by a nationally prominent committee of lawyers and law enforcement professionals. They propose that law enforcement deal more openly with selective law enforcement questions.

Gardiner, John. *Traffic and the Police.* Boston: Harvard University Press, 1969. Gardiner's book describes the effect of different choices in relation to law enforcement values made by neighboring police departments regarding the enforcement of the same laws. This work illustrates the attitudes and other dynamics that formulate law in an active, as opposed to passive, form.

Goldstein, Joseph. "Police Discretion Not To Invoke the Criminal Process." *69 Yale Law Journal*, 543 (1960). This article is perhaps the leading early study in this area. He believes that law enforcement agencies are not, by and large, given the discretion to discriminate between cases where there is conceded to be a technical violation of the law. He suggests that if discriminatory enforcement decisions are to be made, they should be made somewhere other than at the police level. He would favor the stringent enforcement of laws, so that some laws that may have become anachronistic will be confronted by political interests.

Goldstein, Herman. "Police Discretion: The Ideal versus the Real," 23 *Public Administration Review*, 543 (1960). This article is written from the perspective of someone who ha$ been an administrator in an operating system. He notes that discrimination in the application of laws is very much a part of such systems and suggests that administrators have an obligation to face up to their decisions. He describes some of the rationales developed by police executives to avoid direct positions on discriminatory or selective law enforcement questions.

LaFave, Wayne. *Arrest: The Decision to take a Suspect Into Custody.* Boston: Little, Brown, 1965, Chapters 3–8; "Police and Non-enforcement of Laws," *Wisconsin Law Review* (1962). This book deals not only with the laws of arrest, but also with the dynamics of the decision to arrest. In several chapters he discusses the selective and discriminatory enforcement of laws and the control factors that relate thereto. The article represents some of Professor LaFave's earlier thinking in the area.

"Police Discretion and Equal Protection," *14 South Carolina Law Quarterly*, p. 472 (1962). This work discusses the constitutional questions raised by the existence of selective law enforcement policies.

Schiller, Stephen A. "More Light on a Low Visibility Function: The Need to Recognize and Structure Selective and Discriminatory Enforcement of Laws." *Police Law Quarterly*, July 1972, p. 6; October 1972, p. 20; January 1973, p. 17; April 1973, p. 35.

The study of this chapter will enable you to:

1. Describe what we mean by community control.
2. State why some communities are more desirous of control than other communities.
3. List different methods of community control.
4. Compare the effectiveness of different styles of community control.
5. Write a short essay on why some methods of community control are more successfully received than others.

12

Community Control

This chapter will attempt to offer some insight into the interaction that takes place between the criminal justice system and the community. It describes some of the methods of implementing community control, which has an impact on the criminal justice system as a whole. It is not our purpose to advocate any particular model of community control, nor even to convince the reader of the value of such a concept. Rather, it is intended to be an objective description and analysis of some of the methods of community control currently being considered or implemented in the field of criminal justice.

The General Concept of Community Control

Little general agreement exists on a definition of this concept. The term is generally defined to suit the purposes of a specific analysis, and depends to a large extent on what subject is being investigated. Definitions range from meaning the community's absolute control over an organization (of which there are few examples) to the ability of a community to exercise some degree of input (of which there are many examples).

Because the definitions vary so widely, it is important to examine the characteristics of community control. What do we mean when we speak of community and of control? Why are some communities more desirous of control than are others? Why are some methods of community control more successfully received than are others? How do the styles of community control differ?

In order to understand the concept of community control, we must first ask ourselves what we mean by the term *community*. It has been used to refer to a wide range of different groups of people, such as neighborhood (people united because they live near each other); population subgroups (people united because they have common characteristics, such as racial or ethnic origins, socioeconomic status, or political affiliations); and legal jurisdiction (people united because they live in a legally defined area, such as a city, congressional district, county, or state). Some writers have as their theme a community of man, which has international boundaries. Although the definitions vary in their emphases, they are unified by one important element: a community is composed of people interacting with people. The interaction may be conscious or unconscious, deliberate or unintentional, positive or negative. These patterns of interaction may be characterized by cooperation, competition, accommodation, conflict, assimilation, or stratification. However, the type or frequency of interaction, although significant, are not as important as the fact that the interaction is occurring. For the purpose of this discussion, community will be defined to describe groups of people brought together by a common goal. The object of the goal, whether it is to strengthen, alter, or destroy the system, is not central to the definition. Rather, what is emphasized in the definition is its "common-unity".[1] When *community* is used in this manner, it must be recognized that the members of the community may or may not be from the same neighborhood, racial or ethnic background, socioeconomic status, or legal jurisdiction. Instead, they are united by a common interest or purpose.

The use of the word *control* is equally difficult to pinpoint. Some writers have used control in an absolute context to mean "the ability to impose one's views upon others by the threat or use of power." Control can also mean the "opportunity to check, regulate, or keep within certain limits the actions of others." Defined in this manner, control is used in the context of providing an equilibrium and a measure of

[1] Louis A. Radelet, "The Idea of Community," *Police and Community Relations: A Sourcebook*, ed. A. F. Brandstatter and L. A. Radelet (Beverly Hills: Glencoe Press, 1968), p. 82.

accountability. Finally, control can be used more indirectly to include the ability to communicate with, to influence, to vote for, to participate, or to exercise impact with important decision-makers. Used in this manner, control emphasizes the ability to interact with people. Each of these definitions of control can be found to some extent in the criminal justice system. The prisoners' riots at Attica can be reviewed as an attempt to exercise control by threat or use of force. Civilian review boards, developed to handle citizen complaints against the police, are examples of the community's attempt to control by way of regulation and accountability. Recent citizen voting initiatives to reinstate the death penalty, citizen support of community-based correctional and diversionary programs, and citizen participation on criminal justice advisory councils are examples of community control by interaction.

Community control has a multifaceted nature, not an absolute value—it encompasses degrees of involvement. Community control must be regarded as a continuum of citizen participation. The degree of participation varies with the community involved as well as with the target or subject matter of the goal. The type of control used will be determined by the goal of the community. For example, if the community intends to destroy the system, the threat or use of violence might be contemplated as the most effective use of control. The purpose of defining community control by the use of a participation continuum is to create a definition that is flexible enough to incorporate a wide range of activities pursued at various levels of the criminal justice system.

In analyzing community control, the reader should be aware of several key questions related to the basic issue.[2] From what community is the demand for increased involvement coming? How likely is it to persist or mushroom? What type of increased participation does the community desire? How does the demand for increased participation fit into the general framework of American culture and politics? What are the types of interest affected by increased community control? How is the community being defined? What mode of representation or accountability does it seek?

[2] Alan A. Altshuler, *Community Control: The Black Demand for Participation in Large American Cities* (Indianapolis: Pegasus, 1970), pp. VII-IX.

Development of Community Control

There has been a growing demand on the part of citizens to have a greater voice in the governing of urban areas. Charges have been made by all segments of the political spectrum that the government is no longer responsive to the needs of the individual or general community, that the decision-makers are too far removed from the citizens and appear to be immune to public accountability.

The criminal justice system has not remained isolated from these accusations. The police, who are the most visible arm of the government at the community level, are often accused of representing the force of the dominant white class and of employing differential treatment and unnecessary brutality. The courts, too, have been criticized. These criticisms range from accusations of uneven justice to a questioning of judicial standards and accountability. The bail system, plea bargaining, and sentencing criteria are viewed as arbitrary decisions that are no longer responsive to the changing mores of the communities being served. Attacks aimed at the correctional system center around its perceived inability to rehabilitate the criminal so that he is no longer a threat to society.

The demand for increased participation by various communities comes from an apparent realization on the part of the citizens that they have a stake in making the components of the criminal justice system operate at a level responsive to their needs. This realization of citizen responsibility is being translated into citizen action. No longer is the aroused citizen content to permit the professionals to solve alone the problems of the police, courts, and corrections. Instead, the emphasis has seemingly switched from *"They* should do more" to *"We* can do more." Examples of this are numerous. Groups of citizens have organized to monitor the performance levels of the police, courts, and corrections. When the community is dissatisfied, pressure to improve the performance is generated from the community to the relevant administrator or elected official. The pressure is sometimes direct in the form of filing numerous complaints against a specific agency; at other times, it is more indirect and takes the form of citizen ballot initiatives or community support of alternative candidates. Judging from recent municipal, state, and national elections, "law and order" has become a visible issue that few office-seekers can afford to ignore.

The recent report of the National Advisory Commission on Criminal Justice Standards and Goals emphasized the importance of community involvement when it pointed out that:

> Government programs for the control of crime are unlikely to succeed all alone. Informed private citizens, playing a variety of roles, can make a decisive difference in the prevention, detection, and prosecution of crime, the fair administration of justice, and the restoration of offenders to the community.[3]

Thus, citizen and community involvement in the criminal justice system can no longer be viewed as merely desirable: it must be regarded as a necessity.

Community control of the criminal justice system is not a radical concept. Many early American societies required each individual to be responsible for keeping the peace. If a crime was observed, it was the duty of the citizen to arouse his neighbors and pursue the criminal. Peace was kept by the entire community.

Primarily because of increasing job specialization, the community delegated the peace-keeping function to specific individuals in the community. However, advocates of community control argue that the delegation of this responsibility by the community to the criminal justice specialist was not intended to be total abdication of responsibility on the part of the community. The citizen should still retain the right and duty to remain involved in the administration of the criminal justice system.

In its report on *State and Local Relations in the Criminal Justice System* (1971), the Advisory Commission on Intergovernmental Relations added indirect support to this argument by noting that:

> The distance between city hall or county courthouse and the neighborhoods is considerable. As a result, the delivery of services may be slow, communication channels may be cumbersome, and policymakers may be unaware of the real needs of neighborhood areas. Moreover, highly centralized decision-making may deter citizens from participating in crime prevention efforts.[4]

As a consequence, many criminal justice authorities stress that the

---

[3] National Advisory Commission on Criminal Justice Standards and Goals, *Working Papers for the National Conference on Criminal Justice* (Washington, D.C.: Law Enforcement Assistance Administration, January 1973), p. CC-7.
[4] Ibid., p. CC-8.

responsibility and accountability for planning, decision, and action should be placed at the lowest level consistent with sound decision-making—the community. Instead of attempting to wage the war against crime alone, proponents of community control urge professionals in the criminal justice system to work cooperatively with the community.

Problems of Community Control

The recognition of the usefulness of citizen involvement or community control is not universally accepted by either the average citizen or by the professionals employed in the criminal justice system. By its very nature, community control is reactive. It is only when conditions become unacceptable that citizens are aroused from apathy and are motivated to devote time, imagination, and energy to a particular cause. The civil rights movement of the 1960s and the college student demonstrations over the invasion of Cambodia in 1970 are strong examples of an aroused citizenry.

This phenomenon partially explains why some communities in the United States are much more actively seeking to assert control. The city of Berkeley, California, has become integrally involved. In the past four years, the voters of Berkeley have twice attempted to alter drastically the services provided to them by various components of the criminal justice system. The first was a ballot initiative to decentralize the police force into three autonomous units, each under the control of a specific community. The second attempt was to give the lowest enforcement priority to apprehending marijuana offenders. Both of these citizen initiatives will be discussed more extensively elsewhere in this chapter.

What the Berkeley examples point out is that communities react when the services provided are no longer acceptable to them. Even then, it is not the entire community that responds, but rather only the energetic and sufficiently aroused citizen. It is a difficult task to enlist the support of the unaffected citizen. The 1972 report of the National Advisory Commission on Criminal Justice Standards and Goals emphasizes this point and further suggests some of its implications.

There appears to be a widespread assumption that it is the business of the criminal justice system to respond to this demand and to marshall all available resources to choke off crime at its roots. This viewpoint neglects the certainty that unless a worried citizenry can translate its indignation into active participation in the search for and implementation of an effective solution, the criminal justice system must inevitably fall even farther behind in its crime control and rehabilitation efforts. Awakening the conscience of America is a necessity because if the multiplicity of factors that produce crime and delinquency are not recognized and remedied, more crime will occur, more of it will go undetected, and the inadequateness of the system will thus become even stronger incentive to further illegal activity.[5]

Beyond marshaling citizen support and involvement in the criminal justice system, advocates for increased citizen participation point out the need to instill a willingness on the part of the police, courts, and corrections to effectively use the available citizen input. Many studies indicate that the three components of the justice system are reluctant to involve the citizens in their operations. Many employees view such participation as an attempt to minimize their professional expertise.[6] In addition, there is a natural suspicion of outsiders on the part of any organization. It is established public administration theory that much organizational energy is spent in self-sustaining activities. Proposed reforms tend to be evaluated in terms of their efficiency in protecting the organization's welfare and in their ability to minimize the required expenditure of energy.[7] The organization's employees reinforce this tendency by developing patterns of behavior that further insulate the organization from the community. Their members often prefer to maintain the status quo despite public demands for change. They may be more resistant to community input than members of other organizations, because of the fragmentation of their services into separate local units, their method of recruitment and promotion, and their degree of isolation from the general public as well as from one another. Although police, courts, and corrections comprise a system, they are to a large degree isolated from each other in their operations.

Therefore, merely involving the community is not sufficient. When

[5] National Advisory Commission on Criminal Justice Standards and Goals, *Working Papers for the National Conference on Criminal Justice*, pp. CC-2.

[6] President's Commission on Law Enforcement and the Administration of Justice, *Task Force Report: The Police* (Washington, D.C.: U.S. Govt. Printing Office, 1967), p. 104.

[7] Vincent O'Leary, "Some Directions for Citizen Involvement in Corrections," *The Annals*, 381 (January 1969), p. 102.

a community is contemplating making a change in the system, it must recognize the importance of selecting an appropriate method for exerting influence and control. The Vera Institute of Justice in New York City provides a positive example of a private group of citizens working together to improve the criminal justice system. A brief review of their approach to improving the criminal justice system may serve as a model to others who are considering similar actions.

Vera's control strategy has been to identify specific problem areas and to experiment with changes that might benefit both the defendant and the relevant criminal justice agencies (police, prosecution, courts, and corrections). Its first project was bail reform; the second was a police summons project. Both of these projects were successfully incorporated into the operating structure of the New York City Police Department.[8]

The style of participation selected by the Vera Institute is an important facet of their success. Basically, their approach has five steps:

1. The Vera staff identifies the problem, considers the alternatives, and proposes a solution to the affected criminal justice agencies.
2. The Institute then provides the manpower to operate the project on a trial basis, thus minimizing the concerned agencies' expenditure of valuable resources.
3. The Institute assumes responsibility for the trial phase and continues to remain in close contact with the involved agencies.
4. When the trial phase has been evaluated and is considered to be a success, the Institute assumes an advisory role and permits the involved agency to take control of the project.
5. Although no longer formally involved with the project, the Institute remains in close association with the agency, available to discuss problems as they arise.

This example illustrates that bureaucratic inaction or citizen apathy need not hamper the development of effective community involvement in the criminal justice system.

It is now appropriate to turn our attention from the major theoretical foundations of community control and involvement to an analysis of examples of community control in the criminal justice system. Two general categories of community control have been developed. Each

[8] J. W. Doig, "Police Problems, Proposals and Strategies for Change," *Public Administration Review*, XXVIII (September/October 1969), p. 398.

category requires the citizens and community to assume a different role and involves different definitions of community control. The first category to be discussed will be defined as *pure* community control, based on the community's desire to participate in an "overseeing" capacity. Pure community control attempts to check, regulate, and otherwise keep within defined limits the actions of various components of the criminal justice system. The second category to be analyzed will be called *participative* community control, predicated on the community's willingness to function in the capacity of supplementing and complementing the operations of the criminal justice system. In this context, control encompasses a much larger range of activities. It is used to mean the ability to communicate with, to influence, to participate with, or to exercise impact with important decisionmakers.

Pure Community Control

A unique characteristic of pure community control is that it has been directed primarily at the police, since policing agencies are the most visible force of government at the community level, and police officers the primary initiators of action in the entire justice system. When a policeman makes the decision to arrest, he is making a formal determination of whether or not the potential arrestee should be processed into the criminal justice system. What happens at the police level determines to a greater degree what the rest of the criminal justice system is capable of doing. The initial and most expansive sorting out of "criminals" from "average citizens" is done by the police officer: only those arrested by the police can be adjudicated by the courts and rehabilitated by corrections. For these reasons, much public attention and concern centers around the operations of law enforcement agencies. Also, because police departments are manned by people who often are not required to receive a specialized education, the ordinary citizen perceives himself to be qualified to comment on and participate in police operations. A reason proposed by some to account for the lack of pure community control of the courts and correctional systems is that in both areas some variety of preservice education is required at the operating level. For that reason, the average citizen in the community is hesitant to exert control in these areas.

This section will review briefly five major developments in the area of pure community control of the police. These developments are: (1) the attempt to establish civilian complaint review boards; (2) the attempt to create an ombudsman to review citizen complaints against the police; (3) the attempt to politically and administratively decentralize the police; (4) the attempt to ride patrol on the police in the community; and (5) the attempt to affect the establishment of enforcement priorities.

Civilian Review Boards

Before discussing civilian review boards, it is important to understand the characteristics of internal police review boards. Most law enforcement agencies have regularized procedures and machinery for processing allegations of misconduct on the part of its officers, whether those charges originate inside or outside the department.

Internal complaint boards typically consist of high-ranking or, in some cases, nonsworn departmental officials who investigate the facts of the alleged misconduct and make recommendations to the departmental administrators. The department administrator, usually the chief or the sheriff, has the authority and responsibility to take disciplinary action. When this internalized system is operating fully and fairly, it succeeds both in disciplining misbehaving officers and deterring others in the department from misbehaving. The effectiveness of enforcement rests on the relative autonomy which society invests in the police. In the eyes of most police administrators, the exposure of police behavior to public scrutiny would politicize the operations of the police and thereby irreparably damage law enforcement's ability to act impartially.[9]

Civilian review boards were developed because of a general dissatisfaction with internal police review procedures. Many citizens, particularly members of minority communities, urged the establishment of civilian review boards to determine the validity of citizen complaints against the police. Civilian review boards were established in Washington, D.C. (1948), Philadelphia (1958), Minneapolis and York (1960),

[9] Harry W. More, Jr., ed., *Critical Issues in Law Enforcement* (Cincinnati: W. H. Anderson Company, 1972), p. 243.

Rochester (1963), and New York City (1966).[10] Boards have been proposed in most other large cities throughout the nation. Some state legislatures have considered bills requiring that large cities within their jurisdictions form such boards.

The creation of civilian review boards has generated controversy and heated debate. The President's Task Force Report on the Police documents the stormy history of the civilian review boards.

> The boards in Philadelphia and Rochester have been the subject of court suits and injunctions against their operation during part of their lives. The board in Washington, D.C., was severely criticized for inaction and was reorganized in 1965. The boards in Minneapolis and York never actually operated, and the board in New York City, after a very heated campaign, was rejected by the electorate and has been replaced by a board composed of civilian police employees.[11]

The size, composition, and staffing have varied with each civilian review board. Generally, however, the size of the boards ranged from seven to nine members, with the civilian membership in the majority. Usually, the civilian members were appointed by the mayor and the police members were appointed by the police commissioner. The staffing patterns varied considerably with each board. The New York Civilian Complaint Review Board had an administrative staff of 6 and an investigating staff of 50 police officers.[12] Italian, Spanish, and Chinese interpreters were available as well as adequate secretarial and office support services. In terms of their jurisdiction and power, the boards were advisory in nature and had no disciplinary power over the police.

Pro. Although the concept of civilian review boards is no longer advocated strongly, it is important to understand the arguments advanced by its advocates. Primarily, the board created a climate in which citizens were less fearful of stating their complaints regarding alleged police misconduct. The board also provided for conciliation by an impartial agency. It educated the public regarding their legal rights as well as what constituted good police behavior, and provided for public exoneration of a police officer by an impartial agency. Finally, the board's investiga-

---

[10] *Task Force Report: The Police*, p. 200.
[11] Ibid.
[12] Algernon D. Black, *The People and the Police* (New York: McGraw-Hill, 1968), p. 80.

tion of the complaint would be impartial and characterized by a quest for truth.

Con. Counteracting these positive aspects of the civilian review board are the arguments advanced by the opponents to the board, specifically, police officers and administrators. They argued that the board tied the hands of the police administrator by usurping his authority to investigate and discipline his officers; that it had a demoralizing influence on the police department, causing many men to seek other employment. Another side effect was that it fostered inaction on the part of the department since, by exercising discretion, an officer ran the risk of having a complaint lodged against him. Finally, the board was ineffective because civilians are not qualified to judge the performance of police officers. The civilian membership on the board was perceived as possessing a likely bias in favor of the complainant.

The responsibility remains with the reader to critically appraise the merits of each side's arguments and come to his own conclusions regarding the value of the concept of the civilian review board.

Ombudsman

Some cities and states have explored the idea of establishing an ombudsman as an alternative to the civilian review board concept. The ombudsman concept in government is fairly new to Americans, but it has been in existence in Sweden since 1809.

The ombudsman concept is similar to the civilian review board in that it is external to the police department and has the power to act upon any complaints received from aggrieved citizens. It differs from the civilian review board in the sense that it handles complaints lodged against all governmental agencies, including the city manager's office, fire department, and department of public works. The department or agency named in the complaint is obligated to assist the ombudsman in the investigation of the complaint. If the complaint is found to be justified, the ombudsman notifies the concerned agency and advises the proper administrator of the action required to relieve the situation. The administrator reports back to the ombudsman when the corrective steps have been taken. At this point, the ombudsman notifies the complainant of the disposition of his complaint.

The ombudsman approach appears to have several advantages in terms of the community. Again, like the civilian review board, it provides the opportunity for citizen complaints to be aired in an environment of seeming impartiality. A measure of government accountability is inherent in the process.

The opposition to the concept has primarily been from law enforcement. The police argue that their work is unique, especially when compared to that of firemen, public works employees, the city manager's office, or even city councilmen. Law enforcement administrators question whether someone unfamiliar with police practices can adequately appraise what would constitute correct police procedure in a given situation.[13]

Political and Administrative Decentralization of the Police

In response to various communities' demands for greater participation in the functioning of law enforcement, many police administrators have initiated structural changes in their organization that are designed to bring the officer into closer contact with the community being served. These changes have taken a number of forms, many of which fall under the name of "team policing." Team policing has been successfully implemented in communities as diverse as Washington, D.C., New York City, Detroit, Syracuse, Los Angeles, Palo Alto, Holyoke, Dayton, and Louisville. The basic goal of team policing is to return greater responsibility to those doing the actual policing. Consequently, it involves a certain measure of administrative decentralization. Patrolmen and first-line supervisors are assigned in a semipermanent capacity to a particular neighborhood and are encouraged to develop a positive rapport with the residents of the community.

The team-policing approach was designed to bring the police and the community closer together. Augmenting this is a police strategy designed to decentralize their services. This decentralization of services has led to the creation and development of police "storefront" operations, which have been gaining popularity in recent years. Several large police agencies have established storefront centers in an attempt to pro-

---

[13] Ibid., p. 255.

vide greater public access to a wide range of referral services. The Los Angeles Police Department has recently established a storefront operation in East Los Angeles, an area heavily populated by Mexican-Americans. Bilingual officers man the center 12 hours a day. The sole purpose of the project is to help the community's residents handle their problems. If the staff cannot assist adequately, the resident is referred to an appropriate agency, and follow-up telephone calls are made to determine that the problem has been resolved. To date, the results have been good, but long-term evaluations will be necessary to evaluate the project's effectiveness.

The Berkeley Model. The residents of Berkeley, California, developed an extension of the team policing model, which sought to politically decentralize the police. An amendment to the city charter was proposed which "would rearrange city government to permit direct control of the police by the people in three administrative (and neighborhood) districts."[14]

Supporters of the Berkeley charter amendment believed that the citizens were unable to effectively control the city's police department under the existing system, in which the city manager and city council rarely exercised their legally constituted authority over the police. Consequently, the proponents argued, the police department was insulated from the public. To overcome the situation, the proponents advocated splitting the city into three neighborhoods: the black community; the campus/youth community; and the middle-class Northside/Hill community. It was realized, however, that none of these communities were distinct, but that they were more common than uncommon. Each of these three communities was to be divided into precincts on a population basis. A precinct representative would be elected by the residents of that area to sit on a district police council, which was to be represented proportionally according to population. Fifteen precincts comprised a district, and there were five districts in Berkeley. Each district was entitled to elect a commissioner to a five-man police commission for the city of Berkeley.

It was the responsibility of the district council to perform the following duties: a continual review of all policies of the police depart-

---

[14] Richard A. Myren, "Decentralization and Citizen Participation in the Criminal Justice System," *Public Administration Review*, XXXII (October 1972), p. 726.

ment; the formulation of recommendations to the police commission for policy changes when the needs or will of the neighborhood they served were no longer being met by the policies; the creation and operation of a grievance procedure to hear complaints against the police; and discipline of members of the police department for violations of law and policy in their district.[15]

Administrative coordination of the three essentially autonomous neighborhood police departments was the responsibility of the five-member police commission. Their duties would be similar to those normally assumed by a police chief. The police commission set police policy, established criteria for employment, determined salary levels, and handled all of the other administrative duties associated with normal police operations. Financing would continue to be through appropriation from the city council, and would be distributed to the three forces according to population.

The Berkeley charter amendment failed at the polls in April 1971. The arguments against implementing the Berkeley charter initiative were similar to those against civilian review boards. That is, police morale would deteriorate, which would deter the recruitment and retaining of qualified police officers; there would be a decline in police stature and prestige; and that only a police-trained robot could function under the proposed Berkeley initiative.

Citizen and Community Alert Programs

In August, 1966, a civic group was organized in San Francisco called "Citizens Alert." This program was developed as an alternative to police review boards, and was composed of people interested in police work. Its purpose was to facilitate communication between the police and the community and to collect, analyze, and report police misconduct. One method used was to have someone on call day and night who could respond to complaints of alleged police misconduct. Legal and medical services were also available. The organization investigated the complaint independently and registered its findings with the relevant police agency.

[15] Ibid., p. 727.

The proponents of the group emphasize the importance of its independent status and its grass roots appeal. The opponents stress its ineffectiveness in handling complaints; since the group is not present at the incidents, their investigations are based solely on the testimony of the complainants.

The "Community Alert Patrol" is similar in some ways to the "Citizen Alert." The former has augmented its approach by using community residents to follow police cars in the neighborhood to observe and document police activity. The participants use "community alert" cars and carry flash cameras, tape recorders, and two-way radios. This approach was developed in the Watts community of Los Angeles, and has been implemented in several other communities.

Community Control of Enforcement Priorities

Another development in community control took place in Berkeley in April 1973, when the voters passed an initiative calling for police to give the "lowest priority" to enforcing laws against possession, use, or cultivation of marijuana and to obtain district police council permission to make arrests for violation of those laws.[16] The city council further voted to instruct the city manager to comply with the provisions of the marijuana initiative. In effect, the police department has been directed to no longer enforce those California laws that make it a crime to possess, use, or cultivate marijuana.

Law enforcement authorities hold that the council did not have the power to prohibit police from making arrests for violations of state law. The effect of the city council's support of the initiative is that a challenge to the initiative's legality must originate from outside sources.

What this example illustrates is the extent to which a community can exert control. The initiative passed by the Berkeley voters has placed the city in violation of the state law. And the police department is caught in the middle. Should the police, being a local entity, respond to the directives of the voters, city council members, and the city manager, or should they continue to be guided by the state law prohibiting mari-

[16] Philip Hager, "Berkeley Council Votes to Ease Up on Pot Arrests," *Los Angeles Times* (May 3, 1973), Section 1, p. 3.

juana? What the police decide to do will have impact on the functioning of the entire criminal justice system in Berkeley. As mentioned earlier, the decision to arrest on the part of the police officer activates the balance of the justice system. The Berkeley situation raises some critical questions that, at least in California, have yet to be resolved.

Although most efforts in pure community control have been directed towards the police, the student should be aware that some measure of control has also been aimed at the courts. Some communities have developed "Court Watcher" programs. These programs are composed of interested and concerned citizens who sit in on various court sessions and monitor the performance of the presiding judge and prosecutor. The program is still in its initial stages of growth, but it has a great potential as a restraint of the power of the judiciary. Since many judges, district attorneys, and city attorneys are elected, the court watcher program could become a workable method for making the judiciary more responsive to the community.

Participative Community Control

Participative community control has been defined as the community's willingness to function in the capacity of supplementing and complementing the operations of the criminal justice system. Four key roles may be identified as being central to participative community control. They are: the volunteers—those who work directly with the person being assisted; the social persuaders—persons of influence or elite status in the dominant social system who are willing to persuade others to support criminal justice programs; the gatekeepers of opportunities— those who control the access to important social systems; and intimates —persons who possess a common background or understanding of the problems confronting the person to be assisted.[17] The effective balancing of these roles by a program coordinator can be of valuable assistance in generating a successful program in the community.

Unlike *pure* community control, *participative* community control

[17] O'Leary, p. 99. "Some Directions for Citizen Involvement in Corrections," *The Annals*, 381 (January 1969), p. 99.

is directed toward augmenting and providing supportive services to the justice system. The most obvious examples of participative control are found in the support and development of diversionary and community-based treatment facilities. Although diversionary programs and community-based treatment programs overlap, each topic will be discussed separately.

Diversionary Programs in the Community

Diversion refers to the official or unofficial practice of diverting people away from and out of the justice system prior to conviction. Action taken after conviction is not diversion because, at that point, the prosecution has already reached the determination of guilt. The major characteristic of diversion is that it prevents the person's penetration further into the justice system.

The decision to divert an individual from judicial proceedings is affected by many factors: the nature of the offense, the circumstances of its commission, the attitude of the victim, and the character of the accused.

Diversion of persons from the criminal justice system has long been practiced in the United States and throughout most of the Western world. Unfortunately, it has been carried out in a covert manner since many people feel that it violates the classic arrest, conviction, and punishment model that the justice system is supposed to follow. However, if a considerable degree of discretion was not exercised by the police, prosecutors, and the judiciary, the system would be swamped by its own activities. If all law violators were processed according to the classic model, our criminal justice system would collapse both from voluminous caseloads and community opposition. Consequently, the practice of diverting law violators on a formal and informal level must be viewed as a realistic adjustment on the part of the justice system.

Basically, the argument for diversion is an argument against the existing system. The primary thesis of diversion assumes that the present justice system has so many negative aspects that any alternative for diverting persons out of it is better than any that will move the person

[18] Robert L. Smith, "Diversion from the Juvenile and Criminal Justice Process" (unpublished paper, 1972), p. 12.

further into it.[18] Based on current research and knowledge in the field, there is much evidence to support the thesis that the further a person penetrates into the justice system and the more frequently he is recycled through it, the greater the likelihood that he will continue his illegal behavior.

A variety of diversionary programs have developed in the community to handle the increasing numbers of people being diverted from the system. Some of these programs are described in the following pages.

The Manhattan Bowery Project

In one of our largest states, one out of three arrests is for the offense of nontraffic drunkenness. It is estimated that the cost for handling each case—involving police, courts, and corrections—is approximately $100 per arrest. The official processing of these offenders is ineffective both in terms of deterrence and rehabilitation, and achieves only the offender's temporary removal from public view. This is accomplished, however, at an expense of $44 million per year to the taxpayer and the placement of an enormous burden on the criminal justice system.

In an attempt to free these criminal justice resources for use in a more constructive manner, the Vera Institute of New York developed a program designed to keep persons arrested for drunkenness out of the justice system. The program operates in Manhattan's Bowery district; one of its major objectives is to find a way to treat alcoholics without burdening the police with an arrest procedure. Additional project goals include a reduction in the permanent burden on the courts and jails caused by drunk-related arrests, and the rehabilitation of as many of the men as possible.

To implement these goals, the Vera Institute established a detoxification center, medical clinic, and aftercare unit for Bowery residents. All three units were housed in a large shelter located within the district. Teams of civilians riding in unmarked police vehicles patrol the area, offering services to anyone who appears intoxicated or otherwise debilitated. Police officers also bring cases to the medical unit, but they are careful to avoid giving the appearance of making an arrest. Nearly two-thirds of the men approached by these teams accept the invitation to enter the center, and a greater number enter on their own.

Treatment in the Bowery detoxification center is similar to that offered by other centers. After detoxification, referrals are made to other agencies that can provide an expanded range of services. Follow-up indicates that nearly 75 percent of the referrals are pursued by the patients. Because of the aftercare unit, patients may continue treatment at the center if they wish.

The approximate cost of serving the client is $40 per day for detoxification and a lesser cost for aftercare. The Bowery project has assisted in reducing the number of men processed through the criminal justice system. In addition, it has provided a nonpunitive environment that emphasizes treatment and rehabilitation.

Family Crisis Intervention Project

There are indications that the police, by identifying conflict-ridden situations at an early stage of development, can prevent the escalation of violence and the necessity of making arrests, thereby diverting persons from becoming involved in the criminal justice system.

To test this hypothesis, the New York City Police Department established a family crisis intervention unit. Officers stationed in high-crime neighborhoods were trained to intervene in family disturbances. Interracial teams of officers responded to all family disturbance calls and attempted to mediate or resolve the conflict on the scene. If unsuccessful, they referred the antagonist to various community agencies that could provide the necessary counseling services. The New York program has been implemented in other urban areas, including Chicago, Denver, and Oakland.

During the trial phase of the unit, not one homicide occurred in the 926 family crisis situations handled by the intervention teams, nor was a single officer injured.[19] Families who had experience with the teams referred other families to the project. Many troubled individuals even sought out team members for advice. As an unintended consequence, the relationship between the police and the community improved. The most important result of this program is that officers were

[19] Ibid., p. 55.

able to prevent the escalation of incidents to the point at which arrests would have been required.

Youth Services Bureau

The concept of a youth service bureau was developed as an alternative to social control by the criminal justice system. Although the concept is not new, it gained recent official support by the President's Crime Commission, which urged that such bureaus be developed in all communities to provide programs and services to youths. These bureaus are designed to divert children and young adults from judicial processing into social services. Because of regional differences in the types of delinquent acts, and resources available in communities, the nature of the programs and services vary from one community to another. Nevertheless, all youth service bureaus strive to involve the entire community, its agencies and its resources, in effective programs of crime prevention, diversion, rehabilitation, care, and control.

Community Responsibility Programs

Community responsibility programs are related to the concepts of the youth service bureaus, and are increasing in popularity. Frequently located in predominantly low-income, ethnic, and racial communities (particularly in California, Illinois, New York, and Puerto Rico), these projects are designed to assist troubled and delinquent youths. The main focus of the program is community involvement and responsibility for its own youth. A panel of community residents, both adults and youths, serve as judges, listening to cases of young offenders who have been referred by various justice agencies. Minors who have committed violations of the law appear before the citizen panel, which determines the minor's responsibility. If the panel finds that the offender is guilty, the youth may be required to carry out some supervised work for the good of the community. He may also be asked to participate in a counseling program.

Not only do community responsibility programs reduce crime and delinquency in their area, but they are also proving to be an effective method for diverting youthful offenders out of the juvenile justice system.

Drug-Related Diversion Programs

Because of the magnitude and nature of drug abuse and addiction, a wide variety of programs have been developed to divert and treat drug offenders. There are residence facilities, hospital programs, and outpatient treatment clinics, each requiring a different kind of community support.

Synanon is a good example of a residential drug treatment facility. Residents of the home have usually asked to be helped, which is an important aspect of the Synanon program. The program uses reality therapy and the communal residential unit to assist in the rehabilitation of the individual. Drug addiction is treated as a sickness—not a crime. A unique characteristic of Synanon is that once cured, the individual is free to remain in the Synanon environment for as long as he likes.

New York City's Metropolitan Hospital has a community program for addicts in which addicts are detoxified by a methadone-substitution method and placed in a rehabilitation ward for a period of four weeks. They may sign themselves out at any time. Major emphasis is placed on aftercare; including family, financial, and housing services, legal advice, recreation, and vocational counseling.[20] The hospital program is associated with local neighborhood agencies who work with addicts and ex-addicts.

Experience with outpatient care of addicts is more recent. A major development has been the proliferation of methadone maintenance centers, at which addicts are given daily doses of liquid methadone. It is reported that individuals maintained on methadone are able to adjust satisfactorily to normal community life. However, there is some controversy over the value of sustaining individuals at an addicted state. The clients of methadone treatment centers are primarily referrals from courts and prisons. In order to remain on the methadone program, an addict must cooperate with the staff, come to the center daily, and refrain from any criminal activity.

Community-Based Correctional Facilities

For over two centuries, most attempts to rehabilitate the offender have occurred in prisons, reformatories, and training schools. Today, however, there is increasing recognition that these efforts have been inef-

[20] Eleanor Harlow, J. Robert Weber, and Fred Cohen, *Diversion from the Criminal System*, Washington D.C.: U.S. Govt. Printing Office, 1972), p. 13.

ficient and ineffective. Disillusionment with traditional correctional institutions as rehabilitative tools appears justified. Substantial research data supports the belief that lengthy incarceration in correctional institutions does not deter crime or recidivism. In fact, some writers have argued that our institutions are "schools of crime," which encourage the development of further criminal behavior. The President's Commission on Law Enforcement and the Administration of Justice has reported that "life in many institutions is at best barren and futile, at worst unspeakably brutal and degrading. . . . The conditions in which [inmates] live are the poorest possible preparation for their successful reentry into society, and often merely reinforce in them a pattern of manipulation or destructiveness."[21]

The practice of handling offenders outside the institution is not new. For several years, theorists and practitioners have stated that community-based correctional programs will be required if corrections is to realize the goal of making law-abiding citizens out of convicted offenders and delinquent youths. It has been estimated that over 70 percent of all offenders can be placed immediately in community-based correctional facilities instead of being institutionalized.[22] However, the accomplishment of this task requires a major strengthening of probation and parole departments and integration of correctional activities with general community rehabilitative activities. In order to bring about these changes, political leaders, judges, public interest groups, and the media will have to be educated in the value of community-based corrections.

The key element of community-based corrections is citizen participation from the mainstream of society. A noncriminal link between society and the offender needs to be developed in order for these programs to be successful. The importance of citizen participation is underlined by the President's Task Force on Corrections.

The task of corrections therefore includes building or rebuilding solid ties between offender and community integrating or reintegrating the

[21] President's Commission on Law Enforcement and Administration of Justice, *The Challenge of Crime in a Free Society* (Washington, D.C.: U.S. Govt. Printing Office, 1967), p. 159.
[22] Milton Burdman, "Realism in Community-Based Correctional Services," *The Annals*, 381 (January 1969), p. 71.

offender into community life—restoring families ties, obtaining employment and education, securing in the larger sense a place for the offender in the routine functioning of society. This requires not only efforts directed toward changing the individual offender, which has been the exclusive focus of rehabilitation, but also mobilization and change of the community and its institutions.[23]

Before this can happen, the community must believe that offenders can be successfully reintegrated into society. This requires public efforts to provide supportive services in the areas of employment, education, housing, and friendship. Each of these areas requires involvement by citizens in the roles previously mentioned.

The term *community treatment* has been applied to probation and parole (these being the traditional noninstitutional correction measures); aftercare and halfway houses designed to bridge the gap between the institution and free society; community-based institutions (located within the community with some degree of interaction with the public); noninstitutional boarding arrangements, such as foster care of small group homes; and a number of daycare programs, outpatient clinics, and nonresidential work/group therapy programs. The common feature of these programs is that they provide an alternative to institutionalizing the offender as well as a means for retaining the offender in the community. Community-based treatment programs are both publicly and privately operated. Each type requires a great degree of community support.

The following pages briefly discuss the variety of programs that fall under the heading of community-based corrections. For the purpose of this discussion, the programs have been divided into two subgroups: programs that have been developed to treat offenders as a condition of probation, and those that were developed to help ex-inmates return to society. Both types emphasize the importance of peer group dynamics and community support.

Programs as a Condition of Probation. Programs of this nature usually provide a supportive environment to the offender. Depending upon the

---

[23] President's Commission on Law Enforcement and the Administration of Justice, *Task Force Report: Corrections*, Washington D.C.: U.S. Govt. Printing Office, 1967, p. 7.

level of supervision deemed necessary and the resources available, the offender will either be directed to a day-care center, foster home, or group home program.

The attendance, or day-care, center represents an alternative to institutionalization for probation failures and for offenders who require more intensive care than probation offers, but who do not require formal incarceration. Programs of this nature permit the offender to live at home. Emphasis is placed on providing educational and counseling opportunities designed to help the offender reenter society. Placement usually results from a court order.

Some jurisdictions have realized that many offenders and delinquent youths require greater supervision than day-care centers can provide. Either because the home environment does not lend itself to correctional treatment or because the offender poses a potential threat to the security of the community, 24-hour-a-day supervision of the offender is thought to be necessary. Foster home and group home programs have been established to rehabilitate correctional clients who fall into this category.

The concept of foster home programs is dependent upon the willingness of private families to volunteer their services to care for juveniles in a family setting. The underlining thought of foster home care is that children who show signs of disturbed behavior can be placed and treated successfully in a supportive family environment; therefore, the selection of qualified foster parents is of central importance to the ultimate success of the program. In most jurisdictions, clients are referred to foster home care by the juvenile court.

The group home concept differs from foster care in several ways. Generally, less family atmosphere is present since most of the staff are salaried employees. The activities of the residents are supervised by a paid professional caseworker. Educational and vocational training are available to the residents as well as group and individual counseling. Access to the community may be controlled, depending upon the nature and type of program implemented in the group home.

Programs Developed to Assist the Ex-Inmate. If ex-inmates are to be effectively reintegrated into the community, a positive link must be provided between the offender and society at large. This is a task that cannot always be successfully accomplished by the offender himself. Consequently, programs are needed to assist the offender through the post-institutional transitional phase. Primary developments in this area are halfway houses and work-release programs.

The introduction of the community treatment center, or halfway house, in its present form, is less than 10 years old. The major function of the halfway house is to provide a residential setting to which offenders may be referred after release from an institution. It is the responsibility of the staff to create an environment which supports the offender in his attempt to reestablish ties with the community. The main thrust of the center is outward. Halfway houses are intended to provide a setting in which residents can test their skills and measure their expectations against reality. Access to the community is planned and controlled. Professional staff is available to help each resident adjust to his new job, to his family, and to his duties as a citizen. In order to facilitate this adjustment; educational, recreational, and vocational opportunities are stressed.

Another correctional development designed to ease the offender's reentry into society is the work-release program. This program permits offenders to have jobs in the community while serving the remaining portion of their sentence in the institution. Work-release programs are oriented toward the offender's discharge. The program provides an opportunity for the offender to test the new work skills he developed in the institution and to save money for use after his release. There are two major benefits of the program. First, an offender's performance in a work-release setting can provide a practical measurement to parole authorities of the offender's readiness for release.[24] Second, the program can prepare the offender for his eventual release from the institution.

There are a number of benefits accompanying a well-managed community-based treatment program. Most program coordinators recognize that the community, if adequately prepared, has a vital role to play in assisting the offender to reenter society. When the community becomes directly involved with offenders on their jobs and in training situations, the citizens develop an improved understanding of the potentialities and problems of ex-offenders. So far as the offender is concerned, community-

---

[24] H. G. Moeller, "The Continuum of Corrections," *The Annals*, 381 (January 1969), p. 87.

based corrections permits him to reestablish ties with the community prior to his total release from correctional supervision.

Summary

This discussion of community control in the criminal justice system has pointed out that there are several stages at which the concerned citizen can become involved. The stage, level, and manner of involvement are determined both by the resources available and by the individual's concern and motivation.

Throughout this chapter we have tried to avoid advocating any particular model of citizen control or commenting on that model's effectiveness. Instead, we have attempted to remain impartial and to point out that the use of a particular model is most often determined by the unique characteristics of the community, its citizens, and its criminal justice clientele. The responsibility remains with the student to critically appraise the efficiency and effectiveness of community control exerted in the criminal justice system.

Student Checklist

1. Are you able to describe what we mean by community control?
2. Can you state why some communities are more desirous of control than other communities?
3. Can you list different methods of community control?
4. Are you able to compare the effectiveness of different styles of community control?

Topics for Discussion

1. Discuss what we mean when we speak of community control.
2. Discuss why some communities are more desirous of community control than others.

3. Discuss different methods of community control and their effectiveness. Are there disadvantages to these methods, and if so, what are they?

ANNOTATED BIBLIOGRAPHY

Altshuler, Alan A. *Community Control: The Black Demand For Participation in Large American Cities.* Indianapolis: Pegasus, 1970. Analyzes recent demands emanating from the black community for political decentralization of government services. A major distinction is drawn between administrative and political decentralization. Critical questions are discussed thoroughly in this book.

Black, Algernon D. *The People and the Police.* New York: McGraw-Hill, 1968. Review of the success and failure of the New York City Civilian Complaint Review Board as remembered by the chairman of the board. The author offers his thoughts regarding the strengths and shortcomings of the Board.

Harlow, Eleanor; J. Robert Weber; and Fred Cohen. *Crime and Delinquency Topics: Diversion From the Criminal Justice System.* Public Health Service Publication No. 2129, Washington, D.C., 1972. Designed to inform readers of significant developments in the area of diverting offenders away from the formal criminal justice system. The history and theoretical basis of diversion are discussed and specific programs in various communities are presented.

Harlow, Eleanor; J. Robert Weber; and Leslie T. Wilkins. *Crime and Delinquency Topics: Community-Based Correctional Programs.* Public Health Service Publication No. 2130, Washington, D.C., 1972. Analyzes the development of community-based correctional facilities as an adjunct to the more institutionalized aspects of the correctional process. This monograph provides a quick review of the types of correctional programs existing in various American communities.

More, Harry W. Jr. *Critical issues in Law Enforcement*. Cincinnati: W. H. Anderson Company, 1968. Provides an excellent discussion of basic problems confronting the police officer in contemporary society. Alternatives to the existing police–community relationship are presented and questions are raised regarding their validity.

Myren, Richard A. "Decentralization and Citizen Participation in the Criminal Justice System." *Public Administration Review*, October 1972. Offers some excellent thoughts regarding developing trends in the area of decentralizing police services at the community level. Alternatives ranging from "team-policing" to the Berkeley, California, referendum to politically decentralize police services in that community are presented. The article primarily focuses on the police, but has relevance to the other components of the criminal justice system.

National Advisory Commission on Criminal Justice Standards and Goals. *Working Papers for the National Conference on Criminal Justice*. Law Enforcement Assistance Administration, 1973. Culmination of a one-year study by recognized criminal justice specialists from various components of the criminal justice system. Specific recommendations designed to improve the operations of this system are directed at police, court, and correctional administrators. These papers were used as the basis for discussion at the January 1973 National Conference on Criminal Justice held in Washington, D.C.

O'Leary, Vincent. "Some Directions in Citizen Involvement in Corrections." *The Annals of the American Academy of Political and Social Sciences*, January 1969. Discusses the various roles available to concerned citizenry who are interested in improving the correctional component of the criminal justice system. The author identifies four key roles: the correctional volunteer; the social persuader; the gatekeepers of opportunities; and the intimates. These roles induce both supportive and resistant forces within the correctional system and in the community. Consequently, the successful utilization of these roles depends upon the strategies used to recruit and train these volunteers.

The study of this chapter will enable you to:

1. Define the right to dissent under the U.S. Constitution.
2. List the findings of the Violence Commission.
3. Identify different views of acceptable dissent.
4. Describe strategies of dissent and strategies of response.
5. Identify the significant aspects of escalation and de-escalation.
6. Write a brief essay on the resolution of social conflicts.

13
Militant Organizations and Dissident Groups

To understand militant organizations and dissident groups it is necessary to place dissent into a perspective that will help us understand the dilemmas of dissent and political response. To properly grasp the concept of dissent, it is necessary:

1. To understand a variety of views toward dissent.
2. To study current social conflicts as they relate to both the strategies of dissent and the strategies of response by political authorities.
3. To understand the processes of escalation, de-escalation, and resolution of social conflicts.
4. To understand how the agencies and people in the criminal justice system are involved in these social conflicts.
5. To understand the political consequences of these involvements.

One of the problems in political history is the conflict between change and order. It is difficult to say that any specific historical time was in a "state of order" because the patterns of conflict and resolution that were current then have led to new conflicts. This process will continue to occur. Our present society is complex, technologically communicative, and composed of many groups of people who have different interests, lifestyles, and values. Our political reality is that we are essentially a society of groups rather than of persons. These groups are pressing for change at an accelerating rate because more and more individuals feel they cannot bring about change unless they represent, or are represented by, a power base.

Why are so many groups seeking changes? The answer, perhaps, can be found by examining our culture. Our contemporary culture places great emphasis on achievement but it also emphasizes dissatisfaction with one's present state. Thus, achievement and its companion value, individual self-determination, make the rights to protest and to have grievances addressed—indispensable elements of a "free society."

The First Amendment protects the freedom of speech, press, the right of the people to peacefully assemble, and the right to petition the government for a redress of grievances. The amendment protects not only the *individual's* right to dissent, but also the right of *groups* to dissent, assemble, petition, and demonstrate. The First Amendment is a principle—a symbolic commitment by our government to permit dissent and debate on public issues. Dissent, in the words of the National Commission on the Causes and Prevention of Violence, is the "catalyst of progress." The survival of our democratic system is dependent upon accommodating dissent, solving disagreements, peacefully containing social conflicts, righting wrongs, and modifying the structure of the system as conditions change. Although these changes are necessary to keep the government alive, the organization of government itself is fundamentally resistant to change. This resistance by the government to peaceful change leads to violence, a problem that the Violence Commission found has occurred throughout the history of the United States. The Commission concluded that:

1. *America has always been a relatively violent nation. Considering the tumultuous historical forces that have shaped the United States, it would be astonishing were it otherwise.*

2. *Since rapid social change in America has produced different forms of violence with widely varying patterns of motivation, aggression, and victimization, violence in America has waxed and waned with the social tides. The decade just ending, for example, has been one of our most violent eras—although probably not the most violent.*

3. *Exclusive emphasis in a society on law enforcement rather than on a sensible balance of remedial action and enforcement tends to lead to a decaying cycle in which resistance grows and becomes ever more violent.*

4. *For remedial social change to be an effective moderator of violence, the changes must command a wide measure of support throughout the community. Official efforts to impose change that is resisted by a dominant majority frequently prompt counter-violence.*

5. *Finally, Americans have been, paradoxically, both a turbulent people but have enjoyed a relatively stable republic. Our liberal and pluralistic system has historically both generated and accommo-*

dated itself to a high level of unrest, and our turmoil has reflected far more demonstration and protest than conspiracy and revolution.[1]

Views of Acceptable Dissent

Our current concern with militant and dissident groups involves the strategies they use to apply pressures in an attempt to bring about changes in society. The men who wrote the Constitution did not define "acceptable dissent tactics" in the First Amendment. Therefore, the meaning of what is considered acceptable strategies of dissent constantly changes. For example, the acceptability of such protest strategies as civil. disobedience, direct action, violent confrontation, sit-ins, boycotts, parades, and draft-card burnings varies greatly, depending upon who is defining these actions. Such tactics may be acceptable to a protest leader or even a bystander, but not to a Supreme Court justice or a policeman. Even legal scholars concede that drawing constitutional lines on acceptable dissent procedures is a difficult task.

A model definition of acceptable dissent was developed by former Supreme Court Justice Abe Fortas, who wrote:

> ... *the First Amendment protects dissent if it is belief and not acts, if it is speech and does not create a clear and present danger of injury to others, if it is against a specific law or enforcement thereof by silent and reproachful presence, in a place where the dissenter has every right to be. Violation of a valid law is not justified by either conscience or a good cause.*[2]

A similar position was taken by Archibald Cox, who said that the Constitution guarantees a wide variety of public actions to express sentiment, dramatize a cause, and to demonstrate aroused indignation, power, or solidarity. As Cox explained: "One may disregard with legal impunity, the commands of civil authorities if what the authorities forbid is in

---

[1] The National Commission on the Causes and Prevention of Violence, *To Establish Justice, To Insure Domestic Tranquility* (Washington, D.C.: U.S. Govt. Printing Office, 1969), p. 1-2.

[2] Abe Fortas, *Concerning Dissent and Civil Disobedience* (New York: New American Library, 1968), pp. 106-111.

truth only the exercise of a privilege guaranteed by the Constitution."[3] Such action does not involve a violation of law in the ultimate sense because the orders given by the authorities are not law at all. However, the Constitution does not give us the right to disobey *valid* laws. Conducting a sit-in demonstration in someone's office, for example, would plainly violate valid and constitutional laws. The Constitution does not give anyone the privilege to violate a law even if the protest demonstration is designed to test the law's constitutionality. Citizens cannot pick and choose which laws they will obey without destroying the whole concept of law. The privilege of freedom and the right to peaceful change are eroded by such lawbreaking, although some changes have occurred as a result of such tactics.

Most of the members of the Violence Commission took a similar position. They said that no matter how a person feels about the dissenters' cause, he must not violate valid laws. In their view, respect for the judicial process is a small price to pay for the civilized hand of law, which alone can give meaning to constitutional freedom. The Violence Commission suggests that the best way to challenge the constitutionality of a law is by initiating legal action, and while the judicial test is in progress, all other dissenters should abide by the law.[4] Every time a court order is disobeyed and each time an injunction is violated, the effectiveness of our judicial system is eroded. Defiance of the law is the surest road to tyranny. Disobeying valid laws does not contribute to the emergence of a more humane society, but leads instead to the emergence of a totalitarian state.

The views described above are legalistic and assume that the Constitution and law are static at any given time. In summary, these views:

1. Hold that protest actions weaken the bonds of law.
2. Compel the state to resort to its power.
3. Make a distinction between laws that are violated through the actions involved in protest demonstrations (such as trespass laws and traffic laws, even though these specific laws are not themselves

---

[3] Archibald Cox, "Direct Action, Civil Disobedience and the Constitution," Grossman and Grossman, *Law and Change in Modern America* (Pacific Palisades, Calif.: Goodyear, 1971), p. 386.
[4] The National Commission on the Causes and Prevention of Violence, *To Establish Justice, To Insure Domestic Tranquility*, pp. 90-91.

being protested) and laws that are violated as the object of dissent.
4. Are committed to the symbolic belief that law and legal institutions are the only viable mechanisms for change in a democracy.

In contrast to the legalistic positions taken by Fortas, Cox, and the Violence Commission, others feel that (1) the traditional methods of dissent are insufficient or have fallen on deaf ears; (2) dissent is often focused on organizational policies or administrative decisions and not laws; and (3) the dissent issue is often not negotiable to those in the power structure. Thus, one cannot legally protest those procedures or institutional practices which the legal system assumes to be "correct." For example, there are few legal options available to people who want to alter school curriculums or textbooks that devalue the role of minority groups in American history. Conversely, a person can protest discriminatory employment practices through the law but not through the economic system itself.

Both the legalists and the advocates of dissent agree that creative disruptive tactics are legitimate, yet they also realize that many protest strategies pose a serious political problem: how to avoid social disorder while at the same time avoiding total social control.

One advocate of increased civil disobedience, Howard Zinn, argues that in order to avoid either tyranny or massive violence it is necessary to accept strategies of dissent that go beyond what is now legally acceptable.[5] In his view, a new politics of protest, designed to put pressure on the national leaders, is needed to balance the interests of the state and the individual, since the balance thus far has been mostly in favor of the state. Zinn feels that the state is not sacred; it should be watched, scrutinized, criticized, opposed, changed, and overthrown and replaced when necessary, since it is an artificial device not synonymous with the people of a country. He argues that the government has abdicated its duty to meet the needs of the people in order to meet the needs of those persons who have power.

Zinn maintains that the Supreme Court should rule on the most fundamental questions posed to it regarding dissent and social change.

It should, therefore, be constantly reinterpreting the Constitution in such a way as to augment the natural rights of the citizen, thus moving

[5] Howard Zinn, "The Need for Increased Civil Disobedience," *Disobedience and Democracy: Nine Fallacies on Law and Order* (New York: Random House, 1968).

away from the deification of precedent and toward bold interpretations. Why should not the equal protection clause of the Fourteenth Amendment be applied to economics, as well as race, to require the state to give equal economic rights to its citizens: food, shelter, education, medical care. Why should not the Thirteenth Amendment barring involuntary servitude be extended to military conscription? Why should not the cruel and unusual punishment clause of the Eighth Amendment be applied in such a way as to bar all imprisonment except in the most stringent of cases, where confinement is necessary to prevent a clear and immediate danger to others? Why should not the Ninth Amendment, which says citizens have unnamed rights beyond those enumerated in the Constitution, be applied to a host of areas: rights to carry on whatever family arrangements (marriage, divorce, etc.) are desired, whatever sexual relationships are voluntarily entered into, whatever private activities one wants to carry on, so long as others are not harmed (even if they are irritated).[6]

In Zinn's opinion, the courts should stand for law sometimes and justice always. Therefore, he offers the following guidelines to help decide when to obey and when to disobey law through dissent activity.

1. *Civil disobedience is the deliberate, discriminate, violation of law for a vital social purpose. It becomes not only justifiable but necessary when a fundamental human right is at stake, and when legal channels are inadequate for securing that right. It may take the form of violating an obnoxious law, protesting an unjust condition, or symbolically enacting a desirable law or condition. It may or may not eventually be held legal, because of constitutional law or international law, but its aim is always to close the gap between law and justice, as an infinite process in the development of democracy.*

2. *There is no social value to a general obedience to the law, any more than there is value to a general disobedience to the law. Obedience to bad laws as a way of inculcating some abstract subservience to the "rule of law" can only encourage the already strong tendencies of citizens to bow to the power of authority, to desist from challenging the status quo. To exalt the rule of law as an absolute is the mark of totalitarianism in a society which has many of the attributes of democracy. To urge the right of citizens to disobey unjust laws, and the duty of citizens to disobey dangerous laws, is of the very*

---

[6] Ibid., pp. 115-116. (Reprinted with permission of Random House)

essence of democracy, which assumes that government and its laws are not sacred, but are instruments, serving certain ends: life, liberty, happiness. The instruments are dispensable. The ends are not.

3. *Civil disobedience may involve violation of laws which are not in themselves obnoxious, in order to protest on a very important issue. In each case, the importance of the law being violated would need to be measured against the importance as the life of a child run over by a car; illegal trespass into offices is nowhere as serious as the killing of people in war; the unlawful occupation of a building is not as sinful as racism in education. Since not only specific laws, but general conditions may be unbearable, laws not themselves ordinarily onerous may need to be violated as protest.*

4. *If a specific act of civil disobedience is a morally justifiable act of protest, then the jailing of those engaged in that act is immoral and should be opposed, contested to the very end. The protester need be no more willing to accept the rule of punishment than to accept the rule he broke. There may be many times when protesters choose to go to jail, as a way of continuing their protest, as a way of reminding their countrymen of injustice. But that is different than the notion that they must go to jail as part of a rule connected with civil disobedience. The key point is that the spirit of protest should be maintained all the way, whether it is done by remaining in jail, or by evading it. To accept jail penitently as an accession to "rules" is to switch suddenly to a spirit of subservience, to demean the seriousness of the protest.*

5. *Those who engage in civil disobedience should choose tactics which are as nonviolent as possible, consonant with the effectiveness of their protest and the importance of the issue. There must be a reasonable relationship between the degree of disorder and the significance of the issue at stake. The distinction between harm to people and harm to property should be a paramount consideration. Tactics directed at property might include (again, depending on efficacy and the issue): depreciation (as in boycotts), damage, temporary occupation, and permanent appropriation. In any event, the force of any act of civil disobedience must be focused clearly, discriminately on the object of protest.*

6. *The degree of disorder in civil disobedience should not be weighed against a false "peace" presumed to exist in the status quo, but against the real disorder and violence that are part of daily life, overtly expressed internationally in wars, but hidden locally under*

that facade of "order" which obscures the injustice of contemporary society.

7. *In our reasoning about civil disobedience, we must never forget that we and the state are separate in our interests, and we must not be lured into forgetting this by the agents of the state. The state seeks power, influence, wealth, as ends in themselves. The individual seeks health, peace, creative activity, love. The state, because of its power and wealth, has no end of spokesmen for its interests. This means the citizen must understand the need to think and act on his own or in concert with fellow citizens.*[7]

Strategies of Dissent and Strategies of Response

The positions described above differ in many critical respects, but they all recognize the need for "justice," "order," and "change" and agree that dissent must be analyzed in relation to crises in American institutions. This factor was also recognized by the Violence Commission. In a staff report, the Commission suggests that mass protest is an outgrowth of social, economic, and political conditions and the violence that occurs in these protests arises from an interaction between protesters and the authorities. Therefore, according to the Violence Commission, militant organizations and dissident groups must be viewed in the context.

1. *That what is "violent" is established through political processes. That whoever has the superior resources for disseminating and enforcing his definitions blames the other party for the violence.*

2. *That authorities and protesters often exaggerate the violence conducted against them as a means of discrediting the other party, as a means of gaining sympathy with a third party, or as a means of covering their own violence.*

3. *That interplay of protest and violence by authorities cannot be understood solely through an analysis of demonstrators and police. It must be seen in the light of the surrounding structure of authority and power and the conceptions which authorities hold on the nature of protest and the proper uses of official violence.*

Ibid,, pp. 119-122. (Reprinted with permission of Random House)

*4. That the participants in mass protest today see their grievances as
rooted in the existing arrangement of power and authority in contemporary society, and they view their own activity as political
action, on a direct or symbolic level, aimed at altering those arrangements of dependency and external control.*[8]

In most issues of social conflict, there are a variety of groups and
individuals with different demands and different strategies of dissent.
These dissenters, however, generally have much less power than the
political authorities or other parties whose actions, beliefs, policies, or
laws the dissenters are protesting. Because dissenters usually have the
least amount of power in a social conflict, the views of the more powerful authorities or organizations generally become the accepted ones.

The authorities, or those who have power (the "establishment"),
generally label dissenters as "militants." This label may be applied to
whole groups of dissenters or to individual spokesmen for a particular
group of dissenters. There are, however, no clearcut definitions for the
word militant. This label has been used by the opponents of a movement to discredit everyone in the movement; it has also been used selectively by persons who partially agree with the objectives of the movement but who regard some of its demands as nonnegotiable. For example, Lewis Killian states that some designated militants are regarded as
fanatics or as having an untractable position and, consequently, are not
acceptable to the authorities for negotiations; on the other hand, these
designated militants may be viewed as the most effective negotiators or
leaders by the people in the movement.[9] Thus, they are regarded as the
most dangerous by the authorities. In line with Killian's statements,
Gary Marx found that black citizens generally define black militants as
those who: approve of violence as a tactic; are pessimistic about the
changes that have occurred and are expected to occur; support separatist
goals; are hostile to and mistrust whites; and support black control of

---

[8] Jerome Skolnick, *The Politics of Protest: Violent Aspects of Protest and Confrontation*, A Staff Report to the National Commission on the Causes and Prevention of Violence (Washington, D.C.: U.S. Govt. Printing Office, 1969),
pp. 1-6.
[9] Lewis M. Killian, "The Significance of Extremism in the Black Revolution,"
Social Problems, Vol. 20, No. 1 (Summer 1972), pp. 41-49.
[10] Gary Marx, *Protest and Prejudice* (New York: Harper Torchbooks, 1969),
pp. 216-231.

black communities.[10] Although these findings specifically concern the black movement, it is generally agreed that militants (1) talk or act with approval of violence as a tactic in protest; (2) are hostile toward their adversaries; and (3) do not accept the legitimacy of the structural system or its institutions.

These definitional elements fit in with a typology of dissent strategies. These strategies can be called the *strategy of order*, the *strategy of disorder*, and the *strategy of violence*. The strategies of dissent differ on the basis of their concern with (1) the nature of the changes to be achieved (the issue); (2) adherence to the rules of the system (the means); and (3) the persons who defend the system (the persons). In the *strategy of order*, dissidents divide their attention between the changes to be accomplished and the accepted rules regarding legitimate ways of bringing about change; dissidents who use this strategy follow the rules. In the *strategy of disorder*, dissidents have less interest in both the given rules and the powerful persons who stand in the way of change; they focus strongly on the changes needed. In the *strategy of violence*, dissidents divide their attention between the changes needed and the powerful persons who stand in the way of change; dissidents who use this strategy attack their enemies.[11] Presumably, we can define any particular dissident group's strategy at any given time simply by analyzing its rhetoric and observing its deeds.

However, to understand the dynamics of these dissent strategies, we must also understand the strategies of response utilized by political authorities or other parties who are the targets of dissident groups. The orientations and response strategies of those in political power or those whose job it is to respond to dissident groups can vary as widely as the orientations and strategies of protest groups. In fact, there is often conflict between the courts, police, legislators, and others in authoritative power positions concerning how to respond to the different strategies of dissent. Thus, the strategies of response also differ on the basis of their concern with: (1) the nature of the changes demanded (the issue); (2) adherence to the rules of legal response (the means); and (3) focus on the persons who are dissenting (the persons).

The strategies of response can be classified as the *response of law*, the *response of order*, and the *response of violence*. In the *response of*

[11] Arthur Waskow, *From Race Riot to Sit-In* (New York: Doubleday, 1966).

law, authorities do not respond at all or they respond only in a protective manner when dissenters are utilizing legal strategies of protest (*strategy of order*); if, however, dissenters are using illegal dissent strategies, such as disorder or violence, then the *response of law* strategy involves arresting the dissenters and processing them in a legally acceptable manner—the authorities follow proper legal procedures. In the *response of order*, authorities respond to legal dissent (*strategy of order*) with either no response or with a protective response. They respond to illegal dissent by creating a system of response procedures that encourages nonviolent bargaining of the social conflict. In the *response of order*, authorities place less emphasis on the demanded change (the issue) and more emphasis on maintaining order or preventing violence. This response seems to occur more frequently when the government or legal authority is not one of the parties to the conflict (such as labor–management disputes and student–administration problems). In the *response of violence*, authorities tend to be concerned with the issue in conflict and respond by focusing on the dissidents regardless of the nature of the strategy (legal or illegal); authorities attack their enemies.

These strategies of response by authorities correspond to the strategies of dissent groups. It is the interaction of these different orientations and strategies of action in social conflict situations that produce (1) changes in the orientations and strategies of the conflicting parties; (2) violent actions; and (3) "resolution" of the conflicts.

Social and political conflicts have a history and a dynamic structure. Specific social conflicts, dissent and response, must be viewed in the context of the conflict's past history of action and reaction. For example, a concern with the legitimacy of the means of protest and the symbolic goodness of the law has characterized a considerable amount of recent dissent. The civil disobedience of Martin Luther King and the Vietnam War draft resisters reinforced law and respected law. When dissenters openly and peacefully disobey a law that they believe to be unjust and are willing to assume the consequences, then law, as an institution, is upheld. This strategy of dissent, which includes confrontation of conscience, conversion of nonbelievers, dignity, and symbolic reverence of law, is to them an adventure of educating the public sensitivities, drawing attention to the issues of dissent, and pressing for legal or administrative change. Police response to this type of dissent has varied, from the *response of order* to the *response of violence*. A familiar *response of violence* strategy, for example, involves an attempt by the authorities to divert attention from the issues by casting the dissidents (in a counter-educational campaign) as riffraff, communists, militants, kooks, or common criminals. Consequently, many law enforcement officials do not distinguish between civil disobedience and crime when they disagree with the issues involved in the protest movement.

Whatever the strategy of dissent or the strategy of response, a recurring concern is the effect that such strategies will have on third parties. Peace demonstrations met by police violence, or voter registration attempts met by arrest, recruited many third party allies. Third parties are extremely critical when there are great power differences among the conflicting parties. When power differences are great, the weaker party can achieve its goals or obtain a compromise only if strong third parties become allies.[12] Therefore, each adversary tries to win over third parties. Each plans tactics, publicity, and media communications to influence specific third parties—the issue in conflict critically affecting the allies or third parties. In the issue of black civil and voting rights, for example, the goal the protesters sought was inclusion in the political system; thus, these groups aimed their messages at not only the black persons directly affected, but also at third party persons sympathetic to these goals, and those who believed in the legal inclusion of blacks in the political system. As a result, media coverage and the violent response of political authorities to the black civil rights movement had the consequences of: affecting third party intervention by the federal government, expanding the issues in conflict, and obtaining both participants in the movement and allies.

Because media coverage is so necessary, the outcome of the conflict is critically affected by which conflict situations are given press coverage and how the parties are portrayed. Both parties to the conflict attempt to use the media to their advantage through well-planned dissent activity and well-planned response activity.

Dissenters often create events for the media. If the public is not aware of the conflict, the dissenters' position will remain poor with regard to the outcome of the conflict; the dissenters need good press coverage in order to increase their bargaining power. Political authori-

---

[12] Louis Kriesberg, *The Sociology of Social Conflicts* (Englewood Cliffs, N.J.: Prentice-Hall, 1973), p. 227.

ties, on the other hand, attempt to (1) control the media and its contents by increasing control over regulatory agencies or by putting political pressure on local media; (2) control the sources of information by making government documents secret; (3) infiltrate dissident groups with spokesmen; (4) cut dissident groups off from media visibility; or (5) attack the media itself and its "underdog" bias. Thus, when political authorities are seriously pressed by dissent, freedom of the press increasingly comes under fire.

Escalation and De-Escalation of Conflict

Conflict, its resolution, and the selection of strategies for its conduct, especially those that contribute to increased or decreased coercion or violence, must be viewed in the context of the process that occurs during a struggle. While this process is occurring, the issues, the conflicting parties, and the relationships between the conflicting parties and third parties become altered. The interaction of the strategies of dissent and response contribute toward escalation or de-escalation of conflict and ultimately affect the outcome. However, the outcomes of one conflict often create further struggles or expand the issues. For example, the outcomes of the early civil rights struggle, especially the implementation of school busing, heightened the conflict and dissent activities of powerless white groups toward blacks and toward the authority of the central government.

Once conflict has started, each conflicting party tends to undergo changes that lead to escalation. Feelings of loyalty and commitment to one's position increase, especially if the other side responds with coercion, threats, or injuries. Increased commitment leads to and justifies further efforts toward the attainment of one's goals, creates anxiety, and heightens a sense that *now* is the time to act. For example, dissident or militant leaders state, "Seize the time!" "Freedom now!" "Peace now!," or:

> This is our last gasp as a sovereign people, and if we don't get these treaty rights recognized, then you might as well kill me because I have no reason for living.[13]

[13] Russell Means, American Indian Movement, *Chicago Express*, Vol. 1, No. 38, 1973.

My hunger is for liberation of my people, my thirst is for the ending of oppression. I am a political prisoner, jailed for my beliefs that black people must be free. . . . Death can no longer alter our path to freedom. For our people death has been the only known exit from slavery and oppression. We must open others. Our will to live must no longer supersede our will to fight, for our fighting will determine if our race shall live. . . . Brothers and sisters, and all oppressed peoples, we must prepare ourselves both mentally and physically, for the major confrontation is yet to come. We must fight.[14]

Reacting to intensified conflict by dissidents, political authorities maintain that they must "nip dissent in the bud" with a display of force. For example, this occurred during the revolt at Attica State Prison.

Why then did the state order the assault? The decision was based upon the belief that basic principles—not just lives (of the keepers and the kept)—were at stake in the uprising. From the outset, the Governor (Rockefeller) perceived the Attica uprisings as more than a prison riot. The uprising constituted an insurrection against the very authority of the state, and to tolerate it was to concede a loss of sovereignty over the rebels. The Governor testified that he expected the Commissioner to follow "the usual patterns" of reestablishing order without negotiation. Choosing the unorthodox alternative course, Oswald, was therefore, negotiating not only with inmates, but against time. Sooner or later, the state's paramount interest in restoring order would have to be asserted. The decision to retake the prison was not a quixotic effort to rescue hostages in the midst of 1200 inmates; it was a decisive reassertion of the state of its sovereignty and power.[15]

Once conflict begins, it often escalates because leaders acting as representatives of an entire collectivity usually persist on a course of action, even if no success is achieved. Mistakes are rarely admitted by either the dissenters or the responders. However, admission of mistakes does tend to occur when the group's constituency changes, when the futility of the strategy becomes apparent, or when escalation and reaction reaches the point where survival of the group is threatened. Thus, the Black Panther party retracted its focus on the police when party programs were seriously threatened by police actions. Party leaders recog-

[14] Rap Brown, *The Black Panther*, March 1968.
[15] New York State Special Commission on Attica, *Attica, The Official Report of the New York State Special Commission on Attica* (New York: Bantam Books, 1972), p. 329.

nized that other authorities are more important than the police, and began to concentrate more deeply on the issues.

Another factor influencing the escalation of conflict is the withdrawal of members who are unwilling to participate in more intense conflict behavior, leaving the group in the command of those who are more eager to engage in hostile actions.[16] In addition, if one party to the conflict is threatened, it tends to respond with hostility and aggression toward the other. Thus, if the police see a group of dissidents as a threat or as a source of violence, they tend to respond with violence; consequently, the dissident group tends to increase its violent activities. However, it is also possible that a response of lower magnitude by the authorities may further escalate violence by the dissident group in the hopes of achieving greater success from a seemingly weakened "enemy."

Conflict cannot escalate indefinitely. The processes of de-escalation are imbedded in those of escalation. Although participation in conflict behavior produces greater commitment to the group and willingness to escalate conflict, it also becomes increasingly costly if the attainment of the group's demands are not in sight. Coercion by one side can lead to de-escalation by the other side in several ways:

1. By having superior coercive power and exercising it.
2. By repressing the opposition via harassment or imprisonment of its leaders.
3. By splitting the conflict, or by being devisively conciliatory and thus lessening the ability of dissident groups to form coalitions. Ending military conscription can be viewed as an example of devisive conciliatory action since it encouraged many active students to withdraw from the peace movement even though it did not address the issue of peace itself.
4. By creating other issues that achieve precedence or involve new third parties (for example, raising the P.O.W. issue brought in new third parties to the Peace movement). The intervention of third parties also can have a de-escalating impact by (a) enlarging dissident groups to form a broad-based movement, thus allowing these groups to obtain more power, increasing the political costs to the authorities of continuing the practices which are being protested; (b) acting as a mediator or negotiator of the conflict; or (c) enlarging power groups, thereby quickening conflict resolution.

[16] Kriesberg, *The Sociology of Social Conflicts.*

De-escalation is also furthered when the conflict has reached militant proportions; moderate leaders thus appear to be more "reasonable," and their bargaining power increases if, of course, the authorities have not repressed the entire movement.

Successful dissident groups tend to have either a specific goal or a broad goal that can realistically be applied, such as equality of opportunity or peace (for example, a specific percentage of construction jobs; or an end to the bombing in Indochina). Furthermore, successful dissident groups have an identifiable target (landlord, administration, political leader, group, or company) who is capable of granting the goal sought.[17] The demands of dissident and militant groups and the responses of conflict parties or authorities must be viewed in this context. Some demands are defined as nonnegotiable by the conflict authority (e.g., state sovereignty, capitalism, or student control of school administration), and some demands are not grantable by the targets chosen (e.g., police, mayor).

Outcomes

Power differences seem to be the major determinant in the outcome of social conflict. Extreme power differences almost invite domination and repression if the conflict has escalated to highly coercive strategies. In general, the greater the power difference the more the outcome is likely to be withdrawal or domination of the dissidents. The outcomes of different conflicts vary according to the perceived permanence of the conflict. The Vietnam War has ended, but other social conflicts, such as the status of black Americans and Indians, seem to be permanent and painfully direct. The report of the National Advisory Commission on Civil Disorders suggests that white institutions created the ghetto, white institutions maintain the ghetto, and white sociey condones the ghetto. However, the Report focuses its attention on individual white attitudes and ghetto conditions and not on white institutions. Racial containment has always had its counter-theme of sabotage, protest, and resistance.

[17] James Q. Wilson, "The Strategy of Protest: Problems of Negro Civic Action," *Journal of Conflict Resolution*, Vol. 5, 1961.

According to Stokely Carmichael and Charles V. Hamilton, the time has been long overdue for the black community to redefine itself, to set forth new values, and to organize.[18] *Black Power* has been a call for black people to unite, to recognize their heritage, to build a sense of community, to define their own goals, to lead their own organizations, and to reject the oppressive institutions and values of racist society. *Black Power* rests on a fundamental premise that group solidarity is necessary before a group can bargain from a position of strength. Thus, the direction of "colonized" groups today is one of self-defense, cultural autonomy, and community control. "Militant" groups pursuing these ends have (1) served as a constant corrective to illusions of progress through their critical and pessimistic attitudes; (2) served to identify unresolved crucial issues facing the movement through futile, if not suicidal, confrontations; (3) radicalized movement membership and increased the polarization between the movement and its opposition; and (4) created a new sense of injustice and awareness in nonmovement third parties through direct acts.[19] Local community control of schools, police, housing, business, welfare, and social services are the likely issues and targets of this arena of dissent. Schools, because of their socialization-identity function and their abject "failure," have been the first issue.[20] The police, viewed as one of the most critical institutions maintaining these "colonized" states, are another target.

Criminal Justice Theaters

From the preceding discussion, it becomes apparent that the theaters of criminal justice—the police, courts, and prisons—often become arenas for dissent and response These organizations and their personnel often become and are perceived as instruments of power rather than of law. In their daily conduct or in crisis situations, depending on one's perspec-

[18] Stokely Carmichael, and Charles V. Hamilton, *Black Power: The Politics of Liberation in America* (New York: Vintage Books, 1967), p. 44.
[19] Killian, "The Significance of Extremism in the Black Revolution," *Social Problems*, Vol. 20, No. 1.
[20] Robert Blauner, "Internal Colonialism and Ghetto Revolt," *Social Problems*, Vol. 16, No. 4, Spring 1969.

tive, these institutions are asked to deal with social conflict as if it were a criminal and not a political matter.

The Police

In dissent situations and "colonial" dramas, the police frequently find themselves in the position of acting as substitutes for necessary political and social reform. Labor history demonstrates that the police served as the main bulwark against the labor movement. Picket lines were violently dispersed; meetings were disrupted, and organizers and activists were shot, beaten, and jailed. Police harassment of unions, such as the United Farm Workers, exists today. Denial of strikers' legal rights; physical and verbal abuse; detaining organizers for long periods of time; encouraging workers to cross picket lines; and arresting strikers for trespass, unlawful assembly, secondary boycott, and illegal picketing are current episodes of old alignments. The police have also sought to prevent the political organization of Mexican-Americans in New Mexico and blacks in our major cities by harassing and intimidating organization members and arresting leaders.

In some of our larger cities, tenant unions, students, war protesters, and blacks have drawn similar responses from the police. For example, some highly publicized *responses of violence* occurred at the 1968 Democratic Convention and in police confrontations with the Black Panther party. The shooting outbreaks between Panthers and police in New Orleans, Detroit, Toledo, Philadelphia, New York, Houston, and Chicago were touched off by harassment (the Panther view) or minor offenses (the police view). These incidents involved the selling of a Panther newspaper on a Detroit street corner, the assault upon two police infiltrators in New Orleans, and the stockpiling of weapons in the other cities. The Black Panthers argue that police respond violently because (1) police departments include high percentages of individual "racists"; (2) few minority persons serve on police forces; (3) police are isolated from the people they police; (4) police are ill-trained for their sensitive peacekeeping jobs; and (5) police have a special view of dissent and dissenters.

The special view of police toward dissent and dissenters considers protest to be unequivocally illegitimate. The police have a tendency to view organized protest as the conspiratorial product of authoritarian

Figure 13-1. In dissent situations, the police frequently find themselves acting as the alternatives for necessary political and social reform.

agitators, communists, rabble-rousers, rotten and permissively-raised kids, outsiders, or anarchists. This view comes down from the highest officials, does not distinguish dissent from subversion, and lumps all dissent strategies into one category.[21] Thus, the police tend to be hostile to most strategies of dissent and tend to make the reduction of dissent their goal. However, this view that dissent is caused by agitators, communists, and personal enemies leads the police to underestimate both the number of people involved and the emotionality of dissent. This view also calls for the arrest of leaders or speakers at mass rallies, an action which heightens the cycle of escalating violence. The views of the police tend to move them into a position of equating the law with their own situational power. These escalating attitudes and actions are not, however, held by the majority of policemen in many cities.

Violent dissent and violent response are generally an interactional product of short-term situational escalation or of a history of unsuccess-

[21] Skolnick, *The Politics of Protest: Violent Aspects of Protest and Confrontation,* p. 198.

ful dissent and/or response strategy. However, escalation to violence also emanates from the positions taken by some violence-oriented dissent groups; these groups purposely provoke police hostility and violence in order to gain attention, to raise "anti-imperialist" consciousness, to enlist third parties, to increase membership, and to show how "violent" the political system is. The militant factions of Students for a Democratic Society (SDS) and the Youth Against War and Fascism were two groups utilizing this approach in the recent antiwar movement. The greater resistance that these groups encountered from authorities, the greater their motivation to continue their perceived "just" cause became. In such cases, the labels of communist, outsider, agitator, radical, militant, and criminal become symbols of integrity, courage, morality, and honor. Consequently, for persons highly committed to expressive behavior, threats of punishment have little deterrent value.[22]

The *response of order* is more likely to occur if the power of the dissenting group approaches that of the powerful group. While the *response of violence* was a more frequent response in the infant stages of the antiwar movement, when large numbers of people became involved and when the goals became specifics (such as getting the ground troops out of Vietnam), the police *response of order* became more frequent. Thus, the strategies of dissent also de-escalated. Although the peace movement continued, much dissent had de-escalated as a result of the concession of ground troop removal, an end to military conscription, and the return of the P.O.W.'s. Many third parties abandoned the movement, leaving only the highly committed dissident groups and individuals to deal with the larger issues of foreign policy in Indochina. It appeared that the basic foreign policy itself was nonnegotiable, while negotiations on numerous side issues tended to diffuse the strength of dissent.

The police are only the most visible, direct responders to these confrontations, dissidents, and "out" groups in general. Their visibility provides only an overt understanding of how the people in power handle situations where repressive action is considered necessary, but in which few people are willing to do what the "powers" want done.[23] For exam-

[22] William J. Chambliss, "Types of Deviance and the Effectiveness of Legal Sanctions," *Wisconsin Law Review*, Summer 1967, pp. 703-719.
[23] Lee Rainwater, "The Revolt of Dirty Workers," pp. 435-437, Skolnick and Currie, *Crisis in American Institutions*, Second Edition (New York: Little, Brown, 1973).

ple, many Americans feel that blacks and dissenters must be controlled and confined. Yet, these same citizens prefer not to know what the police, school teachers, the real estate industry, or other authorities do to control and confine blacks or dissidents. As a result, this self-imposed insularism by the public makes the police the scapegoats of the political system. Although the police are the recipients of powerful socialization efforts by political authorities, who encourage them to cast undesirable dissent into the categories of "criminal" or "subversive," they are now beginning to revolt against the "dirty work."[24] "Dirty workers" are marginal men caught between those persons who desire their "dirty work," and the objects of "dirty work" who refuse to tolerate control and confinement. When the orchestrated attitudes of the police and other "dirty workers" are coupled with comparable attitudes by other political authorities (legislatures, judges, city councils, and the like), and further coupled with perceived provocation (either symbolic or coercive acts) by dissenters, a *response of violence* is probable. Nevertheless, the police are, in the final analysis, only one group of actors in the drama of restricting political challenge and creating social change. They do the "dirty work" of the larger power structure, deflecting dissent, and helping to discredit not only the dissenters but the issues as well.

Legislative and judicial bodies reacting to dissent have seemingly forced the police, often unwillingly, into inevitable violence-prone confrontations. A commission investigating an April 1968 Peace Rally in Chicago indicated that city officials denied the dissenters a permit to use the bandshell, denied a parade permit, and denied the use of the Civic Center Plaza because they disagreed with the antiwar rally.[25] City councils have amended parade ordinances to require a permit if five or more persons desired to parade, and have enacted ordinances restricting pickets to business hours. Furthermore, city councils have at times broadened parade ordinances to require a permit for virtually every use of the streets and sidewalks, and stated that no permits would be issued for demonstrations. For example, in 1964 the Mississippi legislature, reacting to the voter registration drives, enacted criminal measures which pro-

[24] Ibid.
[25] *Dissent and Disorder: A Report of the Citizens of Chicago on the April 27, Peace Parade*, August 1, 1968 (The Sparling Commission Report).

militant organizations and dissident groups   **329**

hibited the printing or distribution of materials advocating boycotts, and prohibited people from advocating, teaching about, or participating in criminal acts (demonstrations) designed to effect any political or social change.[26]

The police are not the only actors who equate dissent with subversion. The view that dissenters are either a tool or a dupe of foreign manipulation calls for the creation of intelligence agencies to conduct surveillance of dissent activities. This surveillance is conducted not only by the police but also by the FBI, the Army, the CIA, the IRS, the Secret Service, the Civil Service Commission, the Department of Justice, and many others. Despite the efforts of intelligence officials to keep the objectives of intelligence systems secret, there is little doubt that one of their purposes is the political control of dissent.[27] Political surveillance has become so commonplace and its targets so numerous that presidential candidates, senators, and large segments of the population are its subjects.

The intelligence infiltrator often becomes the agent provocateur, who commits provocative acts because he must both gain entry to planning circles and must also produce results in the form of concrete evidence of illegal activity. Frank Donner reports that at least six agents of the New York City Police Department infiltrated the Black Panther party and appeared as witnesses in the trial of the Panther 21.[28] He further reports that three members of the Chicago Police Department infiltrated the Chicago Peace Council and that one exposed another to enhance his credibility; the chairman of the Peace Council said that these infiltrators took militant positions, trying to provoke the movement from its nonviolent thrust.[29]

When the "national security" is believed to be at stake, political intelligence sweeps up dissenters of all styles. To protect the "national security," all groups and individuals committed to social or political change, however peaceful, nonviolent, or legal, must be scrutinized

---

[26] U.S. Commission on Civil Rights, *Enforcement: A Report on Equal Protection in the South* (Washington, D.C.: U.S. Govt. Printing Office, 1970).
[27] Frank Donner, "The Theory and Practice of American Political Intelligence," pp. 444-460, Skolnick and Currie, *Crisis in American Institutions.*
[28] Ibid.
[29] Ibid.

because they may be "subversive." These intelligence activities are designed to demoralize, intimidate, and frighten citizens into not dissenting. The harassment, invasion of privacy, prosecution on drug charges, vandalism of offices and homes, blacklisting, or illegal searches, are chilling. When a covert force plays an important role in political decisions, the selection of candidates, the publication of false opinion polls, and the conducting of "smear" campaigns, then this nation's stated democratic political processes cease to exist. The First Amendment becomes meaningless when dissenting individuals are not allowed to exercise their rights. If there are great personal costs involved in the process of dissent, then there is no freedom. Driving political activity underground tends to escalate strategies to the more organized forms of violence, paramilitarism, terror, sabotage, assassination, guerrilla warfare, espionage, counter-intelligence, and extreme political repression.[30]

The Courts

The intelligence collectors often provide information for the court trials of dissenters-conspirators-subversives. The passage of laws that attempt to stifle dissent, such as the riot conspiracy laws, the mob action laws, and administrative laws (Selective Service System draft policy toward draft-card burners), all make the court a scene of the politics of protest. Intelligence-gathering, selective prosecution, and the *response of violence* move the theater from the street to the courtroom. When this occurs, the courts are asked to perform tasks for which they are not suited. The courts have been designed to handle cases which do not contest the authority or legitimacy of the courts.[31] The court process assumes that the activities defined as crimes are disapproved of by the community as a whole. In contemporary dissent situations, however, these conditions may not be met. As dissent increases and as a strategy of dissent gains acceptability, a majority of the citizens may not define the activity as criminal. Moreover, they may not accept the court's authority to decide the dispute. This presents a crisis for the courts and

[30] L. W. Pye, "The Roots of Insurgency and the Commencement of Rebellion," H. Eckstein ed., *Internal War* (New York: Praeger, 1964).
[31] Skolnick, *The Politics of Protest: Violent Aspects of Protest and Confrontation*, p. 243.

the legal system. The court becomes and is perceived as a theater in which the actors attempt to win third parties to their side; it becomes a political arena.

It is difficult for the court to function as an impartial arbiter of conflict when the government itself is a conflicting party. When civil disorders occur, lower courts have a tendency to set aside their independence and become an instrument of political need, without regard for legality. For example, during recent civil disorders the courts tended to take the view that:

1. *Civil disorders represent a time of extreme and dangerous emergency, requiring extraordinary measures of control and resistance.*
2. *The efforts of the police, military, fire department, and other public agencies must be actively supported to restore order as quickly as possible.*
3. *The presumption of guilt of defendants is made necessary by the presence of troops in the city, the sight of "fires on the horizon," and a common-sense appreciation of the danger and inherent criminality of a "riot" or "uprising."*
4. *High bail is required to prevent rioters returning to the riot.*
5. *The nature of the emergency and the overwhelming number of defendants preclude the possibility of observing the niceties of due process.*
6. *Due process will be restored as soon as the emergency has been terminated. Both the courts and the police seek to prevent growth of the disorder to distinguish the leaders, and to control the mob. The courts attempt to control the mob by detaining rioters until order is restored, by displaying power and resolve in the processing of defendants, by observing strict security precautions (having troops and police in court buildings and courtrooms, limiting access to prisoners, and checking credentials of lawyers), and by coordinating policies with other public agencies.*[32]

Even more crisis-producing for the court as an institution of due process, independence, and impartiality have been the trials of dissidents such as Dr. Spock et. al., The Chicago Seven, the Panther Twenty-one, Angela Davis, and numerous others.

During the early phases of dissent against the Vietnam War, the strategy of dissent, such as pouring blood on, or napalming draft files

[32] Ibid., p. 237.

(Milwaukee 14, Catonsville 9), served to dramatize moral intolerance of the war's violence. The dissenters were willing to accept the legal penalties for their acts to raise the moral issues of the war. However, while this dissent was symbolic and dramatic, it also aroused outrage and "patriotic" counter-dissent. The burning of draft cards and the definition of these actions as "patriotic" by applauding adults was one activity that heightened conflict and response and dissent strategies. The government's main purpose in conducting the Spock trial was probably to deter draft resistance and adult support of this resistance. But the trial was also used to symbolically discredit these dissenters, to blame dissent on Spock for his permissive child-rearing philosophy, and to rally patriotic third parties to the government's side of the conflict. Criminal convictions were probably of limited concern. The Spock trial, however, seemingly produced the opposite effect—the trial was used for and became a rallying point for the entire movement; an inducement for third parties to join the defendants in not surrendering one's conscience to the state. The trial became a theater for informing citizens about the war.

Political trials become educational and political forums. Most of the recent political clients—Spock, Ellsberg, the Berrigan brothers, and The Chicago Seven—used their trials as a tool for organizing. In such trials, defense is not a primary concern. The defendants prevail upon their attorneys to emphasize (1) the presentation of the conflict issues, and (2) the court as an instrument of an oppressive system determined to preserve itself at all costs.[33] Though some judges have remained impartial, many have, through their actions, served to reinforce and give greater credence to this last view. As a consequence, the reality of court operation becomes a part of the trial's political education. How are jurors selected? What is a peer? Are judges impartial? Do prosecutors seek truth, convictions, or exposure for their political careers? Is bail not preventive detention? What is the meaning of defending one's self or having counsel of one's choice? Who should determine who should testify? What the judge sees as contempt or premeditated disruption of courtroom procedures, the clients view as further indications of racism, repression, and politicalization of the courts. According to the

[33] Fred Cohn, "Soldiers Say No," pp. 300-309, Robert Lefcourt ed., *Law Against the People* (New York: Vintage Books, 1971).

radical lawyer's point of view, it was clear, from the evidence presented and from the treatment the Chicago Seven conspiracy trial was given by the government, that the defendants were on trial because of who they were, what they advocated politically, what they wore, how they looked, and the challenge they posed to government policy. Of the total number of "conspirators," only some were chosen to be prosecuted, and they represented the full spectrum of the antiwar movement.

A further example of the shift of issues to the structure of the court itself occurred in the Panther Twenty-one conspiracy trial. This trial charged members of the Black Panther Party with conspiring to bomb police stations, department stores, railroads, and other places, and attempting to murder policemen. During the long, turbulent pretrial hearings, the behavior of the defendants led Judge John M. Murtaugh to recess the hearings until the defendants would promise to deport themselves with "good conduct." While the hearings were recessed, the defendants prepared a lengthy critique of American justice, concluding that:

> In light of all that has been said, in view of the collusion of the federal, state, and city courts, the New York City Department of Correction, the city police, and district attorney's office, we feel that we, as members of the Black Panther party, cannot receive a fair and impartial trial without certain preconditions conforming to our alleged constitutional rights. So we state the following: we feel that the courts should follow their own federal Constitution, and when they have failed to do so, and continue to ignore their mistakes, but persist dogmatically to add insult to injury, those courts are in contempt of the people. One need not be black to relate to that, but it is often those who never experience such actions on the part of the courts who believe they, the courts, can never be wrong.
>
> So, in keeping with that, and the social reality to which that principle must relate, we further state:
>
> 1. That we have a constitutional right to reasonable bail, and that a few of us would, if they were white, be released in their own custody. We demand that right, and the court's consistent denial of that right in effect is in contempt of its own Constitution.
> 2. We demand a jury of our peers, or people from our own community, defined by the Constitution.
> 3. We say that because the grand jury system in New York City systematically excludes poor black people, it cannot be representative of a cross-section of the community from which we come. So, in

effect it is unconstitutional and nothing more than a method of wielding class power and racial suppression and repression. We demand to have a constitutional and legal indictment, or be released, for we are being held illegally, by malicious and racist unethical laws.

4. *We demand that the unethical practice of the police and D.A.'s office in their production of evidence, lying, and misrepresentation, be strictly limited by the introduction of an impartial jury of our peers for all pretrial hearings, to judge all motions and evidence submitted, subsequent to a new constitutional indictment.*

Therefore, since you have effectively denied by your ruling of Wednesday, February, 25, 1970, our right to a trial, and since this ruling will affect the future of black and white political prisoners, we have directed our attorneys to do everything in their power to upset this vicious, barbaric, insidious and racist ruling, which runs head-on in contrast with the promise of the Thirteenth and Fourteenth Amendments of your U.S. Constitution.

Let this be entered into all records pertaining to our case.

All power to the people![34]

Thus, the court itself was on trial. The political dissent issues began to take a back seat. Could the criminal justice system deal impartially with a black political defendant accused of serious violent acts?[35]

The Angela Davis trial also raised issues involving the administration of justice, specifically the court issues of the grand jury, the death penalty, bail, and an impartial judiciary. The grand jury is composed of leading citizens, persons who are often the targets of dissent. Grand jury secrecy serves as a protection for people under investigation who have not been indicted, but, because only state evidence is presented, it also serves as a disadvantage to the political dissenter. High bail hampers political defendants from gaining political and monetary support for their cause, and from using their "on trial" status to obtain the support of third party allies. High bail also drains the monetary supply of small movements and dissident groups. After finding an impartial judge, Angela Davis was acquitted in a case heavily affected by a Supreme

[34] The Panther Twenty-one, "To Judge Murtaugh," pp. 185-205, Robert Lefcourt ed., *Law Against the People.*
[35] Jerome H. Skolnick and Steven A. Brick, "A Fair Trial for Angela Davis?" pp. 501-509, Skolnick and Currie, *Crises in American Institutions.*

Court of California case (death penalty) which made her eligible for bail. Did this trial prove that a fair trial is possible for dissidents? Did the court have to demonstrate this to retain its institutional and symbolic reverence? If the court has successfully defended itself and its independence, have the original issues of dissent been resolved? In the Angela Davis case, the goals of the "criminal" actions taken by the dissenters were either to free political prisoners or to ameliorate prison conditions by negotiating the return of hostages. The theater of dissent thus turns to prisons.

The Prisons

One of the points of the Black Panther party's ten-point program of black liberation is the demand of freedom for all black persons held in prisons or jails. The Panthers argue that all black persons are political prisoners of a system of justice designed neither to protect them as citizens nor to guarantee their constitutional rights. Black men are viewed as imprisoned victims of a society designed for genocide or for chaining black men to criminal statuses. Prisons are the theater of despair and the school of militancy.

Setting aside the myths of rehabilitation, American prisons are institutions of punitive confinement. Prisons are autocratic institutions which purport to teach men how to live in a "free" and pluralistic society, an impossible objective in view of the prison's atmosphere. Secure custody and control of the prisoners is extended even to the thoughts of prisoners. For "colonized" persons, prison is a more concentrated and undiluted version of the outside world, where poverty, meaningless work, repression, physical abuse, violence, theft, lack of protection, drugs, oppressive education, and powerlessness prevail.[36]

Prisoners are subjected to degradation ceremonies, deprived of social contact, confined to an enclosed space, and limited to highly restricted communication. Prisons are the places of "dirty work," since the citizenry attempts to ignore and avoid prisoners. Citizens want "deviants" disposed of safely, quickly, and invisibly. This invisibility

---

[36] Herman Schwartz, "Prisoners' Rights: Some Hopes and Realities," pp. 47-63, Roscoe Pound—American Trial Lawyers Foundation, *A Program for Prison Reform: The Final Report,* June 1972.

Figure 13-2. *Prison may be, for some, an undiluted version of the outside world—a place where poverty, repression, violence, and powerlessness prevail.*

makes prisoners escalate the strategy of dissent so that they can obtain attention. Most prison dissent—hunger strikes, building takeovers, hostage-taking—is directed toward making third parties aware that "just" ideals are perverted both inside prison and out. Prisons are the breeding grounds of the *strategy of violence* and the marketplace of the *response of total control.*

One reaction to prison life is that of docility, cooperativeness, and uncomplaining conformity; another reaction is to demand liberty and rebel. Philip Zinbardo writes that dissent in prison results because prisoners feel that to be subject to the arbitrary exercise of power is to be

Figure 13-3.   The aftermath of a riot.

a slave, a prisoner, a black man.[37] Conversely, prison authorities feel
that prison dissent is caused by a small band of militants, the circulation
of militant, revolutionary literature, the influence of militant lawyers,
and the strategies of dissent occurring outside the institution. Thus, they
respond by transferring inmates, placing them in solitary confinement,
censoring mail and reading materials, and limiting legal contacts.

The demands and aftermath of Attica provide insight into these

[37] Philip G. Zinbardo, "Pathology of Imprisonment," *Society*, April 1972.

competing explanations and the resulting strategies of dissent and response. The original demands of the inmates were:

1. *We want complete amnesty. Meaning freedom for all and from all physical, mental, and legal reprisals.*
2. *We want now speedy and safe transportation out of confinement, to a nonimperialistic country.*
3. *We demand that the federal government intervene, so that we will be under direct federal jurisdiction.*
4. *We demand the reconstruction of Attica prison to be done by inmates and/or inmate's supervision.*
5. *We urgently demand immediate negotiation thru Wm. M. Kunstler, Attorney-at-Law—588 Ninth Avenue, New York City., Assemblyman Arthur O. Eve, of Buffalo, New York. The Solidarity Prison Committee, Minister Farrekhan of M. S. Palante, the Young Lords Party Paper, the Black Panther party. (Clarence Jones, of Amsterdam News). Tom Wicker, of the New York Times, Richard Roth from the Courier Express, the Fortune Society, Dave Anderson of the Urban League of Rochester, New York, Blond Eva-Bond Nicap, and Jim Ingram of Democratic Chronicle of Detroit, Michigan.*[38]

The demands for amnesty and safe transportation out of confinement to a nonimperialistic country were drastically altered during the negotiation period. The death of a guard, the legal squabble over amnesty, the autocratic inmate society, fear of dissent, the public attention, the killing of three inmates, and other elements made the following negotiated points unacceptable to the autocratic inmate leaders.

Proposals acceptable to Commissioner Oswald:

1. *Provide adequate food, water, and shelter for all inmates.*
2. *Inmates shall be permitted to return to their cells or to other suitable accommodations or shelter under their own power. The observers' committee shall monitor the implementation of this operation.*
3. *Grant complete administrative amnesty to all persons associated with this matter. By administrative amnesty, the state agrees:*
    a. *Not to take any adverse parole actions, administrative proceedings, physical punishment, or other type of harassment such as holding inmates incommunicado, segregating any inmates, or keeping them in isolation or in 24-hour lockup.*

[38] New York State Special Commission on Attica, *Attica, the Official Report of the New York State Special Commission on Attica*, p. 205.

b. *The state will grant legal amnesty in regard to all civil actions which could arise from this matter.*

c. *It is agreed that the State of New York and all its departments, divisions, and subdivisions, including the State Department of Corrections and the Attica Correctional Facility, and its employees and agents shall not file or initiate any criminal complaint or act on complaints in any criminal action of any kind or nature relating to property, property damage, or property-related crimes arising out of the incidents at the Attica Correctional Facility during September 9, 10, 11, 1971.*

d. *The District Attorney of Wyoming County, New York, has issued and signed the attached letter as of this date.*

4. *Establish by October 1, 1971, a permanent ombudsman service for the facility staffed by appropriate persons from the neighboring communities.*

5. *Recommend the application of the New York State minimum wage law standards to all work done by inmates. Every effort will be made to make the records of payments available to inmates.*

6. *Allow all New York State prisoners to be politically active, without intimidation or reprisal.*

7. *Allow true religious freedom.*

8. *End all censorship of newspaper, magazines, and other publications from publishers, unless there is determined by qualified authority which includes the ombudsman that the literature in question presents a clear and present danger to the safety and security of the institution. Institution spot censoring only of letters.*

9. *All inmates, at their own expense, to communicate with anyone they please.*

10. *Institute realistic, effective rehabilitation programs for all inmates, according to their offense and personal needs.*

11. *Modernize the inmate education system, including the establishment of a Latin library.*

12. *Provide an effective narcotics treatment program for all prisoners requesting such treatment.*

13. *Provide or allow adequate legal assistance to all inmates requesting it or permit them to use inmate legal assistance of their choice in any proceeding whatsoever. In all such proceedings, inmates shall be entitled to appropriate due process of law.*

14. *Provide a healthy diet; reduce the number of pork dishes; increase fresh fruit daily.*

15. *Reduce cell time, increase recreation facilities and equipment, hopefully by November 1, 1971.*
16. *Provide adequate medical treatment for every inmate; engage either a Spanish-speaking doctor or inmate interpreters who will accompany Spanish-speaking inmates to medical interviews. (See point 11 above.)*
17. *Institute a program for the recruitment and employment of a significant number of black and Spanish-speaking officers.*
18. *Establish an inmate grievance commission comprised of one elected inmate from each company, which is authorized to speak to the administration concerning grievances, and develop other procedures for inmate participation in the operation and decision-making processes of the institution.*
19. *Investigate the alleged expropriation of inmate funds and the use of profits from the metal and other shops.*
20. *The State Commissioner of Correctional Services will recommend that the penal law be changed to cease administrative resentencing of inmates returned for parole violation.*
21. *Recommend that Menechino hearings be held promptly and fairly.*
22. *Recommend necessary legislation and more adequate funds to expand work-release program.*
23. *End approved lists for correspondence and visitors.*
24. *Remove visitation screens as soon as possible.*
25. *Paroled inmates shall not be charged with parole violations for moving traffic violations or driving without a license, unconnected with any other crime.*
26. *Institute a 30-day maximum for segregation arising out of any one offense. Every effort should be geared toward restoring the individual to regular housing as soon as possible, consistent with safety regulations.*
27. *Permit access to outside dentists and doctors at the inmates' own expense within the institution, where possible, and consistent with scheduling problems, medical diagnosis, and health needs.*
28. *It is expressly understood that members of the observers' committee will be permitted into the institution on a reasonable basis to determine whether all of the above provisions are being effectively carried out. If questions of adequacy are raised, the matter will be brought to the attention of the Commissioner of Correctional Services for clearance.*[39]

[39] Ibid., pp. 251-256.

Further reasons given for the rejection of the 28 points were that: (1) amnesty for crimes against persons was not negotiable; (2) the inmates had no system for approving or disapproving the points; (3) an inmate leader ripped up the 28 points; (4) some inmates felt that they had achieved so much so fast, that they could achieve more; and, most critical (5) the inmates had a deep mistrust of the white establishment, the political system, and anyone associated with them. Could they believe and trust the promises of Commissioner Oswald? Would they really be protected from reprisals? What assurance did they have that there would be no mass prosecutions?

Thus, the negotiations broke down. The time had come for the *response of violence*. After the unrestrained violence that regained the "state's sovereignty," the prisoners indeed received no protection from reprisals.

Conclusions

Dissent consists of acts by the powerless to bring about social and legal change. The new politics of dissent creates activities that revive direct citizen participation in politics. The common thread of current dissent is a desire by people to shape their own destiny, to be more active in the processes and structures that affect their lives. The new politics of dissent requires the organization of people into groups, with deep commitments of time and emotion. The processes of action involved in dissent make politics more immediate and relevant. This is the dissent of mass society.

The response of political authority can be one that adapts and becomes responsive to change. These authorities can encourage the adoption of necessary changes in order to alleviate the conditions which are the objects of dissent. On the other hand, the authorities can strengthen their systems of forceful control. The current political response has generally been toward strengthening the systems of control. However, the response of direct violence will decrease as the political authorities become more sophisticated in their abilities to handle conflict by utilizing the techniques of persuasion, reward, or compromise. One response designed to avoid instituting changes focuses on the use of the media, the schools, and other institutions of socialization (information). Another nonchange response is avoiding the problem by intensifying the infiltration of dissident and militant organizations. In counter-reaction to this, sophisticated dissident groups form consumer networks, attempt to outadminister the authorities (breakfast programs, health clinics, legal bureaus), or organize to control local communities. If the authorities respond to these counter-reactions by using force to maintain the political order, it is possible that prisonlike reactions will occur. Most persons will be docile while others will participate in terrorist or guerrilla activities.

Perhaps an increased readiness by the authorities to respond to the issues raised by dissenters will transform our institutions. Conversely, if these issues are considered to be nonnegotiable and the authorities' response is one of escalated, sophisticated control techniques, then the society will move itself into a destitute state. Coercive control is not acceptable to people with long-standing and legitimate grievances. As Jerome Skolnick stated, "This nation cannot have it both ways; either it will carry through a firm commitment to massive and widespread political and social reform, or it will develop into a society of garrison cities where order is enforced without due process of law, and without the consent of the governed."[40] Democratic political institutions are not viable under massive control circumstances. They become prisons.

Student Checklist

1. Can you define the right to dissent under the U.S. Constitution?
2. Can you list the findings of the Violence Commission?
3. Do you know the different views of acceptable dissent?
4. Are you able to describe the strategies of dissent and strategies of response?
5. Can you identify the significant aspects of escalation and de-escalation?

[40] Skolnick, *The Politics of Protest: Violent Aspects of Protest and Confrontation*, p. 261.

Topics for Discussion

1. Discuss the conflict between the right to dissent and the need to maintain order.
2. Discuss the strategies of dissent and strategies of response.
3. Discuss the limit of escalation of conflict.

ANNOTATED BIBLIOGRAPHY

Bienen, Henry. *Violence and Social Change: A Review of Current Literature.* Chicago: The University of Chicago Press, 1968. This is a good review of the literature on violence and social change. Internal warfare is discussed. Violence in the ghetto, guerrilla war, revolution, and totalitarianism are analyzed.

Blumer, Herbert. "Social Problems as Collective Behavior," *Social Problems, 18,* Winter 1971. Rather than studying objective conditions for an analysis of social problems, Blumer focuses on the processes of collective definitions. How does a problem arise, will it be legitimated, how is it shaped, how is it addressed in official policy, and how is it redesigned in practical application?

Carmichael, Stokeley and Charles V. Hamilton. *Black Power: The Politics of Liberation in America.* New York: Vintage, 1967. An excellent book analyzing the colonial view of the black struggle and the need for black political and cultural self-determination and autonomy.

Carnoy, Judity, and Marc Weiss. *A House Divided, Radical Perspectives on Social Problems.* Boston: Little, Brown, 1973. This is a book which the student can use to find lists of demands by "radical" protest groups. More critical, it deals with the crisis of political authority.

Denisoff, R. Serge, and Charles H. McCaghy. *Deviance, Conflict, and Criminality.* Chicago: Rand McNally, 1973. An excellent book of readings which attempts to bring together conflict theory with the concepts of deviance and criminality.

Douglas, William O. *Points of Rebellion*. New York: Random House, 1969. This member of the Supreme Court analyzes dissent and warns of the necessity of change or else impending revolution.

Eckstein, Harry, ed. *Internal War*. New York: Macmillan, 1964. An excellent book of articles on internal conflict. See especially the articles by Feldman, Gerschenkron, Kornhauser, Levy, and Pye.

Fanon, Frantz. *The Wretched of the Earth*. New York: Grove Press, 1963. This has been an extremely influential book. It analyzes the politics and psychologies of colonialism and anticolonialism.

Fortas, Abe. *Concerning Dissent and Civil Disobedience*. New York: New American Library, 1968. The book provides a classical legal statement on acceptable constitutional dissent.

Grossman, Joel B., and Mary H. Grossman. *Law and Change in Modern American*. Pacific Palisades: Goodyear Publishing, 1971. This is a good reader on law as an instrument of social change, of controlling deviant behavior, of securing justice, and of dealing with dissent.

Gusfield, Joseph R. "Moral Passage: The Symbolic Process in the Public Designations of Deviance," *Social Problems, 15*, Fall 1967. This is one of the best articles illustrating the importance of the symbolic nature of law. It also makes the point that public definitions of deviance have a history and that the "deviant as enemy" is most likely to escalate response strategies because he challenges the legitimacy of the definers.

Horowitz, Irving Louis, and Martin Liebowitz. "Social Deviance and Political Marginality," *Social Problems, 15*, Fall 1968. The article addresses the merger of social deviance and political marginality. The consequences of the politicalization of "deviant" subcultures is analyzed.

Kriesberg, Louis. *The Sociology of Social Conflicts*. Englewood Cliffs, N.J.: Prentice-Hall, 1973. Presents a very comprehensive analysis of conflict. Contemporary struggles: women's liberation, the cold war, collective bargaining, student protests, the Mid-East, and racial conflict, are analyzed. The analysis covers the underlying bases of conflict, the alternative strategies of conflict, escalation processes, and the termination, outcome, and consequences of the conflict.

Lefcourt, Robert, ed. *Law Against the People, Essays to De-mystify Law, Order and the Courts.* New York: Vintage, 1971. This is an excellent book demonstrating the perspective of "movement" lawyers, how they work to de-mystify law and challenge law as an institution which works against the people. An excellent annotated bibliography.

Lindenfeld, Frank. *Radical Perspectives on Social Problems*, 2nd Ed. New York: Macmillan, 1973. This is a social problem reader which attempts to present "radical" perspectives on current social problems. Specifically applicable to this subject matter are the articles by Mills, Horton, Kropotkin, Milgram, Cleaver, and Marcuse.

Malcolm X. *The Autobiography of Malcolm X.* New York: Grove Press, 1966. The life of one of the most influential black leaders. He has had enormous impact on current black conflict.

National Advisory Commission on Civil Disorders. Washington, D.C.: U.S. Govt. Printing Office, 1968. The Kerner Commission Report detailing the history of civil rights conflicts. It places blame on white institutions, but studies only ghetto conditions and individual white racism.

New York State Special Commission on Attica. *Attica, The Official Report of the New York State Special Commission on Attica.* New York: Bantam Books, 1972. This is the commission's version of the complete story of the events leading up to and the aftermath of the Attica prison disaster. Prison life and conditions as well as the ideologies of political authorities are analyzed. A must for understanding prisons.

Skolnick, Jerome. *The Politics of Protest: Violent Aspects of Protest and Confrontation.* A Staff Report to the National Commission on the Causes and Prevention of Violence. Washington, D.C.: U.S. Govt. Printing Office, 1969. This is an excellent document. A must for understanding dissent, violence, and the history of recent conflict issues. Sections on the police and courts are very valuable. An excellent annotated bibliography.

Skolnick, Jerome and Elliott Currie. *Crisis in American Institutions.* 2nd Ed. Boston: Little, Brown, 1973. This is one of the better social problems readers. It has a section on police and one on criminal law and connections among the many institutions treated.

To Establish Justice, To Insure Domestic Tranquility. Final Report of the National Commission On the Causes and Prevention of Violence. Washington, D.C.: U.S. Govt. Printing Office, 1969. The commissioner's summary, debate, and conclusions of the vast amount of research produced regarding violence in the United States.

Turk, Austin T. *Criminality and Legal Order.* Chicago: Rand McNally, 1969. The first three chapters of this book present a power perspective for analyzing which conflicts come to be reacted to as "criminal." Excellent beginnings for an analysis of conflict parties' interaction and outcomes.

U.S. Commission on Civil Rights. *Enforcement: A Report on Equal Protection in the South.* Washington, D.C.: U.S. Govt. Printing Office, 1965. This report considers the denials of constitutional rights in the South. It makes recommendations for civil and criminal remedy.

U.S. Commission on Civil Rights. *Mexican-Americans and the Administration of Justice.* Washington, D.C.: U.S. Govt. Printing Office, 1970. An analysis of the current plight of minority groups. The legal system, politicians, and police abuse are addressed.

Zinn, Howard. *Disobedience and Democracy: Nine Fallacies on Law and Order.* New York: Random House, 1968. Zinn presents an analysis of dissent and encourages new forms of dissent to place pressure on political authorities such that changes occur which meet the needs of "the people."

The study of this chapter will enable you to:

1. Identify several alternatives to arrest.
2. Write a short essay describing the defusement process.
3. List three ways to develop close communication between the police and the community.
4. List the functions of teams in a police department conflict management program.
5. Understand how conflict management actually operates in typical situations needing police intervention.

14
Conflict Management

This chapter will discuss an important, but neglected, aspect of police–community relations—alternatives to arrest. Although the usefulness of arrest has been questioned, it would be difficult to find an intelligent person who believes that arrest should be completely discarded. Yet, society is continually groping for an understanding of the proper position of arrest in the fulfillment of its needs.

The power to arrest is often used by communities as an easily accessible device for controlling deviancy. However, the complex nature of today's world requires that we consider the development of alternatives to arrest. Some people argue that if police officers could arrest and incarcerate all of the law violators in their community, there would be a pronounced effect on the volume of crime. But the community's reaction would be prompt and negative, because mass arrest has always been associated with the suspension of individual rights. In the area of mass dissent and civil disobedience, the line that separates the positives and the negatives is even less clear, especially since the ranks of dissenters have been joined by college professors, congressmen, religious leaders, and other noncriminal citizens. Thus, it is reasonable to assume that many arrests may aggravate, rather than resolve, impending problems.

Since the late 1950s, police agencies in the United States have been especially attuned to the difficult and critical problem of maintaining an orderly community. But how do we maintain an orderly community? Unfortunately, there is no prescribed formula to tell us how to accomplish this task. Each situation is unique and must be resolved through intricate knowledge of the community—its concerns and its priorities. Before a police agency can develop an effective order-maintenance program, it must first initiate a program of self-critical analysis;

the goal of this program is to scientifically and rationally place the police role into proper perspective as it relates to community needs, tolerances, and expectations. Such an analysis must include the realization that police–community relations means responsive, effective, considerate police operations.

Therefore the primary consideration of police operations should be the concerns and changing priorities of the community's citizens. The police department must make an effort to provide the community with staff assistance directed toward identifying and resolving the causes of crime and violence, whether those causes are legal or social.

Policemen are involved in a balancing act between rigid enforcement and community tolerances, which is complicated by their own personal beliefs. Before any alternatives, contingencies, or strategies are developed, the department must first acquire an in-depth knowledge of the community and its problems, which can only be accomplished by police operating as a part *of*, and not apart *from*, the community. In addition, the community must be convinced that its police department is operating objectively and is serving the community's legitimate interests to the best of its ability. A partnership must exist between the police and the community. This partnership is one step in laying the groundwork for an accommodation within the department and the community for developing and internalizing alternatives to arrest.

One method of establishing a partnership is through community organization, information, and education efforts initiated by the police. This chapter will focus on one successful effort in community organization and leadership—a conflict management program established by the Dayton, Ohio, Police Department in 1970. Dayton's program was designed to develop conflict alternatives, improve police–community relations through community involvement, and quell disturbances without mass arrest. This program illustrates how arrest alternatives can be developed and internalized into standard operating procedures.

Program Design

The first step in the development of Dayton's conflict management program was the recruitment of a conflict management unit staff. The program's design called for eight police officers and four civilians with professional skills in areas not commonly found in the police ranks; this mixture of sworn and civilian personnel is a facet of the program's objective of police–community interaction. Recruitment of the staff was primarily accomplished by incorporating the former community relations unit into the new unit's structure. Unit members were selected on the basis of their ability to work competently without close supervision, their sensitivity and adaptability to change, and their commitment to change through rational means.

After staff members were selected, they met with the program director in a series of informal seminars where a number of concepts, including intergroup relations, personal attitudes, and problems relating to police-community interaction were reviewed and discussed. Gradually, a statement of objectives and procedures was developed. It gave the unit a "checks-and-balances" structure and provided a means of coordinating activities and measuring progress. The statement, however, was written broadly enough to permit flexibility in developing police responses appropriate to each new situation.

As planning progressed, Dayton divided its conflict management unit into three specialized teams: conflict intervention, community

Figure 14-1.   The conflict management unit.

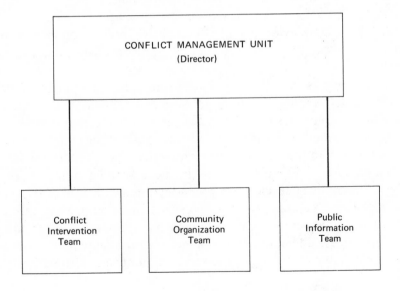

organization, and public information. The operations of these teams are described below.

Conflict Intervention Team

The conflict intervention team is responsible for seeking out, identifying, and intervening in areas of potential conflict, before they become serious disruptions. The police department may not be able to recognize conflict before it reaches major proportions unless the department develops close communication and contact with the community. Thus, the primary responsibility of the conflict intervention team is to develop and nurture this kind of close contact. Team members spend most of their time in the community in an effort to create the open exchanges of opinion that are necessary for a working police–community interaction. The team members meet with ministers, presidents and chairmen of neighborhood organizations and service clubs, directors and staff members of service agencies, business and industrial leaders, school administrators and faculty, leaders and members of paramilitary and youth groups, gang members, and others who have no formal connections to anyone or any group, but who can still exert influence over a large number of people.

These relationships give team members a chance to learn about the conflicts and community problems that might lead to violence and confrontation situations. The relationships play a major role in the so-called defusement process—a conflict management technique employed to smooth over potentially abrasive police–community interaction when a large group forms, either spontaneously or as a planned demonstration.

The first aspect of conflict intervention, then, is to identify conflict and potential conflict situations in the community and to respond to potentially explosive situations as they arise in the community.

The second aspect is to actually intervene in the conflict and work out a solution to the conflict situation so that the necessity for forceful police response is eliminated. This includes keeping command officers advised as conflicts develop and preparing a number of alternatives that the department can adopt in handling each situation. During this stage, the conflict intervention team acts as a resource and research arm for the department, attempting to find a means of responding that will maintain a maximum of order, yet not result in an open confrontation.

At other times, intervention may mean going immediately into the problem area and bringing initial relief to the community through defusement before developing the longer term solution. This permits the department to control a situation through conflict management techniques using only six officers, and to alleviate problems that might otherwise call for a more extensive use of force. The ability of the team to defuse potentially dangerous situations illustrates the value of a conflict management approach toward law enforcement. The conflict intervention unit is not only a specialized task force that acts as a planning source for the department; it is also a practical, on-the-street operation that intervenes in crises as they arise. Its approaches are those of mediation, communication, and advocacy. When a conflict and its participants have been identified, a meeting or series of meetings is arranged between the team and those community members who are parties to the conflict.

The team has intervened as a mediator in such varied disputes as two quarreling neighbors, two youth groups, labor and management during a strike situation, and a group of college students hostile to the school administration.

In many cases, a conflict results from a lack of proper services from some other public agency. Advocacy by the conflict intervention team is often necessary to see that the proper service is rendered. This concept is also employed during intensive conflict situations when an in-depth study is necessary to discover the causes of the conflict and develop recommendations for action.

The concept of the policeman as a mediator, communicator, and advocate has shown a degree of success in Dayton. It allows the department to maintain as neutral a position as is possible in the community, preventing the kind of open, police-citizen confrontation that leads to ineffective police–community relations which injure the welfare of the cities themselves.

When the conflict management unit was first established, its design called for a separate youth aid team, which has since been incorporated into the conflict intervention team. The original youth aid team was responsible for juvenile counseling and other youth-related activities, as well as the comprehensive school safety program, but its activities overlapped with the work of the conflict intervention team in problem areas, investigations, and program solutions. Because of this overlap, the conflict management unit's director decided that the interests of the overall program would be better served by consolidating these two team areas.

Because of this transfer of duties, the conflict intervention team's work now includes the counseling of juveniles who reach the department as delinquents or potential delinquents. Efforts are made to informally discuss delinquency problems with parents, school officials, and the young people themselves. The goal is to improve the youngsters' attitudes toward police, school, and authority in general.

The school safety program has been expanded from the traditional elementary school activities to include visits to secondary schools, where team members conduct discussions on such topics as civil disobedience, community behavioral patterns, the American system of law, and the responsibility to achieve change through nonviolent, legal means. A central theme in these lectures pertains to the police role in society and police-community interaction. Through a school safety program of this sort, the department has established a good relationship with a much broader range of young people.

Community Organization Team

The community organization team works to develop a sound relationship with the community by establishing contacts with neighborhood organizations. The community organization specialist, a civilian, provides the technical assistance needed for improved community involvement, and organizes meetings and workshops in the neighborhoods between the police and the residents. These meetings provide the opportunity to explain both the problems and priorities of the police and the attitudes and grievances of the community.

Public Information Team

The public information team, headed by a former journalist, is designed to alleviate the stigma attached to one-way public relations programs and provide for complete, open, and honest dissemination of information, even if that information is negative. The Dayton Police Department believes that this type of open dissemination is necessary to win the trust and confidence of the community. The information specialist plays a number of roles associated with his position; as the department's spokesman, he responds to questions pertaining to departmental programs, policy, decisions, and actions. His most significant role is that of the dissemination of information during tense situations.

Conflict Management in Action

Since 1970 the conflict management unit and its three specialized teams have developed many unique and common-sense approaches to problem-solving. The following pages describe several of these situations and the unit's response.

Labor–Management Problem

Situation. A labor–management dispute was taking place at the city's largest hospital. Unskilled hospital workers were seeking union representation but were denied it by the hospital, who claimed that the majority of the workers were satisfied with the existing labor–management arrangement. The workers campaigning for union membership then sought an election so that the wishes of the majority might be determined, but the hospital refused to sanction the election and said that it would not recognize it. The dispute continued throughout the summer of 1970. But it emerged into open conflict one morning when about 50 workers confronted the hospital administrator in his office and demanded the election.

Potential. The workers were an angry, volatile group and said that they would not leave the office until either the election was granted or they were arrested by the police. In addition, they said that they would resist arrests and would have to be forcefully carried from the office and the hospital. The potential for the department to be drawn into a confrontation with the workers was clearly evident.

Conflict Management Unit Response. Two conflict management unit officers were dispatched to the hospital and began the so-called defusement process. Employing this technique, the officers were able to move the workers into an adjacent hallway and out of the administrator's office. This brought about the immediate relief that was needed to give the officers an opportunity to work with the situation. The officers explained to the workers that they would not be "taking sides," but were there only to protect life and property and assure that hospital services would not be interrupted.

Then the officers stayed with the workers and talked about how the arrest process would be carried out and what it might mean to the workers (possible injuries and arrest records). While the officers talked to employees, the conflict management unit director was buying time from the hospital administration.

By demonstrating this kind of patience and concern, the two officers were able to reduce both the size and hostility of the group; they eventually won an agreement—the protestors would submit themselves to voluntary arrests.

Thus, when the hospital administration invoked a trespassing ordinance, the remaining workers were cooperative. Uniformed patrolmen were called to the hospital to carry out the arrest process, which was orderly and quick.

Evaluation. A hostile, angry group engaged in a peaceful protest. There were no injuries, property destruction, or interruption of hospital services. A more traditional police response could have committed the department to a confrontation with the workers. But there was no confrontation, and—with the exception of five minutes during the arrest process—only two officers were needed.

Operation Stop-Drag

Situation. About 400 teenagers and older people gathered in a residential neighborhood on weekend evenings to drag-race down a long, sliding hill. The participants were endangering their own lives, as well as public safety. In addition, the noise generated by the drag-racing and the onlookers was seriously detrimental to peace and tranquility in the neighborhood.

Potential. Neighborhood residents were becoming increasingly irritated with the situation, and there were indications that they would take action on their own if police were not able to alleviate the problem. Some of the residents were arming themselves, and others were talking about putting nails and broken glass in the street. Such action would have created an enduring scar on the neighborhood, and evoked a police response that would have required many troops, an expenditure of departmental resources, and a serious deterioration in police–community relations. A confrontation and disturbance of major proportions were in the making.

Conflict Management Unit Response. The conflict management unit's response was broken into two segments. The first called for documentation of the incidents. One team member went into the area during the week following initiation of the response, discussed the residents' observations, and assured them that the department was involving itself in the situation.

Following this, the officer made a personal inspection of the drag-racing, documenting illegal actions, determining what the team's best action might be, and where the department would encounter the most problems. This segment of the operation was handled by the public information team. Through use of the media, primarily radio, team members explained the problems being created in the particular community, and asked that the drag-racing be stopped before police action would be necessary. This action gave comfort to the troubled neighborhood and also "put the word out on the streets" that, in the interests of a peaceful community, the department would not tolerate the drag-racing.

The second and final segment of the operation was the actual defusement process. Using conflict management techniques, the conflict intervention team went into the area on the first night of the weekend that was selected. Officers walked among the drag-racers and general crowd and explained the problems and what the department would have to do if the activity were not stopped.

On the second night of the weekend, the size of the crowd was greatly reduced. The team once again talked with the people there and stopped the drag-racing before it started. After a few hours, most of the crowd was gone.

Six arrests were made at the very end of the evening when a group of youngsters refused to stop their activity. After that the entire activity ceased. And the drag-racing problem has never since arisen in that neighborhood.

Evaluation. Although six arrests were made, had the department responded with traditional means, many more arrests would have been necessary, and a serious confrontation might have taken place. Overall, a potentially explosive situation, where danger to life and destruction to property could have occurred, was eliminated. Residents in the neighborhood were given the relief to which they were entitled, and only a token number of officers was needed.

The Gangs

Situation. Several paramilitary and loosely organized youth groups were responsible for considerable apprehension in the city's neighborhoods and for assaults and destruction to property.

Potential. Due to the quick, "hit-and-run" nature of gang activities, only rarely were witnesses and victims able to identify assailants or provide enough information to effect arrests. It was virtually impossible for the department to legally halt such activities.

However all gangs do not engage in antisocial behavior, nor are all members of a gang that engages in antisocial behavior destructive or violence-oriented. Indeed, some of these groups have assisted the department in keeping tense situations from exploding. Therefore, an attempt by the department to "get the gangs off the streets" by gathering intelligence information and making arrests would have been both unfair and of little value in reaching the real sources of trouble. Additionally, such police action has proven to be disastrous; it serves as a recruiting mechanism for the gangs and, as experience across the country has shown, further alienates young people, drawing police into an imaginary "war" with the youths. Neither does such action offer more than stopgap measures. It only commits the department to respond to gang activities again and again.

Conflict Management Unit Response. The conflict management unit recognized its double predicament. The gangs were becoming more influential in Dayton, and a confrontation with them would heavily drain the department and the city of vital resources. Therefore, the conflict management unit sought to develop a longer lasting solution to this problem area.

Operating under the premise that "if you can't lick 'em, join 'em," two conflict intervention team officers have practically become gang members. But this is not an intelligence or undercover operation. The two officers wear their police uniforms and ride marked police motorcycles in their interaction with the gangs. This gives the team a chance to meet the gangs "on their own grounds," developing an honest relationship with them which allows the officers to become familiar with gang leaders, their habits, and other related matters. The officers caution the gang members if they are causing trouble, and explain the consequences of their behavior.

Evaluation. This relationship between the officers and the gangs has proven to be valuable. The department has been able to reduce the late night noise caused by gangs, the general vandalism and littering, and the roughhousing that often leads to assaults on innocent people. It has prevented a potential gang–police confrontation and has reduced the need to investigate complaints due to gang activities. In addition, the conflict management operation has provided the community with a visible police presence, assuring residents that the department is monitoring gang activity.

Sporadic problems with gangs still develop, but the volatility has disappeared, and beat officers are able to handle the problems with little difficulty.

The Tenant–Landlord Disputes Program

Situation. Private disputes occur between tenants and landlords, usually in low-income apartments or houses.

Potential. Traditionally, there has always been friction between tenants and landlords. Tenants often take advantage of landlords who do not carefully supervise and maintain rental property, and landlords often take advantage of tenants who do not understand the legal technicalities of rental contracts or landlord obligations. Disputes are common occurrences. The police have traditionally regarded such disputes as strictly civil matters that do not call for police involvement, and often one of the participants falls victim to the other. The tenant may suffer unfair landlord practices, ranging from illegal rent increases to eviction. Or the landlord may have his rental property completely destroyed by the tenants. When landlord–tenant disputes continue over a period of time, criminal acts often occur. These may be property destruction, assaults that may result in serious injuries or death, and other types of violence.

Disputes in many cities reach proportions where angry groups of tenants or a civil rights organization enter into large-scale demonstrations against the landlord; as a result, there is a breakdown in order. This means that in many tenant–landlord disputes police become involved at one point or another, with a considerable expenditure of man-hours in the conducting of investigations or quelling disorder.

Conflict Management Unit Response. The conflict management unit has established a program to intervene in tenant–landlord disagreements at the initial stage. The program is an on-going crime and violence prevention project, a definite police responsibility.

This program requires part of one conflict management officer's time. Upon being notified of a dispute (either by a beat officer who identifies a dispute during his course of duty or by a call from one of the parties involved), the officer meets with the tenant and landlord to find out what the problem is. Then, employing his training in this area, he informs both participants of their mutual obligations and of what they legally can and cannot do. He keeps in contact with the cases to see that both sides reach reasonable and satisfactory agreements. Often he is able to handle a dispute quickly by referring the tenants and landlords to the proper service agencies or by informing the agency that a dispute exists.

Evaluation. This program deals with police responsibilities (crime and violence prevention) at a level traditionally ignored by police. The program has saved the Dayton Police Department countless manhours that would otherwise have been expended.

The Housing Projects

Situation. A number of low-to-moderate income housing projects, many racially mixed, exhibit unrest.

Potential. There is often considerable apprehension among housing project residents, especially in racially mixed projects; white residents believe that favors are being given to black residents and the blacks believe that they are being subjected to unfair treatment by police and the project management. Both black and white residents have problems in their relationships with the residents of the single family dwellings which adjoin many of the projects; the people who live in these private homes regard the project tenants as "invaders." The degree of apprehension that exists among housing project residents, coupled with the strained relationship between these residents and nearby neighbors, creates a potential for serious conflict. The slightest incident can trigger a large group situation.

There have been many cases in which the traditional police response to "break up" such situations backfires, and draws police into the middle. When this occurs, the police become the object of confrontation. Additionally, these kinds of confrontation are frequent and consume excessive departmental resources.

Conflict Management Unit Response. One of the primary needs among housing project residents is that of communication. An exaggerated rumor can, within minutes, produce unpleasant, large group encounters. To prevent this type of situation from occurring, conflict management unit members have developed a communications apparatus to enable project residents to identify problems and dispel rumors. In a series of meetings at the project, Dayton police told the residents that they, themselves, must be responsible for finding solutions to their problems. However, in order to assist the residents, the conflict intervention team mediates disputes between the residents and the project management, identifying areas where residents have exceeded housing rules and regulations or violated housing contracts, or where the management has not rendered proper and expected services. Acting both as mediators and advocates, team members have also worked to alleviate some apprehensions between project residents and private homeowners. The techniques employed by the team members have successfully warded off potential explosions.

Evaluation. By developing a means of interaction among project residents, management, and single-family homeowners, many problems that would have eventually called for police involvement have been checked in their initial stages. By placing the responsibility for problem-solving directly upon the project residents, the residents have been given a sense of pride and self-achievement in being able to handle their own problems. The need for police response has been practically eliminated; what have been regarded as tense housing areas have become rational, stable, and peaceful communities.

The High Schools

Situation. Growing urban schools, beginning to integrate, and the complex problems of young people experiencing the first challenges of responsibility have been a source of difficulty. This is complicated by racial antagonisms, often reflected in the homes and carried into schools by the students, apprehension on the part of city residents who live in school neighborhoods, and the fear of "new" people (integration).

Potential. There is a real strain on intergroup relations among students in the public school system, and even unintentional acts can produce confrontations between black and white youngsters. Traditional responses—sending in troops to separate and disperse youngsters—have resulted in making the police the object of the confrontation and creating just as serious a problem. In many cases, this type of response only aggravates the situation and makes it necessary for the department to return to the school on a continual basis, which places an exhausting strain on departmental resources. It also irritates students, who resent massive police presence at the schools and are drawn more and more into the situation.

Conflict Management Unit Response. Recognizing that the Dayton Police Department could not afford to respond day after day to such situations, yet realizing that the department has an obligation to assure that the schools remain peaceful learning centers, the conflict management unit sought to develop longer lasting solutions.

Conflict intervention team members met with students in seminars, assemblies, conferences, workshops, classrooms, and street parties to explore and dissect myths, rumors, false and malicious statements, and ignorant beliefs. This has brought about an understanding on the part of both black and white students that the fast-moving pace of our times calls for interdependence. These discussions have been expanded to include parents and the residents of the school neighborhoods. In addition, the team members have promoted the establishment of student-faculty-administration councils, which bring normally separated people into a more positive alliance.

The team also developed a special course that is taught to high school students in civic classes. This course is led by a conflict management officer who discusses such topics as the laws of search and seizure, the American system of justice and constitutional rights, police responsibilities and limitations, and basic police operations.

Evaluation. The Dayton Police Department has been able to maintain a healthy learning atmosphere in the schools, reducing the negative attitudes that students often have toward police. Racial tensions and hostilities among students and in school neighborhoods have been reduced, and the department no longer has to contend with continuous, abrasive contacts between students and neighborhood residents.

The County Fair

Situation. A week-long county fair with an attendance of 132,000, has grown over the years into a cycle of predictable violence. The fairgrounds are located in Montgomery County, adjacent to Dayton, and policing of the fairgrounds is the responsibility of the county sheriff's department. However, the Dayton Police Department must respond to fair-related violence, since the fairgrounds are located only eight blocks from Dayton's downtown business area.

Potential. In September 1968, during Fair Week, there were incidents of property damage, crowd disorders, and hostility between fair patrons and the police. Again, in September 1969, similar problems occurred; in addition, a large group of antagonized and hostile youths were driven from the fairgrounds into downtown Dayton, where they caused thousands of dollars in damage to local businesses and homes. As a result, the relationship between the police and the community sank to an all-time low.

Analyzing the problems that occurred in 1968 and 1969, the Dayton Police discovered that many of the violent situations were caused by young people from the inner-city poverty areas. These teenagers, who could not afford the price of admission to the fair, would gain entry to the fairgrounds by climbing over fences. Once inside, they wandered around aimlessly, grabbed prizes from concessionaire booths, assaulted people, and threw rocks and bottles at exhibits. The police response was to arrest these youngsters, or chase them out of the fairgrounds, but it was discovered that this type of action did not have any impact on stopping the violence. In addition, the Dayton Police found that those young people who were not causing trouble themselves were being irritated by concessionaires, who took advantage of the youngsters by shortchanging them, changing game rules when a teenager demonstrated skill at a particular booth, and calling the youngsters derogatory names. The hostility and tension would then be transferred to other people at the fair, especially when sheriff's deputies began dispersing crowds by ejecting large, disorderly groups from the fairgrounds. These groups would then walk to downtown Dayton and create trouble.

Thus, as the 1970 fair drew near, the Dayton Police realized that they had to devise alternative methods of handling the problems associated with the fair in order to prevent the violence of previous years.

Conflict Management Unit Response. To prevent violence at the 1970 fair, the conflict management unit director recruited 14 additional officers from the department to help coordinate police activities during Fair Week, increasing the unit's strength to 21. In addition, the director obtained assistance from paramilitary groups, such as the Black Guard and the Republic of New Africa, as well as the churches and civic groups. The paramilitary groups agreed to patrol the fairgrounds and intervene in situations where black teenagers might be causing trouble. They agreed to work closely with the Dayton Police Department in the coordination of efforts, and were given police radios to facilitate communications.

In addition, the conflict management unit asked the department to assign 200 officers to downtown streets during the late evening hours when there was a possibility that large groups would move into that area. This allowed for a show of police force, an important consideration in conflict management techniques.

Even though the conflict management unit tries to arrive at a peaceful alternative to conflict, using arrest as a last resort, it is advantageous to have a large reserve force effectively deployed in order to defuse situations that may erupt into violence.

As the fair date drew near, three teams of six officers each were formed to report directly to the conflict management unit director. These teams met with officials of the city, fair board, and sheriff's department, as well as the news media, to outline plans. In addition, they met with concessionaires and ride operators to explain police concerns and obtain their cooperation in preventing violent situations.

Each day before the teams went into the fairgrounds, they met with both the paramilitary and the citizens groups at the Dayton Public Safety Building to discuss what had happened the day before, what might happen that day (due to weather, crowd sizes, or the events of the previous day), the kinds of responses that were working, and other alternatives that could be used.

The officers, wearing uniforms, circulated freely at the fair, playing games, going on rides, and buying tickets for those youngsters who did not have money (several donations had been made by local businesses and industries for this purpose). By circulating, talking with people, and observing what was happening, the teams were able to identify those youngsters causing trouble and, employing a variety of conflict management techniques, assist them in leaving the fair and going home.

Unfortunately, however, there were some groups determined to leave their mark somewhere before the summer's end. On one occasion, an unorganized group of black youngsters was running around the fairgrounds, yelling and bumping into people. Patrons began to grow irritated, and there was talk of retaliation by some white teenagers. The conflict management teams were able to take control of the situation and talked the youngsters into leaving the fair and going home. On the night before the fair closed, about two dozen members of a youth gang appeared at the gate, then walked inside and began moving about the midway. Almost immediately, the conflict management unit members began walking and talking with them. The two groups threatened to close down the fair. They moved into a shelter underneath the grandstands and were joined by the unit's director, who launched a "summit conference" with them. After an agreement was reached between the police and the gangs, the gang members left the fairgrounds.

The last night of the fair presented the most difficult problem. The final scheduled activity was a demolition derby, and when it ended, all the booths, exhibits, and rides were closed. About 2500 youths who had just finished watching the derby had nothing to do but head for the streets. The crowd formed outside the fairgrounds on Main Street, and began marching toward the downtown area.

Conflict management unit officers decided to walk downtown with the youngsters, talking with them and trying to reduce the level of hostility. The officers walked inside the crowd, rather than alongside, using first names and joking. By the time the crowd reached the downtown area, most of the hostility was gone. With the loss of hostility and the appearance of the uniformed policemen in the downtown area, the youths simply lined up at the bus stop and went home.

The news media, in covering the police activities at the fair, called the conflict management team the "Daisy Squad." That label came about because the officers wore large plastic daisies inside their revolver holsters. The purpose of the daisies was to open up communication with people who might otherwise resent the presence of uniformed policemen or with people who would assume that the presence of a policeman meant that there was trouble. The presence of the flower relieved a great amount of apprehension and tension, and brought about an atmosphere of cooperation.

In succeeding years, the conflict management unit has handled fair activities in the same manner, eliminating the types of violent activities that plagued the 1968–69 fairs.

Evaluation. During the 1970 fair, there were three potentially explosive situations and some minor moments of tenseness, but there were no arrests, no assaults, no property damage incidents, and no detour in police–community relations. In addition, the work performed by the conflict management unit at the fairs has improved the unit's relationship with other units in the Dayton Police Department, enabling patrol officers to see the value of conflict management techniques in action.

Conclusions

Each of the problem situations described above were solved as the result of careful planning and training. At present, as each new problem develops, a deliberate attempt is made by the conflict management unit to keep the community's leaders aware of the problem's potentials. In addition, citizens who do not agree with the police are sought out to discuss their differences.

The Dayton experience has not solved all the problems related to arrest alternatives. But it illustrates that the initiation of such alternatives cannot be casual. The objectives of the conflict management program must support overall departmental goals. Tools and resources are then identified, from which a careful, thorough planned design should emerge, custom-fitted to the department's priorities and directions.

For example, in the inventory of tools that the department has at its disposal, one would consider its cohesive powers, its power of discretionary judgment (the ability or sanction to do nothing when faced with conflict), and its power to issue warrants or warning tickets. These are all alternative tools. As far as resources are concerned, the news media, churches and civic organizations, regulatory agencies, neighborhood organizations, and movements for a particular case are all community resources, which are usually at the disposal of a requesting agency, such as the police. Additionally, the department develops its own internal resources, primarily by training specialized personnel.

It is imperative that arrest be viewed from a reasonable and proper perspective. There are too many persons in the police service and within our communities who view arrest as the final problem-solver. This simplistic point of view has served as an inhibiting factor in allowing police to increase their options for response. The cohesive powers of the police are certainly necessary for the performance of their duties; however, those same cohesive powers (arrest) sometimes contribute to the chaotic conditions in today's communities. Police, as the community's resource in the control of deviant behavior, must look beyond traditional ways so that their contribution to society may be even more effective.

Student Checklist

1. Can you identify several alternatives to arrest?
2. Are you able to write a brief essay describing the defusement process?
3. Can you list three ways to develop close communication between the police and the community?
4. Can you list the functions of teams in a police department conflict management program?
5. Do you understand how conflict management actually operates in typical situations requiring police intervention?

Topics for Discussion

1. Discuss the organizational structure of a conflict management program.
2. Discuss the advantages to police of having such a program.
3. Discuss how members of such a program can explain its advantages to the rest of the police department.

The study of this chapter will enable you to:

1. Describe the current status and the prospects of police–community relations programs in the United States.
2. Understand the difficulties that surround a new police–community relations program.
3. Describe what incorporating police–community relations into police work generally does not mean.
4. Write a short essay telling why police officers must understand and help parole officers, social workers, teachers, and psychiatrists and yet not do their work for them.

15

The Impact of Police-Community Relations on the Police System

A reasonable estimate of prevailing attitudes is that the concept of police–community relations has gained a secure level of acceptance in the law enforcement establishment and in urban government. By "acceptance" we mean that proposals to establish and maintain such programs tend to have a fair chance of success. Nor are there any organized factions publicly opposing police efforts to open and cultivate channels of communication with the public generally, and with civic groups and social movements particularly. Whether those who were aligned against such attempts are now merely silent for the time being, or whether they have changed their views, is an open question. But there is no doubt that the activities included under the heading of police–community relations have achieved respectability, and that a large and growing number of police officials in positions of responsibility have come to view them as indispensable for effective law enforcement and peace keeping.

The acceptance of these views is a sign of progress, a remarkable achievement. In less than two decades the most insular of all institutions in American society has become committed, at least in principle, to a program of ongoing exchanges about its mandate and practices. Secrecy and institutional separation have ceased to be a defensible position, although they have not completely disappeared.

It is important to begin the assessment of the current status and the prospects of police–community relations programs with this realization in order to place the review of actual practices in proper perspective. It is, of course, much easier to agree with the reasonableness and justice of a proposal than to implement it and live with the consequences of its implementation. Above all, when the task is to decide what must and can be done, it is important to measure aspirations against resistance and inertia. Thus, for example, despite the acceptance of the principle of police–community relations, no actually functioning police–community relations programs are fully deserving of the name. The very best among them have barely succeeded in laying the foundations for their own existence. Yet it should not be concluded that the entire attempt is nothing more than an exhibition of institutional hypocrisy. It would be more productive to begin with the hypothesis that newly functioning programs are somewhere in the middle of being accepted in principle and putting into operation the kind of activities the total acceptance would lead one to expect.

Therefore, it follows that we must look at the difficulties and risks that surround a new community relations program. We must also examine the far-reaching consequences of the ways in which these difficulties and risks are met. From this perspective, it becomes clear that the advocates of the police–community relations program face a real dilemma: They have to ask for recognition with appropriate modesty, and with a "live-and-let-live" attitude to prevent themselves from being rebuffed at the outset; yet they also must reckon with the fact that what is granted to them now will later be cited as the fairly negotiated limitations on the scope of their undertaking. The difficulty of this situation is compounded because claims, acceptances, and negotiations tend to be provisional and vague, and accommodations are reached in an informal process of give-and-take that leaves open the question of whether positions once given in to can be retracted or not. Thus, many programs tend to take shape because of circumstance, occasion, or passing expediency, but are later often spoken of as if they had been the product of planning and deliberate intentions.

Moreover, and perhaps more importantly, new programs face the problem of having to be advanced in the face of tight finances, against the claims of other existing programs that are oriented towards meeting long-established obligations. Thus, for example, in many police departments it is often said that at a time when there is a need for increased resource allocation to crime control, traffic, training, and the like, the new effort, which even enthusiasts admit is of uncertain promise, constitutes a difficult-to-defend drain on the budget. Such arguments create pressures upon the advocates of the program to produce quick evidence that the program is good. The first line of defense in this regard is to show a lot of activity; at the very least this demonstrates that the personnel assigned to the police–community relations unit are not idle. In addition, it indicates that they are busily engaged in work that needs to be done. This is, of course, a quite common practice in all bureaucratically organized settings. Its existence in this case generally would not be of great interest, except that such defense tactics, undertaken initially to silence inside critics, can become permanent features of programs. Thus, problems that are attacked initially merely because they are easily available targets of opportunity become *preferred* targets. Dealing with them becomes routinized, and interest in them prevents the pursuit of more hazardous, but probably more important, ventures. A good example of this tendency is found in the widespread practice of many of the police–community relations programs that establish and maintain contacts with civic groups who are known to be receptive to police influence. Another example is the even more frequent practice of producing ceremonial occasions of contact between the police and citizens, which typically use public relations techniques and salesmanship.

Although the foregoing remarks contain some examples of simple organizational analysis that might be helpful in assessing police–community relations programs, what has been said could apply to any program, whatever its orientation. That is, any undertaking will have to be initiated with consideration of its practicality. The project may, however, suffer from having set its sights too low at the outset. Thus, being exposed to the hard task-master of success, it is consequently channeled into easy accomplishments. But police–community relations programs face certain difficulties that appear to be uniquely particular to them. Nothing has been said about this yet. Therefore, in the following sections we will discuss some of these difficulties and attempt to show how they can be resolved. First, we will look at how police–community relations programs have developed in an asymmetrical form. To do this, the following discussions will totally disregard simple one-way public relations efforts that do not even pretend to be reciprocal; they are not worthy of consideration as genuine forms of police–community relations. Instead, we will concentrate on those activities in which authentic exchanges take place. Next, we will consider the form that an exchange between the police and the community might take if the police establishment as a whole were to participate in it, instead of merely sending out envoys to certain limited constituencies. It will become apparent that the serious

.

consideration of drawing the entire police department into police–community relations will add new dimensions to the idea—both in terms of who participates in these relations, and in terms of the substance around which these relations are organized. Finally, we will discuss why the concept of police–community relations has had consequences that were not initially envisioned: the police–community relations concept has gone beyond its initial objectives. Perhaps this should not come as a surprise, since communication produces change.

Before proceeding to a discussion of these points, we should clarify that everything said here is offered primarily as an argument; that is, it is offered for consideration. It is provisional simply because it deals with a continually changing condition; more importantly, it is provisional because, in the final analysis, the time will have to come when police will have to speak for themselves, not from prepared statements in textbooks.

Background of Police–Community Relations Program

Many of the aspects of police–community relations programs can only be properly explained by considering the circumstances that gave rise to them. As with all things, we are not compelled to accept what the past has handed down to us, but we can neither accept it nor reject it without first understanding the substance of the heritage.

Contrary to what is generally assumed, the idea of police–community relations is not altogether the brainchild of the second half of the twentieth century. The Metropolitan Police Act for the City of London, of July 19th, 1829, and the procedural instructions subsequently attached to it, made it quite clear that the new police department was a civil force seeking to attain the objectives of peace, order, and crime control in cooperation with the people. No aspect of police work was quite as strongly stressed in these documents as the duty of every member of the force to protect the rights, service the needs, and earn the trust of the population he policed.[1] These principles were specifically imported from England into American police departments. This is clear

---

[1] T. A. Critchley, *A History of Police in England and Wales 1900-1966* (London: Constable, 1967).

from a review of the events preceding the establishment of the municipal police in New York in 1844, upon which most other departments were modeled.[2] The significance of this point can not be overstated. The establishment of the police was strenuously opposed in England and in the United States because of fears that it would become an organ of executive government, indifferent to public influence, and functioning against the people. The opposition was finally silenced by assurances that the new institution would function as the people's police.

It is an amazing testimonial to our short memory that we generally forget that World War II, and the so-called Cold War, were struggles against what were known as "police states." At the time, in many European countries and in the United States, the police worked hard to disassociate themselves from these tainted practices. Thus, in the 1950s, in many European countries, as well as in the United States, police departments established public relations campaigns to portray themselves as open institutions, to gain public understanding, and to actively seek public support of a nonpolitical character.[3] Since these efforts were established at a time when political propaganda and commercial advertising became professionalized and used highly technical methods of salesmanship, it should come as no surprise that these arts played a decisive role in "selling the police to the people." Although these tactics now seem misguided and misleading, it appeared at the time, even to people of genuinely good will, that it was more important to "keep the product on the market" than to improve its quality. Nevertheless, some of the most effective propagandists of the police at the time, such as the late Chief William Parker of Los Angeles, were also engaged in vigorous efforts to purge the departments of corruption, sloth, and indolence.

While the specter of the police state has been kept alive by Hollywood, the majority of Americans have never experienced the use of police force as in Stalin's Russia or Hitler's Germany. Instead of playing a part in national partisan politics during the first century of their existence, the police forces in the United States were simply a corrupt pawn of corrupt urban government. Thus, the reformers of the 1950s felt that it was necessary to overcome the attitudes of contempt that middle-class

[2] C. Astor, *The New York Cops: An Informal History* (New York: Scribners, 1971).
[3] G. E. Berkley, *The Democratic Policeman* (Boston: Beacon, 1969).

citizens held toward police. This was done by sending speakers to high schools, to businessmen's luncheons, to meetings of civil organizations, to ladies clubs, and so on. These speakers argued that the police are the "thin blue line," the last bulwark of defense against the dark forces of crime and disorder. Though we can see how selectively these police–community contacts were chosen, in the 1950s they did constitute a movement away from the exclusive dominance of police departments by city-hall bosses.

There is little doubt that the American police moved into the 1960s with a solid sense of promise. They had moved toward freeing themselves from machine politics; and they had succeeded to a notable degree in rebuilding the image of the policeman, even if only in the minds of urban and suburban middle classes. But in the turmoil of the 1960s all this turned out to be of little use. As far as the police were concerned, whole segments of society, who, in the past, never had a voice in public affairs and whose fate was traditionally decided "by their betters," rose "out of the blue" in what could only be described as a wholesale revolt. Blacks, young people, the poor, and recent immigrants explosively announced their claims to new freedoms. Most of all, they demanded freedom from oppression and from want. And, although their quarrel was with society as a whole, or with the "system" as it came to be known, the confrontation took place between them and the police. In most cities the first impulse of the police was to resort to a show of force, and to the use of force, to control the varieties of the liberation movements. But the equipment of the police did not entirely consist of tear gas, bullets, and chemical mace. Some departments also had ongoing public relations programs.

It seemed proper to put these public relations programs to deal with the unforeseen troubles. Thus, it was in the heat of struggle, parallel with efforts to gain control over urban disorders by sheer armed force, that public relations became tortuously adapted to new tasks. Now, however, these programs were directed toward people who were hostile to the police.

A few additional remarks should be made about the transition from the earlier public relations approach to the new programs. An example of the process might help make it clearer. In the mid-1950s, the Metropolitan Police Department of St. Louis, Missouri, established a public relations division that became known as one of the best functioning programs of its kind in the country.[4] The division contained a speakers' bureau, published a newsletter, organized citizens' councils, and maintained school contacts, all of which were considered to be effective in accordance with their aims. There were also police and community relations committees in housing projects, which, in the department's own estimate, did not function well even as late as 1966. Nevertheless, the undertaking as a whole had an enviable reputation. In 1962, Chief Thomas Cahill of San Francisco visited St. Louis to help obtain answers to his own problems. Chief Cahill realized that it was important to use other resources, not just force, to deal with outbreaks of discontent. His department was faced with student protests against hearings being conducted by the House Un-American Activities Committee in the San Francisco City Hall. Chief Cahill took the new director of his community relations program, Lieutenant Dante Andreotti, to St. Louis to study their methods. While Cahill and Andreotti went to St. Louis to learn because they had a problem on their hands, their problem, however, was quite different from the situation that had motivated the St. Louis department. The St. Louis program was formulated primarily to address the "solid citizens." No one considered the program seriously impaired by the fact that the project that was directed toward working with the disadvantaged and the aggrieved did not function.

In the ensuing years, Lieutenant Andreotti developed a program in San Francisco which was vastly different from the St. Louis program. The direction of work that was permitted to lie fallow in St. Louis became the central interest of the San Francisco community relations unit. While Andreotti commanded the unit, "community relations" meant working primarily with the disadvantaged and the aggrieved segments of the population. The unit's officers were attached to organizations such as the Youth Opportunity Center, which served ghetto youngsters, and the Office of Economic Opportunity. They also exerted themselves in trying to meet with, talk and listen to, and help people living in the tenderloin, the skid row, and the ghetto. The activities of the San Francisco unit are illustrated by the following example.

A robbery and beating of a white grocery store operator in a minority

---

[4] *A National Survey of Police and Community Relations*, School of Police Administration and Public Safety, Michigan State University (Washington, D.C.: U. S. Govt. Printing Office, 1967).

group neighborhood resulted in community-wide concern and tension. As a result of the efforts of the police and the community relations unit, together with minority group leaders, a group of youngsters (many of whom had juvenile records) were organized into a picket line which marched back and forth in front of the store carrying signs condemning violence and stating that they were ashamed of what had happened. Although the boys picketing were not involved in the robbery or the beating, they offered verbal apologies to the family of the victim for the act done by members of their race. The publicity given this parade by the various media communications resulted in an almost immediate lessening of tensions.[5]

This incident should not be taken as indicating the scope of the unit's program nor even its focal concerns. The routine work of the officers assigned to the unit concentrated much more on everyday kinds of predicaments, such as protecting persons who were not resourceful on their own, or helping persons with police records find employment or lodgings. What the officers did was to act upon the realization that life in the city has many conditions, circumstances, and troubled people, and when troubled people are left to themselves, they are likely to cause, or get into, great calamities of various sorts. The officers worked on the assumptions that ex-cons without jobs are likely to commit crimes again; inter-group tension may lead to violent confrontations; children without recreational facilities tend to get into mischief, and so on. According to this assumption, when such potential is not checked, it leads to consequences that will sooner or later have to be handled by detectives, riot squads, or juvenile officers, depending on the specific situation.

In all fairness, it must be admitted that the men in the San Francisco community relations unit were not the first police officers ever to help a former criminal find a job, nor were they the first to succeed in preventing a public disorder. The innovation must be found in two additional aspects of their work: first, they did not simply go out to solve some problem; rather, they always dealt with problems in conjunction with other community resources. In the example cited earlier, they worked together with minority group leaders. The main point is that the cooperation was not simply a convenient expedient. Rather, it involved an established and ongoing, mutually cooperative arrangement between

[5] Ibid., p. 49.

members of the police and members of the community. Second, the men in the unit felt that providing services to citizens was their primary job. In the past such services were rendered on rare occasions and only after the officers took care of more demanding crime control problems.

In conclusion, the establishment of the community relations unit in San Francisco meant that manpower resources were specifically assigned to the task of working cooperatively with the people. More important, the chief of the department referred to the existence of the unit with pride. He claimed credit for creating it, and he gave weight to its importance by having its commanding officer report directly to the office of the chief, rather than through the chain of command. Nevertheless, some commanding officers and several line officers did not like the unit. Yet, even though the unit did not have total acceptance within the department, it gained momentum. It soon was regarded locally and nationally as conspicuously successful.

Although others considered the unit to be a success, its commander, Lieutenant Andreotti, recognized the problems that still had to be faced. Speaking at a law enforcement conference in 1968, he said:

> It is my belief that there isn't a successful police–community relations program anywhere in the country today, in terms of commitment by all members of the law enforcement agency. There have been successful police–community relations units, but practically all of them have been frustrated in their efforts to get the rank and file involved to the point of a genuine, personal interest and commitment.[6]

Since this remark comes from a man who has been one of this country's leaders in police–community relations, it deserves to be seriously considered. Andreotti does not find that those who work in the field have fallen short of the mark. Rather, he feels that they are not receiving the necessary support from their own agencies. Therefore, it is safe to assume that, even under the best circumstances, community relations programs suffer both from neglect and from being given low priority by the police department. At worst, these programs are resisted and condemned by personnel of all ranks.

The absence of commitment by all members of the police depart-

[6] D. A. Andreotti, "Present Problems in Police Community Relations," C. R. Chormache and M. Hormachea, eds., *Confrontation: Violence and the Police* (Boston: Holbrook, 1971), p. 120.

ment indicates that the department believes that social problems are not "proper" police business. Then, when long-standing tensions in the community result in violence, the police must address these problems directly rather than attempting to deal with the underlying causes. According to this view of the police role, the division of labor among the several agencies of municipal government assigns to the police the duty of preventing people from violating the law and to bring them to the bar of justice when they do. The responsibility for helping people to lead decent lives is assigned to other agencies; their personnel are specially trained and they have chosen social service work as their vocation.

Conversely, commitment to the principles of police–community relations by all members of the department means that the department considers it foolish to define the police role within narrow limits. Although an individual police officer may occasionally be justified in sticking to a narrow conception of his duties and thereby avoid dealing with a problem he might possibly solve, the problem will fall back into the lap of the police. To say that only social workers should deal with these problems is similar to arguing that a champion swimmer should not pull a drowning person from the water unless he has a Red Cross Life Saving Certificate. Commitment to the principles of police–community relations means acting on the assumption that the police are a service organization dedicated to keeping the peace, to the defense of the rights of the people, and to the enforcement of laws. In all these fields they are not merely an independent instrument of government; rather, they must work with individuals, community groups, and community institutions to achieve the desired objectives.

It was this latter attitude that governed the intervention of the San Francisco community relations unit in the incident mentioned earlier. This incident is a good example of commitment to the principles of police–community relations on the level of departmental organization. It is important to emphasize that the case is used only for the purposes of illustration. Because a full record of the case is not available, many of the factors will be introduced as unproven assumptions. However, it does not matter whether these assumptions were true in this instance. What matters is that the assumptions we shall make about the case are generally true.

Even the most uninitiated reader of the account of the case must have noticed that it is incomplete; details are lacking in one crucial aspect. What about the principals in the case, the victim and the assailants? It could be said that one does not expect to hear much about victims in such cases no matter how they are handled. What, then, of the assailant? It must be assumed that the assailant would have become the concern of the departmental unit dealing with this type of crime, and that procedures would have been set into motion leading to his apprehension and trial. It is fair to say that at this point the involvement of the community relations unit with the case stopped. That is, from this point on the community leaders would be told to stay out of it and let the experts take over. The community relations unit men would understand that the case had been taken away from them and that they should move on to the next case.

All this seems in good order and as it should be. One does not expect citizens to be involved in catching crooks; in fact, when they insist on becoming involved, they are more likely to cause harm than to do good. No doubt this is the view of policemen. But, perhaps more importantly, it is also the view of most judges, public prosecutors, city councilmen, and citizens. Indeed, as long as one thinks in terms of isolated offenses, it is difficult to reason otherwise. Thus, even those who are in favor of genuine police–community relations are forced to agree that the work must be assigned to special units which work independently while the rest of policing takes its ordinary course. In other words, progressive departments establish external units to deal with the community, but these units must follow the department's conditions. In still different terms, it appears that accepting the principles of police–community relations in its present exclusively outward-oriented direction (somewhat in the way nations send envoys to other nations) does not mean that two-way police–community relations are the norm (or, to continue the analogy, that the other nations send their envoys).

Before we explore this onesidedness, it should be pointed out that this situation is not unique. The police are not alone in thinking that they can communicate adequately with the people by means of external ambassadors. Indeed, they have done better with this approach than other institutions. The educational system, for example, keeps parents at arms length while pretending to allow for involvement by letting assistant principals of schools deal with the P.T.A. Similarly, institutions that deliver medical services often do not even pretend to communicate with the people they serve. In each of these cases, it is argued that lay people could not possibly contribute to solving the case of a slow-learning child or a diabetic patient, just as it is said that lay people could not be helpful in solving a robbery.

All communities have educational needs, health needs, and law enforcement needs. It is neither proper nor efficient for the specialists alone to define the nature of these needs or the way in which they will be met. The specialist brings competence and skills to bear on meeting these needs, but he must communicate with lay citizens to determine what their needs are.

The establishment of police–community relations units is a first, long step in recognition of the usefulness of bringing needs and special resources together in a harmonious relationship. Nevertheless, it is just that—a first step. The establishment of *community–police relations*, in a much broader sense, is a logical next step. An example might help in making clear what this involves. It is commonly accepted that the black ghettos of our cities produce a disproportionately large number of people who engage in criminal activities and that the people living in the black ghettos are exposed to a far greater risk of being criminally victimized than other citizens. Finally, it is no secret that people living in the ghettos distrust the police and are often reluctant to help officers in their efforts to control crime. What would be more sensible than for the police to consider these three facts, together with their present ways of dealing with black suspects and black victims, as systematically related? Joint consideration of the larger problem suggests that a successful attack on the problem can come only from the establishment of a program of trusting and fully cooperative relations between the black community and the police.

The reversal of terms from police–community relations to community–police relations was not done simply to coin a new term. It could not matter less what the arrangement is called! What matters is that the full effectiveness of the program cannot be attained by merely having a special unit to implement it. At best such units can only succeed in doing an occasional good deed and putting out an occasional fire, while leaving the rest of the police department's work unaffected by even these accomplishments.

We have come a long way from the public relations programs that were popular in the post-World War II years through the unit-based police–community relations programs of the 1960s. We have learned that if the principles embodied in these programs are to be carried out fully, they cannot be assigned to special units. They must be incorporated into, and become an integral part of, every aspect of police work. Nevertheless, it would be totally irresponsible to leave it at that. Even if the example of crime in the black ghetto were to be accepted as the truth, an example like this should never be offered as proof of anything. After all, it is one thing to let a few police officers work in community relations, but if all police officers are required to be community relations officers as well, will anybody ever get around to catching crooks, stopping fights in bars, and attending to the endless variety of other emergencies?

Perhaps it would be easiest to explain what incorporating police–community relations into police work generally means by discussing what it does not mean. First, it does not mean requiring entire departments to do what their police–community relations units are doing now. In fact, the only reason that these units are now free to concentrate exclusively on their present activities is because they are special units, counting on other units to do the rest of the work.

Second, it would be totally wrong to think that the adoption of police–community relations principles into police work might somehow weaken commitment to criminal law enforcement. Contrary to what is often said, viewing crime as a social problem does not imply that the criminal should be let go, or let off easily. In fact, it is not unreasonable to assume that the police might become more strongly dedicated to crime control than they are now, especially the control of some crimes they presently fail to consider. That is, they may come to act upon the moral contained in the ancient ditty:

> The law locks up both man and woman
> Who steal the goose from off the common
> But lets the greater felon loose
> Who steals the common from the goose.

Third, although police–community relations programs have in the past primarily been supported by more liberals than conservatives, it would be a grave mistake to tie the fate of the program to partisan politics. Taken by itself, police–community relations involves a technique, a method of doing police work. But this method also implies a greater openness to all community situations. Therefore, it calls for extensive and explicit reckoning with the distribution of political forces and with the often controversial play among them. This becomes evident at two levels. On the one hand, the police, as an institution of city government, will need to gain public support and the support of city hall for its own modernization. Conversely, police officers need to mobilize support for specific police–community relations peace-keeping and law enforcement programs.

Fourth, it cannot be denied that opening police work to inputs from all segments of the community contains the risk of putting it in an impossible situation, requiring it to bend to different influences, while being driven into inactivity and ineffectiveness in this storm of conflicting demands. But this risk can be easily contained if it is kept in mind that being responsive to community needs and demands does not involve bargaining away the police mandate. In fact, because openness is a two-way street, the risk will become an opportunity for citizens to understand and respect the police mandate in society.

Fifth and finally, fears have been expressed that police–community relations programs turn polciemen into social workers. These fears have gained some acceptance from observations of the activities of members of functioning special units. But these units should not be taken as models. These special programs allow the police officer to become a more effective public servant while retaining his full range of duties and responsibilities.

So much, then, for what is not true, or, in some instances, should not be permitted to be true. What does it mean to incorporate principles of police–community relations into police work generally, rather than assigning them to special units?

Above all, it means reviving the basic idea on which modern, urban police departments were founded; specifically, that these departments be the "people's police" rather than merely an arm of executive government. It could be said, of course, that executive government also belongs to the people. But executives tend to develop certain internal needs that are not all for the public good. For example, elected officials have a well-known tendency to want to remain in office; nothing strengthens their hand in this respect quite as much as the ready and unquestioned availability of the police. If being a "people's police" means anything, it means that the needs for the police service cannot be decided only from above. Determining the needs of the people and ways of meeting these needs must be continuously monitored in ongoing consultations between the people and the police. However, executive city government is a community structure too, probably the most important one the police must deal with. Police–community relations does not mean that the police should fight the power, the authority, and the needs of City Hall.

Next, the acceptance of police–community relations means putting the work of policing on a reasoned basis. This is a far more complex and difficult matter than it is usually thought to be. Many people want to believe that the structure of police work is completely determined by what is written in the penal codes, in municipal ordinances, and by the evident situational needs present in the vast variety of emergencies police officers deal with. According to this view, the police officer simply moves from arresting a rapist, to taking a suicidal person to the county hospital, to quelling a campus disorder, to administering first aid to an automobile accident victim, to intervening in a domestic dispute, to investigating a reported burglary, and so on. In each case he does what needs to be done, and he never looks beyond the level of the clearly present situational necessity. But every police officer knows that these are not random events. He knows that each results from a complex network of problems. But under traditional constraint, he is required to act as if it was beyond his intellectual capacity to recognize such interests. Instead, he is supposed to assume the "I-just-work-here" attitude of someone who merely does what he is told to do. It should be mentioned, however, that the most skillful and most experienced police officers do go beyond the limitations of traditional constraint and handle complex matters in complex ways.[7] But this practice is not officially recognized and certainly not officially encouraged. A reasoned approach to police work requires that these practices be examined, debated, and assessed according to their merits.

Finally, the police–community relations approach calls for a widespread understanding, both in the community and among police, that the

[7] Bittner, "The Police on Skid Row: A Study of Peace Keeping," *American Sociological Review*, **32**, 1967, pp. 699-715.

police are entitled to and are required to take an interest in human life before they are called to pick up its shattered pieces. This, too, sounds like a stilted formula. But if we disregard the sentimentality in this statement, it means very little more than what effective police officers already do in their dealings with people. These men already do this generally as a personal expression of humanity, but it should be considered part of their work. Nevertheless, it would be foolish to expect that all police officers would be idealists, just as it would be foolish to expect that all teachers would take a genuinely sympathetic interest in children. But teachers are not free to flaunt their contempt for people, not even for people who are contemptible. Thus, hypocrisy is put into the service of virtue. But among police it is often assumed that it is proper to maintain an attitude of cynicism toward human life. This attitude must be overcome, not only in the interest of virtue, but also in the interest of effectiveness. Taking an interest in human life, especially those aspects of life that are in need of interest—such as poverty, discrimination, racism, and exploitation—does not mean undertaking to solve them. It only means joining the struggle to solve them.

Conclusions

The police–community relations programs of today took a form that was appropriate to the circumstances of their origin. First, they began to build on the foundations of the already existing public relations programs, adopting their exclusively outward orientation. This meant working with various segments of the community outside the department in ways that did not produce any substantial changes in the operation of the rest of the police system. Second, in accordance with the beliefs of the 1960s, the work concentrated on cultivating relations with the segments of the community that were most neglected by the earlier public relations approach. New partners to the exchange called for new forms of exchange. It is obvious that responsiveness to a civil rights organization is a much different matter than responsiveness to the chamber of commerce.

Third, in keeping with the overall tendencies of our age, the task came to be viewed as a technical specialty. The drift toward specialization was further strengthened by the almost irresistible tendency of bureaucracies to compartmentalize tasks in special units. Fourth, the 1960s were a time in which the presence of injustice, discrimination, and poverty aroused the conscience of America. Under these circumstances it seemed more important to get going in whatever way possible, rather than to begin with careful analysis and planning.

But starting with what was at hand, and focusing on those problems that were most obviously in need of being attended to, was not just the beginning. The establishment of the original and timely police–community relations programs eventually revealed things about the police that were not recognized at the time. Above all, it brought into full recognition the enormous isolation of the police in society. It became clear that policemen were strangers not only in the ghettos of our cities, but that they were also strangers in the hospitals, in the universities, in the union halls, in the various agencies of government and, most important, in the institutions of the criminal justice system.

Thus, having police–community relations officers working with tenants' councils in public housing, with representatives of civil rights movements, and with activists in the war on poverty was merely the beginning of a far more thoroughgoing reconstruction of the relations of the police to the community. Two things became clear as the result of the work of the special units. First, holding the fort of isolation was an exercise in stubbornness, keeping the police stationary in a rapidly changing society. Second, the maintenance of ongoing dialogues with all members of society could not be achieved without involving all members of the police system. The methods of some officers had to be built into the methods of all officers. The need for this is most evident in the relations of the police with other segments of the criminal justice system.

Though it is quite commonly assumed that the police are a part of the criminal justice system, it is more correct to say that they function apart from it.[8] While it may appear to the uninformed observer that policemen, prosecutors, judges, and corrections officers are united in the struggle against crime, they are, in fact, only very poorly coordinated. The police, especially, engage in a sort of take-it-or-leave-it relationship with the rest of the system. No better evidence for this fact exists than the recent history of the so-called exclusionary rules. These rules provide

[8] E. Bittner, *The Functions of the Police in Modern Society* (Washington, D.C.: U. S. Govt. Printing Office, 1970).

that when a criminal complaint is based on illegally obtained evidence, judges are obliged to dismiss it, in accordance with a series of Supreme Court decisions. These decisions were handed down to teach the police a lesson in the principles of legality.[9] But this form of teaching has led to nothing but frustration.

The problem of the exclusionary rules is a matter of delicacy, involving the independence of the judiciary in our system of government. Yet the frequently prevailing situation of the police and the judiciary working at cross-purposes is plainly in need of attention. But it must not be thought that the problem will be properly attacked by bringing police chiefs and presiding judges together into administrative conferences. The formal agreements that result from such conferences rarely affect actual practices, and virtually never affect underlying attitudes. The only hope seems to lie in the establishment of a mutual understanding, an understanding not only about the exclusionary rules but about many other matters as well.

In the complex network of relations between the police and the criminal justice system, the case involving the judges is by far the most difficult one. Police relations with probation and parole officers are more easily approached. In fact, policemen and probation officers assigned to juvenile law enforcement tend to work closely together. But this kind of cooperation is not the norm for the rest of the police department and probation. Some of the difficulties arise from the fact that in recent years probation practices have been heavily influenced by teachings drawn from casework practice—at this point the traditional aloofness between police work and social work comes into play.

When one says that the police must be open toward psychiatrists, judges, educators, civil rights activists, social workers, poverty warriors, and probation officers, and that they must somehow come to understand their concerns and work with them, this does not mean that policemen must adopt their attitudes, assume their methods, and ultimately do their work. Far from becoming like the groups, professions, and agencies with which police–community relations units function, the police will, in these interactions, find a more distinct and more clearly defined role for themselves. In the context of open relations, a clearer definition of the police role will be achieved.

[9] F. P. Graham, *The Self-Inflicted Wound* (New York: Macmillan, 1970).

Student Checklist

1. Can you describe the evolution of police–community relations programs in the United States?
2. Are you able to list some of the difficulties that surround a new police–community relations program?
3. Do you know why police officers should understand and help social workers and psychiatrists and yet not try to do their jobs?
4. Can you list some of the dysfunctions of the criminal justice system?
5. Can you compare the likely benefits of a meeting between police staff officers and presiding judges with benefits from changing attitudes?

Topics for Discussion

1. Discuss the difficulties encountered by all new programs and compare them with problems of new police–community relations programs.
2. Discuss why police officers should understand and help psychiatrists, social workers, and teachers, and yet not try to do their jobs.
3. Discuss the merit of formal meetings between police administrators and presiding judges and compare this with the need to change attitudes in these parts of the criminal justice system.

ANNOTATED BIBLIOGRAPHY

Alex, N. *Black in Blue: A Study of the Negro Policeman*, New York: Appleton-Century-Crofts, 1969. Though not dealing directly with the problem of police–community relations, this study is of the first order of importance for a reasoned approach to the topic. The work is written with commendable care and richly documented.

Berkley, G. E. *The Democratic Policeman*. Boston: Beacon Press, 1969. An effort to explain the mandate of the police in relationship to the political structure of the democratic state. Especially valuable because it draws on observations about several European police systems, comparing them to conditions prevailing in the United States.

Bittner, E. *The Functions of the Police in Modern Society*. Washington, D.C.: U.S. Govt. Printing Office, 1970. A short account of the development of the police idea in England and the United States, and an attempt to relate the actual duties policemen perform with reform proposals, especially in the areas of training and community relations.

Black, A. D. *The Police and the People*. New York: McGraw-Hill, 1968. A very informative and well reasoned account of the creation, work, and abolishment of the Civilian Complaint Review Board in New York City, written by a man who is in the midst of the development. Very useful as a source on a topic that is shrouded in more mystery than it should be.

Hewitt, W. H., and C. L. Newman, eds. *Police–Community Relations: An Anthology and Bibliography*. Mineola, N.Y.: Foundation Press, 1970. A generous selection of readings from a wide variety of sources. The materials deal mainly with background factors, with regard to which practices must be organized, rather than with the organization of practice. The bibliography lists approximately 1500 items of literature in the police field.

A National Survey of Police and Community Relations. School of Police Administration and Public Safety, Michigan State University. Washington, D.C.: U.S. Govt. Printing Office, 1967. Prepared by the staff of one of this country's foremost institutions of police study and training, the report was submitted to the President's Commission on Law Enforcement and Administration of Justice. Perhaps the most extensive and most authoritative work on the topic of police–community relations in the recent past. Indispensable.

Rubinstein, J. *City Police.* New York: Farrar, Strauss & Giroux, 1973. The most recent of a large number of recent books about the work of the uniformed patrol of urban police. Confined to the description of the Philadelphia Police Department, the work is, however, of far greater significance because the author concentrates on the pressures under which patrolmen work, which are alike in all metropolitan centers.

Glossary

Perhaps the fastest way to gain a general knowledge of a particular vocation is to acquire an understanding of the terminology used. Law enforcement uses many unique words and phrases in carrying out its duties. Many of the most frequently used terms will be defined in this glossary. It must be emphasized that the definitions presented here are not intended to be complete interpretations of the words. For a complete explanation, consult a law dictionary.

Abet
To encourage or advise another to commit
a crime. To aid by approval.

Accessory
One who aids or conceals a criminal so that he
may avoid arrest or punishment.

Acquit
To find a person not guilty of the crime charged.

Addict
Usually a person who is addicted to the taking
of narcotics in some form.

Admission
A statement by a defendant tending to prove
his guilt. Not a complete confession.

Affidavit
A written statement made under oath.

Alias
A false or assumed name.

Alibi
The defense that the accused was in some place
other than that where the crime was committed.

Alienist
A person who specializes in the study of
mental diseases.

Appeal
The transfer of a case to a higher court, in which
it is asked that the decision of the lower court
be altered or reversed.

Appellant
One who makes an appeal or who takes an
appeal from one court to another.

Appellate Court
A court that has jurisdiction of review
and appeal.

Arraignment
A court proceeding in which the defendant is
informed of the charge against him, advised
of his constitutional rights, and at which he may
enter a plea or deposit bail.

Arrest
Detaining a person in a manner authorized
by law, so that he may be brought before a

court to answer charges of having committed
a crime. Both peace officers and private persons
may make the arrest.

Arson
Willfully burning property.

Assault
An unlawful attempt to physically hurt another
person. If the person is actually struck, the act
is called "battery."

Bail
Security, in the form of cash or bond, deposited
with a court as a guarantee that the defendant,
if released, will return to court at the time
designated to stand trial.

Ballistics
The science of the study of bullets and firearms.

Barratry
The unlawful practice of initiating lawsuits or
police complaints without just cause.

Battery
The unlawful use of force or violence against
a person without his consent.

Bertillon System
A method of identifying criminals by body
measurements and descriptions. *See* **Portrait parle.**

Bigamy
The crime of being married to two persons
at the same time.

Blackmail
The extortion of money from a person through
threats of accusation or exposure of an
unfavorable nature.

Blue Laws
Rigid laws regulating activities on the Sabbath.

Bribery
The offering or accepting of any undue reward
to or by a public official in order to influence
his official actions.

Brief
A summary of the law pertaining to a case,
which is prepared by the attorneys for
submission to the judge. Useful in police work
for case law reference.

Brothel
A house used for the purpose of prostitution.

Bunco
A type of theft perpetrated by the use of false
or misleading representations.

Burglary
The crime of entering a building with the intent
to steal or commit some felony. Not to be

confused with robbery, which is a theft from the
immediate presence of the victim through force
or fear. In burglary, the victim is seldom present
at the time.

Capital Crime
A crime punishable by death.

Certiorari (*writ of certiorari*)
An order issued by a higher court to a lower
court directing that a case be transferred to
the higher court for review or trial.

Change of Venue
A change of the place of trial in a criminal
or civil proceeding.

Circumstantial Evidence
Evidence tending to prove a fact through a
logical association of other facts, but without
an actual witness to the act to be proven.

Citation
An official summons issued by a court or peace
officer directing a person to appear before the
court for some official action. Frequently
referred to as a ticket.

Civil Action
A law suit to recover damages or correct some
wrong between two parties. Does not usually
involve a crime and is apart from a criminal
action. A person may be convicted in a criminal
court and also sued in a civil court for the same

act. Example: A drunk driver may be sentenced
to jail in a criminal proceeding and then sued
in civil action by the owner of a car damaged
by the drunk driver.

Commitment

An official court order directing that a person
be taken to a jail, prison, hospital, or other
location (usually a place of confinement).

Common Law

The basic, unwritten concepts of English and
American law. In many states, there are no
so-called common law crimes. For an act to
be a crime, there must be a specific, written
statute so declaring it.

Complaint

The formal accusation of crime presented
to the court, which acts as the formal
commencement of a criminal prosecution.

Compounding a Crime

The unlawful act of accepting money or other
reward for agreeing to refrain from prosecuting
a crime—concealing it from the authorities or
withholding evidence.

Compromising a Crime (misdemeanors only)

The proceeding by a court whereby a person
charged with a misdemeanor may be discharged
without prosecution upon payment of damages
to the party injured.

Confession
A voluntary declaration admitting the commission of a crime.

Confidential Communication
Communications between a person and his attorney or clergyman, or between husband and wife, which may be legally concealed in court testimony.

Conspiracy
A secret combination or agreement between two or more persons to commit a criminal act.

Contempt of Court
Disobedience to the court by acting in opposition to the authority, justice, or dignity thereof. Punishable as a crime.

Conviction
The finding of a person guilty of a criminal charge.

Coroner
A county official whose principle duty is to determine the manner of death of any person.

Corpus Delicti
The complete set of elements necessary to constitute a particular crime.

Crime
An act committed or omitted in violation of a law forbidding or commanding it, for which a punishment is provided.

Criminal Action
A court proceeding instituted and prosecuted
by the state for the punishment of crime.
Not to be confused with civil action.

Criminology
The science that deals with crimes, their causes,
and their prevention and punishment.

Criminal Procedure
The method prescribed by law for the
apprehension, prosecution, and determination
of punishment for persons who have
committed crimes.

Defendant
The person sued or charged in a court action,
whether criminal or civil.

Demurrer
A plea made to the court that the actions
alleged in the complaint, even if true, do not
constitute a crime.

Deposition
The written testimony of a person, who, for
some reason, cannot be present at the trial.

District Attorney
A county official whose principal duty is to
act as attorney for the state in prosecution of
criminal cases.

Double Jeopardy
The act of placing a person on trial a second
time for a crime for which he has already been
tried once (forbidden by criminal procedure).

Duces Tecum
A subpoena whereby a person summoned to
appear in court as a witness must bring with him
some piece of evidence (usually a written
document).

Dying Declaration
A statement made by a dying person regarding
the cause of his injuries. Acceptable evidence
in a homicide prosecution. Based on the theory
that a person about to die will be inclined to
be truthful in any statements he makes.

Embezzlement
The crime of stealing property or money
that has been entrusted to one's care.

Et Al.
And others. For example: "*People* v. *Jones*,
et al." indicates that Jones and others are the
defendants in a criminal case. This form is used
to prevent repeating the names of all persons
involved every time the case is referred to.

Evidence
Testimony, physical objects, documents, or any
other means used to prove the truth of a fact
at issue in a court proceeding.

Ex Post Facto
After the facts. Usually refers to a law that
attempts to punish acts that were committed
before it was passed.

Extortion
Similar to blackmail.

Extradition
The surrender by one state or nation to another,
on its demand, of a person charged with a
crime by the requesting state.

Felony
A major crime punishable by death or
imprisonment in a state or federal prison.
All other crimes are called misdemeanors.

Fence
A person who makes a business of purchasing
or receiving stolen goods from criminals.

Fine
The financial punishment levied against a
lawbreaker that is paid to the government funds.

Fingerprints
A reproduction of the ridge formation on the
outer joint of the fingers. Although a definite
identification can be made using only one finger,
it is usually necessary that the prints of all ten
fingers be available for a successful search of
fingerprint files.

Forgery
Any of several crimes pertaining to the false making or alteration of any document with intent to defraud.

Former Jeopardy
Same as double jeopardy.

Fugitive
One who has fled from punishment or prosecution.

Grand Jury
A group of men and women whose duty it is to make inquiries and return recommendations regarding the operation of local government. They also receive and hear complaints in criminal cases, and if they find them sustained by evidence, to present an indictment against the person charged. It is called a grand jury because it is composed of a greater number of jurors than a regular trial jury.

Habeas Corpus (writ of)
A court order directing that a person who is in custody be brought before a court in order that an examination may be conducted to determine the legality of the confinement.

Habitual Criminal
Many states have statutes providing that a person convicted a certain number of times may be declared an habitual criminal and, therefore, is unsuited for attempts for rehabilitation.

A person so declared may then be sentenced to life imprisonment for the protection of society.

Hearsay Evidence
Evidence that deals with what another person has been heard to say. This evidence is usually excluded in a trial.

Heroin
An opium derivative drug. It is a coarse white or gray powder that is taken hypodermically, orally, or by sniffing. It is completely outlawed for any purpose in the United States.

Homicide
The killing of a human being by another human being.

Fratricide—killing of one's own brother
Matricide—killing of one's own mother
Infanticide—killing of a child
Patricide—killing of one's own father
Uxoricide—killing of one's own wife

Impeachment
The process whereby a public official may be removed from office through judicial proceedings. Also, the discrediting of a witness in order to show that his testimony is probably false.

Indeterminate Sentence
A court- or board-imposed sentence with neither minimum nor maximum limits.

Indictment
An accusation in writing, presented by the grand
jury, charging a person with a crime.

Informant
One who supplies information leading to the
apprehension of a criminal.

Information
An accusation in writing, presented by a
prosecuting official; i.e., district attorney,
city attorney, or others, charging a person
with a crime.

Injunction
A court order whereby a person is ordered to
do, or restrained from doing, a particular thing.
Not enforced by the police without an additional
court order to that effect.

Inquest
An inquiry with a jury conducted by the
coroner to establish the cause of death.

Intent
In general, there must be a concurrence between
a person's acts and his intentions in order to
constitute a crime. A person cannot be convicted
of a crime if he committed the act involuntarily,
without intending injury. If a person acts
negligently, however, without regard for the
rights of other people, this is sufficient in itself
to establish criminal intent. Thus, the drag racer
who kills an innocent party may be convicted of

manslaughter, even though he did not intend the death or injury of anyone.

Interrogation
The art of questioning or interviewing, particularly as applied to obtaining information from someone who is reluctant to cooperate. May apply to the questioning of witnesses, victims, suspects, or others. Requires the use of psychology, salesmanship, good judgment, and a knowledge of human nature. The use of physical force to obtain information has no legitimate place in modern law enforcement.

Jail
A place of confinement maintained by a local authority, usually for persons convicted of misdemeanors. The terms prison or penitentiary apply to such institutions operated by the state or federal government, usually for more serious offenses.

Judiciary
That branch of the government concerned with the administration of civil and criminal law.

Jurisprudence
The science of laws.

Jury
A group of men and women whose duty it is to determine the guilt or innocence of persons charged with a crime.

Juvenile Court
Generally, a special court or department of another court that hears cases involving

juveniles. Proceedings are less formal and the primary objectives are rehabilitation and protection, rather than punishment.

Kleptomania
An abnormal desire to steal.

Larceny
Same as theft. The unlawful taking of the property of another. Divided into grand theft and petty theft. Grand theft includes the taking of money or goods in excess of $200; the theft of any item from the immediate possession of another; theft of an automobile of any value; the theft of certain domestic animals; and the theft of certain fruits, vegetables, and fowl over the value of $50. All other theft is petty theft.

Libel
The circulation of written matter that tends to discredit or injure the character of another. It is not necessary that the material be false. The prime consideration is the motives under which it was issued. Slander is of the same nature except it is verbal rather than written. Note: There are few criminal prosecutions for libel or slander. It has become largely a civil matter.

Limitations, Statute of
The statutory time limit within which a criminal prosecution must be begun. For felonies, this is usually three years from the date the crime was committed. For misdemeanors it is one year. There are some crimes that have a longer time

404 *community relations and the administration of justice* limit and a few, such as murder, that have no time limit.

Lynching
In popular usage, the killing of an accused criminal by a mob that has taken him from the authorities by force. Technically, it is the act of a group unlawfully taking a person from the custody of a peace officer for any purpose.

Magistrate
A judicial officer having authority to conduct trials and hearings in criminal and civil matters and to issue writs, orders, warrants of arrest, and other legal documents.

Maim
The crime of willfully disfiguring another.

Mala in Se and Mala Prohibita
A basic grouping of crimes according to the nature of the act. *Mala in se* means "bad in itself" and refers to those crimes such as murder, robbery, and rape, that are deemed to be wrong in almost all civilized societies. *Mala prohibita* means "bad by prohibition" and refers to those offenses, such as building and safety regulations and certain traffic violations, established by statute for the public convenience, that are not immoral or bad in themselves.

Mandamus (writ of)
An order issued by a court, directed to a government agency or to a lower court, commanding the performance of a particular act.

Mann Act
The federal statute relating to the interstate
transportation of females for immoral purposes.

Manslaughter
The unlawful killing of a human being without
premeditation or intent to take life.

Marijuana
A narcotic produced from the East Indian
hemp plant (*cannibis sativa*). The leaves and
flowering tops are ground into a form resembling
tobacco, but which is drier and coarser. It is
then rolled into cigarettes and smoked.

Misdemeanor
A crime punishable by other than
imprisonment in the state prison.

Modus Operandi
Literally, method of operation. Refers to the
habit of criminals to continue to pursue a
particular method of committing their crimes.
Through study of a criminal's habits (or *modus
operandi*) it is possible to link several crimes
committed by the same person and even to
determine where he can be expected to commit
his next crime.

Murder
The unlawful, deliberate, or premeditated killing
of a human being. It is not required that the
premeditation be of any specific length of time.
The instant of time necessary to form a specific
intent to kill is sufficient.

Nolle Prosequi

A motion by the prosecuting attorney in which he declares that he will not prosecute a case. Used when extenuating circumstances in a case indicate that, although a crime has been committed, it is in the best interests of justice to forego prosecution.

Notary Public

A public officer authorized to administer oaths, witness signatures, and acknowledge the genuineness of documents.

Oath

Any form of attestation by which a person signifies that he be bound to perform a certain act truthfully and honestly. A person making a false statement while under oath to tell the truth may be prosecuted for perjury.

Opium

A narcotic substance prepared from the juice of the original poppy. It is further refined to produce morphine, heroin, and other narcotics. Opium is normally found as a dark, sticky mass that is smoked in special pipes. Opium smoking is decreasing in the United States in favor of the much stronger derivative, heroin.

Ordinance

Term used to designate any law enacted by a local governmental legislative body.

Panel

A group of men and women summoned for jury duty. A panel of approximately 25 prospective jurors is examined by attorneys for both sides prior to the start of a case. Through this examination, 12 are selected to hear and decide the case.

Pardon

An act of grace, proceeding from the power intrusted with the execution of the laws, which exempts the individual on whom it is bestowed from the punishment the law inflicts for a crime he has committed.

Parole

The conditional release of a prisoner from jail prior to the completion of his sentence, usually on the condition that he remain under the supervision of a parole officer.

Peace Officer

General term used to designate a member of any of the several agencies engaged in law enforcement.

Penal Code

A collection of statutes relating to crimes, punishment, and criminal procedures. This is the portion of the law most frequently used by police officers.

Perjury

The crime of knowingly giving false testimony in a judicial proceeding while under oath to tell the truth. Subornation of perjury is the crime of procuring or influencing someone else to commit perjury.

Plaintiff
In a civil action, the party initiating the suit;
one who signs a complaint or causes a complaint
to be signed. The other party to the suit is the
defendant.

Plea
The answer that the defendant makes to the
charges brought against him.

Pleadings
Written statements reciting the facts that show
the plaintiff's cause for bringing the action and
the defendant's grounds for defense to the
charges. These are prepared by the attorneys
for each party and are presented to the judge.

Policy
In gambling, a game in which bets are made
on numbers to be drawn in a lottery.

Portrait Parle (word picture)
Method of identification established by
Alphonse Bertillion wherein a description of
physical characteristics is used to identify a
person. This is one of the identification methods
used in America today.

Posse Comitatus
The authority of the sheriff to assemble all
able-bodied male inhabitants of the county to
assist in capturing a criminal, keeping the peace,
or otherwise defending the county. Refusal to
obey the summons is a criminal offense.

Post Mortem   (after death)
Refers to the examination of a body after death.
Also called an autopsy.

Precedent
A parallel case in the past that may be used as
an example to follow in deciding a present case.

Preliminary Hearing
An examination before a judge of a person
accused of a crime in order to determine whether
there is sufficient evidence to warrant holding
the person for trial.

Prima Facie
"On its face" or "at first view." Refers to
evidence which, at first appearance, seems to
establish a particular fact, but which may be
later contradicted by other evidence.

Principal
A person concerned in the commission of a
crime, whether he directly commits the offense
or aids in its commission. All principals to a
crime are equally guilty. The driver who waits
in the getaway car during a robbery is as equally
guilty of murder as the accomplice inside the
building who fires the fatal shot.

Private Person's Arrest
The authority granted to a private party to make
an arrest under certain conditions. It is
sometimes referred to as a "citizen's arrest,"
although it is not limited only to citizens.

Privileged Communication
See **Confidential Communication.**

Probate Court
A court that establishes the legality of wills
and that administers the distribution of the
estate of a deceased.

Probation
Allowing a person convicted of a criminal
offense to go at large under the supervision of
a probation officer rather than confining him
to prison or jail. The probationer must comply
with certain conditions set forth by the court
and must be on good behavior. Failure to
comply with these conditions will cause the
probationer to be placed in jail to serve his
sentence.

Proof
The establishment of a fact by evidence.

Prosecutor or Prosecuting Attorney
A public officer whose primary duty is to
conduct criminal prosecutions as attorney on
behalf of the state or people. The district
attorney and city attorney are examples.

Prostitute
A woman who engages in sexual relations
for hire.

Pyromania
An unnnatural, overpowering attraction to fire.

Rape

Unlawful sexual intercourse with a woman
against her will, usually accomplished by
physical violence, but it may be committed
when the woman is drunk, unconscious, feeble-
minded, or otherwise unable to resist. Statutory
rape is when the female is under the age of
eighteen, even though she has given her consent
to the act.

Recidivist

An habitual criminal.

Recognizance

Official recognition of some fact by a court.
In criminal procedure, it applies to a person
accused of an offense being released on his own
recognizance without being required to post
bail, on his promise to appear for trial. It is
employed where the accused is well known to
be reputable or is charged with a minor offense.

Res Gestae (things done)

Facts and circumstances surrounding a
particular act. Refers particularly to acts or
exclamations overheard by a third party that
would be inadmissible in court under normal
rules of evidence but, because they occurred
at the moment of the particular act in question,
are admissible under the rules of *res gestae*
evidence.

Resisting an Officer

Any person resisting, delaying, or obstructing
a public officer in the discharge of his duties
is guilty of a misdemeanor.

Return
A short account in writing made by an officer
in respect to the manner in which he has
executed a writ or a process.

Reversal
The setting aside or annulment of the decision
of a lower court made by a higher court.
See **Appeal.**

Rigor Mortis
The stiffening or rigidity of the muscles and
joints of the body that sets in within a few
hours after death.

Robbery
The unlawful taking of personal property in
the possession of another, from his person or
immediate presence, against his will, and
accomplished by use of force or fear.

Search Warrant
An order to a peace officer, issued by a court,
directing that a certain location be searched and
that certain specifically described property, if
found, be seized and delivered to the judge.

Seduction
The offense of inducing a woman to engage in
sexual relations under a false promise of
marriage.

Statute Law
A written law enacted and established by the
legislative department of a government.

Stay of Execution

An order of a court postponing the carrying out
of the penalty or other judgment of the court.

Stipulation

An agreement between opposing attorneys
relating to certain portions of a case. Usually
refers to minor points in a case that are accepted
without demanding proof, in order to shorten
the time of trial.

Subpoena

An order issued by a court commanding
the attendance of witnesses in a case.
See **Duces tecum.**

Summons

In a civil case, an order directed to the defendant
giving notification that an action has been filed
against him, giving instructions as to how
and when he may answer the charges. Failure
to answer the summons will result in the case
being awarded to the plaintiff by default.

Supreme Court

Highest court of appeal, either state or federal.

Suspended Sentence and Judgment

Suspended sentence occurs when no sentence is
pronounced by the court, and the offender is
released after being found guilty on condition
that he abide by certain rules laid down by the
court, such as making restitution to the victim.
Suspended judgment occurs when the offender is

released as above after sentence has been
pronounced. In either case, the offender may
be returned to court at any time to be sentenced
or, in the case of suspended judgment, have the
sentence carried out.

Testimony
Oral evidence given by a witness under oath.

Theft
See **Larceny.**

Tort
A civil wrong. An invasion of the civil rights
of an individual.

Transcript
A printed copy of a court record, including the
verbatim testimony of witnesses.

Trauma
An injury to the body caused by
external violence; a mental shock.

Trial
That step in the course of a judicial proceeding
that determines the facts. A judicial examination
in a court of justice. May be held before a judge
and jury, or a judge alone.

Valid
Having full legal force and authority.

Versus   (against)
Abbreviated "vs." or "v."

Waive

To surrender or renounce some privilege or right.

Warrant

A written order from a court or other competent authority, directed to a peace officer or other official, ordering the performance of a particular act, and affording the civil protection for the person executing the order. Examples are a warrant of arrest and a search warrant.

Witness

A person who has factual knowledge of a matter. One who testifies under oath.

Subject Index

Adjudication, 287
Admission, 196, 390
Advisory Commission on Intergovernmental
    Relations, 283
Affirmation, 17
Aggression, 81, 97, 114–124, 323
    aggressive tendencies, control of, 114, 115,
        117, 119
    expression of, constructive and beneficial
        aspects of, 120–124
    need for, 115–117, 118, 119
    and hostility compared, 115, 119, 120
    projected, 108
    scapegoating and, 158, 160
Alcoholism, 47, 172, 297
    social implications of, 160, 161
Alienation, 72, 73, 134
    between police and community, 78, 233, 234,
        240, 243, 244
    between police and youths, 358
    social, 34, 35, 36, 37, 39, 223
    see also Isolation from society; Police, isola-
        tion from society
Allport, Gordon W., 158, 160
American Bar Association, 193, 270
Anomie, 37
Antiwar movement, 315, 334; see also Protest
    movement
Anxiety, 118, 162
Arrest, 39, 287, 298, 319, 320, 391
    alternatives to, 349, 350, 355, 356, 357, 358,
        366, 367
    circumstances of, 197, 266
    of dissident groups, 326, 327
    drunk-related, 297
    effect of, 259, 260, 261, 263, 264
    police, 46, 77, 91, 189, 192, 195, 196, 244
    power of, 92
    police discretion and, 251, 255, 256, 261
    of youthful offenders, 169, 363, 364
Arrestee, 287
Attica State Prison, 281
    revolt at, 328
        aftermath of, 338–342
Attorney, district, 195, 397
Attorney, U.S., 252
Attorney General, state, 211, 213

Attorney General's Advisory Commission on
    Community–Police Relations, 211, 212,
    215

Badge, police, 76, 79, 161; see also Uniforms,
    police
Bail, 392
    excessive, 18
    for political defendants, 332, 333, 334, 335,
        336
    system, 282
        reform in, 286
Ballistics, 196, 392
Behavioral modification, 61, 62
    change theory, 59–60
    learning principles, 60–61
Berkeley, California, Berkeley Model commun-
    ity control, 292, 293
    community control at, 284, 294
Berrigan brothers, trial of, 333
Biases, active, 159
    community, 262, 290
    police, 255, 256
Bible, the, 6, 10, 11
Bill of Rights, 4, 17–18, 193, 199, 310, 311,
    314, 331
Black Panther Party, 330, 334, 336
    Panther Twenty-one conspiracy trial, 330,
        332, 334
    police confrontations with, 322, 326
Black police officers, 56–58; see also Police,
    role concept of
Blacks, 77, 144, 364, 374
    Black Power, 325
    community, 169, 170, 171, 292, 380
    constitutional rights and, 334, 335, 336
    discrimination against, 159, 160
    group solidarity, 111, 112, 126, 127, 128
    impact of police enforcement decisions, 261,
        262
    militant, 317, 318
    police and, 49, 50, 54, 326, 329
        attitudes toward police, 163, 164
    social status of, 324
    struggle for social and legal equality, 56, 57,
        320, 360
    see also Ghettos, black; Minority groups

417

Body language, 140–145, 148; *see also* Communication, interpersonal
Boycotts, 315
Brandeis, Louis, Justice, 23, 29
British policeman, comparison of role with American police, 77, 78
Burger, Warren E., Chief Justice, 19

California Attorney General's Office, 211, 213
California law enforcement agencies, 215
California State Highway Patrol, 83
Capital crimes, 18, 394
Central Intelligence Agency, 330
Chicago Police Department, 256, 330
Chicago Seven conspiracy trial, 332, 333, 334
Cincinnati Police Division, 163, 164
Citations, 239, 394
  traffic, 78, 242, 244
Citizen and community alert programs, 293–294
Civil disobedience, 354
  arrests in, 349
  degree of disorder in, 315, 316
  distinguish between crime and, 319, 320
  justifications for, 312, 313, 314
Civil disorders, 200
  and crisis for courts and legal system, 332
  media coverage of, 203
  National Advisory Commission on Civil Disorders, 324
Civil Liberties Union, American, 194
Civil matters, 359
Civilian review boards, controversy over creation of, 288, 289
  opponents to, 290
Civil rights, 7, 15, 199, 243, 284, 360, 384, 385, 386
  demonstrations, media coverage of, 201
  movement, 75, 320, 321
  U.S. Commission on Civil Rights, 330
Civil service, 87, 330
Code of Hammurabi, 11
Code of laws, 31
Codes of conduct, 8, 10, 11, 12, 18
Codes of ethics, 26, 27, 90; *see also* Ethics
Coercion, 321, 322, 323, 329; *see also* Dissent, strategies of
Commandments, 10, 11, 27, 76
Common law, rules of, 18, 395
  wisdom of, 12, 13
Communication, between community and

police, 50, 133, 352, 361
  blocks to effective, 155–182
    community distrust of police, 155, 169
    police false perception of community, 155, 156
    police organizational structure, 156–158
    poor training of police, 156
    removing, suggested programs for, 162–182
    scapegoating, phenomena of, 158–162
  distortion ine, 135, 139, 142, 145
  levels of, 134–148
    interpersonal, 134, 135
      art of effective listening, 134, 145–149
      concept of nonjudgmental, 146, 147
      efficiency of, 147
      nonverbal cues, interpretation of, 140–145
      verbal cues, importance of, 134, 135–140
    intrapersonal, 134
  process of, 134, 135
  quality of, 149–151
Community, 3
  community communication net, 173, 174
  community survey, 169–171
  expectations of police role, 50, 51, 52
    see also Police, role of
  influence of on police enforcement decisions, 261, 262
  law enforcement in, role of, 53–54, 62
  size of, and police duties, relationship between, 46
  see also Police–community relations; Society, changing
Community-based corrections, *see* Corrections, community-based
Community control, 169, 325
  advocates for, 283, 284, 285
  concept of, 279–304
  definition of, citizen participation continuum, 279, 280, 281, 287
  demand for, 281
  development of, 282–284
  by interaction, examples of, 281
  problems of, 284–287
  styles of, 281, 286, 287
    participative, 287, 295–304
      community-based correctional facilities, 300–305
      diversionary programs in community, 296–304

418   *subject index*

drug-related diversion programs, 300
family crisis intervention project, 298-299
Manhattan Bowery Project, 297-298
Youth Services Bureau, 299
pure, 287-294
characteristics of, 287
citizen and community alert programs, 293-294
civilian review boards, 288-290
decentralization of police, political and administrative, 291-293
development of police "storefront" centers, 291-292
enforcement priorities, community control of, 294-295
ombudsman, concept and advantages of, 290-291
team-policing approach, 291, 292
Community relations, as compared to public relations, characteristics of, 212, 214, 218, 219, 221, 222, 225
differences between, extent of citizen involvement, 220, 221, 224
philosophical differences, 217, 221, 222, 224
concept of, 213, 214
defined as philosophy of police administration, 212, 213, 220
historical development of, 211, 212
problem-avoidance and problem-solving mechanisms as primary strength, 221, 222
processes of, balance of self-serving and citizen-serving, 219, 220
programs of, rapid growth of, 211, 215, 217
purposes of, 214, 215, 217
image enhancement purpose, 214, 215, 216, 218
interrelated and overlapping, 217, 221, 225
public information category, 216
tendency toward public's needs, 219, 220
use of public relations concept, to gain public support and cooperation, 215, 216, 217, 218, 219
see also Public relations
Complaint, 196, 395
Confession, 196, 198, 275, 396
Confinement, 338, 339
Conflict management, 349, 350
in action, 355-366
county fair, 363-366

gangs, 358-359, 365
high schools, 362-363
housing projects, 360-361
labor-management problem, 355-356
operation stop-drag, 356-358
tenant-landlord disputes program, 359-360
defusement process, 352, 353, 355, 357
program design, 350-355
community organization team, 354
conflict intervention team, 352-354, 362
public information team, 354, 355
value of, 353
Conformity, 162, 337; see also Groupism
Congress, United States, 14, 17
Constitution, U.S., 4, 13, 18, 265, 266, 334, 335
philosophical antecedents, 6-10
right to dissent defined under, 310, 311, 312
new interpretations demanded, 313, 314
Constitutional rights, 26, 274, 363
blacks and, 334, 335, 336
violation of, 3, 4
Contraband, 197
confiscation of, 252, 260
Conviction, 46, 192, 194, 251, 296, 396
criminal, 259, 333
Corrections, 71, 75, 282, 285, 286, 287
community-based, 281, 296, 300-305
importance of citizen participation in, 301, 302
Corruption, 84, 85
police, 268, 269, 373
removal of, 234, 235
Counsel, defense, 193, 199
right to assistance of, 18, 197
Counseling services, 298
of juveniles, 353, 354
Courts, 71, 92, 256, 260, 286
attitude toward strategies of dissent, 318
juvenile, 25, 303, 403
Cox, Archibald, 311, 313
Crime, 4, 18, 23, 33, 36, 51, 274, 395, 396
in black urban neighborhoods, 50, 381
capital, 18, 394
causes of, 71, 72, 350
classifications of, 239
concept of, 263
coverage of in media, see Media
definition of, 104, 240, 331
deterrence, 301
drug addiction and, 160, 161

fighting, 160, 161
    effects of crime news in newspapers on,
        187, 189
    investigation of, see Investigation of crimes
    prevention of, 24, 38, 173, 175, 192, 193,
        215, 240, 244, 284, 299, 360
        control of, 283, 285, 370
    property, 358, 359, 363
    rate increase in, 118
    rate of, community responsibility programs
        and, 299
    rising, 71, 91, 223
    reporting, 155, 207
    scene of, 198
    as social problem, 381
    specialists, 178
    violent, 118, 189
Criminal, 92, 376
    apprehension of, 3, 4, 46, 187, 188, 192, 196,
        240
    common, dissidents as, 320, 328, 329
    definition of, 331
    police perception of, 259
    prosecution of, 23, 27
    sorting out of, 287
    vagrancy laws and, 243
Criminal acts, 39, 359, 380
Criminal code, 104
Criminalization, 259, 261
Criminal justice, changing society and, 23-40
    citizen responsibility in administration of,
        282, 283
    ethical needs of, 40, 41
    see also Criminal justice system
Criminal justice system, criticism of, 282
    historical perspectives on, 3-19
    impact of dissent on, 325-342
    isolation from each other among segments of,
        285, 385, 386
    profession of, liabilities to, 162
        professionals in, 23, 25, 26, 29, 31, 39, 40,
            74, 75, 83, 134, 282, 284
        trend toward human services emphasis, 32,
            33, 34, 35, 36, 37, 40
    public and, 91, 92
        effects of relationship between community
            and law enforcement agencies, 62
        public confidence in integrity of, 250, 255,
            259
    social conflicts, effects of, 309, 310, 317,
        319, 321, 324-325

Criminal law, see Laws, criminal
Criminologist, 63, 397
Criminology, School of, at Berkeley, 87
Cruel and unusual punishment, 18, 314
Culture, impact of on social changes, 309, 310;
        see also Social changes; Values
Custody, 196, 197, 198, 334, 336

Davis, Angela, impact of trial on criminal justice
        system, 332, 335, 336
Davis, Kenneth C., 270, 271
Dayton, Ohio, Police Department, 350-366;
        see also Conflict management
Death penalty, 281, 335, 336
Decentralization of police service, advantages
        of, 237, 238
    at Berkeley, California, 284
    versus centralization, 234, 236, 237
    concept of, 237
    police resistance to, 237
    political and administrative, 291-293
    social benefits versus efficiency and costs, 238
Declaration of Independence, 4, 14, 17
Defendants, 196, 197, 265, 266, 272, 286, 397
    behavior of, 334
    political, 332, 333, 335
    prior criminal record of, 197, 198
    rights of, 193, 194, 195
Defense, 194, 265
    in political trials, 333
    defense counsel, 193, 199
Dehumanization of mankind, 35, 36, 37, 149
Delinquency, see Juvenile delinquency
Delusions, of grandeur, 105, 106
    of persecution, 105, 106
Demonstrations, 260, 312, 329
    student, 284
    see also Dissent; Protest movement
Depression, 114, 115, 125
Detectives, 169, 376
    authority of, 250, 253
    professional status and prestige of, 181,
        239
    selective law enforcement and, 264
Discretion in justice system, 273
    police exercise of, 20, 91, 92, 150, 182, 234,
        238, 239, 252, 253, 256, 265, 268, 269,
        270, 274, 290, 296
    control of, 264, 270
    prosecutorial, 252
    see also Law enforcement, selective

Field training, 59
Fifth Amendment to the Constitution, 18
Fines, 18, 239, 399
First Amendment to the Constitution, 17, 193, 310, 311, 331
   Supreme Court interpretation of, 199
Fortas, Abe, Justice, 311, 313
Foster home programs, concept of, 303
Fourteenth Amendment to the Constitution, 314, 335
Fourth Amendment to the Constitution, 17
Freedom, 322, 331
   for blacks, 336
   constitutional, 312
   individual, 8, 9, 24, 40, 41
      see also Liberty
   of press, 321
      see also Media; Police–press relations
Freud, Sigmund, 108, 114
Fromm, Erich, 113

Gambling, 92
   selective law enforcement and, 249, 257, 262, 263
Gangs, conflict management approaches to problems of, 358–359, 365
Gesture, 143, 148; see also Communication, interpersonal
Ghettos, black, 54, 77, 261, 262, 324, 375, 380
   community control of police service in, 238
   crimes in, 381
   perceptions of, 126, 127, 128
   police–community relations in, 97, 101, 102, 103, 104, 106, 107, 109, 124, 125
      see also Blacks; Minority groups
Government, civil, 8
   power in, 9, 13
   system of, 6, 8, 14, 16
      conflicts between natural rights of citizen and, 313, 315, 316
Grand jury system, political dissent issues and, 334, 335
Groupism, 112, 126, 127, 128
   need for, 162
   see also Solidarity
Guerilla warfare, 199, 331

Habeas corpus, 12, 400
Halfway houses, 304; see also Corrections, community-based

Hallucinations, 105; see also Perceptions, distorted
Homicide, 39, 51, 401
Homosexuality, 38
Hoover, J. Edgar, 190
Hostility, see Aggression
Humanoids, 34
Human relations, 89, 163, 384

Imprisonment, 314, 338
Incarceration, 301
Individual freedom, 8, 9, 24, 40, 41; see also Liberty
Individual rights, 3, 9, 11, 12, 14, 31; see also Constitutional rights
Informants, use of, 263, 402
Injunction, 312
Injustice, 315, 316, 325, 385
   created by selective law enforcement, 257, 258
Inmate, 105, 106, 120, 123, 322, 338, 339, 342
   paroled, 341
   programs developed to assist, 303–305
Institutionalization, 303
Internal Revenue Service, 330
International Association of Chiefs of Police, 54, 90
   Training Key, 176
Interrogation, 402
   use of, 274, 275
Investigation, of crimes, 45, 46, 87, 91, 155, 192, 194, 195, 196
   protection for people under, 335
Isolation from society, 97, 233
   police, see Alienation; Police, isolation from community

Jails, 297, 315, 326, 336, 403
Judges, 379, 385, 386
   administration of law, 9, 15, 18, 19
   emblems of authority of, 82, 83
   impartiality of, 333
   interpretation of common law, 12
   selective law enforcement and, 263
   trial, 195
Judicial system, effects of defiance of laws on, 312
Judiciary, 5, 13, 194, 386, 403
   impartial, 335
   power of, 9, 15, 295

Jurisdiction, 213, 226, 252, 253, 266, 275, 303
  of civilian review boards, 289
Jurors, 196, 197
  selection of for political trials, 333
Jury system, 7, 19
Jury trials, right to, 12, 15, 18, 193
Justice, application of to American justice system, 15, 193, 195, 267, 314, 334, 335, 336, 363
  effect of selective law enforcement on, 249, 255
  gap between law and, 314
  role of police in, 19, 40
  equal, denial of, 265, 266, 282
  ideals of, 59
  meaning of, 5, 7, 16, 19, 39
Justice Department U.S., 195, 199, 201, 336
Juvenile, 24, 25, 50, 195, 259, 376
  counseling of, 353, 354
  in foster home, 303
Juvenile courts, see Courts, juvenile
Juvenile delinquency, 169, 172, 285, 299, 354
  increasing rate of, 24, 25, 31
  law enforcement of, 386
  parental alcoholism and, 161

Katzenbach Guidelines, 195, 199
Kidnapping cases, 190, 191, 193
King, Martin Luther, civil disobedience of, 319
Knowledge and information explosions, 27;
      see also Society, changing; Technology
Kunstler, William M., 339

Law enforcement, 4, 18, 25, 26, 27, 31, 34
  discretionary, 234, 239
    see also Law enforcement, selective
  juvenile, see Juvenile; Juvenile delinquency
  philosophy, 61
  professionalization of, 75, 86, 87, 89, 90
  professionals, 89, 90, 211, 238, 250
    see also Criminal justice system; Professions
  role concepts of, 61, 62
  selective, 92, 249, 250
    administrative problems created by, 267-268
    discriminatory application of laws, 249-273
      administrative policies and operational level choices of, 250-253
    explanations for, at administrative level, 253-256

community pressures for priorities, 253, 254, 255, 261
    at operational level, 257-264
    "trading" advantages of law enforcement value, 263-264
    guidelines on, need for, 268, 274
    legal authority for, 264-267, 269
    official denial of, reasons for, 268-269
    recommendations for, 270-273
      the courts, 272
      to establish enforcement policy boards, 270, 271, 272
      internal review, 272, 273
      official recognition of, need for, 270, 273
    situational ethics and, 29, 30, 31, 34
    social changes and, capabilities of for coping with, 92
Law Enforcement Code of Ethics, 26
Law and order, maintenance of, 24, 38, 192, 193, 251
  as political issue, 282
Laws, application of, 265, 266, 267, 272
  changing, 29, 35
  concept of, 312
  constitutionality of, 312
  criminal, administration of, 4, 23
    police officer's knowledge of, 3, 61, 89
    police resources to enforce, 91, 92
  definition of, 7, 8, 9, 10
  development of, 10, 11, 12, 18, 32
  interpretation of, effect of selective law enforcement on, 250, 257, 258, 259, 260, 262
  natural law, 7, 8, 9, 12, 13, 14, 15, 16
  rules of, 314
  social compact, 9, 10
  strategy of dissent and, 319
    see also Dissent, strategies of
  unjust, 31, 314
  violation of, valid and constitutional, 312, 313, 314, 315
Legislature, 5, 9, 10, 13, 15, 16
  authority and power of, 9, 15, 269, 271, 272
  legislators' attitude toward strategies of dissent, 318
  purpose of legislation, 258
  selective law enforcement and, 249, 255, 256, 257
Liberty, 59, 315, 337; see also Freedom
Listening, art of effective, 134, 145-149; see also Communication

Los Angeles, 373
  Watts community of, 294
Los Angeles Police Department, 38, 239, 242,
    292

Magna Carta, legal significance of, 11, 12
Mandamus, writs of, 266
Manhattan Bowery Project, 297-298
Mapp v. *Ohio,* 261
Marijuana, 294, 295, 406; *see also* Drugs
Media, news, 51, 199, 200, 376
  coverage of dissent activities, 320, 321
  crime coverage in, 188, 189, 190, 191, 192,
      193, 194
    overcoverage and sensationalizing of, 189,
        190, 191, 193, 194
    public demands and, 188, 190, 193, 194
  impact of, on citizens, 187
  and police, news coverage of police in, 216;
      see also Police-press relations
  pretrial publicity and, 192-198
Menlo Park, California, Police Department,
    community survey, 169-171
  organizational development, 173, 175-177
  police philosophy of, 177-180
  ride-along programs, 164-168
  uniform change, 180-182
Mental health, contributions of to law enforce-
    ments, 74, 75
  importance of aggression in, 118, 120
Metropolitan Police Act for the City of London,
    372
Militant organizations, 311, 316, 322, 324,
    325, 328, 343; *see also* Dissent
Militants, 336, 338
  black, 317, 318, 322
  definitions of, 317, 318
Minority groups, 104, 111, 228, 288, 313, 375,
    376
  defined, 79, 80
  the disenfranchised, 97
  discrimination against, 160
  police and, 54, 62, 111
    mutual alienation between, field interroga-
        tions and, 243, 245
    problems in communicating between, 142,
        212
    see also Police-community relations
  in police forces, 326
  policeman as, 78-81
    see also Isolation from society

social status of, 324
stereotyping of, 114
vagrancy laws and, 244
Miranda v. *Arizona,* 261, 274
Misdemeanor, 406
  alcohol-related, 161
  citizen preference for handling of, 260
  crime classifications of, 239
Mob action laws, 331, 332
Murtaugh, John M., Judge, 334
Myrdal, Gunnar, 76

Narcotics, *see* Drugs
National Advisory Commission on Civil Disor-
    ders, 201, 262
National Advisory Committee on Criminal
    Justice, U.S., 261
National Advisory Commission on Criminal
    Justice Standards and Goals, 282, 283,
    284, 285
National Commission on the Causes and Preven-
    tion of Violence, 54, 75, 310, 311, 312,
    313, 316
National Council on Alcoholism, 160
Networks, guidelines, 201, 202, 203; *see also*
    Media, news; Police-press relations; and
    Television
Newspapers, *see* Media, news
New York City Police Department, 56-58, 82,
    87, 286, 298, 330
  suicide rate in, 81
New York Daily News, 188, 191
Niederhoffer, Arthur, 37, 38, 49, 85
Ninth Amendment to the Constitution, 18,
    314
Nolle prosequi, plea of, 252, 407
Nondelegation doctrine, 271
Nuisance, 243, 263

Oath, 17
Office of Economic Opportunity, 375
Ombudsman, concept and advantages of, 290-
    291
Oppression, *see* Projection
Ordinances, 256, 329, 356, 383, 407
  vagrancy, 266
Oregon Bar-Press Broadcasters Code, 194, 198
Organizational development (OD), 173, 175-
    177

Paranoia, 82

responsive to environmental stress, 83, 84, 85
practices, destructive, 233–244
   see also Scientific management
professionalism, 3, 4, 55, 74, 75, 85, 86, 159, 273
   August Vollmer, work of, 86–89
   influence of scientific management on, 234, 235, 236, 237, 238
professional status and prestige of, 25, 26, 74, 78, 80, 86, 181
   low pay, 78, 84, 88, 124
   see also Police, promotions and raises
promotions and raises, 84, 87, 90, 159, 239, 251
   internal police review boards, 288
   value systems in, 237, 239–240
public attitudes toward, 73, 75, 76, 163, 164, 373, 374
   see also Police–press relations
recruitment and selection of, 23, 163, 267, 273, 350, 351
   improving, 124
role of, 3, 5, 75, 78, 101, 117, 181, 182, 236, 244, 252, 350, 378
   in changing society, 24, 25, 27, 28, 29, 31, 32
   community expectations, 39, 101, 102, 103, 104
   conflicts in, 77
     adjustment to, 57
     social changes and, 71, 73, 74, 75
   definition of, 386
   public misperceptions about, 216
   in terms of duties, "crime fighter" versus social service role, 45–47, 48, 58, 216
role concept of, 47, 49, 353, 354
   citizen's expectations, 51, 52
     definition of, 49–50
     factors that affect, 51, 52, 55, 58
   conflicts in, 52–55
     black police officers, 56–58
   historical concept of, 233
   realistic, 58–62
training of, 20, 52, 54, 207, 267, 273, 326
   in constitutional law, 156
   in human relations, 124, 149, 156, 163, 212
   improving, 124
   in minority history, 156
   police training school, 87

in psychology, 117, 118, 124, 125, 156
realistic, 8, 90, 91
in social theory, 156
use of violence, 77, 84, 162, 182, 320, 374
   brutality, 282
   see also Police system
Police system, 286
   historical development of, 372, 373, 374
   impact of police–community relations on, 369–384
   police organization, 156, 161
     historical development of, 234
     paramilitary organization structure, disadvantage of, 157, 158, 177, 178
   reforms in, 81, 89
     organizational, 270
     professionalization of, 75
       significance of higher education, 87, 88, 89, 90
     technological changes and, 89–91
   relations with other segments of criminal justice system, 285, 385, 386
Police–community relations, 349, 350, 351, 352, 354, 366
   aggression, police perception of, 97, 117, 118, 119
   see also Aggression, expression of
   communication between, lack of, 233, 268
   see also Communication, blocks to effective
   conflicts between, 97, 98, 155, 156, 162, 239, 273
     community expectations and needs, 58, 62
     created by police enforcement decisions, 55, 56, 261
     differences in priorities, 240
     enforcement patterns, 238–239
     false perception, of community, 155, 156
       of role of police, 101, 102, 103, 104
     police goals of efficiency, 236, 237, 241, 242, 243
     see also Decentralization of police service; Scientific management
     police value systems and community values, 237, 239, 240
   definition of, 213, 214, 221
   harmonious relationship, 46, 380
     to achieve effective partnership relationship between, 63, 125, 298, 349, 350
     cooperation between, 190, 191, 192
     to develop positive rapport by administrative decentralization, 291

as personalized form of perception, 110–114, 126

positive, characteristics of, 112, 113

Self-incrimination, privilege against, 252; *see also* Witness

Sentencing, 189
  criteria for, 282
  suspended, 243, 252

Seventh Amendment to the Constitution, 18

Sheriff, 83, 163, 195, 207, 265, 288, 363, 364
  office of, in police–community communication net, 174

"Situation ethics," 29, 30; *see also* Ethics; Police, ethics

Sixth Amendment to the Constitution, 18, 193

Skolnick, Jerome, 77, 233, 263, 264

Social changes, 91, 330
  implications of, 71, 72, 73, 74, 75, 87
  and order, conflict between, 309, 310, 311, 313
  right to peaceful, 312

Social conflict, 317, 319
  as criminal versus political matter, 325, 326
  outcome of, 321, 324–325
  political consequences of, 309, 310

Social workers, 382, 386

Society, changing, criminal justice and, 23–40
  new morality of, 27, 28, 29, 30, 282
  political reality and, 309, 310
  tensions within, 73
  free, 310
  and law, relationship between, 5, 7, 9
  law enforcement and, 37

Sociology, police preparation in, 61, 89

Sociopathic behavior, 34, 35, 36, 37

Solidarity, 311
  community, absence of, 72
  group, 112, 325
  police, 77, 84, 233

Spock trial, 332, 333

Standards Relating to the Urban Police Function, 270

Stare decisis, 13

Statutes, 264, 265, 266, 268, 272, 413
  nonenforcement of, 258, 259
  penal, 259

Statutes of limitations, 265, 268, 404

Stereotyping, 113, 114, 124
  of minority groups, 114
  of police, 75, 76, 77, 137

Stress, consequences of, 81–83, 84, 85;

see also Suicide

Subculture, police, 78

Subpoena, 158, 414

Suicide, 39, 383
  as form of aggression directed to self, 118
  meaning and significance of, 82
  police suicide rate, 81, 83

Summons, 49, 286, 414

Supreme Court, United States, 207, 386, 414
  interpretation of First Amendment, 199
  issue of unequal protection under the law, 265, 266, 274
  Miranda decision, 261
  Sheppard decision, 193, 194
  views of right to dissent, 311, 313

Surveillance, political, 330, 331, 358

Tabloid thinking, danger of, 160, 161

Task Force Report on the Causes and Prevention of Violence, 159

Task Force Report on Corrections, 301

Task Force Report of the President's Commission on Law Enforcement and the Administration of Justice, 75, 76, 91, 92, 285, 289

Team policing, 292
  basic goal of, 291
  defined, 178

Teams, function of, in conflict management, 351, 352, 353, 355, 358, 361, 362, 364

Technology, 24, 27, 34, 88
  advances of, 73, 75, 87, 88, 89, 309
  electronic, 27, 32, 36
  see also Society, changing

Television, 187, 197
  restraining influence of on violence, 200, 201, 202
  see also Media, news; Police–press relations

Ten Commandments, 10, 11, 27, 76

Tenth Amendment to the Constitution, 18

Testimony, 47, 155, 192, 196, 271, 333, 415

Therapy, reality, 300

Third Amendment to the Constitution, 17

Thirteenth Amendment to the Constitution, 314, 335

Totalitarianism, 312, 314

Traffic law enforcement, 3, 45, 46, 47, 50, 51, 77, 78, 90, 140, 158, 169, 268, 312, 370
  citations, 242, 244

impact of delective law enforcement on, 255, 257
patterns of, 251
traffic inspectors, 180
Trespass, 315, 326, 356
Trials, 197, 415
criminal, 195
of dissidents, 331, 332, 333, 336
fair, 334
for dissidents, 336
right to, 193, 194, 195
historical development of, 18, 19
jury, right to, 12, 15, 18, 193
political, 333
right to speedy, 18, 335
"Trying up," 52, 53

Uniforms, police, 55, 76, 80, 130, 137, 239, 358, 365
change of, 180–182
patrolmen's, 356

Vagrancy, laws, 243–244
ordinances, 266
Values, 86, 159, 309, 310, 314
conflicts between community values and law enforcement value system, 236, 237, 238
counterculture, 72, 73
democratic system of, 35, 36
gaps between group, 126
of social system, 27, 29, 38, 59
Vandalism, 240, 331, 359
Vera Institute of Justice in New York, 286, 297
Vice laws, 255
Vietnam War, dissent against, 319, 324, 332
Violence, 23, 33, 62, 118, 262, 326, 342
alcohol-related, 161
causes of, 350
official, 316
police use of, 77, 78, 162, 176, 320, 374
prevention of, 358, 359, 360, 363, 364, 368
in protest demonstrations, 316, 323, 328
cycle of escalating, 327, 328, 329

as tactics of dissenters, 281, 316, 317, 318, 319, 320, 337
restraining influence of television coverage on, 200, 201
social changes and, 310, 313, 315, 336
spread of, law enforcement and, 211
Vollmer, August, 86, 87
work of, 86–89
Volunteers, importance of in community involvement to improve criminal justice system, 295

Warrants, 17, 196, 413, 416
Watergate scandals, impact of on law enforcement, 30
White House Conference on Children, 1970, 24, 25
Wickersham Commission Report, 274
Wilson, James Q., 71, 76, 85, 113, 237, 240, 251, 254, 257, 263, 270, 324
Winters v. *U.S.*, 258
Wisconsin Commission guidelines, 195, 196, 197, 198
Witness, 18, 46, 158, 358, 416
against himself, 252
testimony of, 192, 196
World War II, 373, 381
impact of on police professionalization, 87
social changes after, 27, 30
Writs of mandamus, 266

Yick Wo v. *Hopkins*, 265, 266
Youth groups, 72, 164, 292
attitudes toward police, 354
impact of police enforcement decisions on, 260
in police–community communication net, 174
police handling of, in conflict management programs, 352, 353, 357, 358, 362, 363, 364, 365
see also Juveniles
Youth Against War and Fascism, 328
Youth Opportunity Center, 375
Youth Services Bureau, 299